Postmodern Environmental Ethics

Postmodern Environmental Ethics

Edited by
Max Oelschlaeger

State University of New York Press

Published by
State University of New York Press, Albany

For information, address State University of New York Press,
State University Plaza, Albany, N.Y. 12246

Production by M. R. Mulholland
Marketing by Bernadette LaManna

Library of Congress Cataloging-in-Publication Data

Postmodern environmental ethics / edited by Max Oelschlaeger.
    p.   cm.
    Includes bibliographical references and index.
    ISBN 0-7914-2547-9. — ISBN 0-7914-2548-7 (pbk.)
    1. Environmental ethics.   I. Oelschlaeger, Max.
GE42.P67   1995
179'.1—dc20
                                                    94-32139
                                                    CIP

10 9 8 7 6 5 4 3 2 1

For E.C. Hargrove

Contents

Introduction

The essays gathered here were originally published in *Environmental Ethics*, recognized as the leading journal in the field, indeed, as almost defining environmental ethics as an area of philosophical inquiry (Fox 1990). The maturing of environmental ethics and its increasing acceptance into the philosophical community are manifest in several ways, such as the growth of professional societies, other journals, specialized graduate programs, and increasing numbers of academic books on environmental ethics. Perhaps the leading indicator that the field has arrived is the appearance of environmental ethics anthologies from trade publishers. I find collections that are potpourris, as well as ones that emphasize deep ecology, ecofeminism, animal rights, and so on; to date, no anthology has emphasized postmodern themes. So the collection here is unique, and it may be useful in opening up postmodern approaches to those who have not heretofore considered the possibility. I have confined my selections to essays that have already been refereed and published in *Environmental Ethics,* although there are many other possibilities, on the premise that others will find postmodern approaches more acceptable if they see that ecophilosophy is already being done that way.

Postmodernism is notoriously difficult to define, finding a multiplicity of meanings within the natural and social sciences as well as architecture, literature, art, and the humanities (Natoli and Hutcheon 1993). Postmodern currents run through disciplines as disparate as environmental history, ecotheology, literary criticism, nonlinear thermodynamics, ecophilosophy, and chaos theory. Postmodernism is methodologically open; postmodernists employ a wide variety of techniques in their work, such as critical rhetoric, poststructuralist methods, and discourse theory. Although some common themes run across postmodern thought, such as the opposition to essentialism (the idea that there are timeless, universal truths), it cannot be claimed that a postmodern paradigm exists.

Accordingly, no definition can be given for postmodern environmental ethics, not even in terms of a broad methodological statement. Any such definition would be too narrow and thereby exclude some of the essays anthologized here. Perhaps its methodological and definitional openness indicates that postmodernism is more than anything else a transformational process that is helping to reshape modern culture. Clearly, as an avalanche of scientific data makes clear, we live in a time of ecocrisis. If the modern trajectory continues, the likely outcome will be the collapse of our social and natural ecology (Firor 1990; Wilson 1992; Kennedy 1993). Life will go on, but civilization will no longer be a possibility. The question postmodern environmental ethics faces is that, paradoxically, of defining itself through the very transformational process that leads toward sustainability (Wright 1992).

Regardless of the problems inherent in defining postmodernism, the essays gathered here can be contextualized in two ways: positively, in terms of the so-called linguistic turn and its implications; and negatively, in terms of the kind of ethical theory to which postmodern environmental ethics is a reaction. The following section offers an account of the linguistic turn, followed by an account of two general postmodern approaches, the deconstructive or negative and reconstructive or affirmative. In the ensuing section I develop an account of postmodern environmental ethics as effective discourse; so conceptualized, when postmodern environmental ethics has run its course, we will find ourselves living in a new age (and the term *postmodernism* will pass out of usage). In the final section I contextualize each chapter to show, insofar as possible, that there is a coherence through difference to the postmodern project. Readers will have to decide for themselves if such a context is useful, that is, offers advantages relative to other interpretive frames.

The Linguistic Turn and Postmodernism

Paradoxically, it may seem, my approach to postmodern environmental ethics begins with the scientific revolution and its consequences for the theory of language. My rationale is simple: no adequate description of postmodern environmental ethics can be given apart from language. Modern science has had an enormous effect on the way in which language is conceptualized. Indeed, it can be claimed that modern science engendered the so-called linguistic turn. Thus, modern science has also had an enormous effect on postmodern environmental ethics, since it explicitly takes the linguistic turn. But I am getting ahead of the story.

Painting with a broad brush, it is permissible to say that prior to the twentieth century most modern people, including intellectuals, believed that a sure and certain knowledge of the world was theoretically possible, if not actualized in practice. So-called modernists typically believe that human reason—epitomized by modern science—is supreme, that it exists without limits, as it were, that the whole world lies open to disclosure by human intelligence. It is also characteristic of modernists to consider religion as a mythic form of consciousness, the hangover from a premodern worldview that combined Greek speculative philosophy with Hebraic cosmology. The modern worldview, thus, overturned a view of language that saw nature as a divinely constructed semiosis—literally, the words (works) of God. Interestingly, as many commentators argue, as modern science came into being it initially traded on the legitimacy of religion, on the premise that scientific language was not a threat to religious belief but simply a more accurate description of nature. Today science no longer justifies itself through the claim that it more accurately reveals the underlying principles of the creation. Further, religious narrative has been excluded from the modern worldview; nature is no longer thought of as an expression of a divine semiosis but as nothing more than objectively described matter in motion.

Which is to say that a designative theory of language (also called *representationalism*) now dominates the modern mind (Taylor 1985). Scientific language is conceptualized not as constitutive but as representative of a nature that stands apart from the human enterprise as an object to be objectively known and technologically appropriated. Accordingly, true statements are understood as the mirror of nature, conceived as veridical accounts (in the case of true knowledge) of reality represented through scientific law and description (objective knowledge). The rest is history, a cultural trajectory dominated by instrumental reason and utilitarian values that culminates in global ecocrisis and, as Herman Daly and John Cobb, Jr., (1989) remind us, social crisis.

However, a number of unsettling events, some engendered by natural science itself, have weakened the modern worldview. With the rise of evolutionary thinking and nonlinear thermodynamics, some members of the scientific community came to believe that the cosmos was better described in Heraclitean than Parmenidean terms (Bohm 1957; Prigogine 1980). A number of philosophers, including C. S. Peirce, Henri Bergson, and Alfred North Whitehead (Griffin 1993), can be read as being among the postmodern avant garde, that is, as initiating a sustained critique of the modern worldview and affirming an alternative or postmodern worldview. Quantum theory and the theory of indeterminacy also contributed to the unravelling of modernism, implying that not only was the world in process, but that various aspects of the process influenced or co-determined other aspects. Even the most basic or atomic level of reality appears indeterminate. Further, events are more participatory interminglings than subjective perceptions of objective things standing apart from human consciousness.

In the wake of scientific discovery came increasingly refined observations of scientific behavior, both longitudinally, that is, the process of scientific discovery over time, and sociologically, that is, the behavior of scientists in groups. Scientists themselves, like Albert Einstein (1954), Erwin Schrödinger (1952), and C. F. von Weizsäcker (1949), argued vigorously that science is incomprehensible apart from a culture that gives it meaning, purpose, a raison d'être. Historians and philosophers of science, like T. S. Kuhn

(1970) and Mary Hesse (1980), made evident that scientific inquiry is an ongoing social practice carried out through symbolic means. Knowledge itself is socially constructed, subject to the ongoing historical and linguistic processes of conjecture and refutation. Today, science is conceptualized by a generation of postmodern scholars as a narrative practice operating in and through language (Locke 1992).

To say that science itself is linguistically and historically constructed is not only permissible, but perhaps the only defensible position. A scientific account of the world is no more and no less than an explanation proffered at a particular place and time that is judged by a particular community of researchers to be true. Nonetheless, at some future time almost any scientific belief may find itself to be perfectly apropos of nothing. This does not mean, of course, that scientific truth does not exist, or that we are caught up in a world of vicious relativism, where whatever anyone says is true just because it has been said. Rather it means that scientific truth exists relative to a community of practitioners who have created a variety of procedures that guide research and criteria by which truth claims are evaluated. Further, as Prigogine and Stengers (1984) insist, alternative communities exist and therefore alternative descriptions for any natural process can always be offered.

Given this brief account of science and its situatedness in language, it is little wonder that postmodern currents run even more swiftly and deeply in the humanities generally and philosophy specifically. Although it is to some extent arbitrary to contextualize postmodern philosophy in terms of the linguistic turn, it is necessary in an abbreviated account such as this introduction. Suffice it to say that, after Wittgenstein's (1953) *Philosophical Investigations,* no claim that philosophical knowledge is apodictic can be sustained any more than it can be claimed that scientific knowledge is an isomorphic representation of reality. Even formal logic itself (as well as mathematics, though I do not discuss mathematics here), long believed to be a province of timeless laws of thought and transcendental forms of argument, has been reconceptualized. Postmodern thinkers such as Stephen Toulmin (1958) and Andrea Nye (1990) have made the social construction of logic evident. Again, as with charges from positivists that postmodernists relativize science, such recontextualization of logic is often misunderstood as tantamount to irrationalism. In truth, postmodern accounts of logic do not deconstruct so much as recontextualize the understanding of argumentative discourse. We now realize both what logic is, the indispensable formalization of argument forms that vary across discipline (rather than knowledge of field invariant criteria that determine valid inferences in all cases at all times), and what it is not, that is, not the only mode of human cognition or reason. Indeed, the cogency of postmodern prose depends upon the appeal to logical criteria, such as the notion that the plausibility of conclusions hangs on supporting evidence.

Reconstructive postmodernists, such as Steven Connor, David Griffin, and Richard Rorty, *affirm in different ways* the importance of linguistic conventions that frame rational discussion and the possibility of collective projects. Rorty (1991) finds it difficult to imagine any discussion of solidarity that is consistent with political freedom outside the narrative tradition of democratic liberalism. Griffin (1988) argues that nihilistic deconstruction ignores the basic truth that the past conditions the future. However problematic life may be, no generation is free to entirely repudiate the past and invent the future ex nihilo. The question, Griffin argues, is what kind of a worldview postmodernism is going to create. Connor (1989) makes a convincing case that nihilistic deconstructionists refute themselves, because they presuppose criteria for critical analysis, rational argumentation, and even the inherent structure (grammar) of language in their writing.

After Wittgenstein, *reality* is a word that increasingly finds itself between quotation marks: "reality." The modern project aimed to discover and elucidate reality objectively, that is, in a way that required no quotation marks, so that all people in all places at all times might uniformly agree that, for example, green grass is really green. The problem, post-Wittgenstein, post-Prigogine, and so on, is that even those spots out there in the "real world" that we call green grass needed naming, needed designation. But this does not mean that reality is a contest among a welter of claims and counterclaims to determine who can "yell" the loudest. Rather it is an affirmation that humans grasp the world and their relations to the world in and through language. Humans, regardless of place or time, can never stand outside language to offer descriptions to each other of the thing itself (although they often claim to do so).

So stated, the linguistic turn appears to entail a new paradigm, that is, a reflexive comprehension of language that has consequences across all areas of human endeavor, including science, religion, and philosophy (Lawson 1985). Language is more and more seen as ontogenetic, that is, as constitutive of the *meaningful* world that humans inhabit, and less and less seen as representative of an independent reality. Science itself is viewed as a form of discourse through which our own society typically constructs its picture of the world, the things in the world, and the relations among the things in the world, including our own ecosocial processes of production and reproduction (Locke 1992).

As with science, so with religion. Religious discourse is viewed as constitutive, offering a frame for meaningful self-conceptualization as well as a language through which disparate individuals achieve a sense of community (Lindbeck 1984; Griffin 1989; Burnham 1989). As David Tracy (1987) notes in *Plurality and Ambiguity: Hermeneutics, Religion, Hope,* stable texts have been replaced by unstable readers, that is, readers who are willing to risk ambiguity and plurality in interpretation of their faith (or the narratives that carry faith) because they find themselves in a culture at risk.

And as with science and religion, so with postmodern environmental ethics. Although some of the contributors to this volume might disagree, in my reading they all converge upon the awesome implication that we are language animals (Taylor 1985). Which is to say that if the modern story, in all its different guises, is ecologically pathological, then those activities that disclose its problematic aspects are a prelude to the construction of a postmodern, sustainable society.

Deconstructive and Reconstructive Postmodernism

Deconstructive postmodernists believe that the modern age is based on flawed Enlightenment, capitalistic, and scientific narratives that must be repudiated before culture can be constructed anew. Deconstructive analysis, literally, the close reading of a text that exposes its underlying ideology and assumptions (subtexts), has been brought to bear on the reality of history, truth, God, democracy, the soul, objectivity, science, and technology. These ideas are framed as contingencies, textual artifacts, and human inventions maintained through intellectual dogmatism and political and economic power. Deconstructionists decry all foundational claims; thus, they open themselves to charges that they are self-defeating, because the possibility of human existence requires an assumptive framework—cultural leaps of faith—that guides human action. We are, after all, biologically underdetermined.

A number of commentators have explored the insufficiences of deconstructionism. Clearly, this Introduction is not the occasion for a detailed discussion of such issues. If deconstructionism is defined as the radical skepticism of the possibility of coherent meaning in language, then it is self-defeating as charged. However, if deconstructionism is interpreted as a form of critical thinking that reveals the evolutionary potential inherent in all socially constructed realities, it is less objectionable. Again, if deconstruction is interpreted as denying the possibility of critical judgment, such as the claim that "Y is better than Z," on the ground that such claims are logocentric, that is, either establish or conceal binary oppositions (so-called transcendental signifieds, metaphysical claims), then again it is self-defeating. However, if deconstruction is interpreted as a form of discourse analysis that reveals hidden discourses of power by which privileged groups (e.g., males, Europeans) establish and maintain dominance over marginalized groups (e.g., females, Africans), then it is not objectionable. Similarly, if deconstruction denies the reality of history, then it is self-defeating, since deconstruction itself is an intellectual figure that makes sense only against the ground of intellectual history (Megill 1985). Finally, if deconstruction is interpreted as denying legitimacy to scientific truth, it is, in the context of ecocrisis, self-defeating; humankind simply cannot name holes in the stratospheric ozone, the extinction of species, climate change, and other aspects of ecocrisis independent of scientific judgment.

Reconstructive or affirmative postmodernists share with deconstructionists the idea that culture can be read as a text, but differ in that they see textual analysis of, for example, Judeo-Christian or Enlightenment narrative traditions, as a prelude to reconstruction. Tracy's work is exemplary in this regard, that is, in recognizing that in a time of crisis a literate culture must reconsider the meaning of its basic stories, be these scientific, economic, religious, or philosophic. Accordingly, affirmative postmodernists do not deny the importance of scientific truth, but read science as writing, as a textual enterprise that continually reshapes itself through discourse that occurs in communities (Locke 1992). So construed, science is grasped as ontogenetic, that is, as world making: what humans claim to be scientifically true exists, as Whitehead perhaps first discerned, at the boundary of the subjective and objective, a dynamic interface that conditions the reality in which we live.

Similarly, affirmative postmodernists do not deny the reality of power and the necessity of political process, as deconstructionists sometimes appear to do. Rather, affirmative postmodernists use discourse analysis to expose ideological constructs that marginalize some groups and place others at the center; but deconstructive analysis is followed by reconstructive thinking that attempts to move beyond the disclosure of social anomalies to pragmatic issues involved in societal transformation, placing particular emphasis on the transformative role of discourse. Affirmative postmodernists, like Daly and Cobb (1989), offer both critical analysis of dominant socioeconomic and intellectual paradigms as well as reconstructive alternatives that might facilitate new forms of existence. Affirmative postmodernists do not repudiate history as sound and fury signifying nothing other than the momentary triumph of one social group over the other. Instead, they attempt to change the course of history, that is, rework existing social constructions into new forms. As evident in the collected essays, most postmodern environmental ethicists are not repudiating so much as attempting to recontextualize and thus redirect or alter the course of history. Rather than deconstruction, affirmative postmodernists naturalize the category of "history," so that human beings are described as members of the earth community.

If reconstructive postmodern environmental ethics has a constant theme, it is the importance of sustainability—a term distinct from *sustainable development,* which is primarily an apologetic for the continued wholesale exploitation of the earth and Third World peoples by multinational corporations and developed nations (Shiva 1989; Kennedy 1993). Affirmative postmodernists argue that all discourse is subject to the formal requirement of sustainability, because any cultural narrative that leads humans to degrade either natural ecology or social ecology is not a viable strategy for life (Wright 1992). Postmodernists generally revel in diversity and ambiguity, believing that Cartesian certitude and definitive analysis, and thus closure of the processes of discussion and further inquiry, are more illusion than reality. Postmodern ecophilosophers seek to reopen subjects, economic theory being one example, that are generally believed closed. As a deconstructive prelude to such inquiry, they argue that mainstream economic theory is a rhetorical construction modeled on classical physics and maintained by a discourse of power that places socially dominant groups at the center of society while marginalizing others. Alternative forms of economic discourse, such as steady state economics (Daly 1991) or ecological economics (Costanza 1991), are introduced as conceptual strategies for building a sustainable society. Textual analysis discloses that civilization is at the center and nature is at the margin of the dominant cultural narrative; accordingly, the earth is exploited without limit. Thus, transformation to a postmodern age of sustainability entails voicing concerns that the dominant narrative marginalizes.

Postmodern Environmental Ethics as Effective Discourse

The essays collected here are all, in one way or another, forms of effective discourse; that is, the writers are reflexively aware of the linguistic predicament, our human situatedness in language, and working through language to promote societal transformation toward sustainability. The notion of effective discourse presupposes the convergence of a variety of twentieth-century language studies on a postmodern, interdisciplinary theory of language as a form of social behavior, where knowledge is constituted through linguistically framed conventions that guide inquiry and judgment, and where power is socially created and exercised through open-ended conversation that facilitates solidarity (that is, cultural cohesiveness, a sense of guiding principles and broad agreement on policy). From a postmodern perspective, language is the primary means by which human beings come to know and participate in a world, both natural and social. Language is also the means by which culture is reproduced, not only maintained or perpetuated but also transformed in response to natural and social exigencies.

Although no complete description of modern approaches to environmental ethics is possible, postmodern environmental ethicists are critical of so-called systematic environmental ethics. In the first place, they believe that modern ethical theory is linguistically naive. Although ethical theories are constructed from inside and through language, that linguisticality is ignored by modernists, who refuse to step inside the hermeneutic circle, fearing that plurality and ambiguity will overwhelm the possibility of rational discourse.

As Taylor (1985) argues, modern philosophy is based on the premise that language is purely designative; thus, any philosophical system or ethical theory is represented as "pure depiction, utterly undetermined by its place in a potential conversation" (p. 267). Postmodern environmental ethics, in contrast to modernist ethical theory, is always situated in language, especially attentive to linguistic context, socially dominant forms of narrative (final vocabularies), and the potential for realizing change through alternative discourse.

Accordingly, there is a continual oscillation between deconstructive or critical and reconstructive or imaginative moments in postmodern environmental ethics. As the concluding section of the Introduction confirms, some postmodern ecophilosophers tend to be deconstructive and others reconstructive, but they all follow in the wake of the linguistic turn. So framed, postmodern environmental ethicists acknowledge that there are no privileged positions outside language, no foundational places upon which individuals can stand to build apodictic truth. Thus, rather than building master narratives, they are interested in what might be called *performativity* generally and *societal transformation* more specifically. No society can reinvent itself ex nihilo, but rather only move into the future through reinterpretation of its legitimating narratives. Postmodernists place far greater emphasis on communities and collaborative discussion than on individual judgment. Indeed, they would view the notion that a single individual produces theoretical truth good for all other individuals as a remnant of a modern, prelinguistic notion of philosophy.

Postmodernists also criticize modern ethicists for practical failure, because environmental ethics has not been socially effective (Hargrove 1993), as evidenced by the steady decline of the indices of ecosystem health, the continued explosion of human population, and the relentless growth dynamic of industrial society (Brown et al. 1993). This pragmatic failure implies that modern ethics produces arguments that are "hygienically pallid" (Nussbaum 1990) and that lack "moral authority" (McCann 1986). Even worse, perhaps, is Alasdair MacIntyre's (1984) argument that post-Enlightenment ethical discourse is a failed project. "The most striking feature of contemporary moral utterances is that so much of it is used to express disagreements; and the most striking feature of the debates in which these disagreements are expressed is their interminable character" (p. 6). MacIntyre recontextualizes ethics within discourse communities; in short, human beings can judge what is good and bad only from within language, that is, on the basis of narrative traditions that make judgment possible.

Effective discourse is a relatively new concept, and no entirely adequate discussion of it can be offered here (see Lincoln 1989). However, it recognizes that language is inherently social, that is, there are no private languages. Thus, effective discourse, at least in the context of environmental ethics, is discourse that moves people. Even more specifically, as we will discover through these essays, effective discourse should help to move a society in the direction of sustainability. However, if the ecophilosophical project is to be successful in a democratic context, that is, actually help transform the industrial growth society into a sustainable society, then it must meet at least three criteria (Lincoln 1989). Its discourse must be cognitively plausible. Second, it must evoke sentiment. Finally, ecophilosophical discourse must influence people, that is, gain a wide audience and hearing. Insofar as environmental ethics aspires to be effective discourse, then it needs to reconsider its pretense of producing knockdown arguments, philosophical foundations, and master narratives and begin attending to the narratives that actually determine human behavior. For a democratic society to move in a new direction, even if good reasons exist, the people must feel a compelling need to change course and redirect behavior.

Essays on Postmodern Environmental Ethics

Part I. Language and Environmental Ethics

In distinction from ethicists who theorize independently of any consideration of language and its effects on theorizing, the essays collected in Part I represent a step into reflexive, linguistic awareness. These writers may be read as being committed to at least one common premise: any kind of environmental ethics that is linguistically unconscious is basically irrelevant to achieving a sustainable condition of human existence, including the conservation of biodiversity, since the roots of ecocrisis originate through and are sustained by language itself.

The first chapter, "Postmodern Environmental Ethics: Ethics as Bioregional Narrative," by Jim Cheney, has proven itself to be the most catalytic essay in postmodern environmental ethics (at least among those essays published in *Environmental Ethics*). Although not the earliest piece anthologized here, "Ethics as Bioregional Narrative" has attracted considerable attention, being previously anthologized, valorized, and villanized. Several of the essays that follow in Parts II and III respond to Cheney's piece, some affirmatively and some negatively. In my reading, Cheney touches on most if not all of the issues that other postmodern environmental ethicists have taken up.

Cheney's thesis is that there are no solutions for environmental dysfunctions in general, but only in relation to specific ecosystems where human beings have effectively dug in and taken root. Such sustained living in place, Cheney claims, gives humans the opportunity to discover the fundamental rhythms and pace, the structures and dynamics, of particular ecosystems. Bioregional narratives reflect human situatedness in nature and articulate local knowledge of the interrelations between the human and the more than human. They also enable storied residence, where the transcendental subject and the notion that language is solely a vehicle for expression of human intentionality is challenged by individuals who come to self-consciousness in place. Storied residence, an idea that Cheney takes from Holmes Rolston's (1988) work, offers a new way of being in the world, an alternative to the modern worldview that reduces the diversity and particularity of local places to one universal mechanism: nature as matter in motion. Cheney characterizes the modern worldview as totalizing and colonizing: totalizing in that it purports to be a master narrative that is epistemologically normative; colonizing in that it categorizes all places in terms of universals or principles that are indifferent to the texture of place.

One reason that "Bioregional Narrative" has generated so much discussion is that it raises the question of language itself, especially the theory of language and meaning. Interestingly, Cheney has been attacked (see later) for advancing a position that is relativistic. Yet he himself goes to considerable length to criticize such theories, using Richard Rorty as his foil. Cheney claims that Rorty's theory of the contingency of language and his attack on representationalism undercuts the reality of *the other*—that is, nature, the flora and the fauna. To accept the premise that language overdetermines human behavior does not also entail the conclusion, Cheney argues, that reality is "language all the way down." In Cheney's view, thinking of postmodern environmental ethics as bioregional narrative does not reduce the biophysical world to language but rather incorporates that world into human discourse. Cheney uses Heideggerian notions of language to argue that the world can speak through human beings who have taken up being in the world.

"Nature and Silence," by Christopher Manes, can be read as extending the argument advanced by Cheney in a way that helps to recontextualize deep ecology. Manes looks explicitly at the language that posits *Man* as a speaking-thinking subject apart from and in control of the earth. "The language we speak, today, the idiom of the Renaissance and Enlightenment humanism, veils the processes of nature with its own cultural obsessions, directionalities, and motifs that have no analogues in the natural world." Manes also calls systematic environmental ethics into question, because it is an abstraction from the life world of immediate human experience, the gesture of Man who is in control of the planet. Systematic philosophy is characterized by Manes as the discourse of reason that reflects the disembodied ego inherent in modern language; the consequence is the silencing of nature's voice. Manes notes that primary oral cultures have allowed the flora and the fauna "to speak." He valorizes deep ecology as perhaps the most linguistically open form of ecophilosophical discourse, but he carefully qualifies this contention. Humans need to speak a language, Manes argues, that cultivates a sense of ontological humility, reconnects human projects with the larger earth community, and moves us beyond our preoccupation with Man.

The third chapter, "Merleau-Ponty and the Voice of the Earth," by David Abram, brings the resources of continental philosophy to bear on environmental ethics. Working outward toward the world and the reality of lived experience from Merleau-Ponty's posthumously published *The Visible and the Invisible,* Abram attempts to disclose a transcendental signified embedded in the narratives of systematic philosophers: the disembodied thinking subject, the ego cogito, indeed, the environmental philosopher who is held apart from and above the world by *his* reason. Who is this ego that thinks? What is it? The systematic philosopher does not entertain such questions, for *his* language is assumed to be transparent, a virtual mirror of reality. Abram also explores the phenomenology of perceptual experience in a move, somewhat like Manes, to see if there is not a bodily discourse concealed beneath the customary forms of linguistic expression. We are, Abram insists, embedded as organisms in the awesome mystery of the corporeal world. Language itself reflects this primordial reality, the reality of lived experience and participation of the body in the world.

The fourth chapter, "Class, Race, and Gender Discourse in the Ecofeminism/Deep Ecology Debate," by Ariel Salleh, extends the hermeneutic horizon beyond the first three chapters. Although Salleh might agree with Manes and Abram that nature has been silenced, she sees silencing as including women and people of color; thus, the target of her criticism is the privileging of the male, patriarchal voice rather than any gender-free, transcendental ego. Unlike Manes, who identifies the patriarchal voice as Man and who affirms the language of deep ecology as an alternative, Salleh identifies the presence of the patriarchal voice in the language of deep ecology. In her reading deep ecologists still utter words of power by which they remain above both woman and nature. She argues that the narratives of deep ecology reflect the biases of middle class, professional (elite) males who remain enframed by traditional psychosexual mores and the hierarchies of dominant culture that place men over women and nature. Salleh points out that she cannot find anywhere in the deep ecology literature a concern for family, for the labor of women, and for the body itself as a means of finding (knowing) the human place in the world. Salleh also argues that the disdain for, inattention to, and misinterpretation of ecofeminist discourse is further confirmation that deep ecologists are embedded in modern liberalism. Her position, in this regard, is more like Cheney's, who is critical of deep ecology, and less like Manes's, who sees the potential for reform in deep ecology. Salleh ends her chapter, however, on an affirmative note, envisioning the possibility of women and men working together in a lateral-collaborative (or nonhierarchical) way to liberate all creatures, great and small.

"Green Reason: Communicative Ethics for the Biosphere," by John S. Dryzek, closes Part I with an exploration of communication itself—a subject increasingly important in postmodern studies of language. Dryzek is especially interested in how communities create meaning; however, his chapter goes beyond typical modernist communication theory (e.g., J. Habermas), which limits communication to the human sphere. In Dryzek's view, communication also involves the voices of the more than human. Following the lead of what he terms postmodern biology, which views nature as self-creating, Dryzek contends that the modern worldview is wrong, that nature is not mere matter in motion but alive and full of purpose and value. In moves reminiscent of both Cheney and Abram, Dryzek contends that communicative reason is attentive to the peculiarities and specificities of place (bioregionalism). Like Salleh, who finds the language of deep ecology problematic, Dryzek also sees it as wanting, but for a different reason; rather than being patriarchal, Dryzek reads it as mystical, arguing that what is needed is less talk about deep ecological consciousness or the union of self with the world and more ecologically informed discourse that points the way toward solution of specific problems. Embracing the world in "rational terms," Dryzek suggests, thus rescues environmental ethics from its flight from science toward mysticism.

Part II: Environmental Ethics, Postmodern Politics, and the Other

Part II contains essays that, like those in Part I, reflect the linguistic turn; some could be included in Part I. But the chapters in this part generally look at language in terms of its shaping influence on political discourse and thus power. Assuming that postmodern environmental ethicists are actually attempting to facilitate the processes of societal transformation toward a socially just and ecologically sustainable society, such considerations of political power relations are vital—and all the more so in a democratic society.

Chapter 6, "Radical Environmentalism and the Political Roots of Postmodernism: Differences That Make a Difference," by Robert Frodeman, is critical of postmodern environmental ethics. Frodeman argues that the project is epistemologically misguided, politically naive, and thus ultimately self-defeating. The primary target of his critique is Cheney's "Bioregional Narrative." Frodeman reads Cheney as a romantic nature lover who offers slogans rather than meaningful analyses of real power relations. Even worse, according to Frodeman, postmodernists like Cheney remain caught in the political narrative of the Enlightenment; that is, they assume the outmoded political individualism that mirrors the metaphysical atomism of classical physics. The consequence is that the political community is defined by utilitarian relations, where the social good is conceptualized as no more than the aggregate of individual preferences. The politics of Cheney and other postmodernists, in Frodeman's reading, valorizes the inviolability of individual rights and private property. In the concluding part of the chapter, Frodeman suggests that the narratives of deep ecology escape the enframing of Enlightenment political discourse.

"The Incarceration of Wildness: Wilderness Areas as Prisons," by Tom Birch, is a deconstructive analysis that attempts to show how the modern discourse of power—the narrative tradition that posits humankind as the engineer in control of the ecomachine—is hidden within the ideology and politics of wilderness preservation. More so than any other postmodern environmental ethicist, with the exception of Abram, Birch draws on continental philosophy, especially the work of Jean Baudrillard. Like Frodeman, Birch (an environmental activist) is concerned with political power and its implications for the protection of the earth, especially for the conservation of unhumanized land communities. Also like Frodeman, but for different reasons, Birch sees the political discourse of the Enlightenment as being the root of our ecomalaise. Birch argues that the modern narrative which frames political action, like the Wilderness Act (1964), is a discourse of power that privileges human interests over those of the more than human, thus silencing the voice of nature—an argument much like the one Manes trades on. Like Dryzek, Birch is interested in the question of how the other, or the voice of the other, can be represented, validated, and incorporated into political discourse. Birch, as I read him, appears more pessimistic than other postmodern environmental ethicists, because he claims that the West needs "an entirely different story about wildness and otherness." He bases this claim primarily on a keen analysis of wilderness preservations as simulacra, as hyperrealities that deceive us into thinking that we are conserving wild nature when in fact such preservations conceal the gesture of continued domination.

"The Call of the Wild: The Struggle Against Domination and the Technological Fix of Nature," by Eric Katz, can be read as picking up, at least in part, where Birch leaves off. Like Birch, Katz is concerned with the ideology and technology of wilderness conservation and restoration. And like Cheney, Katz believes that nature, if left free of technological manipulation and human intervention, has moral lessons to teach humankind, primarily that there are nonanthropocentric values outside the utilitarian web of economic valuation. Unlike Birch, Katz retains some sense that we can work our way toward sustainability without totally abandoning the past. The call of the wild, as Katz puts it, beckons human attention, reminding us that wild nature is a subject with its own imperatives rather than an object, subject only to human control. Katz's position might be read as a less demanding approach to bioregional living than Cheney's call for storied residence; simply by walking in wild nature and exploring the margins between the wild and the civil Katz believes that we can *dis-cover* the presence of the other, which lies concealed beneath the surface of conventional narratives of ethics, politics, and technology. Thus, wild nature invites each of us to recontextualize ourselves as a member of a moral community of subjects that goes beyond the conventional bounds of civilization (which accords agency only to human beings).

"Rethinking Resistance: Environmentalism, Literature, and Post-structural Theory," by Peter Quigley, is among the more theoretical pieces in this collection (rivaled in its technical argumentation by the chapters written by Cheney, Salleh, and Birch). Quigley argues that Cheney and other post-modern environmental ethicists have ignored the lessons of poststructural theory; he finds transcendental signifieds and hierarchial structures still haunting postmodern environmental ethics, especially in its discussion of things "wild and free" as well as things characterized as "natural." Much as Part I focused on the voice of Man, the ego cogito that silenced nature, Quigley directs us toward the concept of Nature. He finds Cheney's piece at once a conceptual advance and yet problematic: an advance because it brings into question the epistemological difficulties inherent in theories of meaning that depend on designation, but problematic in that his view of language is romantic and logocentric. Like Frodeman, albeit for different reasons, Quigley thinks Cheney's failure to deal with the poststructural analysis of language leads to political naiveté.

Part II closes with a chapter by J. Baird Callicott, "Traditional American Indian and Western European Attitudes Toward Nature: An Overview." Callicott would likely deny that he is a postmodernist (though he recently wrote a paper offering what he terms a *deconstruction*). I read this chapter as postmodern, because Callicott offers a carefully qualified comparison-contrast of two different language games (which he calls *worldviews*). One worldview is that of the primary oral peoples of Turtle Island, as the lands now named North America were called prior to European colonization. Callicott finds an implicit land ethic, or reverential relation to the earth, in the discourse of in-digenous peoples of Turtle Island. The other language game is our own European worldview. Unlike the native Americans, Callicott finds nothing in-herent in our discourse that suggests a reverential or ethical orientation toward the earth. Rather, he argues, we find an ideology of domination that attempts to harness the land to narrowly defined, economic purposes. Therefore, in Callicott's opinion, those of us who find ourselves embedded in Eurocentric discourse have much to learn from the stories of indigenous peoples.

Part III. Systematic Environmental Ethics Reconsidered

Postmodern environmental ethics remains an unfinished project, be-cause the world lurches on toward ecological oblivion. The chapters in Part III are part of the new beginning, suggesting an array of possibilities for soci-etal transformation and movement toward sustainability. In this regard these chapters might be viewed as framed by MacIntyre's (1984) critique of tradi-tional ethical theorizing, the kind of theory that maintains the illusion that it is outside language.

"Before Environmental Ethics," by Anthony Weston, shows its

postmodern colors in a number of ways. He argues that the attempt by environmental ethicists to produce a master narrative is misguided because it remains bound by the modern worldview. Weston detects a number of characteristic gestures on the part of environmental ethicists that belie their embeddedness in modernism. For example, rather than call into question the "boundary" between the human and the more than human, environmental ethicists ask whether we should extend moral considerability to the "nonhuman," thus cementing a socially constructed boundary into metaphysical place. Weston also advises environmental ethicists to become more concerned with social contexts, especially the institutions that direct human behavior and help to shape and maintain values. Today environmental ethics (theory) remains almost totally isolated from practice; tomorrow Weston hopes to see an environmental ethics that coevolves, as he puts it, with institutional practice. Such coevolution, he argues, makes impossible in principle the kind of analyticity that ethicists have traditionally sought in a master theory that stands over and above practice. Weston suggests that a more viable strategy is to lateralize the hierarchy (one that originates in Greek philosophy) that elevates theory over practice. Postmodern environmental ethics, in Weston's reading, is the sustained practice of social reconstruction, where means and ends, theory and practice, coevolve.

"Moral Pluralism and the Course of Environmental Ethics," by Christopher D. Stone, also calls into question the traditional philosophical goal of constructing a master theory, which he terms *moral monism,* that provides an overarching conceptual framework—either a single principle or coherent system—used to make ethical decisions. Stone contends that even a cursory familiarity with the problems faced by humans in their cultural interactions with the natural renders such a quest almost meaningless: any principle is overwhelmed by the great diversity and complexity of environmental problems. In the place of moral monism Stone recommends moral pluralism, that is, the recognition by the ecophilosophical community that a number of different language games are to be played, each guided by different conceptual frameworks that in turn enable different kinds of moral action, be this assuming responsibility for future generations, critical evaluation of policy and legislative oversight, or individual decision making regarding consumption patterns, housing, and recycling. Comparison-contrast of alternative vocabularies reveals what Stone calls *editorial viewpoints;* that is, the diversity and plurality of perspectives inherent in situations that seem simple on the surface but are capable of many different interpretations. Reflecting his background in law, Stone implies that environmental ethics might be more useful if modeled on casuistry rather than on the syllogism, because casuistry takes us down to the level of making good decisions that fit particular situations based on precedents, or antecedently established principles, that are creatively and imaginatively applied in new contexts.

"Cheney and the Myth of Postmodernism," by Mick Smith, is the most recent in the series of critical responses to Cheney's "Postmodern Environmental Ethics: Ethics as Bioregional Narrative" (and there are others not anthologized in this collection). In my reading, Smith's critique is particularly useful in helping us realize the awesome mystery of language; that is, the fact that humans always remain enframed by narrative, that there is no exit, no human position outside of language. In Smith's reading, Cheney lapses in his postmodern project by privileging bioregional narrative and, thus, in making an implicit foundational claim, the hold of modernist epistemology on Cheney's thinking is disclosed. In this sense, Smith defends Rorty's theory that epistemology (as traditionally conceived) is no longer useful, rather it is useful to think of conversation as the context in which knowledge is defined (Rorty 1979). Although Smith also affirms Cheney's emphasis on place or context, he argues that bioregionalism is just one among many possibilities for doing environmental ethics, rather than the one way as Cheney claims. Smith's thesis is that no single language game is a priori privileged over any other because no language gives immediate access to nature. Smith emphasizes, in a move much like Stone's, that the diversity of language games played by environmental ethicists, in their convergence on the importance of place, gives environmental ethics its moral authority rather than any one master theory (such as the putative necessity of "storied residence").

"Quantum Theory, Intrinsic Value, and Panentheism," by Michael Zimmerman, introduces the possibility of a postmodern environmental ethic at the interpretive interface of scientific and religious discourse. For modernists such an argument is impossible, because science and religion are conceptualized as antagonistic, even oppositional forms of discourse, making rival claims about the nature of reality. But the quantum theory, in Zimmerman's reading, undercuts dualism, such as the rigid distinction of facts and values or the objective and the subjective, in favor of an interactive theory of knowledge. But, advancing from J. B. Callicott's argument that quantum theory supports the theory of the intrinsic value of nature, Zimmerman argues that any environmental ethic derived from the language of quantum theory alone is not a sufficient condition, although it may be a necessary condition, to engender the respectful treatment of nature by humans. Zimmerman claims that a postmodern panentheism—a panentheism that draws on the possibility of the reenchantment of nature via quantum theory—offers good reasons for thinking that environmental ethics may become operative in human affairs. The discourse of panentheism, in

Zimmerman's interpretation, builds upon and also goes beyond quantum theory by offering us new interpretive possibilities for religion, such as an affirmation that God the transcendent creator is also present in the creation. "Christian Existence in a World of Limits," by John B. Cobb, Jr., appears last in this collection, but is arguably the first postmodern piece to appear in *Environmental Ethics* (published in the second issue of the inaugural volume). In a radically postmodern move, that only now is being elucidated theoretically (Lindbeck 1984; Burnham 1989), Cobb argues that the Christian narrative tradition, whatever its responsibility and culpability in creating ecocrisis, can renew itself in a time of ecocrisis. Cobb dares to reread the Great Code to see what the implications of the biblical tradition are for the contemporary faith community. Only in the last few years has ecotheological discourse taken off; Cobb was there two decades previously. But Cobb's pioneering work has not been followed up with the care it deserves in the journal. Insofar as environmental ethics aspires to be effective discourse, that is, to actually promote movement toward sustainability, one must wonder why more philosophers have not seriously considered the contributions that religious narrative has to make (Oelschlaeger 1994).

References

Bohm, David. 1957. *Causality and Chance in Modern Physics.* Philadelphia: University of Pennsylvania Press.

Brown, Lester R., et al. 1993. *State of the World 1993: A Worldwatch Institute Report on Progress Toward a Sustainable Society.* New York: W. W. Norton.

Burnham, Frederic B., ed. 1989. *Postmodern Theology: Christian Faith in a Pluralist World.* San Francisco: HarperSanFrancisco.

Connor, Steven. 1989. *Postmodern Culture: An Introduction to Theories of the Contemporary.* Cambridge: Basil Blackwell.

Costanza, Robert, ed. 1991. *Ecological Economics: The Science and Management of Sustainability.* New York: Columbia University Press.

Daly, Herman E. 1991. *Steady-State Economics: Second Edition with New Essays.* Washington, D.C.: Island Press.

———. and John B. Cobb, Jr. 1989. *For the Common Good: Redirecting the Economy Toward Community, the Environment, and a Sustainable Future.* Boston: Beacon Press.

Einstein, Albert. 1954. *Ideas and Opinions by Albert Einstein,* ed. Carl Seelig, trans. Sonja Bargmann. New York: Crown Publishers.

Firor, John. 1990. *The Changing Atmosphere: A Global Challenge.* New Haven, Conn.: Yale University Press.

Fox, Warwick. 1990. *Toward a Transpersonal Ecology: Developing New Foundations for Environmentalism.* Boston: Shambala.

Griffin, David Ray, ed. 1988. *The Reenchantment of Science: Postmodern Proposals.* Albany: State University of New York Press.

————. 1989. *God and Religion in the Postmodern World: Essays in Postmodern Theology.* Albany: State University of New York Press.

————, ed. 1993. *Founders of Constructive Postmodern Philosophy: Peirce, James, Bergson, Whitehead, and Hartshorne.* Albany: State University of New York Press.

Hargrove, Eugene C. 1989. *Foundations of Environmental Ethics.* Englewood Cliffs, N.J.: Prentice-Hall.

————. 1993. "After Fifteen Years." *Environmental Ethics* 15: 291–92.

Hesse, Mary. 1980. *Revolutions and Reconstructions in the Philosophy of Science.* Bloomington: Indiana University Press.

Kennedy, Paul. 1993. *Preparing for the Twenty-First Century.* New York: Random House.

Kuhn, Thomas S. 1970. *The Structure of Scientific Revolutions,* 2d ed. Chicago: University of Chicago Press.

Lawson, Hilary. 1985. *Reflexivity: The Post-Modern Predicament.* LaSalle, Ill.: Open Court Press.

Lincoln, Bruce. 1989. *Discourse and the Transformation of Society: Comparative Studies of Myth, Ritual, and Classification.* New York: Oxford University Press.

Lindbeck, George A. 1984. *The Nature of Doctrine: Religion and Theology in a Postliberal Age.* Philadelphia: Westminster Press.

Locke, David. 1992. *Science as Writing.* New Haven, Conn.: Yale University Press.

MacIntyre, Alasdair. 1984. *After Virtue: A Study in Moral Theory,* 2d ed. Notre Dame, Ind.: University of Notre Dame Press.

McCann, Michael W. 1986. *Taking Reform Seriously: Perspectives on Public Interest Liberalism.* Ithaca, N.Y.: Cornell University Press.

Megill, Allan. 1985. *Prophets of Extremity: Nietzsche, Heidegger, Foucault, Derrida.* Berkeley: University of California Press.

Natoli, Joseph, and Linda Hutcheon, eds. 1993. *A Postmodern Reader.* Albany: State University of New York Press.

Nussbaum, Martha. 1990. *Love's Knowledge: Essays on Philosophy and Literature.* New York: Oxford University Press.

Nye, Andrea. 1990. *Words of Power: A Feminist Reading of the History of Logic.* New York: Routledge.

Oelschlaeger, Max. 1994. *Caring for Creation: An Ecumenical Approach to the Environmental Crisis.* New Haven, Conn.: Yale University Press.

Prigogine, Ilya. 1980. *From Being to Becoming: Time and Complexity in the Physical Sciences.* New York: W. H. Freeman and Co.

———— and Isabelle Stengers. 1984. *Order out of Chaos: Man's New Dialogue with Nature.* New York: Bantam Books.

Rolston, Holmes, III. 1988. *Environmental Ethics: Duties to and Values in the Natural World.* Philadelphia: Temple University Press.

Rorty, Richard. 1979. *Philosophy and the Mirror of Nature.* Princeton, N.J.: Princeton University Press.

————. 1991. *Objectivity, Relativism, and Truth.* Cambridge: Cambridge University Press.

Schrödinger, Erwin. 1952. "Are There Quantum Jumps?" *British Journal for the Philosophy of Science* 3, cited in Prigogine and Stengers, *Order out of Chaos.*

Shiva, Vandana. 1989. *Staying Alive: Women, Ecology, and Development in India.* London: Zed Books.

Taylor, Charles. 1985. *Human Agency and Language: Philosophical Papers I.* Cambridge: Cambridge University Press.

Toulmin, Stephen. 1958. *The Uses of Argument.* Cambridge: Cambridge University Press.

Tracy, David. 1987. *Plurality and Ambiguity: Hermeneutics, Religion, Hope.* San Francisco: Harper and Row, Publishers.

von Weizsäcker, C. F. 1949. *The History of Nature,* trans. Fred D. Wieck. Chicago: University of Chicago Press.

Wilson, Edward O. 1992. *The Diversity of Life.* Cambridge, Mass.: Harvard University Press.

Wittgenstein, Ludwig. 1953. *Philosophical Investigations.* New York: Macmillan Publishing Company.

Wright, Will. 1992. *Wild Knowledge: Science, Language, and Social Life in a Fragile Environment.* Minneapolis: University of Minnesota Press.

Part I

Language and Environmental Ethics

1

Postmodern Environmental Ethics: Ethics as Bioregional Narrative

Jim Cheney

I. Postmodernism and Privileged Discourse

"But you know, grandson, this world is fragile."
The word he chose to express "fragile" was filled with the intricacies of a continuing process, and with a strength inherent in spider webs. . . . It took a long time to explain the fragility and intricacy because no word exists alone, and the reason for choosing each word had to be explained with a story about why it must be said this certain way. That was the responsibility that went with being human . . . and this demanded great patience and love.

—Leslie Marmon Silko (Laguna Pueblo)[1]

The question which this section addresses might be put as follows: in the light of postmodernist deconstruction of modernist totalizing and foundationalist discourse, can we any longer make sense of the idea of privileged discourse, discourse which can lay claim to having access to the way things are? The dominant postmodernist view is that this is not possible, that language can be understood only as either a set of tools created for various human purposes or as the free creation of conscious persons or communities. This being so, it is argued, we should practice ontological abstinence in our beliefs about the relation between language and world. To the extent that the notion of objectivity enters into postmodernist discourse at all it tends to take the form that "truth" is simply the result of social *negotiation,* agreement achieved by the participants in particular conversations.

A more useful conception of objectivity has been suggested by some feminist postmodernists in an attempt to privilege discourses constructed in opposition to the totalizing and colonizing discourses constructed by the

dominant culture. It is within this basic framework that Sandra Harding, for
example, tries to weave a place for a feminist standpoint epistemology within
postmodernism: ". . . if there can be 'a' feminist standpoint, it can only be
whatever emerges from the political struggles of 'oppositional consciousness' oppositional precisely to the longing for 'one true story' that has been
the psychic motor for Western science. . . . The greatest resource for would-
be 'knowers' is our nonessential, non-naturalizeable, fragmented identities
and the refusal of the delusion of a return to an 'original unity.'"[2] Objectivity
is defined negatively in relation to those views which oppositional consciousness deconstructs. A voice is privileged to the extent that it is constructed
from a position that enables it to spot distortions, mystifications, and colonizing and totalizing tendencies within other discourses.

More can be said on behalf of privileged discourses. John Caputo, for
example, has pointed to significant differences in the views of Heidegger and
Rorty, both writers in the deconstructionist tradition.[3] One way of stating
Heidegger's position would be to say that he thinks that postmodernist deconstructionism of the sort exemplified by Rorty must itself be deconstructed;
Rorty is still working within the metaphysical framework he sought to dismantle by deconstructing that framework's foundationalist epistemology.
Rorty has, in effect, accepted the view of language embedded in the correspondence theory of truth, rejecting merely its pretension to be a "mirror of
nature." We are left with the same old dualistic view of language and its relationship to the world, minus only the idea that language mirrors nature. Since
this mirroring was supposed to provide the link between language and world,
language now floats free of the world—it's language all the way down. What
we are left with are conversations sustained only by the criteria of internal
self-coherence and adequacy to the purposes for which they are constructed—
which, of course, are freely constructed purposes of conscious human beings,
not purposes given to us, as it were, by the world. Because it's language all the
way down, Heidegger would deconstruct these language games as well.

Exposing the errors in the correspondence theory of truth and its foundationalist epistemology exposes the bankruptcy of the view that language is
rooted solely in conscious human projects and validated solely by reference
to canons of internal consistency and adequacy to those projects. Rorty dis-
mantles the correspondence theory of truth, with its hope of finding a way for
the transcendental subject to touch the world with its words only to leave the
transcendental subject in place, freely creating world upon world of words—
finally not taking responsibility for its words, but merely pouring them forth
in conversation after conversation. Surely a thoroughgoing postmodernism
would deconstruct the modernist transcendental subject along with the foundationalist epistemologies modernism has constructed in its attempt to regain
the world.

When this transcendental subject is also deconstructed, we are left with the world and words in it, emergent from it. Heidegger, for example, opts for a new relation to language altogether, one which results from a "meditative openness" to the world. The world speaks through us when we let go of the metaphysical voice. Language of this sort is a "listening," a "gift in which things come to presence." Language doesn't trap us in a world of words but is the way in which the world is present to us. The difference in the languages Heidegger describes is said to be a difference between "primordial" language, as a way in which the world discloses itself by our being rooted in the world, and "fallen" language, which constructs itself as a mirror of nature and uproots itself from the world by employing the criteria of adequacy to human purposes and internal coherence (not problematic in themselves) at the expense of faithfulness to experiential embedment in the world—a loss of hearing in the hegemony of constructed vision, a hegemony that did not abate, as it should have, with the rise of postmodernism.

Language as so conceived does not pretend to be giving the "one true story" any more than language does on Rorty's view. Just as a particular wolf is only one of the ways in which the world has expressed itself, so the stories and narratives which emerge in various physical, cultural, and linguistic settings give expression to human "being-in-the-world" in various ways. In the end even instrumental rationality gives expression to the world in this way, though it is a distorted expression, distorted precisely through denying its own origins as a particularized expression of the world and setting up shop as a "mirror of nature" certified by a foundationalist epistemology or by cutting itself free from the world altogether. Like the conscious ego which has turned its back on the id out of which it grew, such language becomes subject to bad dreams, neurosis, and psychosis—the return of the repressed. The truth of "It's language all the way down" must be understood in light of the equal truth of "It's world all the way up"—though it gets perverse in its upper reaches as the world as language closes in on itself, becoming inbred and pretending to totalization and foundationalist philosophy.

The possibility of totalizing, colonizing discourse arises from the fact that concepts and theories can be abstracted from their paradigm settings and applied elsewhere. Although these abstractions are fully intelligible only within the paradigm settings which gave birth to them, such abstractions achieve a life of their own; they can be articulated in accordance with canons of coherence and made into apparently self-contained wholes ready for export and application to a variety of situations. The situations to which a theory is deemed applicable, however, are specified within the theory, by the theory as articulated in abstraction from its paradigm setting. The danger is that the theory when applied to a situation specified *by* the theory will serve not to *articulate* that new situation, that is, bring it to experiential and moral coherence, but rather will serve as a mechanism of *de facto* repression of at least some of the experiential dimensions of the situation and lead to confusion and bafflement at the level of action and conscious attempts to understand one's situation and what one is about.[4] Vine Deloria, Jr. and other Native American writers make this point about Christianity, for example, and contrast it with Native American spirituality, which is closely tied to place and, for that reason, is not thought of as exportable.[5] To prepare a theory, religion, or culture for export is to turn it into a potential tool for the colonization of the minds of other people.

The effect of totalizing language is to assimilate the world to it. Totalizing language provides an abstract understanding that cuts through individual differences when these are irrelevant to its purposes. Nested, logically related concepts are employed to draw the (to it) idiosyncratic up into language and give it a place in its schema of the real. Contextual discourse reverses this; it assimilates language to the situation, bends it, shapes it to fit. Contextual discourse is not fundamentally concerned with issues of overall coherence. Or, rather, the kind of overall coherence for which it strives is different: a mosaic of language which serves as a tool of many purposes at once. In the life of a tribal community, for example, it must articulate a sense of those processes which bind the community together and to the land; and it must do this in a language which functions effectively to call forth appropriate responses. It must provide a means whereby individuals can come into their own in nonrepressive ways; yet, individual identities must be articulated in a language that makes these individuals intelligible to the community. Culturally understood conceptions of self, that is to say, must come to articulate individual experience without being imposed on individuals in a way that sets up psychic splits. The language must also articulate a process of human interaction with the land which ensures the health[6] both of the land and the community. Contextualized language is tuned to quite specific situations and forgoes the kind of totalizing coherence with which we have been so preoccupied in the modern world.

Tom Jay, in his lyrical essay, "The Salmon of the Heart," is concerned with just such contextualized language. He reports that ". . . the 'flash' in our phrase 'flash of inspiration' is etymologically grounded not in lightning but in the flash-splash of a fish. Ideas do not flash like lightning but rise like trout to caddis flies."[7] Here we have a lovely image of the difference between the totalizing overlays of which I have been speaking and contextualized languages which percolate upward through the contexts they are bringing to voice in language shaped by this percolating process.[8] A striking feature of contextualized language, particularly in traditional cultures such as those of Native Americans, is that it ". . . bridges subject and object worlds, inner and outer. Language is the path, the game trail, the river, the reverie between them. It shimmers there, revealing and nourishing their interdependence. Each word *bears* and *locates* our meetings with the world. A word is a dipped breath, a bit of spirit (*inspire, expire*) wherein we hear the weather. Our 'tongues' taste the world we eat. At root [this] language is sacramental."[9] This observation is commonplace concerning discourse in traditional cultures. The construction of the modernist subject has been a long time in the making. It took much time and cultural effort to generate the intuitive "obviousness" of the Cartesian privatized self. The modernist period in philosophy, with its creation of absolute subjectivity and the need for a foundationalist epistemology to regain connection with the world, is only the latest installment in the story of the cultural construction of the subjective self. We can now tell coherent stories of this cultural construction which take us back to the agrarian revolution, some nine or so millennia ago. As we read these accounts, contextualized discourse seems to emerge as our mother tongue; totalizing, essentializing language emerges as the voice of the constructed subjective self, the voice of dissociated, gnostic alienation.[10]

As an example of language which "bridges subject and object worlds" Tom Jay refers to the place of the salmon in the lives of Northwest Coast Indians, the way in which what is said and done in relationship to salmon incorporates an understanding, including a *moral* understanding, of health—health in self, community, earth, and the relationships between these:

. . . [S]almon . . . are literal *embodiments* of the wisdom of the *locale,* the resource. The salmon are the wisdom of the northwest biome. They are the old souls, worshipful children of the land. *Psychology without ecology is lonely* and vice versa. The salmon is not merely a projection, a symbol of some inner process, it is rather the embodiment of the soul that nourishes us all. . . . [T]o the original peoples of the Pacific Northwest, salmon were not merely food. To them, salmon were people who lived in houses far away under the sea. Each year they undertook to visit the human people because the Indian peoples always treated them as honored guests. When the salmon people traveled, they donned their salmon disguises and these they left behind perhaps in the way we leave flowers or food when visiting friends. To the Indians the salmon were a resource in the deep sense, great generous beings whose gifts gave life. The salmon were energy: not "raw" energy, but intelligent perceptive energy. The Indians understood that salmon's gift involved them in an ethical system that resounded in every corner of their locale. The aboriginal landscape was a democracy of spirits where everyone listened, careful not to offend the *resource* they were a working part of.[11]

This understanding of the salmon performs a major integrative function in Northwest Coast Indian society. It is this integrative function which is the criterion which guides development of the image. In the interest of fulfilling this function the account does forgo another sort of "truth," but this should not blind us to the fact that there is truth here, too, a truth which, perhaps, *must* be embodied in some such way as this.

The epistemological function of contextualist discourse is underscored in Robin Ridington's account of the place of myth in the life of the Beaver Indians, a northern hunting people. Ridington points out that for nomadic people such as these, survival "depends upon artifice rather than artifact. They live by knowing how to integrate their own activities with those of the sentient beings around them." It is what we call *mythic* thinking which carries this knowledge. "Their dreaming provides them access to a wealth of information. Their vision quests and their myths integrate the qualities of autonomy and community that are necessary for successful adaption to the northern forest environment." As Ridington points out, "the true history of these people will have to be written in a mythic language."[12]

Paula Gunn Allen (Laguna Pueblo/Lakota) refers to the Western "meta-myth" that "there is such a thing as determinable fact, natural—that is, right—explanations, and reality that can be determined outside the human agency of discovery and fact finding." The account she gives of myth, ritual, and vision in her tribal culture is distinctively postmodern. She notes that "myth" is synonymous with "fable," not "belief," and that it has the connotation of "moral story." Myth, she says, "is an expression of the tendency to make stories of power out of the life we live in imagination." Here she is noting the intimate connection between myth and ritual—myth as "a language construct that contains the power to transform. . . . Of course it reflects belief . . . but it is at base a vehicle. . . ." Myth, then, is knowledge shaped by transformative intent: "Myth may be seen as a teleological statement, a shaped system of reference that allows us to order and thus comprehend perception and knowledge. . . ."[13] We in the postmodernist West are only beginning to see such possibilities in language. Postmodernism makes possible for us the conception of language conveying an understanding of self, world, and community which is consciously tuned to, and shaped by, considerations of the health and well-being of individual, community, and land and our ethical responsibilities to each. This postmodernist possibility is an actuality in the world of tribal myth and ritual.[14]

The current emphasis in contemporary feminist thought on contextualism, narrative discourse, standpoint epistemologies, and "cultural and discursive birthplaces"[15] helps give us access to the discourse of tribal peoples, with which it has significant affinities. In addition, the role of the land in tribal discourse as well as the details of its narrative and mythic style can significantly inform postmodernist thought on discourse. The postmodernist account of ethics as bioregional narrative which I explore in the next section owes much to meditation on the role of land in tribal discourse.

II. Environmental Ethics as Bioregional Narrative

The landscape and the language are the same,
And we ourselves are language and are land.

—Conrad Aiken[16]

I can only answer the question What am I to do? if I can answer the prior question 'Of what story or stories do I find myself a part?' . . . Mythology, in its original sense, is at the heart of things.

—Alasdair MacIntyre[17]

An environmental ethic does not want to abstract out universals, if such there be, from all this drama of life, formulating some set of duties applicable across the whole. . . . The logic of the home, the ecology, is finally narrative. . . . If a holistic ethic is really to incorporate the whole story, it must systematically embed itself in historical eventfulness. Else it will not really be objective. It will not be appropriate, well adapted, for the way humans actually fit into their niches.

—Holmes Rolston, III[18]

    In *A Sand County Almanac,* Aldo Leopold offers the following general principle: "A thing is right when it tends to preserve the integrity, stability, and beauty of the biotic community. It is wrong when it tends otherwise."[19] Holmes Rolston, III, suggests that we understand this principle as "deeply embedded in [Leopold's] love for the Wisconsin sand counties,"[20] that we understand it as belonging to Leopold's "storied residence" in those counties. Rather than view it simply as a universal norm perhaps *suggested* to Leopold by his life and work, we are urged to understand it as inflected by historicity, as *essentially* tied to place and Leopold's narrative embedment in, and understanding of, the sand counties of Wisconsin.

    Rolston's notion of "storied residence" can be understood as urging environmental ethicists to make the postmodern turn. It can also be understood in the spirit of Alasdair MacIntyre's recent insistence upon the central importance of narrative to ethical thought, an insistence which is, likewise, a rejection of modernist ethical thought. In this section I pick up on Rolston's suggestion in an indirect way by sketching a path for a postmodernism which makes use of certain notions current in contemporary environmentalism. In so doing, my hope is that this transformed postmodernism will, in turn, have a transformative effect on environmental ethics which, protestations to the contrary notwithstanding, has almost always been conceived of in modernist ethical terms. In reconstructing postmodernism I am at the same time setting an agenda for reconceiving environmental ethics in contextual and postmodern terms.

In a recent article, Biddy Martin and Chandra Talpade Mohanty state with admirable clarity both the limitations and potential of postmodernism for feminist discourse in particular (and, by implication, for any discourse aimed at the deconstruction of totalizing and colonizing discourse). In discussing the work of Minnie Bruce Pratt, Martin and Mohanty contrast her insistence upon "our responsibility for remapping boundaries and renegotiating connections" with

> . . . the more abstract critiques of "feminism" and the charges of totalization that come from the ranks of antihumanist intellectuals. For without denying the importance of their vigilante attacks on humanist beliefs in "man" and Absolute Knowledge wherever they appear, it is equally important to point out the political limitations of an insistence on "indeterminacy" which implicitly, when not explicitly, denies the critic's own situatedness in the social, and in effect refuses to acknowledge the critic's own institutional home.

The project that emerges from the acknowledgement of situatedness while refusing modernist essentialism and totalization is that of initiating a "complicated working out of the relationship between home, identity, and community that calls into question the notion of a coherent, historically continuous, stable identity and works to expose the political stakes concealed in such equations." This is accomplished by grounding the narrative account not in a "coherent, historically continuous, stable identity" but rather ". . . in the geography, demography, and architecture of the communities that are [Pratt's] 'homes'; these factors function as an organizing mode in the text, providing a specific concreteness and movement for the narrative." Further, "Geography, demography, and architecture, as well as the configuration of her relationships to particular people . . . serve to indicate the fundamentally relational nature of identity and the negations on which the assumption of a singular, fixed, and essential self is based." Relations to people are elaborated "through spatial relations and historical knowledges," the importance of which "lies in the contextualization of [those relations], and the consequent avoidance of any purely psychological explanation."[21]

Narrative is the key then, but it is narrative grounded in geography rather than in a linear, essentialized, narrative self. The narrative style required for situating ourselves without making essentializing or totalizing moves is an elaboration of relations which forgoes the coherence, continuity, and consistency insisted on by totalizing discourse. Our position, our *location,* is understood in the elaboration of relations in a nonessentializing narrative achieved through a grounding in the geography of our lives. Self and geography are bound together in a narrative which locates us in the moral space of defining relations. *"Psychology without ecology is lonely* and vice versa."[22] *Mind*scapes are as multiple as the *land*scapes which ground them. Totalizing masculine discourse (and essentializing feminist discourse) give way to a contextualized discourse of place.

Why a discourse or narrative of relation to place? And what is meant by "place" here? We can work toward an answer to these questions by considering some of the possible alternatives for a contextualizing narrative as the means for locating oneself in a moral space out of which a whole and healthy self, community, and earth can emerge.

The fragility of the inturning process, the internal narrative in isolation from community and world is obvious. A particularly poignant example of this fragility is related by Edith Cobb in her book *The Ecology of Imagination in Childhood.* She relates the story of Alice, a child she describes as "surrounded by empty psychological space"; her narrative construction of self had to operate entirely within the confines of her own interior space. The result (or actuality) of this is schizophrenia. In extreme cases such as this it is brought home to us that what we take to be the interior space of the self, our individual essence, is really an internalized landscape or, better, one term of a constructed narrative of self-in-place. Cobb's account of Alice's life brings this out clearly. In one situation only is Alice embedded in a geography larger than her own closed-in self. This occurs in yearly visits to the family summer home, when a "sea change" comes over her in the context of an immersion in the natural world. Alice's lyrical portrait of these summers poignantly illustrates the necessity of landscape for the coherent construction of a self:

Canoes. Water against the paddle pushing ahead, home late, moon on the water, crickets singing, stumbling up the path carrying blankets. . . . Michigan and Michigan again, always different, each year it changed—it didn't change, I did, a new me in the same place. Each summer I would wonder what would happen . . . each one with something new, unexpected, exciting, for me to have and to remember, never lose it, always have it, in me, never forget it, just think about it, relive it over and over, love it and keep it, part of me. . . . for me, *is me.*

As the reality of the natural world of Alice's summer home slips away, leaving Alice "surrounded by empty psychological space," the writing changes: ". . . twisting, revolving, rotating, squirming, wriggling, slithering, shakey . . . water breaking, sliding past, new water passing by, turning white, turning black, turning green, turning blue, going far away, never come back, off to nowhere. . . ." The writing deteriorates further: "dissipation," Cobb says, "of all solidity into shapeless feeling; helpless longing follows, ending on a note of bewildered exhaustion."[23] The necessity of landscape for the construction of self is clear—"psychology without ecology is lonely."

What happens when the landscape includes only the human community and its institutions? Here Martin and Mohanty's analysis of Pratt's autobiographical narrative is illuminating. We have looked at the positive side of narrative contextualized by reference to geography. There is a negative aspect, however, when that geography is one of human making: ". . . the very stability, familiarity, and security of these physical structures are undermined by the discovery that these buildings and streets witnessed and obscured particular race, class, and gender struggles. The realization . . . politicizes and undercuts any physical anchors she might use to construct a coherent notion of home or her identity in relation to it." This cultural geography serves as well to indicate

> . . . the negations on which the assumption of a singular, fixed, and essential self is based. For the narrator, such negativity is represented by a rigid identity such as that of her father, which sustains its appearance of stability by defining itself in terms of what it is not. . . . The "self" in this narrative is not an essence or truth concealed by patriarchal layers of deceit and lying in wait of discovery, revelation or birth.
>
> It is this very conception of self that Pratt likens to entrapment. . . .[24]

When "unity is exposed to be a potentially repressive fiction"[25] in this way, one of the critical functions of narrative is to undercut such identities, such "homes":

> "The system" is revealed to be not one but multiple, overlapping, intersecting systems or relations that are historically constructed and recreated through everyday practices and interactions, and that implicate the individual in contradictory ways. . . .
>
> Community, then, is the product of work, of struggle, it is inherently unstable, contextual, it has to be constantly reevaluated in relation to critical political priorities. . . . There is also, however, a strong suggestion that community is related to experience, to history. For if identity and community are not the product of essential connections, neither

are they merely the product of political urgency or necessity. For Pratt, they are a constant recontextualizing of the relationship between personal/group history and political priorities.[26]

Within the geography of human landscape the contextual voice can emerge in clarity and health only through a "constant recontextualizing" which prevents the oppressive and distorting overlays of cultural institutions (representing a return of the repressed) from gathering false, distorting, and unhealthy identities out of "the positive desire for unity, for Oneness."[27]

Is there any setting, any landscape, in which contextualizing discourse is not constantly in danger of falling prey to the distortions of essentializing, totalizing discourse? Perhaps not. A partial way out might be envisioned, however, if we expand the notion of a contextualizing narrative of place so as to include nature—nature as one more player in the construction of community. My suggestion is that a postmodernist emphasis on contextualism and narrative as a means of locating oneself offers us an alternative mode of understanding bioregionalism and, conversely, that bioregionalism is a natural extension of the line of thought being developed by those advocating a view of ethics as contextualist and narrative. What I propose is that we extend these notions of context and narrative outward so as to include not just the human community, but also the land, one's community in a larger sense. Bioregions provide a way of grounding narrative without essentializing the idea of self, a way of mitigating the need for "constant recontextualization" to undercut the oppressive and distorting overlays of cultural institutions.

Listen to the following passage concerning the Ainu, the indigenous people of Japan (The Kamui referred to are spirits of natural phenomena—everything is a Kamui for the Ainu.):

The Ainu believed that the housefire was an eye of the Kamui that watched and welcomed all game that entered through the hunting window. As game entered through the hunting window . . . the fire reported its treatment back to the appropriate Kamui community. Fire is the appropriate witness for the *resource,* flickering warm light rising from the broken limbs of trees. . . . The mythic images circle and knot together into a reality that is a story, a parable, where facts are legendary incidents, not data.[28]

One significant feature of this passage is that it locates moral imperatives in the watchful eye of the housefire. The reality that is knit together as story and parable carries not the "intrinsic value" so much discussed in the literature in environmental ethics, but rather actual moral *instruction.* An important aspect of the construction or evolution of mythic images is their ability to articulate such moral imperatives and to carry them in such a way that they actually *do* instruct; that they *locate* us in a *moral* space which is at the same time the space we live in physically; that they locate us in such a way that these moral imperatives have the lived reality of fact. In the case of the Ainu this is achieved, in part, by including all of nature within the moral community. For a genuinely contextualist ethic to include the land, the land must *speak* to us; we must stand in *relation* to it; it must *define* us, and we it.

It has often been noticed that mythical cosmologies carry thought, that they are the vehicles of richly textured understandings of human nature and community cohesion. John Wisdom and Paul Ricoeur, for example, have noted the quite sophisticated and complex understandings of human psychology embedded in Christian cosmology.[29] The difficulty with that cosmology in particular is in its relationship to the land. It has been argued by Shepard[30] and others that although the religion of the Desert Fathers *was* a response to the desert landscape, it was one of denial, one which set culture over and against nature, history over and against cyclical mythologies firmly embedded in place. James Hillman has noted that monotheism functions as a mechanism to deny the voices of polytheism, those voices which speak from all dimensions and aspects of one's experience of, and relation to, the world; voices which, if allowed to speak, would tell not only of distortions, but of the health that is there, or might be there.[31] These voices can also be found in a monotheistic cosmology, but they come through indirection or as background, subliminal, buried, as in dreams. The monotheistic overlay, the narrative of a totalizing history, a salvation history rooted in the beyond of a father god distinct from his creation, is a rejection of precisely those elements which make mythical images bearers of health, images which gather to themselves knowledge of place and its health, community and the dynamics of community health—all woven together in a narrative that *instructs* by locating us in a moral space in which moral imperatives are present to the community with the force and presence of reality, of fact. The mythic images and narratives which gather to themselves knowledge of place and community and the health of each must be free of the influence of such world-denying and self-truncating projects so they can be responsive to world and self. In addition, they must be rich and complex enough to articulate an understanding of both self and world and to weave them together into a unity in which an understanding of self and community *is* an understanding of the place in which life is lived out and in which an understanding of place *is* an understanding of self and community.

Where are *we* to find those "mythic images" which "circle and knot together into a reality" that is life-giving, healthy, liberating? Where we must look is to the *mind*scape/*land*scape which emerges from our narrative and mythical embedment in some particular place. This begins with the inscribing of the nervous system *in* the landscape; the body is the instrument of our knowledge of the world.[32] With language comes a taxonomy of the world, an ordering of our cosmos, and a positioning of ourselves within this matrix. Eventually the cosmos comes to express a moral order—it instructs us in virtue of its very manner of containing us. Shepard argues for the critical importance of the early taxonomic stage, the first ordering of one's cosmos. It is critical that just as the infant passes from the nurturing womb into a nurturing relationship with the first caretaker(s), so the child must pass from this to a sense of embedment in a nurturing cosmos. The claim is that without this there is fixation at the earlier developmental level, a fixation on ambivalences engendered in relation to one's first nurturer(s) which would have been resolved by passing into what he calls the "earth matrix." This second "grounding" or "bonding" to the earth matrix nourishes the growing child in ways that the earlier bonding cannot achieve by itself. By satisfying emerging urges, the earlier bonding is incorporated in the latter bonding; the ambivalences which begin to emerge do not become objects of fixation. The result is not an *identification* with nature; identification is an essentializing move motivated by attempts to deal with ambivalence. As Shepard notes, the lovers of the earth and the destroyers of the earth often have one thing in common: the attempt to handle ambivalence without resolving it, using the defective tools of identification or dichotomization, respectively.[33] What one should do is *relate* to nature as "satisfying other."

Shepard's account of the ways in which we have lost this bioregional connectedness is instructive, for it points to the difficulties that must be faced in the "constant recontextualization" discussed by Martin and Mohanty as well as to some features of "storied residence" that might temper these difficulties. The central claim is that when social structures emerged in an agrarian society which no longer allowed for the broadening of the child's relationship from the human nurturer to nature as the nurturing other in a wider sense, rather than establishing relationships to nature as nurturing other, the image of the mother, with all its ambivalence, was *projected* onto nature. The result was a representation of the mother rather than a clear vision of nature as nurturer but *not* mother. The whole complex of Mother Earth imagery is the result of this projection, making Mother Earth the object of highly ambivalent attitudes and behavior. The love-hate relationship to nature and the need to dominate nature seems to begin precisely with the rise into prominence of Mother Earth imagery. To resolve this particular problem it should not be necessary to return to a preagrarian, gatherer-hunter life. It *is* necessary, however, that we do not take existing, humanly constructed models such as machines, words, and human society as our models and metaphors of order, for these already embed our projections and carry with them the return of the repressed. One consequence of this tendency is a literalization of nature at the conscious level and its use as a projection screen by unconscious processes. Bioregionalism could help turn this around if it were understood in light of the kind of contextualist approach I have been advocating.

The cosmos constructed as a result of a sense of embedment in the "earth matrix" first nourishes and later instructs. "Through myth and its ritual enactments," Shepard says, "natural things are not only themselves but a speaking." Passage into adolescence *not* marked by ambivalence and fixation at earlier levels precludes perception of the world as an illusion to be transcended. Rather than graduating "*from* the world," Shepard says, the child graduates "into its significance."[34]

That this second grounding is in the natural world is important. As the ground out of which we have evolved, it can be satisfying in a way that no substitute for this matrix could be. What is desired is a complex system of images or myths of the human-land community which *instructs* and does so in a way that is felt to be both obligatory and fostering of individual and community health. These purposes can be accomplished best when the community has before it a coherent model of health to draw on. When this model is the one within which, and in interaction with which, both the individual and the community must live, we get precisely the images we need to mediate our relationships to one another and to the land. But nature must be transformed in image to perform this function. A Western scientific description of the specifics of the ecosystem within which one lives is not adequate. It provides the wrong kind of myth. It can and ought to *inform* our construction of appropriate mythical images, but it cannot function as the centerpiece of a viable environmental ethic, much less a *mythos* for our times. Elizabeth Bird asks whether we would want "the world [that] ecology would construct for us if it were to win political hegemony in the sciences?"[35] The *mythos* into which modern ecology is drawn in the minds of many radical environmentalists is that of organicism, the "dream of natural (unforced) community":

> For many radical and antiliberal thinkers, including many feminists considering sciences and technologies, [organicism] has . . . appeared to be an alternative to both antagonistic opposition and to regulatory functionalism. It is easy to forget that organicism is a form of longing for a spontaneous and always healthy body, a perfect opposite to the technicist and reductionist boogey man. . . . Organicism is the analytical longing . . . for purity outside the disruptions of the "artificial." It is the reversed, mirror image of other forms of longing for transcendence.[36]

The integrity of the objective scientific model must, for the purposes I have been sketching (but not for all purposes), give way to the requirement of the health and well-being of individual, community, and land in the construction of an image of nature (with us in it) which effectively instructs. If value is implicit in our descriptions of the world and our place in it, then the narratives we construct will embody value and orient us.

What we want then is language that grows out of experience and articulates it, language intermediate between self and world, their *intersection,* carrying knowledge of both, knowledge charged with valuation and instruction. This is language in which "the clues to the meaning of life [are] embodied in natural things, where everyday life [is] inextricable from spiritual significance and encounter."[37] The vision received in the Native American vision quest, for example, is a culturally mediated intersection of self and world. It is a gift and must be located in the world. It is important not to conceive of these images as projections; they are intersections, encounters. This way of putting it acknowledges both our active construction of reality and nature's role in these negotiations. We should say with Aiken that "The landscape and the language are the same, / And we ourselves are language and are land."[38] Such language mediates experience and the world with language alive and responsive to our interaction with the world, language which articulates not the *logos* of the system as we in the West have come to understand this, but our *telos* within it. It is a language of instruction; and in order to instruct it must embed an understanding of self and world and the relation between the two. The task then is to tell the best stories we can. The tales we tell of our, and our communities', "storied residence" in place are tales not of universal truth, but of local truth, bioregional truth.

The notion of a mythic, narrative, and bioregional construction of self and community, and the "storied residence" out of which action proceeds, has a close affinity with, and relevance to, feminist postmodernist attempts to deal with the "fractured identities" of multiple female voices in the wake of the deconstruction of patriarchal totalizing and essentializing discourse. Listen to the following comparison of Australian aboriginal people with the villager/farmer: "[For the aboriginal peoples the] topographic features and creatures were diffused throughout a vast region. They were not all visible at once and human products were always mixed with the nonhuman. The villager[s by contrast] did not rove through these physical extensions of the self; [they] occupied them. [The aborigine] seemed to inhabit the land like a blood corpuscle, while the farmer [by contrast] was centered in it and could scan it as a whole."[39] The gatherer-hunter who wanders through "physical extensions of the self" "like a blood corpuscle" is certainly not subject to many of the essentializing pressures brought to bear on "civilized" people since the agrarian revolution. The "centered" point of view of the farmer and the diminished natural landscape available for articulating both self and community (as well as its virtual replacement by a humanly-contrived world) are simply the first of many such pressures. The totalizing, essentializing discourse of patriarchal consciousness is the latest of such pressures. Dismantling patriarchal discourse is not likely by itself to eliminate the forces of essentialization and totalization. If the above description is right, the price that was paid by the human move away from the gatherer-hunter condition was precisely the setting in motion of those forces of essentialization and totalization. In the modern world the constant "recontextualization" that Martin and Mohanty speak of is likely to be an ever necessary feature of attempts to produce health and well-being. The concept of "storied residence" or "bioregional narrative" that I have been articulating seems increasingly important once we see the omnipresent nature of the forces of essentialization and totalization. In fact, "storied residence" seems to be a necessary part of the deconstructive process, the dismantling of the manifestations of these forces.

But beyond the project of deconstruction is the goal of health and well-being, which is the primary reason for introducing the idea of bioregional narrative. Authentic existence is not a matter of discovering a "real" self (it is still a social self, a construct); there is just the project of bringing into being healthy communities, healthy selves—an *achievement,* not a discovery of something that is hidden, covered over. But landscapes can be hard, or diminished and distorted, and the health in them and, consequently, in us comes at a price and only with much labor.

What has emerged is a conception of bioregional truth, local truth, or ethical vernacular.[40] The fractured identities of postmodernism, I suggest, can build health and well-being by means of a bioregional contextualization of self and community. The voices of health will be as various and multiple as the landscapes which give rise to them—landscapes which function as metaphors of self and community and figure into those mythical narratives which give voice to the emergence of self and community. The notion of socially constructed selves gives way to the idea of bioregionally constructed selves and communities. In this way, bioregionalism can "ground" the construction of self and community without the essentialization and totalization typical of the various "groundings" of patriarchal culture.

III. Conclusion

My objective in this paper has been to suggest a direction for postmodernism which at the same time sets an agenda for any environmental ethic that opts for the postmodern turn. The central notion of such an ethic, I have suggested, is that of bioregional narrative. In setting this agenda I have for the most part bypassed the difficulties attendant upon the satisfactory articulation of this notion and its embedment in an environmental ethic. Bioregional narratives are normative; and they are the subject of social negotiation. What I *have* been at pains to do is to avoid the foundationalist suggestion that these narratives are *givens* from which ethical injunctions *follow,* to resist, that is, a form of naturalism which would preclude the social negotiation of the stories we tell and the concepts of health and well-being embedded in them. I have not, in this paper, begun the work of such negotiation for the culture in which I find myself.

Notes

Cheney teaches courses in environmental ethics and American Indian philosophies in the Department of Philosophy, University of Wisconsin—Waukesha. The prairie restoration project at the UW—Waukesha biological field station is the source of important ceremonies in his life. His homes are the tallgrass prairies of southeastern Wisconsin and the mountains and deserts of Idaho. An earlier version of this paper was presented at the "EcoFeminist Perspectives: Culture, Nature, Theory" conference at the University of Southern California, March, 1987. The author wishes to thank the following people for comments and criticism: Sally Abbott, David Abram, Tom Birch, Elizabeth Bird, Alison Jaggar, Carolyn Merchant, Patrick Murphy, Linda Nicholson, Karen Warren, Michael Zimmerman, and two anonymous referees.

First published in *Environmental Ethics* 11, No. 2. Permission to reprint courtesy of *Environmental Ethics* and the author.

1. Leslie Marmon Silko, *Ceremony* (New York: New American Library, 1977), pp. 36–37.

2. Sandra Harding, *The Science Question in Feminism* (Ithaca, N.Y.: Cornell University Press, 1986), p. 193. See also Linda Alcoff, "Cultural Feminism versus Post-Structuralism: The Identity Crisis in Feminist Theory," *Signs* 13 (1988): 405–36.

3. John D. Caputo, "The Thought of Being and the Conversation of Mankind: The Case of Heidegger and Rorty," *Review of Metaphysics* 36 (1983): 661-85.

4. See Jim Cheney, "The Intentionality of Desire and the Intentions of People," *Mind* 87 (1978): 517-32.

5. See Vine Deloria, Jr. (Standing Rock Sioux), *God Is Red* (New York: Dell Publishing Company, 1973); various Native American contributors to Calvin Martin, *The American Indian and the Problem of History* (Oxford: Oxford University Press, 1987); Paula Gunn Allen (Laguna Pueblo/Lakota), *The Sacred Hoop: Recovering the Feminine in American Indian Traditions* (Boston: Beacon Press, 1986). Margaret Atwood's depiction of the overthrow of a colonizing consciousness by immersion in the mythos of indigenous people in her novel *Surfacing* (New York: Popular Library, 1972) is instructive. See also Paul Shepard, *Nature and Madness* (San Francisco: Sierra Club Books, 1982) on the issue of ideas and their habitats.

6. Elizabeth Bird (correspondence) points out that health is a *political* concept;

and so it is. It is not only reality which must be negotiated but also such notions as health and well-being.

7. Tom Jay, "The Salmon of the Heart," in Finn Wilcox and Jeremiah Gorsline, eds., *Working the Woods, Working the Sea* (Port Townsend, Wash.: Empty Bowl, 1986), p. 116.

8. This last statement should not be taken to imply, however, that there is some one true account of each situation. I am not offering an *anti*postmodernist account. Elizabeth Bird, who urged clarification on this point, asks: "Couldn't a single contact percolate multiple accounts?" Yes. Discourse is privileged on this account not in virtue of being the "one true story" certified by a foundationalist epistemology; it is privileged in virtue of arising in such a way as to enhance the possibility of its being free of the distorting influence of totalizing overlays.

9. Jay, "Salmon," pp. 101–102.

10. It is an old, old story. One such account is offered by Hans Jonas (*The Gnostic Religion: The Message of the Alien God and the Beginnings of Christianity* [Boston: Beacon Press, 1963]) of the rise of Gnosticism in the early Christian era. As Jonas shows, the parallels between ancient Gnosticism and the spirit of modernism are, in fact, deep and striking. Another story is told by Julian Jaynes (*The Origin of Consciousness in the Breakdown of the Bicameral Mind* [Boston: Houghton Mifflin Company, 1976]), who locates the creation of a distinctively psychological vocabulary and unified concept of the self as having taken place, for the Greeks, somewhere between the composition of *The Iliad* and the composition of *The Odyssey*. Shepard traces "culturally-ratified distortions of childhood," "massive disablement of ontogeny" (*Nature and Madness*, p. ix) leading eventually to the creation of the modern subject back to the agrarian revolution. A reasonable story can also be told which brings these distortions as far back as the Upper Paleolithic, the time of the cave paintings at Lascaux and elsewhere (see John E. Pfeiffer, *The Creative Explosion* [New York: Harper and Row, 1982]). On the construction of the modernist self, see Susan R. Bordo, *The Flight to Objectivity* (Albany: State University of New York Press, 1987). A fascinating account for the Orient can be found in Herbert Fingarette's reading of the Confucian texts (*Confucius The Secular as Sacred* [New York: Harper and Row, 1972]).

11. Jay, "Salmon," p. 112.

12. Ridington, "Fox and Chickadee," in Martin, ed., *The American Indian*, pp. 134-35. Allen, *The Sacred Hoop*. pp. 103–105.

13. Allen, *The Sacred Hoop*, pp. 103–105.

14. This is not to say, however, that such potential is, in fact, realized by all tribal cultures. There are, even in tribal cultures, various pressures at work which all too often result in, for example, male dominance, erosion of female power, and dramatic increases in the level of inter- and intratribal violence. The anthropologist Peggy Reeves Sanday, in her wide-ranging, cross-cultural study of tribal cultures

(*Female Power and Male Dominance: On the Origins of Sexual Inequality* [Cambridge: Cambridge University Press, 1981]), provides a perceptive account of the conditions under which such deterioration either takes place or is held at bay. Such factors include recentness of migration to a new home, environmental stress, reproductive difference, and the type of story of origin told by the culture. The interaction between these and other factors in producing or precluding domination and violence is complex. Even under the best of conditions some form of culturally constructed vigilance seems necessary. In many Native American tribes this takes the form of the trickster or clown. For excellent literary examples see the works of Anne Cameron, *Daughters of Copper Woman* (Vancouver: Press Gang Publishers, 1981), pp. 107–14, and Hyemeyohsts Storm, *Song of Heyoehkah* (New York: Ballantine Books, 1981). See also, Paul Radin, *The Trickster: A Study in American Indian Mythology* (London: Routledge and Kegan Paul Ltd., 1956), Barbara Babcock-Abrahams, " 'A Tolerated Margin of Mess': The Trickster and His Tales Reconsidered," *Journal of the Folklore Institute* 11 (1975): 147–48, and the following from D. M. Dooling and Paul Jordan-Smith, eds., *I Become Part of It* (San Francisco: HarperCollins, 1992): Barbara Tedlock, "Boundaries of Belief" (pp. 124–38) and Emory Sekaquaptewa, "One More Smile for a Hopi Clown" (pp. 150–57).

15. See Harding, *The Science Question*; Carol Gilligan, *In a Different Voice: Psychological Theory and Women's Development* (Cambridge, Mass.: Harvard University Press, 1982); Terry Winant, "The Feminist Standpoint: A Matter of Language," *Hypatia* 2 (1987): 123–48.

16. Conrad Aiken. Quoted in Edith Cobb, *The Ecology of Imagination in Childhood* (New York: Columbia University Press, 1977), p. 67.

17. Alasdair MacIntyre, *After Virtue* (Notre Dame, Ind.: University of Notre Dame Press, 1984), p. 216.

18. Holmes Rolston, III, "The Human Standing in Nature: Storied Fitness in the Moral Observer," in Wayne Sumner, Donald Callen, and Thomas Attig, eds., *Values and Moral Standing* (Bowling Green, Ohio: The Applied Philosophy Program, Bowling Green State University, 1986), pp. 97–98.

19. Aldo Leopold, *A Sand County Almanac* (New York: Ballantine Books, 1970), p. 262.

20. Rolston, "Storied Fitness."

21. Biddy Martin and Chandra Talpade Mohanty, "Feminist Politics: What's Home Got to Do with It?" in Teresa de Lauretis, ed., *Feminist Studies/Critical Studies* (Bloomington: Indiana University Press, 1986), pp. 193–200. See also Alcoff, "Cultural Feminism."

22. Jay, "Salmon," p. 112.

23. Edith Cobb, *The Ecology of Imagination in Childhood* (New York: Columbia University Press, 1977) 76, 76, 76–77.

24. Martin and Mohanty, "Home," pp. 196–97.

25. Ibid., p. 204.

26. Ibid., pp. 209–10.

27. Ibid., p. 208.

28. Jay, "Salmon, p. 117.

29. John Wisdom, "Gods," *Proceedings of the Aristotelian Society* 45 (1944–45): 185–206; Paul Ricoeur, *The Symbolism of Evil* (Boston: Beacon Press, 1967).

30. Shepard, *Nature and Madness,* ch. 3.

31. James Hillman, *Re-Visioning Psychology* (New York: Harper and Row, 1975).

32. I use the paradoxical-sounding phrase "inscribing of the nervous system *in* the landscape" to avoid the modernist empiricism which would be suggested were I to interchange "nervous system" and "landscape." See David Abram, "The Perceptual Implications of Gaia," *The Ecologist* 15 (1985): 96–103, for an overview of some of the literature concerning the views (1) that perception must be studied as an attribute of an organism and its environment taken together, (2) that psyche is a property of the ecosystem as a whole, and (3) that the intellect is an elaboration of creativity at the level of bodily experience.

33. Shepard, *Nature and Madness,* p. 123.

34. Ibid., p. 9.

35. Elizabeth Ann R. Bird, "The Social Construction of Nature: Theoretical Approaches to the History of Environmental Problems," *Environmental Review* 11 (1987): 262.

36. Donna Haraway, "Primatology Is Politics by Other Means," in Ruth Bleier, ed., *Feminist Approaches to Science* (New York: Pergamon Press, 1984), p. 86.

37. Shepard, *Nature and Madness,* p. 6.

38. See note 16.

39. Shepard, *Nature and Madness,* pp. 23–24.

40. My thanks to Carolyn Merchant for suggesting the wonderful term "ethical vernacular."

2

Nature and Silence

Christopher Manes

A Tuscarora Indian once remarked that, unlike his people's experience of the world, for Westerners, "the uncounted voices of nature . . . are dumb."[1] The distinction, which is borne out by anthropological studies of animistic cultures, throws into stark relief an aspect of our society's relationship with the nonhuman world that has only recently become an express theme in the environmental debate. Nature *is* silent in our culture (and in literate societies generally) in the sense that the status of being a speaking subject is jealously guarded as an exclusively human prerogative.

The language we speak today, the idiom of Renaissance and Enlightenment humanism, veils the processes of nature with its own cultural obsessions, directionalities, and motifs that have no analogues in the natural world. As Max Oelschlaeger puts it, ". . . we are people who presumably must think of the world in terms of the learned categorical scheme of Modernism."[2] It is as if we had compressed the entire buzzing, howling, gurgling biosphere into the narrow vocabulary of epistemology, to the point that someone like Georg Lukács could say, "nature is a societal category"—and actually be understood.[3]

In contrast, for animistic cultures, those that see the natural world as inspirited, not just people, but also animals, plants, and even "inert" entities such as stones and rivers are perceived as being articulate and at times intelligible subjects, able to communicate and interact with humans for good or ill. In addition to human language, there is also the language of birds, the wind, earthworms, wolves, and waterfalls—a world of autonomous speakers whose intents (especially for hunter-gatherer peoples) one ignores at one's peril.

To regard nature as alive and articulate has consequences in the realm of social practices. It conditions what passes for knowledge about nature and how institutions put that knowledge to use.[4] Michel Foucault has amply demonstrated that social power operates through a regime of privileged speakers, having historical embodiments as priests and kings, authors, intellectuals, and celebrities.[5] The words of these speakers are taken seriously (as opposed to the discourse of "meaningless" and often silenced speakers such as women, minorities, children, prisoners, and the insane). For human societies of all kinds, moral consideration seems to fall only within a circle of speakers in communication with one another. We can, thus, safely agree with Hans Peter Duerr when he says that "people do not exploit a nature that speaks to them."[6] Regrettably, our culture has gone a long way to demonstrate that the converse of this statement is also true.

As a consequence, we require a viable environmental ethics to confront the silence of nature in our contemporary regime of thought, for it is within this vast, eerie silence that surrounds our garrulous human subjectivity that an ethics of exploitation regarding nature has taken shape and flourished, producing the ecological crisis that now requires the search for an environmental counter-ethics.

Recognizing this need, some strains of deep ecology have stressed the link between listening to the nonhuman world (i.e., treating it as a silenced subject) and reversing the environmentally destructive practices modern society pursues.[7] While also underscoring the need to establish communication between human subjects and the natural world, John Dryzek has recently taken exception with this "anti-rationalist" approach of deep ecology, which he suspects is tainted by latent totalitarianism.[8] As an alternative, he proposes to expand Habermas' notion of a discursively rational community to include aspects of the nonhuman, to break the silence of nature, but to retain the language of humanism that suffuses the texts, institutions, and values we commonly celebrate as the flowers of the Enlightenment. Others, such as Murray Bookchin, have in like fashion also attempted to rescue reason from its own successes at quieting the messy "irrationality" of nature, to have their *ratio* and ecology too.[9]

It is a dubious task. By neglecting the origin of this silence in the breakdown of animism, the humanist critics of deep ecology reiterate a discourse that by its very logocentrism marginalizes nature, mutes it, pushes it into a hazy backdrop against which the rational human subject struts upon the epistemological stage. It has become almost a platitude in modern philosophy since Kant that reason (as an institutional motif, not a cognitive faculty) is intimately related to the excesses of political power and self-interest. As Foucault puts it, "we should not need to wait for bureaucracy or concentration camps to recognize the existence of such relations."[10] The easy alliance of power and reason that sustains those institutions involved in environmental destruction also sustains their discourses. Thus, at the very least, we should look askance at the emancipatory claims humanists like Dryzek and Bookchin are still making for reason in the field of environmental philosophy.

In this paper, I want to avoid the jaded polemic between rationality and the irrational, and enter the issue "perpendicularly," so to speak, by taking the silence of nature itself (not the desire to rescue reason, the human subject, or some other privileged motif) as a cue for recovering a language appropriate to an environmental ethics. In particular, this approach requires that I consider how nature has grown silent in our discourse, shifting from an animistic to a symbolic presence, from a voluble subject to a mute object. My aim is neither a critique of reason nor a history of Western representations of nature, both of which have been made happily redundant by a century of scholarship. Rather, I offer a brief genealogy of a discourse, including reason, that has submerged nature into the depths of silence and instrumentality.

Heidegger is surely correct when he argues that all language both reveals and conceals.[11] However, our particular idiom, a pastiche of medieval hermeneutics and Renaissance humanism, with its faith in reason, intellect and progress, has created an immense realm of silences, a world of "not saids" called nature, obscured in global claims of eternal truths about human difference, rationality, and transcendence.[12] If the domination of nature with all its social anxieties rests upon this void, then we must contemplate not only learning a new ethics, but a new language free from the directionalities of humanism, a language that incorporates a decentered, postmodern, post-humanist perspective. In short, we require the language of ecological humility that deep ecology, however gropingly, is attempting to express.

In his comprehensive study of shamanism, Mircea Eliade writes: "All over the world learning the language of animals, especially of birds, is equivalent to knowing the secrets of nature. . . ."[13] We tend to relegate such ideas to the realm of superstition and irrationality, where they can easily be dismissed. However, Eliade is describing the perspective of animism, a sophisticated and long-lived phenomenology of nature. Among its characteristics is the belief (1) that all the phenomenal world is alive in the sense of being inspirited—including humans, cultural artifacts, and natural entities, both biological and "inert," and (2) that not only is the nonhuman world alive, but it is filled with articulate subjects, able to communicate with humans.[14]

Animism undergirds many contemporary tribal societies, just as it did our own during pre-Christian times. Indeed, the overwhelming evidence suggests the universality of animism in human history.[15] Even in modern technological society, animistic reflexes linger on in attenuated form. Cars and sports teams are named after animals (as if to capture sympathetically their power). Children talk to dolls and animals without being considered mentally ill, and are, in fact, read fairy tales, most of which involve talking animals. Respectable people shout at machines that do not operate properly. While modern scholarship tends to focus on "explaining" this kind of thinking in psychological or sociological terms, my interest in it lies in the sense it gives us of what might be called the "animistic subject," a shifting, autonomous, articulate identity that cuts across the human/nonhuman distinction. Here, human speech is not understood as some unique faculty, but as a subset of the speaking of the world.

Significantly, animistic societies have almost without exception avoided the kind of environmental destruction that makes environmental ethics an explicit social theme with us.[16] Many primal groups have no word for wilderness and do not make a clear distinction between wild and domesticated life, since the tension between nature and culture never becomes acute enough to raise the problem.[17] This fact should strike a cautionary note for those, such as Bookchin and Robert Gardiner, who illegitimately use modern technological societies to stand for all humanity throughout history in global claims about culture compelling humans to "consciously *change* [nature] by means of a highly institutionalized form of community we call 'society.' "[18] Our distracted and probably transitory culture may have this giddy compulsion; culture per se does not.

In the medieval period, animism as a coherent system broke down in our culture, for a variety of reasons.[19] Not the least of these was the introduction of two powerful institutional technologies: literacy and Christian exegesis.

Jack Goody argues that alphabetic writing "changes the nature of the representations of the world," because it allows humans to lay out discourse and "examine it in a more abstract, generalised and 'rational' way."[20] This scrutiny encouraged the epistemological inference, apparently impossible in oral cultures where language exists only as evanescent utterances, that meaning somehow resides in human speech (more particularly in those aspects of it susceptible to rational analysis), not in the phenomenal world. Down this road lies the counterintuitive conclusion that only humans can act as speaking subjects.

Taking Goody's analysis a step farther, David Abram maintains that our relationship with texts is "wholly animistic," since the articulate subjectivity that was once experienced in nature shifted to the written word.[21] At one time nature spoke; now texts do ("it says . . ." is how we describe writing). As cultural artifacts, texts embody human (or ostensibly divine) subjects, but stand conspicuously outside nature, whose status as subject therefore becomes problematical in ways unknown to nonliterate, animistic societies.

The animistic view of nature was further eroded by medieval Christianity's particular mode for interpreting texts, exegesis. Christian theology was clear, if uneasy, on this point: all things—including classical literature, the devil, Viking invasions, sex, and nature—existed by virtue of God's indulgence and for his own, usually inscrutable, purposes.[22] With this point in mind, exegesis, the branch of religious studies dedicated to interpreting the Bible, concluded that behind the *littera,* the literal (often mundane) meaning of a biblical passage, lay some *moralis,* a moral truth established by God. And beyond that lurked some divine purpose, the *anagogue,* almost certainly beyond the ken of human intellect, unless divine revelation obligingly made it evident.

The cognitive practice of exegesis overflowed the pages of the Bible onto other texts and ultimately onto the phenomenal world itself. By the twelfth century, the German philosopher Hugh of St. Victor could talk about "the Book of nature"—a formulation that would have puzzled a Greek or Roman intellectual of the classic period, not to mention Hugh's own tribal ancestors just a few centuries earlier.[23] Like the leaven or mustard seeds in Christ's parables, the things in nature could thus be seen as mere *littera*—signs that served as an occasion for discovering deeper realms of meaning underlying the forms of the physical world. According to medieval commentators, eagles soared higher than any other bird and could gaze upon the sun, undazzled, because they were put on Earth to be a symbol of St. John and his apocalyptic vision, not the other way round. From this hermeneutical perspective, it was inconceivable that eagles should be autonomous, self-willed subjects, flying high for their own purposes without reference to some celestial intention, which generally had to do with man's redemption. Exegesis swept all things into the net of divine meaning.

Such, at least, was the theory (and although it appears alien to modern thought, we should consider that our relationship with nature, despite its outward empiricism, is not that different; we have replaced the search for divine meanings with other "transcendental" concerns such as discerning the evolutionary *telos* of humanity[24]). Exegesis established God as a transcendental subject speaking through natural entities, which, like words on a page, had a symbolic meaning, but no autonomous voice. It distilled the veneration of word and reason into a discourse that we still speak today.

It is, of course, a simplification to suggest that a period as intellectually and institutionally diverse as the Middle Ages experienced nature in one way only.[25] Nevertheless, in broadest terms, for the institutions that dominated discourse during the Middle Ages (i.e, the Church and aristocracy), nature was a symbol for the glory and orderliness of God. This idea found its cosmological model in the so-called *scala naturae* or "Great Chain of Being," a depiction of the world as a vast filigree of lower and higher forms, from zoophytes to Godhead, with humankind's place higher than beasts and a little less than angels, as the Psalm puts it. Curiously, for the medieval exegete, the Great Chain of Being at times acted as a theological restraint against abusing the natural world, at least within the hushed, abstracted cells of the cloister. Thomas Aquinas invoked the *scala naturae* in an argument that—*mutatis mutandis*—could have been made by a conservation biologist condemning monoculture: "[T]he goodness of the species transcends the goodness of the individual, as form transcends matter; therefore the multiplication of species is a greater addition to the good of the universe than the multiplication of individuals of a single species. The perfection of the universe therefore requires not only a multitude of individuals, but also diverse kinds, and therefore diverse grades of things."[26]

When the Renaissance inherited the *scala naturae,* however, a new configuration of thought that would eventually be called humanism converted it from a symbol of human restraint in the face of a perfect order to an emblem of human superiority over the natural world. Originally a curriculum emphasizing classical learning, humanism came to emphasize a faith in reason, progress, and intellect that would become the cornerstone of modern technological culture.[27] Drawing on humanity's position in the Great Chain between "dumb beasts" and articulate angels, humanism insisted there was an ontological difference between *Homo sapiens* and the rest of the biosphere, infusing a new and portentous meaning to the ancient observation that humans had rational discourse while animals did not. "Man" became, to quote Hamlet, "the beauty of the world! the paragon of animals!" (though Shakespeare, as if aware of the absurdity of the claim, follows this statement with an obscene joke at Hamlet's expense).[28] The tragic soliloquist might have added: the sole subject of the phenomenal world. About the same time *Hamlet* was written, Francis Bacon expressed this teleological craze more bluntly: "Man, if we look to final causes, may be regarded as the centre of the world; inasmuch that if man were taken away from the world, the rest would seem to be all astray, without aim or purpose. . . ."[29]

Strained by the scientific revolution, the celestial links to this chain may have grudgingly come undone in our time (conveniently leaving our species at the apex of the order), but its cultural residue still haunts the human and physical sciences. It is the source of the modern notion that Homo sapiens stands highest in a natural order of "lower life forms"—a directionality that comes straight out of the *scala naturae,* which seems to hover translucently before our eyes, distorting our representations of the natural world into hierarchical modes, while itself remaining all but invisible.[30]

The Great Chain of Being, exegesis, literacy, and a complex skein of institutional and intellectual developments have, in effect, created a fictionalized, or more accurately put, fraudulent version of the species Homo sapiens: the character "Man," what Muir calls "Lord Man." And this "Man" has become the sole subject, speaker, and rational sovereign of the natural order in the story told by humanism since the Renaissance.[31]

Our representations of nature may have undergone a variety of important permutations since the Middle Ages, molding and conditioning our discourse about respecting or abusing the natural world. But the character of "Man" as the only creature with anything to say cuts across these developments and persists, even in the realm of environmental ethics. It is the fiction reiterated by Bookchin in his teleological description of evolution as "a cumulative thrust toward ever-greater complexity, ever-greater subjectivity, and finally, ever-greater mind with a capacity for conceptual thought, symbolic communication of the most sophisticated kind, and self-consciousness in which natural evolution knows itself purposively and willfully."[32] Through humanism, the boisterous, meandering parade of organic forms is transfigured into a forced march led by the human subject.

It is hardly surprising that this subject should demand such an overbearing role in environmental philosophy. Post-Enlightenment emancipatory thought, from idealism to Marxism to Freud, has made the human subject the expectant ground of all possible knowledge. Empiricism may have initiated an "interrogation" of nature unknown to medieval symbolic thought, but in this questioning no one really expects nature to answer. Rather, the inquiry only offers an occasion to find meanings and purposes that must by default reside in us. As the self-proclaimed soliloquist of the world, "Man" is obliged to use *his* language as the point of intersection between the human subject and what is to be known about nature, and therefore the messy involvement of observer with the observed becomes an obsessive theme of modern philosophy.[33] In the form of the Heisenberg Principle, it has even entered the serene positivism of scientific thought.

Postmodern philosophy has rudely challenged this transcendental narcissism, viewing the subject as fragmented and decentered in the social realm, a product of institutional technologies of control rather than the unmoved mover of all possible knowledge.[34] This challenge has set the stage for the reevaluation of the silence of nature imposed by the human subject. In environmental ethics, however, resistance to the tendentious rhetoric of "Man" has come almost exclusively from the camp of deep ecology.

From one perspective, the biocentric stance of deep ecology may be understood as focusing evolutionary theory and the science of ecology onto the idiom of humanism to expose and overcome the unwarranted claim that humans are unique subjects and speakers. Although regrettably silent on the issue, biologists qua biologists recognize that humans are not the "goal" of evolution any more than tyrannosaurs were during their sojourn on Earth. As far as scientific inquiry can tell, evolution has no goal, or if it does we cannot discern it, and at the very least it does not seem to be us. The most that can be said is that during the last 350 million years natural selection has shown an inordinate fondness for beetles—and before that trilobites.

This observation directly contradicts the *scala naturae* and its use in humanist discourse. From the perspective of biological adaptation, elephants are no "higher" than earwigs; salamanders are no less "advanced" than sparrows; cabbages have as much evolutionary status as kings. Darwin invited our culture to face the fact that in the observation of nature there exists not one scrap of evidence that humans are superior to or even more interesting than, say, lichen.

Predictably, we declined the invitation. Not everyone likes being compared to lichen, and traditional humanists in the environmental debate, explicitly or implicitly, continue to affirm the special subject status of "Man." Bookchin, for instance, insists that humans have a "second nature" (culture) which gives them not only the right but the duty to alter, shape and control "first nature" (the nonhuman world).[35] Henryk Skolimowski sounds a similar trumpet of ecological manifest destiny, proclaiming: "We are here . . . to maintain, to creatively transform, and to carry on the torch of evolution."[36] While refreshingly more restrained, Dryzek seems to accept Habermas' position that the essence of communication is reason—which is not coincidently the kind of discourse favored by human subjects, or more precisely by that small portion of them who are heirs of the Enlightenment. Almost all of us, including biologists, refer to "lower" and "higher" animals, with the tacit understanding that Homo sapiens stands as the uppermost point of reference in this chimerical taxonomy. (Contrast this system of arrangement with the decentered and hence more accurate taxonomy of many American Indian tribes who use locutions such as "four-legged," "two-legged," and "feathered.")

It is no exaggeration to say that as a cultural phenomenon, as opposed to a scientific discourse, evolutionary theory has been absorbed by the *scala naturae* and strategically used to justify humanity's domination of nature. Evolution is often represented graphically as a procession of life forms moving left to right, starting with single-celled organisms, then invertebrates, fish, amphibians, and so on up to "Man," the apparent zenith of evolution by virtue of his brain size, self-consciousness, or some other privileged quality. Strictly speaking this tableau, which we have all seen in high school textbooks, only describes *human* evolution, not evolution in general. Nevertheless, for a technological culture transfixed by the presumed supremacy of intellect over nature, human evolution *is* evolution for all intents and purposes. The emergence of Homo sapiens stands for the entire saga of biological adaptation on the planet, so that everything that came before takes its meaning, in Baconian fashion, from this one form.[37]

None of this directionality has any corroboration in the natural world. Rather, it belongs to the rhetoric of Renaissance humanism, even though it has also found its way into environmental ethics. Bookchin, for example, has proudly proclaimed that his philosophy is "avowedly humanistic in the high Renaissance meaning of the term," which he associates with "a shift in vision . . . from superstition to reason."[38] It cannot be emphasized enough, however, that, the velleities of humanist philosophers notwithstanding, in nature there simply is no higher or lower, first or second, better or worse. There is only the unfolding of life form after life form, more or less genealogically related, each with a mix of characteristics. To privilege intellect or self-consciousness, as opposed to photosynthesis, poisoned fangs, or sporogenesis, may soothe ancient insecurities about humanity's place in the cosmos, but it has nothing to do with evolutionary theory and does not correspond to observable nature.

In similar fashion, biocentrism brings to bear the science of ecology upon the exclusionary claims about the human subject. From the language of humanism one could easily get the impression that Homo sapiens is the only species on the planet worthy of being a topic of discourse. Ecology paints quite a different, humbling, picture. If fungus, one of the "lowliest" of forms on a humanistic scale of values, were to go extinct tomorrow, the effect on the rest of the biosphere would be catastrophic, since the health of forests depends on *Mycorrhyzal* fungus, and the disappearance of forests would upset the hydrology, atmosphere, and temperature of the entire globe. In contrast, if Homo sapiens disappeared, the event would go virtually unnoticed by the vast majority of Earth's life forms. As hominids, we dwell at the outermost fringes of important ecological processes such as photosynthesis and the conversion of biomass into usable nutrients. No lofty language about being the paragon of animals or the torchbearer of evolution can change this ecological fact—which is reason enough to reiterate it as often as possible.

Mercifully, perhaps, there exist other touchstones for appraising human worth besides ecology and evolutionary theory—philosophy, literature, art, ethics, the legacy of the Renaissance and Enlightenment, for the most part, that Dryzek, Bookchin, and other humanist environmentalists clamor to preserve. When, however, the issue is the silencing of nature by the rhetoric of "Man," we need to find new ways to talk about human freedom, worth, and purpose, without eclipsing, depreciating, and objectifying the nonhuman world. Infused with the language of humanism, these traditional fields of knowledge are ill-equipped to do so, wedded as they are to the monologue of the human subject.

Bill Devall, coauthor of *Deep Ecology,* once suggested that deep ecology involves learning a new language.[39] Indeed, environmental ethics must aspire to be more than just an explicit schema of values proclaimed as "true," for ethics are implicated in the way we talk about the world, the way we perceive it. In an attempt to reanimate nature, we must have the courage to learn that new language, even if it puts at risk the privileged discourse of reason—and without a doubt, it does.

A language free from an obsession with human preeminence and reflecting the ontological humility implicit in evolutionary theory, ecological science, and postmodern thought, must leap away from the rhetoric of humanism we speak today. Perhaps it will draw on the ontological egalitarianism of native American or other primal cultures, with their attentiveness to place and local processes. Attending to ecological knowledge means metaphorically relearning "the language of birds"—the passions, pains, and cryptic intents of the other biological communities that surround us and silently interpenetrate our existence. Oelschlaeger has convincingly argued that such relearning is precisely what "wilderness thinkers" such as Thoreau and Snyder are attempting to do.[40]

Dryzek suggests that rational discourse can make an agenda of this listening to place, its requirements and ways. But, as he himself points out, the discourse of reason is not a private attribute, but a communal endeavor. As such, it is enmeshed in the institutions that have silenced nature through the production of various kinds of knowledge—psychological, ethical, political—about "Man."

I am not advocating here a global attack on reason, as if the irrational were the key to the essence of the human being the way humanists claim reason is. I am suggesting the need to dismantle a particular historical use of reason, a use that has produced a certain kind of human subject that only speaks soliloquies in a world of irrational silences. Unmasking the universalist claims of "Man" must be the starting point in our attempt to reestablish communication with nature, not out of some nostalgia for an animistic past, but because the human subject that pervades institutional knowledge since the Renaissance already embodies a relationship with nature that precludes a speaking world. As scholars, bureaucrats, citizens, and writers, we participate in a grid of institutional knowledge that constitutes "Man" and his speaking into the void left by the retreat of animism. Therefore, we have to ask not only how to communicate with nature, as Dryzek does, but *who* should be doing the communicating. "Man," the prime fiction of the Renaissance, will not do.

Perhaps the new language we require can draw upon an earlier practice from our own culture: the medieval contemplative tradition with its sparseness, sobriety, and modesty of speech. Alan Drengson, editor of the deep ecology journal, *The Trumpeter,* has established the Ecostery Project, which hopes to revive a medieval social form: monasteries whose purpose is to promote an understanding of, reverence for, and dialogue with nature. Medieval discourse, for all its absurdities, at times revealed a refined sense of human limitation and respect for otherness, virtues much needed today. The contemplative tradition, too, was a communicating without the agenda of reason.

For half a millennium, "Man" has been the center of conversation in the West. This fictional character has occluded the natural world, leaving it voiceless and subjectless. Nevertheless, "Man" is not an inevitability. He came into being at a specific time due to a complex series of intellectual and institutional mutations, among them the sudden centrality of reason. He could just as inexplicably vanish. To that end, a viable environmental ethics must challenge the humanistic backdrop that makes "Man" possible, restoring us to the humbler status of Homo sapiens: one species among millions of other beautiful, terrible, fascinating—and signifying—forms.

As we contemplate the *fin de siècle* environmental ruins that stretch out before us, we can at least be clear about one thing: the time has come for our culture to politely change the subject.

Notes

Manes is the author of *Green Rage: Radical Environmentalism and the Unmaking of Civilization* (Boston: Little, Brown and Co., 1990), which was nominated for a *Los Angeles Times* book award in science. He is finishing his dissertation in medieval English literature at the University of Oregon.

First published in *Environmental Ethics* 14, no. 4. Permission to reprint courtesy of *Environmental Ethics* and the author.

1. Quoted in Hans Peter Duerr, *Dreamtime: Concerning the Boundary Between Wilderness and Civilization,* trans. Felicitas Goodman (Oxford: Basil Blackwell, 1985), p. 90.

2. Max Oelschlaeger, "Wilderness, Civilization, and Language," in Max Oelschlaeger, ed., *The Wilderness Condition: Essays on Environment and Civilization* (San Francisco: Sierra Club Books, 1992), p. 273.

3. George Lukács, *History and Class Consciousness,* trans. Rodney Livingstone (Cambridge, Mass.: M.I.T. Press, 1968), p. 234.

4. Surely one reason laws against the inhumane treatment of pets have entered our rigorously anthropocentric jurisprudence must be the sense that domesticated animals communicate with us (presumably in ways wild animals do not) and therefore acquire a vague status as quasi-subjects.

5. See especially, Michel Foucault, *Madness and Civilization,* trans. Richard Howard (New York: Vintage, 1973), pp. i–x; "What Is an Author?" *Language, Counter-Memory, Practice: Selected Essays and Interviews by Michel Foucault,* ed. Donald F. Bouchard, trans. Donald F. Bouchard and Sherry Simon (Ithaca, N.Y.: Cornell University Press, 1977), pp. 113–38.

6. Duerr, *Dreamtime,* p. 92.

7. See, especially, John Seed, Joanna Macy, Pat Fleming, and Arne Naess, *Thinking Like a Mountain: Toward a Council of All Beings* (Philadelphia: New Society Publishers, 1988). For an original and enlightening discussion of the interrelationship between language and wilderness, see Oelschlaeger, "Wilderness, Civilization, and Language," pp. 271–308.

8. John S. Dryzek, "Green Reason: Communicative Ethics for the Biosphere," *Environmental Ethics* 12 (1990): 200.

9. Murray Bookchin, *The Ecology of Freedom* (Palo Alto, Calif.: Cheshire Books, 1982).

10. Michel Foucault, *Politics, Philosophy, Culture: Interviews and Other Writings, 1977–1984,* trans. Alan Sheridan (New York: Routledge, 1988), p. 59.

11. Martin Heidegger, *An Introduction to Metaphysics,* trans. Ralph Mannheim (New Haven, Conn.: Yale University Press, 1959), pp. 93–206.

12. I use the term "Renaissance humanism" broadly to include a pastiche of the cultural obsessions mentioned, which have continued through the Enlightenment. The "meaning" of these motifs may change as different institutions use them strategically for different purposes. Nevertheless, they have been consistently deployed in the domination of nature, the issue at hand here.

13. Mircea Eliade, *Shamanism: Archaic Techniques of Ecstacy* (Princeton, N.J.: Princeton University Press, 1972), p. 98.

14. See Robert H. Lowie, *Primitive Religion* (New York: Boni and Liveright, 1924), pp. 99–135. Like humanism, animism may have many "meanings" depending on how institutions use it, but the institutions in animistic societies tend to wield power in a manner too discontinuous and inefficient to dominate discourse the way ours do. See Stanley Diamond, *In Search of the Primitive: A Critique of Civilization* (New Brunswick, N.J.: Transaction Books, 1974).

15. See Edward B. Tyler, *Primitive Culture* (New York: Holt and Co., 1889), p. 425; Louise Bäckman and Åke Hultkranz, *Shamanism in Lapp Society* (Stockholm: Alquist and Wiksell, 1978), p. 27. Although Bäckman and Hultkranz only discuss shamanism, it is well-attested that shamanistic practices depend on an animistic worldview.

16. The Easter Islanders, whose culture was apparently animistic, are the only exception I know of, and their problems probably tell us more about the fragility of island ecosystems than social structures.

17. See Darrell Addison Posey, "The Science of the Mebêngôkre," *Orion* (Summer 1990): 16–23; Jon Christopher Crocker, *Vital Souls: Bororo Cosmology, Natural Symbolism, and Shamanism* (Tucson: University of Arizona Press, 1988).

18. Murray Bookchin, "Social Ecology versus 'Deep Ecology': A Challenge for the Ecology Movement," *Green Perspectives, Newsletter of the Green Program Project* 4–5 (Summer 1987): 27; Robert W. Gardiner, "Between Two Worlds: Humans in Nature and Culture," *Environmental Ethics* 12 (1990): 339–52.

19. Animism had already collapsed in classical Mediterranean cultures with the earlier introduction of literacy and humanism. See Morris Berman, *The Reenchantment of the World* (New York: Bantam Books, 1984), p. 57.

20. Jack Goody, *The Domestication of the Savage Mind* (Cambridge: Cambridge University Press, 1977), p. 37.

21. David Abram, "On the Ecological Consequences of Alphabet Literacy: Reflections in the Shadow of Plato's *Phaedrus*," unpublished essay, 1989.

22. See Arthur O. Lovejoy, *The Great Chain of Being: A Study of the History of an Idea* (Cambridge, Mass.: Harvard University Press, 1950), pp. 67–98. For a contrast between the exegetical and non-exegetical traditions in the Middle Ages, see Cecil Wood, "The Viking Universe," *Studies for Einar Haugen* (The Hague, Paris: Mouton, 1972), pp. 568–73.

23. Hugh of St. Victor, *The Didascalicon of Hugh of St. Victor: A Medieval Guide to the Arts,* trans. Jerome Taylor (New York: Columbia University Press, 1961), p. 64. The metaphor of the world as a book appeared as early as Augustine's *Confessions,* but it did not begin to mold discourse about nature until the later Middle Ages.

24. For a discussion of the "return of exegesis," see Michel Foucault, *The Order of Things: An Archaeology of the Human Sciences* (New York: Vintage Press, 1973), pp. 297–99.

25. As early as the thirteenth century, Albertus Magnus, mentor of Thomas Aquinas, was already writing "natural histories" that were extra-, if not anti-exegetical. Albertus Magnus, *Man and Beast,* trans. James J. Scanlan (Binghamton, N.Y.: Medieval and Renaissance Text and Studies, 1987).

26. Thomas Aquinas, *Summa contra gentiles,* bk. 3, chap. 71. Quoted in Lovejoy, *The Great Chain of Being,* p. 77. Aquinas, of course, meant species in the philosophical, not the biological sense, but the principle is strikingly similar.

27. See David Ehrenfeld, *The Arrogance of Humanism* (Oxford: Oxford University Press, 1978).

28. William Shakespeare, *Hamlet,* act 2, sc. 2, lines 306–10.

29. *The Philosophical Works of Francis Bacon,* ed. Robert Leslie Ellis and James Spedding (1905; reprint ed., Freeport, N.Y.: Books for Libraries Press, 1970), 6:747.

30. For a discussion of this "translucent" quality of representations, see Roland Barthes, *Mythologies,* trans. Annette Lavers (New York: Hill and Wang, 1972), pp. 109–59.

31. The concept of "Man" as a fiction is taken from Foucault, *The Order of Things,* though I have shifted his usage to accommodate the theme of nature's silence.

32. Bookchin, "Social Ecology," p. 20.

33. For a comprehensive discussion of the problematic use of the human subject as the ground of knowledge since the Enlightenment, see Foucault, *The Order of Things,* pp. 303–43.

34. See, for instance, Foucault, "Critical Theory/Intellectual History," *Politics, Philosophy, Culture,* pp. 17–46.

35. Bookchin, "Social Ecology," p. 21. In a recent article, Bookchin truculently denies that he endorses the domination of nature, but then goes on to suggest with a straight face that perhaps humans should someday terraform the Canadian barrens (presumably after removing the polar bears) into something more to our liking (or to the liking of whatever institution is powerful enough to carry out such a bizarre scheme). "Recovering Evolution: A Reply to Eckersley and Fox," *Environmental Ethics* 12 (1990): 253–74.

36. Henryk Skolimowski, *Eco-Philosophy* (Boston: Marion Boyers, 1981), p. 68.

37. Although scientists, of course, are well aware of the difference, and do represent evolution in a more genealogically correct manner, the scientific representation lacks the cultural resonance of the humanized tableau.

38. Bookchin, "Social Ecology," p. 20.

39. Bill Devall, personal correspondence, 17 October 1988.

40. Oelschlaeger, "Wilderness, Civilization, and Language."

3

Merleau-Ponty and the Voice of the Earth

David Abram

I. Introduction

Slowly, inexorably, members of our species are beginning to catch sight of a world that exists beyond the confines of our specific culture—beginning to recognize, that is, that our own personal, social, and political crises reflect a growing crisis in the biological matrix of life on the planet. The ecological crisis may be the result of a recent and collective perceptual disorder in our species, a unique form of myopia which it now forces us to correct. For many who have regained a genuine depth perception, recognizing their own embodiment as entirely internal to, and thus wholly dependent upon, the vaster body of the Earth, the only possible course of action is to begin planning and working on behalf of the ecological world which they now discern.

And yet ecological thinking is having a great deal of trouble taking root in the human world—it is still viewed by most as just another ideology; meanwhile, ecological science remains a highly specialized discipline circumscribed within a mechanistic biology. Without the concerted attention of philosophers, ecology lacks a coherent and common language adequate to its aims; it thus remains little more than a growing bundle of disparate facts, resentments, and incommunicable visions.[1]

It is my belief that the phenomenological investigations of Maurice Merleau-Ponty provide the seeds of a new and radical philosophy of nature that remains true to the diversity of experience within the biosphere of this planet. In this paper I show why a phenomenology that takes seriously the primacy of perception is destined to culminate in a renewed awareness of our responsibility to the Earth, and why the movements toward an ecological awareness on this continent and elsewhere have much to gain from a careful consideration of Merleau-Ponty's discoveries.[2]

I will be, of necessity, simplifying his work. I am not, moreover, interested in merely repeating his ideas twenty-five years after his death; I wish rather to accomplish a creative reading of his writings in order to indicate, not necessarily what Merleau-Ponty knew he was saying, but rather what was gradually saying itself through him. Where this interpretation moves beyond the exact content of Merleau-Ponty's texts, it is nevertheless informed by a close and longstanding acquaintance with those texts. Since I am here interested less in the past than in the future of his project, I have organized this paper in accordance with the plan that Merleau-Ponty himself proposed in the final working note that he wrote down in March 1961, shortly before his unexpected death, in which he projected three major sections for the new book on which he was working: first, "The Visible," then "Nature," and finally "Logos."[3]

II. The Visible

The visible about us seems to rest in itself. It is as though our vision were formed at the heart of the visible, or as though there were between it and us an intimacy as close as that between the sea and the strand.[4]

There must be depth since there is a point whence I see—since the world surrounds me. . . .[5]

The great achievement of Merleau-Ponty's major completed work, *The Phenomenology of Perception*,[6] was to show that the fluid creativity we commonly associate with the human intellect is, in actuality, an elaboration or recapitulation of a deep creativity already underway at the most immediate level of bodily perception. Phenomenological philosophy had, since its inception, aimed at a rigorous description of things as they appear to an experiencing consciousness. Yet the body had remained curiously external to this "transcendental" consciousness. Merleau-Ponty was the first phenomenologist to identify the body, itself, as the conscious subject of experience. Transcendence, no longer a special property of the abstract intellect, becomes in his *Phenomenology* a capacity of the physiological body itself—its power of responding to other bodies, of touching, hearing, and seeing things, resonating with things. Perception *is* this ongoing transcendence, the ecstatic nature of the living body.

By thus shifting the prime locus of subjectivity from the human intellect to what he called the "body-subject" or the "lived body," Merleau-Ponty uncovered the radical extent to which all subjectivity, or awareness, presupposes our inherence in a corporeal world. And this presupposed world is not entirely undefined, it is not just any world, for it has a specific structure—that is, it exists in both proximity and distance, and it has a horizon. More specifically, this always-already-existing world is characterized by a distant horizon that surrounds me wherever I move, holding my body in a distant embrace while provoking my perceptual exploration. It is a world that is structured in *depth*, and from the *Phenomenology of Perception* on, depth—the dimensional spread from the near to the far—becomes the paradigm phenomenon in Merleau-Ponty's writings.

The depth of a landscape or a thing can often be construed by the body-subject in a number of different ways: that cloud that I see can be a small cloud close overhead or a huge cloud far above; meanwhile what I had thought was a bird turns out to be a speck of dust on my glasses. Depth is always the dimension of ambiguity, confusion. The experience of depth is the experience of a world that both includes one's own body and yet spreads into the distance, a world where things hide themselves, not just beyond the horizon but behind other things, a world where indeed no thing can be seen all at once, in which objects offer themselves to the gaze only by withholding some aspect of themselves—their other side, or their interior depths—for further exploration. Depth, this mysterious dimension, which every schoolchild knows as the "third" dimension (after height and breadth), Merleau-Ponty asserts is the *first*, most primordial dimension, from which all others are abstracted.[7] To the student of perception, the phenomenon of depth is the original ambiguity: it is depth that provides the slack or play in the immediately perceived world, the instability that already calls upon the freedom of the body to engage, to choose, to *focus* the world long before any verbal reflection comes to thematize and appropriate that freedom as its own. And so the experience of depth runs like a stream throughout the course of Merleau-Ponty's philosophizing, from the many analyses of visual depth and the incredible discussion of ocular convergence (focusing) in the *Phenomenology of Perception*[8] to the extended meditation on depth in his last complete essay, "Eye and Mind"[9]—a subterranean stream which surfaces only here and there, but which ceaselessly provides the texture of his descriptions, the source of his metaphors. As he himself asserts in a late note, "The structure of the visual field, with its near-bys, its far-offs, its horizon, is indispensable for there to be transcendence, the model of every transcendence."[10]

It is no accident that the crucial chapter of his final, unfinished work is entitled "The Chiasm,"[11] a term commonly used by neurologists and psychologists to designate the "optic chiasm," that place in the brain where the two focusing eyes intertwine. Yet Merleau-Ponty always maintained a critical distance from the sciences that he studied, acknowledging specific discoveries while criticizing the standard, Cartesian interpretations of those findings. Merleau-Ponty was one of the first to demonstrate, contrary to the assertions of a dualistic psychology, that the experience of depth is not *created* in the brain any more than it is *posited* by the mind. He showed that we can discover depth, can focus it or change our focus within it, only because it is *already there,* because perception unfolds *into* depth—because my brain, like the rest of my body, is already enveloped in a world that stretches out beyond my grasp. Depth, which we cannot consider to be merely one perceptual phenomenon among others, since it is that which *engenders* perception, is the announcement of our immersion in a world that not only preexists our vision but prolongs itself beyond our vision, behind that curved horizon.

Indeed, if I adhere to Merleau-Ponty's thesis of the primacy of bodily perception, I must admit that that horizon I see *is* curved around me, as surely as the sky overhead is arched, like a dome, like a vault. Examining the contours of this world not as an immaterial mind but as a sentient body, I may come to recognize my thorough inclusion within this world in a far more profound manner than our current language usually allows. Our civilized distrust of the senses and of the body engenders a metaphysical detachment from the sensible world, fosters the illusion that we ourselves are not a part of the world that we study, that we can objectively stand apart from that world, as spectators, and can thus determine its workings from outside. A renewed attentiveness to bodily experience, however, enables us to recognize and affirm our inevitable involvement in that which we observe, our corporeal immersion in the depths of a body much larger than our own.

Often it takes a slightly unusual circumstance to disturb our metaphysical distance from the corporeal world. On certain days, for instance, when the sky is massed with clouds, I may notice a dense topography that extends overhead as well as underfoot, enclosing me within its layers, and so come to feel myself entirely *inside.* In general, if I pay close attention to bodily perceptions over a period of time, I may notice that the primordial experience of depth is always the experience of a sort of interiority of the external world, such that each thing I perceive seems to implicate everything else, so that things, landscapes, faces all have a coherence, all suggest a secret familiarity and mutual implication in an anonymous presence that subtends and overarches my own. I may discern, if I attend closely, that there is a certain closure which is suggested by the horizon and its vicissitudes, a sort of promise, in the distance, of a secret kinship between the ground and the sky, a fundamental nonopposition, a suggestion that they are not two distinct entities but two layers or leaves of one single power, two leaves that open as I move toward that horizon and that close up, behind me, back there. . . .[12]

The importance of the visible horizon for all of Merleau-Ponty's interrogations has led me to realize that the "world" to which he so often refers is none other than the Earth, that the coherent unity of the "visible" which slowly emerges through Merleau-Ponty's analysis of perception—the "field of all fields," or the "totality wherein all the sensibles are cut out"[13]—is not the abstract totality of the conceivable universe but the experienced unity of this enveloping but local world which we call Earth.

By *Earth*, then, I mean to indicate an intermediate and mediating existence between oneself and "the universe," or, more concretely, between humankind and the Sun, toward which our "pure" ideas seem to aspire directly, forgetful that it is not we, but rather the Earth that dwells in the field of the Sun, the solar system, as we live within the biosphere of the Earth. Much of Merleau-Ponty's work implies a growing recognition of this enveloping existence, which is only local by current scientific standards, but which is truly total for our perception. Hence, in his later writings, he begins to speak not just of the "world" but of "this world" of "our world": "Universality of our world . . . according to its configuration, its ontological structure which envelops every possible and which every possible leads back to."[14]

It is not unlikely that *all* of phenomenology, with its reliance upon the Husserlian notion of "horizon," is tacitly dependent upon the actual planetary horizon that we perceive whenever we step outside our doors or leave behind the city. As Merleau-Ponty has written, using a phrase that summarizes a major facet of his philosophy, "it is borrowing from the world structure that the universe of truth and of thought is constructed for us."[15] His thesis of the primacy of perception suggests that *all* of our thoughts and our theories are secretly sustained by the structures of the perceptual world. It is precisely in this sense that philosophies reliant upon the *concept* of "horizon" have long been under the influence of the actual visible horizon that lies beyond the walls of our office or lecture hall, that structural enigma which we commonly take for granted, but which ceaselessly reminds us of our embodied situation on the surface of this huge and spherical body we call the Earth.

We should not, however, even say "on" the Earth, for we now know that we live *within* the Earth. Our scientists with their instruments have rediscovered what the ancients knew simply by following the indications of their senses: that we live within a sphere, or within a series of concentric spheres. We now call those spheres by such names as the "hydrosphere," the "troposphere," the "stratosphere," and the "ionosphere," and no longer view them as encompassing the whole universe. We have discovered that the myriad stars exist quite far beyond these, and now recognize these spheres to be layers or regions of our own local universe, the Earth. Collectively these spheres make up the atmosphere, the low-viscosity fluid membrane within which all our perceiving takes place.

While science gains access to this knowledge from the outside, philosophy has approached it from within, for again, the entire phenomenological endeavor has taken place within a region of enquiry circumscribed by a tacit awareness of the Earth as the ground and horizon of all our reflections, and

the hidden thrust of the phenomenological movement is the reflective redis-
covery of our inherence in the body of the Earth. We can glimpse this trajectory most readily in certain essays by Husserl such as his investigations of the
"Phenomenological Origin of the Spatiality of Nature," in which Husserl
refers again and again to "Earth, the original ark," and speaks enigmatically
of Earth as that which precedes all constitution,[16] as well as in the later essays
of Heidegger which are a direct invocation of "earth" and "sky" along with
"mortals" and "gods" in "the fourfold."[17] Nevertheless, it is in Merleau-
Ponty's work that the full and encompassing enigma of Earth, in all its dense,
fluid, and atmospheric unity, begins to emerge and to speak.

This new sense of Earth contrasts with Heidegger's notion of "earth" as
that which remains concealed in all revelation, the dark closedness of our
ground which he counterposes to the elemental openness of "sky." The
Merleau-Pontian sense of Earth names a more diverse phenomenon, at once
both visible and invisible, incorporating both the deep ground that supports
our bodies and the fluid atmosphere in which we breathe. In discovering the
body, or in discovering a new way of thinking the body and finally seeing the
body, Merleau-Ponty is providing the entry into a new way of perceiving the
Earth of which that body is a part. To assert, as he did throughout the course
of his life, that the human intellect is a recapitulation or prolongation of a
transcendence already underway at the most immediate level of bodily sensation—to assert, that is, that the "mind" or the "soul" has a carnal genesis—is
to suggest, by a strange analogy of elements that stretches back to the very
beginnings of philosophy, that the sky is a part of the Earth, to imply that the
sky and the Earth need no longer be seen in opposition, that this sky, this
space in which we live and breathe, is not opposed to the Earth but is a prolongation, even an organ, of this planet. If the soul is not contrary to the body,
then human beings are no longer suspended between a dense inert Earth and
a spiritual sky, no more than they are suspended between Being and
Nothingness. For the first time in modern philosophy, human beings with all
of their language and thoughts are enveloped within the atmosphere of this
planet, an atmosphere which circulates both inside and outside of their
bodies: "there really is inspiration and expiration of Being, respiration in
Being. . . ."[18] Although Merleau-Ponty never quite gives the name Earth to
this unity, he does write of "the indestructible, the Barbaric Principle,"[19] of
"one sole sensible world, open to participation by all, which is given to
each,"[20] of a "global voluminosity" and a "primordial topology,"[21] and of the
anonymous unity of this visible (and invisible) world.[22] He writes of "a nexus
of history and *transcendental geology*, this very time that is space, this very
space that is time which I will have rediscovered by my analysis of the visible and the flesh,"[23] but without calling it by name. In another luminous passage he writes of "the prepossession of a totality which is there before one

knows how and why, whose realizations are never what we would have imagined them to be, and which nonetheless fulfills a secret expectation within us, since we believe in it tirelessly. . . ."[24] But again, this totality remains anonymous.

I suspect that Merleau-Ponty had to write in this way because what was anonymous then did not finally lose its perceptual anonymity until a decade after his death, when the first clear photographs of the Earth viewed from space were developed, and our eyes caught sight of something so beautiful and so fragile that it has been known to bring a slight reordering of the senses. It is a picture of something midway between matter and spirit, an image for what Merleau-Ponty had written of as the "existential eternity—the eternal body."[25] Of course, in one sense such images of the Earth present the ultimate "*pensée de survol*," that nonsituated "high-altitude thought" of which Merleau-Ponty was so critical. But we should not be tricked into thinking that he would have brushed them aside on that account. For this philosopher of perception, such photographs (and their proliferation in the world) would undoubtedly have been disturbing indeed, but decisive, like catching sight of oneself in the mirror for the first time.

In any case, it is enough here to recognize (1) that Merleau-Ponty sensed that there was a unity to the visible-invisible world that had not yet been described in philosophy, that there was a unique ontological structure, a topology of Being that was waiting to be realized, and (2) that whatever this unrealized Being is, we are in its depths, and of it, like a fish in the sea, and that therefore it must be disclosed *from inside*. These points are clear from his published notes, where, for example, in a note from February 1960, he writes of his project as "an ontology from within."[26]

III. Nature

It suffices for us for the moment to note that he who sees cannot possess the visible unless he is possessed by it, unless he is *of it, unless . . . he is one of the visibles, capable, by a singular reversal, of seeing them—he who is one of them.*[27]

Do a psychoanalysis of Nature: it is the flesh, the mother.[28]

In the book on which he was working at the time of his death, published posthumously, with working notes, as *The Visible and the Invisible,* Merleau-Ponty makes a significant terminological shift. He refers much less often to the body—whether to the "lived-body," upon which he had previously focused, or to the "objective body," from which it had been distinguished—and begins to speak more in terms of "the Flesh." Indeed he no longer seems to maintain the previously useful separation of the "lived-body" from the "objective body"; rather, he is now intent on disclosing, beneath these two perspectives, the mystery of their nondistinction for truly primordial perception. The singular "objective body," which he so rarely calls upon, has lingered quietly in Merleau-Ponty's writings—a residual concept, and a minor concession to the natural sciences. It was necessary as long as the rest of sensible or "objective" nature remained unattended to in his work, as long as nonhuman nature remained the mute and inert background for our human experience. However, with the shift from the "lived-body" to the "Flesh"—which is both "my flesh" and "the Flesh of the world"—Merleau-Ponty inaugurates a sweeping resuscitation of nature, both human and nonhuman.

As a number of commentators have suggested, it is likely that Merleau-Ponty's move from the lived-body to the Flesh constitutes less a break than a logical continuation of his earlier stylistic move to de-intellectualize transcendence in *The Phenomenology of Perception.*[29] In the language and argumentation of that earlier work, Merleau-Ponty manages to shift subjectivity from the human intellect to the lived-body. In *The Visible and the Invisible,* Merleau-Ponty follows through on that first shift by dislodging transcendence as a particular attribute of the human body and returning it to the entire world of which this body is but a single expression. Merleau-Ponty accomplishes this by describing the intertwining of the invisible with the visible—by demonstrating that the invisible universe of thought and reflection is both provoked and supported by the enigmatic depth of the visible, sensible environment: ". . . the visible is pregnant with the invisible, . . . to comprehend fully the visible relations one must go unto the relation of the visible with the invisible."[30]

Thus, the invisible, the region of thought and ideality, is always inspired by invisibles that are there from the first perception—the hidden presence of the distances, the secret life of the Wind which we can feel and breathe but cannot see, the interior depths of things, and, in general, all the invisible lines of force that constantly influence our perceptions. The invisible shape of smells, rhythms of cricketsong, or the movement of shadows all, in a sense, provide the subtle body of our thoughts. For Merleau-Ponty our own reflections are supported by the play of light and *its* reflections; the mind, the whole life of thought and reason is a prolongation and expansion, through us, of the shifting, polymorphic, invisible natures of the perceptual world. In the words of Paul Eduard, "there *is* another world, but it is *in* this one."[31] Or as Merleau-Ponty himself writes in one note, all the "invisibles," including that of thought, are "necessarily enveloped in the Visible and are but modalities of the same transcendence."[32] The "flesh" is the name Merleau-Ponty gives to this sensible-in-transcendence, this inherence of the sentient in the sensible and the sensible in the sentient, to this ubiquitous element which is not the objective matter we assign to the physicist nor the immaterial mind we still entrust to the psychologists because it is older than they, the source of those abstractions: "There is a body of the mind, and a mind of the body. . . . The essential notion for such a philosophy is that of the flesh, which is not the objective body, nor the body thought by the soul as its own (Descartes), [but] which is the sensible in the twofold sense of [that which is sensed and that which senses]."[33]

The "flesh" is the animate element which Merleau-Ponty has discovered, through his exploration of pre-objective perception, to be the common tissue between oneself and the world:

> The visible can thus fill me and occupy me because I who see it do not see it from the depths of nothingness, but from the midst of itself; I the seer am also visible. What makes the weight, the thickness, the flesh of each color, of each sound, of each tactile texture, of the present, and of the world is the fact that he who grasps them feels himself emerge from them by a sort of coiling up or redoubling, fundamentally homogenous with them; he feels that he is the sensible itself coming to itself. . . .[34]

With this terminological move from the "body" to the common "flesh" Merleau-Ponty dislodges creativity or self-transcendence as a particular attribute of the human body and returns transcendence to the carnal world of which this body is an internal expression.[35] If we now consider the world to which Merleau-Ponty's work refers to be *this* world—that is, the Earth—this move from the "body" to the communal "flesh" suggests that for a genuine perception the human body is radically interior to the "lebenswelt"—the lifespace, or biosphere—of a world-body which is itself in transcendence, self-creative, even—with us—alive: "One can say that we perceive the things themselves, that we are the world that thinks itself—or that the world is at the heart of our flesh. In any case, once a body-world relationship is recognized, there is a ramification of my body and a ramification of the world and a correspondence between its inside and my outside, between my inside and its outside."[36]

Here Merleau-Ponty's investigations anticipated recent work in the sciences and converge with new findings in biology, psychology, and global ecology. I will here mention only one of these developments. The "Gaia hypothesis" was first proposed in the mid-1970s by scientists striving to account for the actual stability of the Earth's atmosphere in the face of a chemical composition recently discovered to be very far from equilibrium. Geochemist James Lovelock and microbial biologist Lynn Margulis have hypothesized that the Earth's atmosphere is being metabolically generated and sensitively maintained by all of the organic life on the planet's surface acting collectively, as a single global physiology. The Gaia hypothesis (named for the Greek goddess of the Earth) provides the only explanation, as well, for the newly recognized evidence that the Earth's surface temperature has remained virtually constant over the last three and a half billion years despite an increase in the Sun's heat of at least 30 percent during the same period. The hypothesis, in short, maintains that the Earth's biosphere is a coherent, living entity regulating its temperature and internal composition much as one's own body metabolically maintains its own internal temperature and balances the chemical composition of its bloodstream.[37] The sensible world that surrounds us must, it would seem, be recognized as a sensitive physiology in its own right.[38]

But let us turn back to Merleau-Ponty, whose work on the "ontology from within" was cut short more than two decades before these developments. There is another, equally important implication of Merleau-Ponty's move from the lived-body to the flesh, for by shifting transcendence, which has been thought to be an exclusively human domain, to the whole of the world of which we humans are but a part, Merleau-Ponty dissolves the traditional division between the human animal and all other organisms of the Earth. The human sentience is indeed unique, but if we follow closely Merleau-Ponty's final writings we will begin to suspect that there are *other* sentient entities in the biosphere—indeed, that each species, by virtue of its own carnal structure has its own unique sentience or "chiasm" with the flesh of the world.[39]

Why then, one might ask, do we not read much more about the flesh of other animals in the pages of *The Visible and the Invisible?* I would answer first that, given the interrupted nature of Merleau-Ponty's text, this absence is not crucial. Since a new recognition of other animals follows directly from his thesis, such a recognition would eventually have emerged. It is clear, nevertheless, especially from our own reluctance to affirm this implication of Merleau-Ponty's work, that to confront and accept this implication twenty-five years ago was to move against the accumulated bias of the entire Western philosophical tradition—a literate tradition that has its origins in the exaltation of a divine ideality beyond the sensory world, a tradition that continues, in the scientific age, as an exaltation of the divine human existent over and above the "mute" and "chaotic" world of nature. It is a tradition that has been formulated almost exclusively by male scholars working within those havens of literacy—the academy and the city—that have been increasingly removed from all contact with the wild and coherent diversity of nonhuman nature. As a result, it is hardly surprising that Merleau-Ponty himself had difficulty accepting the most subversive implication of his phenomenology. It is his reticence on this point—the fact that his thought never quite leaves the city—that is the real stumbling block of his unfinished work.[40]

Let us examine this point more closely. In his course on *Consciousness and the Acquisition of Language*, Merleau-Ponty asserts that his progenitor, Husserl, was unable to abandon the Cartesian conception of a transcendental ego, the Cartesian *cogito* which Husserl "recalls each time we would believe him to be on the verge of a solution."[41] In a similar way we may now discern that Merleau-Ponty, having dropped the Cartesian postulate of a pure consciousness in favor of an embodied subjectivity, found *himself* caught within the more tacit Cartesian assumption of a massive difference between the human body, which for Descartes was open to the intervention of the soul, and all other animal bodies, which for Descartes were closed mechanisms incapable of any awareness.[42] In Merleau-Ponty's final writings we witness him on the threshold of opening his own rich conception of an embodied intersubjectivity to include the incarnate subjectivity of other animals, although never explicitly crossing this threshold—at least not in the fragments we have. Merleau-Ponty comes upon this deep Cartesian opposition between human and other animals, begins to dismantle it, but at the time of his death had not yet stepped through this opposition into a genuinely ecological intercorporeality.

Or had he? In his final working note—the note from which I have taken the plan for this paper—Merleau-Ponty writes that his discoveries "must be presented without any compromise with humanism, nor with naturalism [that is, the naturalism of the natural sciences], nor finally with theology."[43] *Humanism* is the key word here. To accept no compromise with *humanism* was difficult for Merleau-Ponty, for he was, in many ways, a committed humanist, and we can witness him grappling with this compromise throughout his late notes. But then in that same instruction to himself he writes: "Precisely what had to be done is to show that philosophy can no longer think according to this cleavage: God, man, creatures. . . ."[44] This is a powerful statement. From this last note it seems clear that Merleau-Ponty *knew* that he was out to heal the deep wound between humans and the other animals. However, his recalcitrant humanism was letting this happen only very slowly in his writings.

A single example may serve to illustrate Merleau-Ponty's dilemma. In a note from May 1960 he writes that "the flesh of the world is not self-sensing (*se sentir*) as is my flesh—it is sensible and not sentient—I call it flesh, nonetheless, in order to say . . . that it is absolutely not an object." He then goes on to assert that it is only "by the flesh of the world that in the last analysis we can understand the lived body."[45] Here we are left with an immense and ultimately untenable gap between the flesh of the world which is "sensible and not sentient" and *my* flesh which is "self-sensing." It is Merleau-Ponty's recalcitrant humanism that strives to maintain this distinction at the same time that his emerging ecological realism is struggling to assert the primacy of the world's flesh: "it is by the flesh of the world that in the last analysis we can understand the lived body." But it is simply because he is neglecting to consider other animals at this juncture that Merleau-Ponty is still able to assert that the flesh of the world is not self-sensing, for clearly other animals are a part of the perceived flesh of the world, and yet they have their own senses; following Merleau-Ponty's thesis of the reversibility of the sensing and the sensed, they are clearly self-sensing. As soon as we pay attention to other organisms we are forced to say that the flesh of the world is both perceived *and perceiving*. It is only by recognizing the senses of other animals that we can begin to fill up the mysterious gap Merleau-Ponty leaves in this quote. Or, to put it another way, only by recognizing the full presence of other animals will we find our own place within Merleau-Ponty's ontology. (Plants, as well, will come to assert their place, but our concern is first with the animals because they are our corporeal link, animal that we are, to the rest of the Flesh.) In this regard, it is essential that we discern that Merleau-Ponty's thought does not represent the perpetuation of an abstract anthropocentrism, but rather the slow and cautious overcoming of that arrogance. It is only by listening, in the depths of his philosophical discourse, to the gradual evocation of a densely intertwined organic reality, that we will fully understand how it is that the flesh of the world is "absolutely not an object."

Looked at in this way, a great deal of *The Visible and the Invisible* is already about other species, whether or not Merleau-Ponty was aware of their influence. No thinker can really move from his/her bodily self-awareness to the intersubjectivity of human culture, and thence to the global transcendence that is "the flesh of the world," without coming upon myriad experiences of otherness, other subjectivities that are not human, and other intersubjectivities. Indeed, the immediate perceptual world, which we commonly forget in favor of the human culture it supports, is secretly made up of these others; of the staring eyes of cats, or the raucous cries of birds who fly in patterns we have yet to decipher, and the constant though secret presence of the insects we brush from the page or who buzz around our heads, *all of whom make it impossible for us to speak of the sensible world as an object*—the multitude of these nonhuman and therefore background speakings, gestures, glances, and traces which impel us to write of the transcendencies and the "invisibility" of the visible world, often without our being able to say just why. It is likely that Merleau-Ponty, had he continued writing or had he written this text a few years later and witnessed the growing cultural respect for the nonhuman world as both active and interactive, would have had much less difficulty describing his experience of the "invisible" nature of the visible world and the reversibility between humanity and being.

But Merleau-Ponty did not live to read Rachel Carson's revelations about pesticides and the natural world, or the more recent disclosures about animal vivisection and the infliction of animal pain and terror on a grand scale that goes on within contemporary agribusiness and the cosmetics industry—the violent pain and death that unfolds throughout the technological world in its forgetfulness of what he called "Wild Being." It is possible that these disclosures would have been as unsettling to his thought, and as crucial for his rethinking of philosophy, as were the revelations concerning Stalin's purges when these were disclosed in Europe.[46] They would have accelerated his recognition of the nonhuman others and have helped him to welcome these wild, mysterious perceptions into an ontology that was already waiting for them.

IV. Logos

It is the body which points out, and which speaks; so much we have learnt in this chapter. . . . This disclosure of an immanent or incipient significance in the living body extends, as we shall see, to the whole sensible world, and our gaze, prompted by the experience of our own body, will discover in all other 'objects' the miracle of expression.[47]

. . . that things have us, and that it is not we who have the things. . . . That it is being that speaks within us and not we who speak of being.[48]

In *The Phenomenology of Perception,* Merleau-Ponty carefully demonstrated that silent or pre-reflective perception unfolds as a reciprocal exchange between the body and the world. Further, he showed that this constant exchange, with its native openness and indeterminacy, is nevertheless highly articulate, already informed by a profound logos. These disclosures carried the implication that perception, this ongoing reciprocity, is the very ground and support of that more thematized exchange we call "language."[49] Merleau-Ponty's continued focus upon the gestural genesis of language, and upon active speech as the axis of all language and thought—a focus which, as James Edie has written, distinguishes Merleau-Ponty from all other philosophers "from Plato on down"[50]—further served to ground language in the deep world of immediate perception, in the visible, tangible, audible world that envelops us, and of which we are a part.

In a more recent paper Edie maintains that Merleau-Ponty had no place, in his philosophy of language, for a depth linguistic structure such as that which Noam Chomsky has discovered in the years since Merleau-Ponty's death.[51] Now it is true that Merleau-Ponty did not discern any surface and deep structure in the fashion of Chomsky's investigations, but I believe that this is because he was in the midst of uncovering a more primordial structural depth within language, and one which has yet to be understood by other linguists and philosophers. It is that dimension in language correlative to the actual depth of the perceptual world, the deep structure of the sensory landscape.

By starting to show, as he does in his final chapter on "The Intertwining—The Chiasm,"[52] how thought and speech take form upon the infrastructure of a living perception already engaged in the world, Merleau-Ponty carefully demonstrates that language has its real genesis not inside the human physiology but, with perception, in the depth—the play between the esthesiological body and the expressive physiognomies and geographies of a living world. If we follow Merleau-Ponty's argument and agree that language is founded not inside us but in front of us, in the depths of the expressive world which engages us through all our senses, then we need not hunt for the secret of language inside the human physiology. We need not hunt, as Chomsky has suggested, for the ultimate seed of language within human DNA,[53] for this is merely to postpone an inevitable recognition that if the sensible world itself is the deep body of language, then this language can no longer be conceived as a power that resides in the human species, at least no more than it adheres to the roar of a waterfall, or even to the wind in the leaves. If language is born of our carnal *participation* in a world that already *speaks to us* at the most immediate level of sensory experience, then language does not belong to humankind but to the sensible world of which we are but a part. That, I believe, is how we must read Merleau-Ponty's parting note on language: "Logos . . . as what is realized in man, but nowise as his *property*."[54] If we set this insight alongside what we have already found regarding the visible and nature—(1) that man, or woman, is entirely included within the visible, sensible world, and (2) that the sensible world which we are within and of, and which we may suspect is this Earth, is itself sensitive and alive, constituted by multiple forms of embodied awareness besides our own—then some interesting conclusions emerge. We may begin to recognize, for instance, that our language has been contributed to, and is still sustained by, many rhythms, sounds, and traces besides those of our single species.

Since its inauguration in the Athenian *polis,* European philosophy has tended to construe language as that power which humans possess and other species do not. From Aristotle to Descartes, from Aquinas to Chomsky, "language" has been claimed as the exclusive and distinguishing property of humankind; man alone has privileged access to the Logos. Yet this exclusivity rests upon a neglect of the experiencing body, a forgetting of the gestural, carnal resonance that informs even our most rarefied discourse. In this way, it has fostered an abstract notion of language as a disembodied, purely formal set of grammatical and syntactic relations.

At least one contemporary linguist had called this entire tradition into question. Harvey Sarles, in his book *Language and Human Nature,* asks, "Is language disembodied, or just our theories about language?"[55] Sarles argues forcefully that the assumption that language is a purely human property, while providing a metaphysical justification for the human domination of nonhuman nature, nevertheless makes it impossible for us to comprehend the nature of our own discourse. Sarles asserts that "to define language as uniquely human also tends to define the nature of animal communication so as to preclude the notion that it is comparable to human language."[56] However, Sarles claims: "Each ongoing species has a truth, a logic, a science, knowledge about the world in which it lives. To take man outside of nature, to aggrandize the human mind, is to simplify other species and, I am convinced, to oversimplify ourselves, to constrict our thinking and observation about ourselves into narrow, ancient visions of human nature, constructed for other problems in other times."[57] Independent of Merleau-Ponty, yet entirely congruent with Merleau-Ponty's investigations twenty years earlier, Sarles outlines the basis for a more genuine linguistics grounded in a recognition of the "knowing body,"[58] or elsewhere, the "body-as-expression in interaction."[59]

Any such Merleau-Pontian approach to language—any approach, that is, that discloses language's gestural, soundful basis in bodily receptivity and response to an expressive, living world—opens us toward an understanding of the subtle relationship between language and landscape. If it is this breathing body that speaks, writes, and thinks—if it is not an immaterial ego but rather this sensible, sensitive body that dwells and moves within language—then language is at no point a structure of wholly abstract, ideal, or mathematical relations, for it is haunted by all those carnal things and styles to which our senses give us access. Language that has its real genesis in the deep world of untamed perception is language that is born as a call for and response to a gesturing, sounding, speaking landscape—a world of thunderous rumblings, of chattering brooks, of flapping, flying, screeching things, of roars and sighing winds. . . . That is why Merleau-Ponty could write, in the last complete lines of *The Visible and the Invisible,* that "language is everything, since it is the voice of no one, since it is the very voice of the things, the waves, and the forests. . . ."[60] It is even possible that this language we speak is the voice of the living Earth itself, singing through the human form, for the vitality, the coherence, and the diversity of the various languages we speak may well correspond to the vitality, coherence, and diversity of Earth's biosphere—not to any complexity of our species considered *apart* from that matrix.

In any case, we can now hypothesize, following this unique philosopher, a fundamental dynamic behind the ecological and psychological crisis in which human culture now finds itself, for it seems clear that as long as humankind continues to use language strictly for our own ends, as if it belongs to our species alone, we will continue to find ourselves estranged from our actions. If as Merleau-Ponty's work indicates it is not merely *this* body but the whole visible, sensual world that is the deep flesh of language, then surely our very words will continue to tie our selves, our families, and our nations into knots until we free our voice to return to the real world that supports it—until we allow it to respond to the voice of the threatened rainforests, the whales, the rivers, the birds, and indeed to speak for the living, untamed Earth which is its home. The real Logos, after Merleau-Ponty, is Eco-logos.

V. Conclusion

> *Can this rending characteristic of reflection come to an end? There would be needed a silence that envelops the speech anew. . . . This silence will not be the contrary of language.*[61]

What then does Merleau-Ponty bring to the new field of ecology? He brings it a clarified epistemology, and the language of perceptual experience. His work suggests a rigorous way to approach and to speak of the myriad ecosystems without positing our immediate selves outside of them. Unlike the language of information processing and cybernetics, Merleau-Ponty's phenomenology of the flesh provides a way to describe and to disclose the living fields of interaction from our experienced place *within* them.

The convergence of Merleau-Ponty's aims with those of a genuine philosophical ecology cannot be too greatly stressed. I have shown the equivalence between the dimensions of the "world" he discloses and the actual Earth. His *Lebenswelt* is identical to the biosphere of a truly rigorous ecology. He anticipated, I believe, that his perceptual analyses would lead to a clarified description of other embodied forms, other presences which move at rhythms altogether foreign to our own. In one note he writes: ". . . it would be necessary in principle to disclose the organic history under the historicity of truth. . . . In reality all the particular analyses concerning Nature, life, the human body, and language will make us progressively enter into the *Lebenswelt* and the 'wild' being, and as I go I should not hold myself back from entering into their positive description, nor even into the analysis of the diverse temporalities. . . ."[62] Finally, Merleau-Ponty points directly to an Eco-logos by repeatedly referring to the autonomous "*Lebenswelt* Logos," to that "perceptual logic" which reigns underneath all our categories and "sustains them from behind": ". . . the *sensible world* is this perceptual logic . . . and this logic is neither produced by our psychophysical constitution, nor produced by our categorial equipment, but lifted from a *world* whose inner framework our categories, our constitution, our 'subjectivity' render explicit. . . ."[63] It is this mute perceptual logic, recovered in language, that gives birth to ecology. Until today's fledgling ecological science addresses itself to the experience of perception it will remain uncertain of its motives, and unable to find its voice.

Notes

Abram is doing graduate work in the philosophy of biology and phenomenology in the Department of Philosophy, State University of New York at Stony Brook. He is currently teaching courses in phenomenology and the philosophy of ecology. A sleight-of-hand magician, who has done field research on the intertwining of magic and medicine among traditional healers in rural Indonesia and Nepal, he retains a deep interest in tribal culture and indigenous modes of perception. He thanks Claude Lefort, David Allison, and Anthony Weston for many helpful comments, as well as the members of the Merleau-Ponty Circle, before whom an earlier version of this paper was presented in 1983.

First published in *Environmental Ethics* 10, no. 2. Permission to reprint courtesy of *Environmental Ethics* and the author.

1. This is, of course, not to deny the fine work of those few philosophers who have already begun to address themselves to the ecological predicament. See, for instance, the writings of Murray Bookchin, Susan Griffith, Arne Naess, Paul Shepard, Mary Daly, and Theodore Roszak, as well as the philosophers represented in this journal.

2. Merleau-Ponty was perhaps the major philosopher writing in France after World War II; in 1952 he was offered the prestigious chair of philosophy at the College de France, a position that he held until his sudden death in 1961, at the age of fifty-three.

3. Maurice Merleau-Ponty, *The Visible and the Invisible*, ed. Claude Lefort, trans. Alphonso Lingis (Evanston, Ill.: Northwestern University Press, 1968).

4. Ibid., p. 130.

5. Ibid., p. 219.

6. Maurice Merleau-Ponty, *The Phenomenology of Perception*, trans. Colin Smith (London: Routledge and Kegan Paul, 1962).

7. Ibid., p. 256.

8. Ibid., p. 230-33.

9. Maurice Merleau-Ponty, "Eye and Mind," trans. Carleton Dallery, in *The Primacy of Perception,* ed. James Edie (Evanston, Ill.: Northwestern University Press, 1964).

10. Merleau-Ponty, *The Visible and the Invisible,* p. 231.

11. Ibid., p. 130.

12. This common visual experience of the horizon, so rarely attended to, is, I believe, the primary source of Merleau-Ponty's unique metaphor of the two leaves in "The Intertwining-The Chiasm" and in his working notes: "Insertion of the world between the two leaves of my body; insertion of my body between the two leaves of each thing and of the world" (*The Visible and the Invisible,* p. 264). Merleau-Ponty is here affirming Husserl's assertion that, phenomenologically, the perceptual field or landscape has numerous "internal horizons" as well as the "external horizon" that envelops it.

13. Ibid., p. 214.

14. Ibid., p. 229.

15. Ibid., p. 13.

16. Edmund Husserl, "Foundational Investigations of the Phenomenological Origin of the Spatiality of Nature," in *Philosophical Essays in Memory of Edmund Husserl,* ed. M. Farber (Boston: Harvard University Press, 1940).

17. Martin Heidegger, "Building, Dwelling, Thinking" in *Basic Writings,* ed. D. F. Krell (New York: Harper and Row, 1977).

18. Merleau-Ponty, *The Visible and the Invisible,* p. lvi.

19. Ibid., p. 267.

20. Ibid., P. 233.

21. Ibid., p. 213.

22. Ibid., p. 233.

23. Ibid., p. 259.

24. Ibid., p. 42.

25. Ibid., p. 265.

26. Ibid., p. 237.

27. Ibid., pp 134–35.

28. Ibid., p. 267.

29. See, for instance, Gary Madison, *The Phenomenology of Merleau-Ponty* (Athens: Ohio University Press, 1981).

30. Merleau-Ponty, *The Visible and the Invisible,* p. 216.

31. Cited in Morris Berman, *The Reenchantment of the World* (Ithaca, N.Y.: Cornell University Press, 1981).

32. Merleau-Ponty, *The Visible and the Invisible,* p. 257.

33. Ibid., p. 259 (translation amended).

34. Ibid., p. 114.

35. The issue is in fact far more subtle and complex than this admittedly surface analysis suggests. What is immediately evident, however, is that in *The Visible and the Invisible* Merleau-Ponty supplements his earlier perspective—that of a body experiencing the world—with that of the world experiencing itself through the body. Here he places emphasis upon the mysterious truth that one's hand can touch things only by virtue of the fact that the hand, itself, is a touchable thing, and is thus thoroughly a part of the tactile landscape that it explores. Likewise the eye that sees things is itself visible, and so has its own place within the visible field that it sees. Clearly a pure mind could neither see nor touch things, could not experience anything at all. *We* can experience things, can touch, hear and taste things, only because, as bodies, we are ourselves a part of the sensible field and have our own textures, sounds, and tastes. Indeed, to *see* is at one and the same time to feel oneself *seen;* to touch the world is also to be touched by the world. Merleau-Ponty coins the term *reversibility* to express this double or reciprocal aspect inherent in all perception: surely I am experiencing the world; yet when I attend closely to the carnal nature of this phenomenon, I recognize that I can just as well say that I am being experienced *by* the world. The recognition of this second, inverted perspective, when added to the first, leads to the realization of reversibility: "I am part of a world that is experiencing itself," or even, "I am the world experiencing itself through this body."

36. Ibid., p. 136.

37. James Lovelock, *Gaia: A New Look at Life on Earth* (Oxford: Oxford University Press, 1979).

38. For a much more in-depth study of the relation between the Gaia hypothesis and Merleau-Ponty's philosophy, see David Abram, "The Perceptual Implications of Gaia," in *The Ecologist* 15, no. 3 (1985). In that article I also compare and contrast Merleau-Ponty's work with that of the perceptual psychologist James J. Gibson.

39. *Chiasm* is the term Merleau-Ponty selects to describe the blending, the reversible exchange between my flesh and the flesh of the world that occurs in the play of perception. This interweaving, this ongoing communion *between divergent aspects of a single Flesh,* is to be found at every level of experience; it exists already in the body's own organization as the synaesthetic intertwining between one sense and

another, and even within each sense, between the left and the right side of that sense—as in the "optic chiasm."

40. That Merleau-Ponty's thought *was* searching for roots beyond the confines of the city is attested by his increasing fascination with the painter's relation to the natural landscape. See "Cézanne's Doubt," in Maurice Merleau-Ponty, *Sense and Non-Sense,* trans. Hubert Dreyfus and Patricia Dreyfus (Evanston, Ill.: Northwestern University Press, 1964), and also "Eye and Mind," in *The Primacy of Perception.*

41. Maurice Merleau-Ponty, *Consciousness and the Acquisition of Language,* trans. Hugh Silverman and with a foreword by James Edie (Evanston, Ill.: Northwestern University Press, 1973), p. 43.

42. Rene Descartes, *Discourse on Method,* trans. Laurence Lafleur (New York: Macmillan, 1986), pp. 36–38.

43. Merleau-Ponty, *The Visible and the Invisible,* p. 274.

44. Ibid., p. 274.

45. Ibid., p. 250.

46. See Maurice Merleau-Ponty, *Humanism and Terror,* trans. John O'Neill (Boston: Beacon Press, 1969), and *Adventures of the Dialectic,* trans. Joseph Bien (Evanston, Ill.: Northwestern University Press, 1973).

47. From the chapter on "The Body as Expression and Speech," in *The Phenomenology of Perception,* p. 197.

48. Merleau-Ponty, *The Visible and the Invisible,* p. 194.

49. See "The Body as Expression and Speech," in *The Phenomenology of Perception.*

50. See James Edie's "Foreword" to Merleau-Ponty, *Consciousness and the Acquisition of Language,* pp. xvii–xviii.

51. James Edie, "Merleau-Ponty: The Triumph of Dialectic over Structuralism," a paper presented at a conference of the Merleau-Ponty Circle at SUNY—Binghamton in 1982.

52. Merleau-Ponty, *The Visible and the Invisible,* pp. 130–55.

53. Cited in Edie, "Merleau-Ponty: The Triumph of Dialectic over Structuralism." Note that Chomsky is the major contemporary proponent of the view that language belongs to the human species alone.

54. Merleau-Ponty, *The Visible and the Invisible,* p. 274.

55. Harvey Sarles, *Language and Human Nature* (Minneapolis: University of Minnesota Press, 1985), p. 228.

56. Ibid., p. 86.

57. Ibid., p. 20.

58. Ibid., p. 249.

59. Ibid., p. 20.

60. Merleau-Ponty, *The Visible and the Invisible*, p. 155.

61. Ibid., p. 179.

62. Ibid., p. 167.

63. Ibid., pp. 247–48.

4

Class, Race, and Gender Discourse in the Ecofeminism/Deep Ecology Debate

Ariel Salleh

I. Liberal Patriarchalism and the Serviced Society

The separation of humanity and nature is the lynch pin of patriarchal ideology, and both deep ecology and ecofeminism share a desire to dislodge that pin. For deep ecologists, overcoming the division between humanity and nature promises a release from alienation. For ecofeminists, it promises release from a complex set of exploitations based on patriarchal identification of femaleness with the order of nature. Perhaps because most deep ecologists happen to have been men, and middle class, their environmental ethic has had difficulty in moving beyond psychological and metaphysical concerns to a political analysis of the "materiality" of women s oppression. Building on earlier exchanges between ecofeminism and deep ecology, in particular, "The Ecofeminism/Deep Ecology Debate: A Reply to Patriarchal Reason," I amplify the claim that deep ecology is held back from maturation as a Green philosophy by its lack of a fully rounded political critique.[1] To this end, I urge adherents of deep ecology to become more reflexively aware of the sociohistorical grounding of their discourse.

Although there are different emphases among women's groupings internationally, a growing number of ecofeminists now address capitalist patriarchy as an oppressive system of global power relations.[2] They situate both environmentalism and women's struggle against the instrumental rationality and dehumanizing commodity culture that comes with industrial production. Accordingly, ecofeminists of a socialist persuasion are disturbed to hear the father of deep ecology, Arne Naess, claim that "total egalitarianism is impossible," that some human exploitation will always be "necessary."[3] Women's complex treatment as a sexual, reproductive, and labor "resource" is glossed over in the deep ecological agenda. Yet there are, and have always been, people who cultivate and prepare food, build shelter, carry loads, labor to give birth, wash and tend the young, maintain dwellings, feed workers, and mend their clothes. Whether in the First World or the Third World (which is two-thirds of the global population), women's labor "mediation of nature" serves as the infrastructure to what is identified as men's "productive economic" role. This subsumption of women's energies, most often by means of the institution of the family, is homologous to exploitative class relations under the capitalist system. The family is integrally connected with, and makes industrial production possible by "reproducing" the labor force, in the several senses of that word. However, as productivism intensifies with new technologies and the promise of ever greater profits, labor becomes increasingly removed from the satisfaction of basic needs. As a result, under the guise of "development," a new dimension is added to the women's role constellation—that of conspicuous consumer. Moreover, as the economic fetish penetrates personal culture, even sexual relations between men and women come to resemble relations between things, thereby deepening women's exploitation even further.[4]

Deep ecologists do not recognize that women have not been consulted about their interests in this system of social relations. Just as the environment is damaged by "development," women's lives are vitiated by men's systematic appropriation of their energies and time. Writing by Brinda Rao in India, Berit As in Norway, and Barbara Ehrenreich in the United States provides ample documentation of this appropriation.[5] The work of Third World peasant women is fairly obviously tied to "natural" functions and material labor. These women grow most of the world's food and care for their families with a minimum of disruption to the environment and with minimum reliance on a cash economy. They labor with independence, dignity, and grace—and those of us looking for sustainable models may soon want to take advice from such women. In contrast, in supposedly advanced industrial nations, women's maintenance work as housewives or imported guest workers is made dependent on and largely mystified by "labor-saving devices," such as dish-washing machines, blenders, and the like. Nevertheless, cultural assumptions concerning women's apparently universal role of mediating nature still hold. It is for this reason that reproductive rights remain contentious in the United States. Ecofeminists join Dave Foreman's cry to "free shackled river," but more than rivers remain shackled!

Deep ecologist Warwick Fox, who has wondered why ecofeminists have not discussed the class basis of deep ecology, has failed to note that my early ecofeminist criticism in "Deeper than Deep Ecology" refers repeatedly to women's labor as validation of their perspectives.[6] As the sociology of knowledge teaches us, peoples' perception is shaped by their place in the system of productive relations. Nevertheless, the gulf between manual or sustaining productive labor and mental or conceptualizing work is especially profound in industrialized societies. A whole gamut of questions surrounding labor relations is ideologically suppressed, and in the United States it is clouded by the question of race as well. In late capitalism, the middle class, including academics, are "serviced" in their daily needs by hidden workers. Not surprisingly, deep ecology reflects the idealism and individualism of such a privileged group, its preoccupation being "cultural issues" such as meaning, the psychological, and "rights." However, even more invisible as labor, and not even recognized by a wage, are the domestic services of women. Michael Zimmerman's typically middle-class and white articulation of women's lot—he sees them enjoying "the advantages" of a consumer society—illustrates this standard oversight, though the fault is not entirely his, since it largely reflects the liberal feminist attitude he relies on to make his case against ecofeminism.[7] It is not only women's socialization, the various belief systems which shape "the feminine role," but also the very practical nature of the labor which most women do that gives them a different orientation to the world around them and, therefore, different insights into its problems. In both North and South, this labor may include the physicality of birthing, suckling, and subsequent household chores, but is not restricted to such activities. Even in the public work force, women's employment is more often than not found in maintenance jobs—reflecting cultural attitudes to women as "carers."[8]

Radical feminist analyses of the psychodynamic underlying patriarchal social relations, again and again, return to the symbolic killing of mother/nature/woman as the root cause of the "masculine" will to objectify and control other forms of being. Zimmerman's writing is fairly symptomatic in this respect. Although ten or more pages of his "Feminism, Deep Ecology, and Environmental Ethics" are generously given to exposition of the feminist literature, and a concluding paragraph endorses its findings, his article is still querulous. The same observation applies to Fox's response to ecofeminist criticisms of deep ecology. While both Zimmerman and Fox cast doubt on the reality of patriarchal power, Zimmerman's ambivalent article also contains information about how ideology works to protect men from seeing the actual nature of social relations under patriarchy. He quotes the following remark of Naomi Scheman: "Men have been free to imagine themselves as self-defining only because women held the intimate social world together by their caring labors."[9] Similarly, we know that the capitalist entrepreneur sees himself as a man of high achievement, blind to the fact that the wage laborer is responsible for the generation of his surplus. In the patriarchal perspective, self appears to be independent; yet, to quote Jim Cheney, "The atomistically defined self acts as a sponge, absorbing the gift of the other, turning it into capital." Cheney goes on: "This is one way of understanding the frequent feminist claim that males in patriarchy feed on female energy."[10] Capital can be psychological and sexual as much as economic. On the positive side, the actuality of caring for the concrete needs of others gives rise to a morality of relatedness among ordinary women, and this sense of kinship seems to extend to the natural world as well. Consider the reasoning of an Indian peasant woman whose drinking water has been spoiled by village men moving across to a pumped supply for status reasons, or the sensibility of a woman who watches a tree grow over the grave of a child she has suckled. These understandings engraved in suffering make sharp contrast to the abstract philosophical formulations of deep ecology. For ecofeminism, the body is indeed an instrument of our knowledge of the world.[11]

Professional Versus Grassroots Base

As I put it in an earlier critique, ". . . what is the organic basis of [the deep ecological] paradigm shift? . . . Is deep ecology a sociologically coherent position?"[12] One of the most distressing things about the field of environmental ethics is the extent to which it has been taken over by paid professional specialists. What gives authenticity, validity, and "depth" to ecofeminism, in contrast, is that it is implicitly tied to a praxis rooted in life needs and the survival of habitat. Deep ecology is primarily concerned with identification, or rather, re-identification of the so-called "human" ego with nature. For deep ecologists, however, the recommended route for recovering this connected sensuous self is meditation or leisure activities, such as backpacking. How does such activity compare as an integrating biocentric experience with the hands-on involvement of the African subsistence farmer who tends her field with an astonishing knowledge of seeds, water habits, and insect catalysts— and whose land is the continuing staff of the children she has born out of her body? There is surely a large portion of illusion and self-indulgence in the North's comfortable middle-class pursuit of the cosmic "transpersonal Self." Despite Naess careful reformulations, in an age of "me now," the deep ecologists' striving for "Self-realization" demands close scrutiny.

Many deep ecological difficulties in coming to terms with ecofeminism can be traced to the sociopolitical grounding of the deep ecology movement in bourgeois liberalism. Hence, it is probably no surprise that even as deep ecologists put forward their key concept of "ecocentrism" as "the way out" of our environmental holocaust, an implicit endorsement of the Enlightenment rationalist notion of ever upward progress threatens to collide with the principle. For instance, some deep ecologists believe that "anthropocentric" political critiques, such as socialism and feminism, can, in principle, be taken care of by the wider framework of ecocentrism. Fox writes, "Supporters of deep ecology hold that their concerns well and truly *subsume* the concerns of those movements that have restricted their focus to a more egalitarian human society."[13] Not only is Fox's ambitious totalizing program spoiled by the serious gaps in deep ecology's theorization, it is also out of sync with his pluralist claim to respect the unfolding of "other voices" in the universe: the words of women, among others. Fox's attraction to "transpersonal psychology" hangs on the self-actualizing logic of middle-class individualism. Similarly, his assertion that self-interest is fused with that of Gaia as a whole, strikingly resembles the guiding hand behind Adam Smith's libertarian political economy, or Rawls' theory of justice. Despite a will to transcendence, there is an implicit positivism or naive realism in these formulations.[14] Deep ecology has no sense of itself as spoken by a particular group lodged in history. Oblivious to its own cultural context, the deep ecological voice rings out as a disembodied absolute.

Abstract Essences versus Reflexivity

According to Rosemary Ruether, women throughout history have not been particularly concerned to create transcendent, overarching, all-powerful entities, or like classical Greek Platonism and its leisured misogynist mood, with projecting a pristine world of abstract essences.[15] Women's spirituality has focused on the immanent and intricate ties among nature, body, and personal intuition. The revival of the goddess, for example, is a celebration of these material bonds. Ecofeminist pleas that men, formed under patriarchal relations, look inside themselves first before constructing new cosmologies have been dismissed, for example, by Fox, in "The Deep Ecology: Ecofeminism Debate and Its Parallels," as a recipe for inward-looking possessive parochialism and, hence, ultimately war![16] But that would surely only be the case if deep ecologists failed to shrug off their conditioning as White–Anglo–Saxon–Protestant–professional property holders, which they assure us, they are very keen to do. Interestingly, the universalizing, cosmopolitan stance of this particular protest by Fox is somewhat at loggerheads with the deep ecologists' own professed commitment to bioregionalism.

In the name of "theoretical adequacy," Fox's article disregards history. Consequently, his prose blurs who has done what to whom, over the centuries and on into the present. To quote:

[Certain] classes of social actors have . . . habitually assumed themselves to be *more fully human* than others, such as women ("the weaker vessel"), the "lower" classes, blacks, and non-Westerners ("savages," "primitives," "heathens"). . . .

That anthropocentrism has served as the most fundamental kind of legitimation employed by *whatever* powerful class of social actors one wishes to focus on can also be seen by considering the fundamental kind of legitimation that has habitually been employed with regard to large-scale or high-cost social enterprises such as war, scientific and technological development, or environmental exploitation. Such enterprises have habitually been undertaken not simply in the name of men, capitalists, whites or Westerners, for example, but in the name of God (and thus our essential humanity . . .) . . . (This applies, notwithstanding the often sexist expression of these sentiments in terms of "man," "mankind," and so on, and not withstanding the fact that certain classes of social actors benefit disproportionately from these enterprises.)[17]

This passage is a sample of liberal-pluralist mystification in its most blatant form. Its author next goes on to mention Bacon and the rise of science, but without touching on the corresponding elimination of one class of social actors, namely, the 6 million women who perished as witches for their scientific wisdom. Fox believes that all modern liberation movements have had recourse to the same legitimating device—"humanity." Apparently, a belief that this label is available for the use of everyone is the reason why deep ecologists still use the term *man* so persistently.

Zimmerman, in turn, entirely misses the point of ecofeminism by portraying it as an argument about women being "better than men."[18] Ecofeminism does not set up a static ontological prioritization of "woman." Instead, it is a strategy for social action. Equally, men in the Green and the eco-socialists movements, by examining the parallel exploitation of nature and women, are entering into a process of praxis, the results of which will unfold over time. Fox, in his own way, shelves the question of our political responsibility as historical agents by insisting that all people need to understand is that "evolutionary outcomes" simply represent "the way things happen to have turned out," nothing more. For someone concerned with "simplistic" and "facile" political theorization, his familiar charge against ecofeminism beats the lot. Notwithstanding earlier posturing about the "errors of essentialism" in ecofeminist thought, Fox soon emerges as a kind of Spencerian sociobiologist. In fact, the deep ecologists, for all their anxieties about "genetic doctrines" in feminism, seem to be strongly inclined this way. George Sessions too speaks favorably about "the recent studies in ethology and genetics which posit a basic human and primate nature."[19] Is this the old double standard again?

Technology—Productive and Reproductive Relations

When it comes to the question of technology, Zimmerman's text becomes as rudderless as the modern industrial apparatus itself. He notes that some feminists—"essentialists" he calls them, though they remain unnamed—are critical of science and technology, while other feminists, also unspecified, argue that it is not "intrinsically evil."[20] There are, indeed, differences among feminists on technology. Liberal feminists, like their brothers, the reform environmentalists, imagine that solutions to social and ecological problems can be found within "the advanced industrial technostructure." Liberal feminism should not be grouped with ecofeminism, however, any more than resource environmentalism should be grouped with deep ecology. Ecofeminists go further than both liberal feminists, who see technology as emancipatory, and Marxist feminists who argue that technology is neutral and that it is all a matter of who controls it. Ecofeminists observe that the instrumental-rational mode of production inevitably trickles over into the sphere of consciousness and social relations. As a Heideggerian, Zimmerman should know that there are ample reasons for dismantling the techno-monster, given its far-reaching impact into human phenomenology. Yet, he still seems to hold a neutralist thesis, claiming that "Modern science and technology are potentially liberating. . . ." Further, he asks: "While benefiting from the material well-being and technological progress made possible by masculinist science and industry, do women rid themselves of responsibility . . . ?"[21] It is hard to believe that this "growth"-oriented statement should be made in defense of deep ecology. Perhaps Zimmerman genuinely does believe that societies accrue benefit from "advanced" technologies. Perhaps they do for the middle-class men who designed and sold them; nevertheless, the young Korean micro-chip worker steadily going blind at her bench and the California aerospace worker coming down with immune deficiencies have not experienced such well-being. The problem is, and this is a point well-made in Don Davis' article, that deep ecology as a movement has no systematic analysis of multinational-corporate industrial society and its effects.[22]

Equally innocent of the force of contemporary instrumentalism, Wittbecker writes that "human populations are plastic and could probably be decreased without fascism, by economic, religious, or cultural means." Deep ecologist Bill Devall's tone is similarly managerial, preoccupied as he is with population control.[23] The phenomenon of "overpopulation" does need to be seriously examined. However, given the ethical issues of eugenics-genocide and of a woman's right over her own body, the targeting of "population control" by white male environmentalists in the North has both racist and sexist dimensions. Observe how many Americans opposed to abortion in the United States endorse population control programs in Asia and South America. Even as a matter of social equity, where children provide supplementary farm labor for overworked mothers in the South, it is inappropriate for gray-suited international policy advisers to demand population control. Such programs originated in a post-World War II middle-class urban desire to protect the quality of life—that is, high levels of consumerism. These days the argument for population control is formulated more prudently in terms of protecting the

Earth's "scarce" resources. Even this injunction, however, as it is applied to the Third World exclusively, is patently hypocritical. Each infant born into the so-called advanced societies uses about fifteen times more global resources during his or her lifetime than a person born in the Third World. Population restraint may well be called for in the North, hopefully complemented by a scaling back of high technology excess. On the other hand, subsistence dwellers in the South are producers as much as consumers: as "prosumers" they are practical examples of human autonomy in a nonexploitative relation to the land. What much of this talk about population control may express is a projection and displacement of guilt experienced by those who continue to live comfortably off the invisible backs of working women in the Third World. Even deeper, the constant focus on population control may reflect some profound psychosexual fear of that "different" voice.[24]

With regard to biotechnology, Fox agrees with the ecofeminist position that deep ecologists should oppose it; nevertheless, given deep ecology's lack of attention to industrialism and technological rationality, it is not consistently opposed by most deep ecologists. Sessions has said that he believes there "might be a point one day down the road when we can handle genetic engineering." Naess has also defended its use. For example, he has proposed that a genetically engineered microorganism be released in order to counter a mite infecting the eyes of African children.[25] This proposal is a very anthropocentric focus for an ecocentric theory, and it matches oddly with earlier claims by Naess and Sessions that it is better not to approach the nonhuman world reductionistically in terms of its usefulness to humans. Devall's fine tenet that "there is wisdom in the stability of natural processes" is violated here, as is Devall's and Sessions' "refusal to acknowledge that some life forms have greater or better intrinsic value than others." Concern about the unintended consequences of human "hubris" is one level of argument. Feminist critiques of patriarchal science are another. It might be also added, following the logic of Frances Moore Lappé, that if the standard of living—the "vital needs"—of African villages were not decimated by pressures from a predatory white-male dominated international economic order, such children might not succumb to malnutrition and disease in the first place. Given this line of reasoning, genetic engineering can scarcely be justified as a "vital need." In fact, there can be no emergence from this exploitative system as long as humans pursue expensive technological-fix panaceas, such as genetic engineering. Even so, according to Devall and Sessions, "cultural diversity today requires advanced technology, that is, techniques that advance the goals of each culture."[26] Is this why John Seed from the Council of All Beings can be seen traveling with a lap-top computer? What some deep ecologists seem to forget when it comes to the question of technology is that there is no such thing as a free lunch. While Devall condemns "false consciousness" in New Age advocates of genetic engineering and computer technology, one looks in vain for a clear deep ecological praxis on these matters. His discussion of genetic engineering remains descriptive and agnostic in tone, eventually sliding off into renewed denunciation of human overpopulation as the most important "agent of extinction." In other words, women workers in the South can pick up the tab for ecological crisis.

II. Patriarchal Postures and Discursive Strategies

Another metalevel of the debate between ecofeminism and deep ecology is the psychosexual dynamic that runs through it. As with the class and ethnic grounding of deep ecology, gender politics also shapes the context in which philosophical judgments are made. Without an awareness of this fact, the Green, deep ecological, and socialist movements lose reflexivity and run the risk of being partial, single issue, and reformist in focus. Sadly, the deep ecologists' reception of ecofeminist views has been marked by resistance. Perhaps this resistance should be no surprise, since their spokespeople have been men, and the psychological literature suggests that masculine identity is defined by separation rather than closeness. There is certainly nothing uniquely deep ecological in their responses; the strategies used to shore up their standpoints are quite familiar to the experience of women working in male-dominated institutions. As Karen Warren reminds us, "Ecofeminists take as their central project the unpacking of connections between the twin oppressions of women and nature. Central to this project is a critique of the sort of thinking which sanctions that oppression."[27] Elizabeth Dodson Gray and many others have exposed the pervasiveness of the androcentric conceptual frame. Yet, it is not only the epistemology itself that women must attend to, but an armory of discursive techniques that back up and protect the bastion of masculine meaning. Among these, the index to Dale Spender's bibliographic history of feminism names the following common patriarchal procedures for dealing with intellectual and political challenges by women: ageism, appropriation, burial (of contribution), contempt (sexual), character assassination, the double bind, the double standard, harassment, isolation, charges of man hating, masculine mind, misrepresentation, namelessness, scapegoating, and witch hunting.[28] Note that while these postures have no substantive value, they are readily insinuated into the context of evaluation. As late twentieth-century politics moves toward a holistic agenda, it becomes crucial for activist men to be able to identify when they are falling back on these time honored discursive practices.

Denial and Omission

Spender's catalogue is not exhaustive, as we shall see. Fox, a deep ecologist who wants to dissolve "ontological divisions," adds to Spender's list by creating a disposable hierarchy of ecofeminisms. What makes for a "better" ecofeminism? Apparently, it is the work of women building on the theoretical foundations of Buddhism, Taoism, Spinoza, Heidegger, and systems theory![29] Fox's androcentrism is so strong that he remains unembarrassed by the implications of this legitimation device. Because the entire history of patriarchy is an exercise in suppressing the wisdom of women's experiences, deep ecologists would do well to bear this ancient agenda in mind. A related example occurs in the book by Devall and Sessions, whose text echoes snippets of my ecofeminist "Deeper than Deep Ecology" critique, while denying its existence by omitting documentation. Published two years after that unacknowledged essay, the authors respond to the prod with a three-page acknowledgment of women's contributions to ecology. Yet, there is no sign of any effort to integrate ecofeminism within the book's conceptualization as a whole. Chapter One, which reviews environmentalist scenarios—reformist, New Age, libertarian—fails to mention the ecofeminist approach. Chapter Two, which reviews "the minority tradition," including nameless native Americans and "primal peoples," gives eight lines to the "Women's Movement." These remarks mislead because of their brevity, moreover, and risk confusing not only sex and gender stereotypes, but also paradigmatic differences within feminism itself. There is also a short "appendix" on ecology and domestic organization by Carolyn Merchant, whose other published work on patriarchal reason would have resounding epistemological implications for deep ecologists, if they absorbed it.[30] Concerning Devall's later book, Greta Gaard has observed that it "gives the section on Eros, Gender and Ecological Self less than five pages. . . . He devotes an entire paragraph [to] citing a series of feminist analyses, but does not even paraphrase or address their objections to deep ecology. . . ."[31]

   In addition to the documentation of ecofeminist literature being flimsy, the deep ecologists' preparation for debate and grasp of feminist thought is also lacking in respect. Devall and Sessions cite Dorothy Dinnerstein, Susan Griffin, and Jessie Bernard purportedly on how "our culture inhibits the development of psychological maturity in women." In fact, each of these feminist authors discusses the inhibition of "masculine" psychic maturity under patriarchy. Only Griffin is referenced, however, and Bernard's name is given the masculine spelling "Jesse." This lack of respect strongly suggests that the material has been consulted very indifferently, if at all by the deep ecologists.[32] Failing to recognize that women's perspectives are materially grounded in their working lives as carers, Fox and Zimmerman lean heavily on arguments about *essentialism.* No one who responded to "Deeper than Deep Ecology" follows up footnote citations offering a dialectical refutation of the essentialism question. Again, although Fox cites Janet Biehl's critique of deep ecology, he never grapples with it.[33] Given that they are happy enough to set up a normative taxonomy of women's writing, it is remarkable that defenders of deep ecology have read so little ecofeminist literature. Their discussions focus on the writings of a handful of North American authors and myself. No European or Third World material is acknowledged, let alone examined. Perhaps the most damaging instance of denial used by deep ecologists is their disregard of my original ecofeminist endorsement of their ideals. To repeat, *"The appropriateness of attitudes expressed in Naess and Devall's seminal papers is indisputable."*[34] This lapse has deflected the focus of subsequent exchanges between ecofeminism and deep ecology away from constructive mutuality.

Projection and Personalization

Bolstered by adjectives like "simplistic" and "facile"—three or four times on one page in connection with social ecology and what are to him the less acceptable species of ecofeminism—Fox says that the ecofeminist's simplistic analyses are overinclusive and that they target all men, capitalists, whites, indiscriminately as "scapegoats" for what is wrong with the world.[35] His personalization here mirrors the form of those arguments that produce the example of Margaret Thatcher as proof that feminism is wrong. Individual women can be powerful, wealthy, or racist, but their circumstances have no bearing on the structural oppression of the female sex. Conversely, while a class of men may be preserved by entrenched structural privilege, specific individuals may still commit themselves against their class interest. In my discussion of Australian politics in "A Green Party: Can the Boys Do Without One?" I talk, for example, about men working together with women in dismantling patriarchy, and about the potential of conservative churchgoers and corporate wives as catalysts in social change.[36] Fox's tactic of personalization is one to guard against, for it is invariably resorted to by those whose class has a vested interest in ignoring what a structural analysis tells them.

On the same page, Fox claims that "simplistic" ecofeminist analyses are "inauthentic" because they lead to "a complete denial of responsibility" on the part of those who theorize. Because the ecofeminist literature presents an interdisciplinary synthesis of epistemological, political, economic, cultural, psychodynamic and ecological insights, it can scarcely wear the label "oversimplified." The term *essentialism* is also plainly misapplied for the same reason. As for avoiding responsibility, most ecofeminist writers, North and South, have practical experience of movement activism, and that is what stimulates their insights. Women in the thousands have taken up campaigns over toxics, wilderness, and peace, not only in autonomous separatist groupings, but in mainstream environment organizations where they make up two-thirds of the labor force. Women are certainly embracing ecological responsibility, so much so that it has even been remarked that it looks like they are being used all over again in their traditional housekeeping role as unpaid keepers of *oikos* at large.[37] Since women actually receive less than 10 percent of the world's wage, why should they want to maintain this destructive global economy? As women around the world make the connection between sustainability and equality, they are doing just what Fox's either/or logic claims they cannot do. They are becoming "a class in themselves."

When will men lay down their arms? Zimmerman takes up the offensive on behalf of deep ecology with a proposition that perhaps women really accrue benefit from patriarchy:

> . . . feminists try to temper [their] portrayal by saying that *individual* men are not to blame, since they have been socialized. . . . What traits, then, are women projecting on to men? And what benefits accrue to women through projecting such traits? Do women split off from themselves and project onto men violence, aggressiveness, selfishness, greed, anger, hostility, death hating, nature fearing, individuality, and responsibility? And as a result of bearing the projected traits, do men behave much more violently, selfishly, etc., than they would if these traits were withdrawn by women?[38]

I have commented in relation to Fox's work that personalization is invariably used by those who have difficulty thinking about people in groups or classes. Here it is Zimmerman who loses grasp of the structural level of analysis. If women do simply "project characteristics" onto men, that is, if they are ideas only in women's heads, then why do patriarchal statistics corroborate that 90 percent of violent crimes are committed by men? Indeed, are men "responsible" at all for their behavior? What of the wholesale abandonment of 150,000 women and children in the United States each year? What about responsibility in the nuclear industry? What has gone wrong with women's self-fulfilling projection there? According to Zimmerman's "critique of feminism," feminists must realize that men, too, are victims of patriarchy. Of course, I made this point myself in "Deeper than Deep Ecology" with the allusion to masculine self-estrangement. Hilkka Pietila also picks up on it when she writes: "A long process of male liberation is needed . . . in order to meet feminine culture without prejudice. . . . Salleh *still anticipates* a new ally within the personality of men, and it is . . . the feminine aspects of men's own constitution. . . ."[39] Nevertheless, women have all but given up trying to get their brothers into self-discovery through mutually supportive consciousness-raising groups as pioneered by radical feminism in the 1970s. Zimmerman, in contrast, is confident that it is feminism itself which must engage in searching self-criticism. Surely, the emergence of five or six feminist paradigms in the space of two decades already demonstrates the women's movement vitality and openness to renewal. Where is the men's movement and its political, as opposed to psychological, analysis? Women were early to point out how the personal and political intermesh, and hence how nineteenth-century moralizers like "blame" and "accuse" are not apt in a postmodern reflexive culture where people strive to understand their own class implications in repressive social structures. Instead, Zimmerman ponders whether patricentric attitudes become more or less entrenched with "education." As we can see from the present exchange, education, as such, is no panacea. Unless people learn how to recognize the social/personal infrastructure of labor that sustains them daily, a paradigm shift is not likely. Zimmerman is almost there when he remarks that "we are making use of norms and following cultural practices that threaten the future of life on Earth." But who is this "we"? Women's and men's "roles" and values are not everywhere the same. He knows this. After all, he takes hope from the "global awakening of the quest for the feminine voice that can temper the one-sidedness of the masculine voice."[40] Although ecofeminists share this hope, they also want it known that as far as any "quest" goes, a majority of the world's population, North and South, are already "speaking the feminine." The problem is: do they have standing? What is called for now is a move beyond tokenism, an admission of all women into the ranks of humanity.[41]

Caricature and Trivialization

The quest for the "feminine voice" is a recurrent theme in late twentieth-century philosophy, as recent French poststructuralist writing reveals. Alice Jardine's extensive research into this trend suggests, however, that gynesis, or speaking like a woman, is somewhat suspect when it is fashionably pursued by affluent Parisian homosexual *litterateurs*.[42] It deteriorates into parody, and beyond that into an up-market semi-academic export commodity. A revolution in gender relations cannot go anywhere at the level of ideas, language, or ritual alone; it needs an objective "material base." Such professional philosophers as Zimmerman, however, are far removed from this perception. His class-based idealism brings him to conclude that it is "epistemology, metaphysics, and ethics" that have "led to the present exploitation."[43] From an ecofeminist perspective, change demands that relationships of production and reproduction be equably rearranged between men and women and nature—in such a way that freedom and necessity are identically experienced. Equality and sustainability are closely interlinked.

The philosophy of "difference," so poorly served by the deep ecologists cheap paraphrase of ecofeminism—"that women are better than men"—has been widely debated over the past decade among liberal, Marxist, poststructuralist, and ecofeminists. The exploration of this theme marks an important phase in women's political consciousness. It converges both with

men's personal efforts to escape the strictures of patriarchy and with new epistemological directions in science.[44] It is true that some men may still "think
the feminine" in an unreconstructed way. Look at Wittbecker's attempt to dispose of my own critique in the traditional manner: "Hysterical hyperbolism is
a perilous path to consciousness. . . ."[45] Consider, too, the uncritical use of
woman/nature imagery by some early Earth First! deep ecologists, whose
lurid metaphors of familial rape are meant to highlight their manly self-sacri-
fice in protecting "Mother Earth" and her "virgin forests." The thought style
of monkey-wrench politics has tended to reinforce the intrinsic psychosexual
dynamic lying beneath the exploitation of nature, women, and less privileged
peoples. Other men defensively subvert any notion of "difference" by using it
to set up a double bind, affirming "what they knew all along about women."
Zimmerman himself professes concern that arguments based on gender types
"run the risk of simply reaffirming traditional views that women are feelers,
while men are 'thinkers.' "[46] If nothing else, the ecofeminism/deep ecology
debate should put an end to this assumption.

   Fox is especially given to caricature of those he wants to debate, even
when he is not fully cognizant of his terms. While no doubt endorsing wolves
rights to be wolves, he takes my rhetorical line about women being allowed
to "love themselves" entirely out of its context in cultural politics. His next
gambit relies on Wittbecker's poorly reasoned charge that I treat "the sexes
as if they were two species." This alleged dualism is cobbled together with
the playful Irigarayan title "A Green Party: Can the Boys Do Without One?"
in order to illustrate an "oppositional" approach.[47] As Adorno would say, a
totalitarian culture knows no irony. In a related vein, Fox has claimed that
"The extent to which people in general are ready to equate opposition to
human centeredness with opposition to humans per se can be viewed as a
function of the dominance of the anthropocentric frame of reference in our
society."[48] Fox does not see that the extent to which deep ecologists equate
opposition to patriarchy with opposition to men per se can be viewed as a
function of the dominance of their own androcentric frame of reference.

Discredit and Invalidation

   It is easier to think through an issue if there is a clear distinction between "them and us," self and other; hence, Fox "weighs up" the "relative
merits" of deep ecology and ecofeminism. Having polarized the two, he casts
doubt over the value of ecofeminist "anthropocentrics" by means of a footnote reference to racism at Greenham Common in 1987.[49] In fact, the racism
in question was felt to be displayed by socialist women from the Campaign
for Nuclear Disarmament toward Wilmette Brown, an Afro-American legal
aid adviser to ecofeminist activists and a well-known advocate in the wages-
for-housework campaign. As those familiar with ideological crosscurrents

within feminism know, many leftists are antagonistic to the wages-for-house-work campaign, which cuts right across their ideal of socialized domestic production. The confrontation was thus an ideological one, but exacerbated in that a black activist stood at the center of it. Greenham ecofeminists, sensitive to the interconnectedness of all forms of domination—classism, racism, sexism, and speciesism—took all facets of the problem in hand and tried to work them out. Carrying this "inclusiveness" further, an April 1989 meeting of the Woman Earth Peace Institute in San Francisco pioneered an effective model for ensuring racial parity at ecofeminist gatherings.[50] Fox's divisive approach is a dubious one for a radical thinking man in the late twentieth century to engage in. Which brings up another question: where are the Afro-American or Third World "spokespeople" for the deep ecology movement?

Zimmerman writes that "Critics of feminism"—though, since these are not referenced, one must infer it is the author himself speaking—"regard as disingenuous the claim that the real motive of feminism is to liberate *all* people. Such critics contend that feminists have their own power agenda."[51] Obviously, feminists have a power agenda; they are involved in a political struggle designed to redress an inequitable system. Or, if Zimmerman means that individual feminist women are on a "power trip," then there is a margin of truth in that as well, in as much as women attempting to achieve equality alongside male peers have to compete harder to arrive at the same result because of structural discrimination and harassment along the way. However, if he is implying that women only want power, then that is silly. The personal costs of being a feminist in both career and domestic terms are enormous. Nobody would bother with the struggle unless she were committed to the vision of a just society. It may be at least several generations before the community at large even begins to digest what feminists are talking about. Current statistics, for example, indicate that 25 percent of Australian men still believe that it is all right for a man to hit "his" wife. In the United States, a woman is battered every eighteen seconds. In the meantime, there are few benefits for feminists, or even their daughters in the foreseeable future. Ecofeminism is directed toward a long-term transvaluation of values. Women working to this end certainly glean no rewards from the system that they are trying to deconstruct. In a way, deep ecology's "critique of feminism" itself reflects why the ecofeminist sensibility came forward in the first place. In Charlene Spretnak's words, "Ecofeminism addresses the terror of nature and of female power, and the ways out of this mesmerizing condition. . . ."[52]

Ambivalence and Appropriation

While Zimmerman and Cheney, each from their different viewpoints, have observed that convergencies between ecofeminism and deep ecology exist only "at first glance" or "on the face of it," a fraction of the deep ecological mindset still hopes for some sort of I/thou accommodation between the movements. Fox talks about a synthesis and, astonishingly, turns to Cheney's critique and Zimmerman's "evenhanded" examination in defence of his own claim that there is "no real incompatibility."[53] The logic of Fox's turn is incredible, first, in light of Zimmerman's highly ambivalent attitude toward feminism, and second, given Cheney's skeptical thesis that deep ecology may be symptomatic of an inability to identify realistically with others, a manifestation of the patriarchal vacillation between "selfish appetite" and "oceanic fusion."[54] Ecofeminists certainly resist a patronizing subsumption of women's thoughtful labors under the deep ecological umbrella, just as much as they find it offensive to see men raiding and colonizing feminist ideas in order to modernize male dominance. Nevertheless, ignoring our disquiet over the deep ecologists lack of regard for the environmental consequences of technology, economics, race, and gender relations, Fox recommends that in as much as ecofeminists "extend" their concerns to the ecological, then there is no "significant difference." He calls for an alliance with Patsy Hallen, in terms of her paper, subtitled "Why Ecology Needs Feminism," and with Marti Kheel, despite the latter's uncompromising exposé of patriarchal thinking in environmental ethics. On the next page, and relaxing back into the authoritative white, male, academic register, he announces "major problems associated with Kheel's critique."[55] In one important concession, he writes, "Deep ecologists completely agree with ecofeminists that men have been far more implicated in the history of environmental destruction than women."[56] This assertion more or less unhinges Fox's efforts to generate a coherent stand, providing a good example of what liberal pluralism looks like in practice.[57]

Zimmerman also arrives at a point where he is keen "to unite" and finds "no real disagreement on basics," etc., and he adopts the ecofeminist analysis that "So long as patriarchally raised men fear and hate women, and so long as men conceive of nature as female, men will continue in their attempts to deny what they consider to be the feminine/natural within themselves and to control what they regard as the feminine/natural outside themselves."[58] Does he really believe this statement? It seems doubtful, for with the next breath, he writes, "Salleh's critique is, in my opinion, only partly accurate. . . ."[59] This opinion, however, is never demonstrated, for he does not say which "part" he has in mind, or whether the "parts" represent a reader divided within his intellectual/emotional growth. Although intellectual capacities recognize what is true in ecofeminism, emotionally the reader is unsettled by the feminine voice. After all, Zimmerman reads the "Deeper than Deep Ecology" critique as "accusatory," rather than, say, "challenging" or "confronting."[60] Thus, the question is: since ultimately he endorses ecofeminist conclusions, what is Zimmerman defending at such length?

Ambivalence also marks Devall's work. He is happy to take on board the odd ecofeminist insight—for example, Starhawk's revisioning of power, the heroic example of India's Chipko women, or Sarah Ebenreck's farm ethic. He has even come to agree with the ecofeminist premise that "the ecological crisis has complex psychosexual roots." Yet, like other deep ecologists, Devall is anxious to move quickly beyond that messy problem "to explore the ecological self." The emphasis on gender difference runs the risk of "divisiveness," he claims, and "distracts us from the real work." This "after the Revolution" line is a familiar one to feminists who took their first steps hand in hand with brother Marxists. The language is identical, in fact, for what speaks here is the voice of patriarchy. Of course, many men want to avoid doing their personal/political homework; doing so could well upset their comfortable status quo. Nevertheless, humans cannot simply pass over their psychosexual conditioning in this way, as the present textual analysis demonstrates. In Devall's own words, "Healing requires bringing forth that which is suppressed in culture" and leveling with it, however painful and confusing this experience may be. As every deep ecologist knows, band-aid solutions do not work.[61]

III. Conclusion

Richard Ohmann is not himself a deep ecologist, but a man sensitive to the terrain of gender politics that now underlies both daily routine and theoretical work. He approaches our dilemma in this way:

. . . progressive male intellectuals and professionals have arrived at feminism by an inexorable development and by a moral logic that flows from our strongest allegiances. . . . If we are "in" feminism at all, we are dragged into it kicking and screaming, and now that we're there, we should think of ourselves as on extended probation, still learning. What we do there with our experience, our competence, and our gender and class confidence, is a matter to be negotiated with caution, flexibility, improvisation, listening, and often doubtless through a strategic fade into the wallpaper. But I don't see drawing back from the knowledge that feminism is our fight, too.[62]

Clearly there is a long way yet to go. In terms of a Green or eco-socialist political practice, the new politics will demand of men and women more than just rational understanding of their respective positions as bearers of class, race, and gender domination, if they are to recover their shared human complementarity. Men moreover, whose history has taken them on such a destructive path, will need to open up to a deep therapeutic acceptance of the process of mother/nature/woman killing in the making of their own identities. Although the personal and the transpersonal are intermeshed, as far as deep ecology goes, this inner movement has been lacking. Constructed by a class of men that is serviced by both patriarchal and capitalist institutions, deep ecology with its valuable move to "ecocentrism" remains out of touch with the material source of its continuing existence. Significantly, its theorization ignores the place of labor in the creation and sustenance of human life and its pivotal role in our human exchanges with nature. In short, as it is presently formulated, deep ecology reflects the disembodied conditions of its own production. This situation is, and should be, a matter for concern, if not despair, among committed environmental radicals, eco-socialists, and ecofeminists.

Notes

Salleh is an Australian ecofeminist activist and theorist. She writes on convergencies and contradictions between socialism, feminism and ecology and is currently completing a book about ecofeminism and Green politics. She is a coconvener of the Women's Environmental Education Centre in Sydney and an occasional visiting scholar in the Environmental Conservation Education Program at New York University.

First published in *Environmental Ethics* 15, no. 3. Permission to reprint courtesy of *Environmental Ethics* and the author.

1. Ariel Salleh, "The Ecofeminism/Deep Ecology Debate: A Reply to Patriarchal Reason," *Environmental Ethics* 14 (1992): 195–216.

2. For discussion of the international status of ecofeminism and its regional variations, see Ariel Salleh, "From Centre to Margin," *Hypatia* 6 (1991): 206–14.

3. Arne Naess, "The Shallow and the Deep, Long Range Ecology Movement," *Inquiry* 16 (1973): 95–100. A qualification of Naess views appears in *Ecology, Community and Life Style: Outline of an Ecosophy*, trans. David Rothenberg (New York: Cambridge University Press, 1989). Here, the impact of culture and personal experience on ethical intuition is acknowledged in a way that could serve as a model for other deep ecologists.

4. Ariel Salleh, "Epistemology and the Metaphors of Production," *Studies in the Humanities* 15 (1988): 136.

5. Brinda Rao, "Gender and Ecology in India," *Capitalism, Nature, Socialism* 2 (1989): 65–82; Berit As, "A Five Dimensional Model for Change," *Women's Studies International Quarterly* 4 (1980); Barbara Ehrenreich, *The Hearts of Men* (New York: Anchor Books, 1983).

6. Warwick Fox, "The Deep Ecology-Ecofeminism Debate and Its Parallels," *Environmental Ethics* 11 (1989): 14. Compare Ariel Salleh, "Deeper than Deep Ecology: The Ecofeminist Connection," *Environmental Ethics* 6 (1984): 335–41, especially points 3 and 4.

7. Michael Zimmerman, "Feminism, Deep Ecology, and Environmental Ethics," *Environmental Ethics* 9 (1987): 21–44.

8. For an early ecofeminist ethic based on "caring," see Marti Kheel, "The Liberation of Nature: A Circular Affair," *Environmental Ethics* 7 (1985): 135–49. The analysis of caring has since become a veritable growth area for professional philosophers, thus, neutralizing the radical feminist impulse which originally politicized it.

9. Zimmerman, "Feminism, Deep Ecology, and Environmental Ethics," p. 31. The reference is to Naomi Scheman, "Individualism and the Objects of Psychology" in S. Harding and M. Hintikka, eds., *Discovering Reality* (Boston: Reidel, 1983), p. 234.

10. Jim Cheney, "Ecofeminism and Deep Ecology," *Environmental Ethics* 9 (1987): 124.

11. Vandana Shiva, *Staying Alive* (London: Zed, 1989) conveys the voice of Indian women farmers to a Western educated readership. Alternatively, an academic feminist argument connecting pain with political insight is made in Ariel Salleh, "On the Dialectics of Signifying Practice," *Thesis Eleven* 5/6 (1982): 72–84.

12. Salleh, "Deeper than Deep Ecology," p. 339.

13. Fox, "Deep Ecology-Ecofeminism Debate," p. 9 (emphasis added). Since writing this piece, I have discovered that Jim Cheney explicates the totalizing implications of Fox's stand powerfully and eloquently in "The Neo-Stoicism of Radical Environmentalism," *Environmental Ethics* 11 (1989): 293–325.

14. Unfortunately, Robyn Eckersley's recent book *Environmentalism and Political Theory: Toward an Ecocentric Approach* (Stonybook: New York University at Stonybrook Press, 1992) perpetuates Fox's naive realism.

15. Rosemary Ruether, *New Woman, New Earth* (New York: Seabury Press, 1975).

16. Fox, "Deep Ecology-Ecofeminism Debate," p. 12.

17. Ibid., pp. 22–23.

18. Zimmerman, "Feminism, Deep Ecology, and Environmental Ethics," p. 34.

19. Bill Devall and George Sessions, *Deep Ecology: Living as if Nature Mattered* (Salt Lake City: Peregrene Smith, 1985), p. 225. On *essentialism* as red herring, see Salleh, "The Ecofeminism/Deep Ecology Debate," and "Essentialism and Ecofeminism," *Arena* 94 (1991): 167–73.

20. Zimmerman, "Feminism, Deep Ecology, and Environmental Ethics," p. 40.

21. Ibid., pp. 40, 41–42.

22. Don Davis, "The Seduction of Sophia," *Environmental Ethics* 8 (1986): 151–62.

23. Alan Wittbecker, "Deep Anthropology, Ecology and Human Order," *Environmental Ethics* 8 (1986): 269; and Bill Devall, *Simple in Means, Rich in Ends* (Salt Lake City: Peregrene Smith, 1988).

24. This paragraph is adapted from Ariel Salleh, "Living with Nature: Reciprocity or Control," in R. Engel and J. Engel, eds., *Ethics of Environment and Development* (London: Pinter/University of Arizona Press, 1990), p. 251.

25. George Sessions, personal communication; Los Angeles, March 1987; Arne Naess, personal communication, Oslo, August 1987.

26. See Bill Devall and George Sessions, *Deep Ecology,* pp. 71–73.

27. Karen Warren, "Feminism and Ecology: Making Connections," *Environmental Ethics* 9 (1987): 6.

28. Dale Spender, *Women of Ideas and What Men Have Done to Them* (London: Routledge, 1982). See also Margo Adair and Sharon Howell, *The Subjective Side of Politics* (San Francisco: Tools for Change, 1988).

29. Fox, "The Deep Ecology-Ecofeminism Debate," p. 13, n. 20.

30. Bill Devall and George Sessions, *Deep Ecology;* compare Carolyn Merchant, *The Death of Nature* (San Francisco: Harper and Row, 1980).

31. Greta Gaard, "Feminists, Animals, and the Environment," paper presented at the annual convention of the National Women's Studies Association, Baltimore, 1989, p. 10.

32. Devall and Sessions, *Deep Ecology,* p. 180; p. 221, n. 2. The missing references are Dorothy Dinnerstein, *The Mermaid and the Minataur* (New York: Harper and Row, 1976) and Jessie Bernard, *The Future of Marriage* (New York: World Publications, 1972).

33. Janet Biehl's article "It's Deep but Is It Broad?" appeared in *Kick It Over,* Winter 1987, pp. 2A–4A, at a time when she identified herself with social ecofeminism.

34. Salleh, "Deeper than Deep Ecology," p. 339 (emphasis added).

35. Fox, "The Deep Ecology-Ecofeminism Debate," p. 16.

36. Ariel Salleh, "A Green Party: Can the Boys Do Without One?" in Drew Hutton, ed., *Green Politics in Australia* (Sydney: Angus and Robertson, 1987), p. 88.

37. See the special women's issue of *Environmental Review* 8 (1984); and Ariel Salleh, "The Growth of Ecofeminism," *Chain Reaction* 36 (1984): 26–28.

38. Zimmerman, "Feminism, Ecology, and Environmental Ethics," p. 41.

39. Hilkka Pietila, "Daughters of Mother Earth," in Engel and Engel, *Ethics of Environment and Development,* p. 243 (emphasis added).

40. Zimmerman, "Feminism, Ecology, and Environmental Ethics," p. 41.

41. The participation of women from all continents in the 1992 United Nations Conference on Environment and Development is a case in point. Even so, at one point, Third World government negotiators were prepared to "trade off" women's rights, if the United States would concede its high level of resource depletion by leaving references to "overconsumption" in Agenda 21 texts!

42. Alice Jardine, *Gynesis* (Cambridge, Mass.: Harvard University Press, 1985).

43. Zimmerman, "Feminism, Ecology, and Environmental Ethics," p. 44. The same tendency is manifest in his book *Heidegger's Confrontation with Modernity* (Bloomington: Indiana University Press, 1990), even while a "feminist perspective" is incorporated into the last five pages of text.

44. See Benjamin Lichtenstein, "Feminist Epistemology," *Thesis Eleven* 21 (1988).

45. Wittbecker, "Deep Anthropology and Human Order," p. 265, n. 18.

46. Zimmerman, "Feminism, Ecology, and Environmental Ethics," p. 34.

47. Fox, "Deep Ecology-Ecofeminism Debate," pp. 17–18. As well as being poorly informed, notes 33 and 41 of this article are classic examples of misrepresentation by trivialization.

48. Ibid., p. 20.

49. Ibid., p. 14, n. 24.

50. Jacinta McCoy, personal communication, Eugene, Oregon, June 1989.

51. Zimmerman, "Feminism, Ecology, and Environmental Ethics," p. 41.

52. Charlene Spretnak, Address to the First International Ecofeminist Conference, University of Southern California, Los Angeles, March 1987.

53. Fox, "Deep Ecology-Ecofeminism Debate," p. 9, n. 7.

54. Cheney follows Carol Gilligan, *In a Different Voice* (Cambridge: Harvard University Press, 1982).

55. Fox, "Deep Ecology-Ecofeminism Debate," p. 9, n. 7; p. 10, n. 11. Patsy Hallen, "Making Peace with Nature: Why Ecology Needs Feminism," *The Trumpeter* 4, no. 3 (1987): 3–14; Marti Kheel, "The Liberation of Nature."

56. Fox, "Deep Ecology-Ecofeminism Debate," p. 14.

57. In tandem with Fox, Eckersley, in *Environmentalism and Political Theory,* also tries to appropriate ecofeminism for deep ecology. In quite uncritical language, she describes ecofeminist theory as "nesting within" ecocentrism and as an "essential tributary." Moreover, focusing exclusively on the world of ideas, Eckersley sees ecocentrism as waiting to be "fleshed out in a political and economic direction." Women's ongoing political/economic resistance, North and South, remains invisible to her.

58. Zimmerman, "Feminism, Ecology, and Environmental Ethics," p. 24.

59. Ibid., p. 39.

60. Ibid.

61. Devall, *Simple in Means, Rich in Ends,* pp. 56–57.

62. Richard Ohmann, "In, With," in A. Jardine and P. Smith, eds., *Men in Feminism* (New York: Methuen Books, 1987), p. 187.

5

Green Reason:
Communicative Ethics for the Biosphere

John S. Dryzek

I. Introduction

The fields of environmental ethics and politics are currently home to a variety of lively and radical challenges to established institutions, practices, and moralities.[1] Although deep ecologists, animal rights activists, ecofeminists, social ecologists, Heideggerians, pantheists, sociobiologists, and others find much to disagree about, they are united by rejection of the narrowly anthropocentric and utilitarian world views of industrial society and liberal morality. Unfortunately, however, the nefarious aspects of this rejected status quo can creep back in quietly through the back door in the form of what may be termed the subversion of ethics by epistemology. This subversion can be anticipated to the extent that an environmental ethic fails to attend fully to issues of knowledge and rationality. While connections between ethics and epistemology are readily identified (at least at the level of metaethics), in practice (i.e., at the level of applied ethics, or, following MacIntyre,[2] ethics simpliciter) epistemology is often ignored. This neglect may be safe enough in many fields of human endeavor, but when it comes to the environment the oversight is dangerous. In this paper, I seek to correct this oversight and so close the back door.

One may expect the undermining of ethics by epistemology to the extent that an environmental ethic consorts—whether by design, accident, or oversight—with exclusively instrumental notions of reason.[3] The association with instrumental rationality applies most obviously if the ethic in question is seen as providing only the ends for instrumental actions; however, absolute prohibitions and compulsions (concerning, for example, respect for the rights of natural environments) are not immune, for such directives operate and make sense only in an environment of instrumental action—if only as constraints upon this action.

I begin my argument by outlining the threat to both the environment and environmental ethics posed by the lingering grip of instrumental reason. The search for a solution usually begins with the popular nostrum of ecological spirituality. I argue for a different cure, one that expands rationality to encompass communicative practices. Even though contemporary proponents of communicative rationality proceed in exclusively anthropocentric terms, a recognition of agency in the natural world, which a number of recent scientific developments point to, can overcome this limitation and render communicative rationality fit to regulate human dealings with the environment.

II. The Rational Roots of Environmental Decay

It can be argued that instrumental rationality underlies our current environmental predicament. Instrumental rationality, on this account, invokes a Cartesian dichotomy between subject and object. The human mind is subject; all else—including the natural world, and other people—consists of objects, to be manipulated, therefore dominated, in the interests of the mind's desires. Instrumental rationality is therefore abstract, estranged from nature (and society) and estranging to the extent that we subscribe to it.[4] The expansion of this kind of rationality is often associated with the Enlightenment's disenchantment of the world,[5] which paves the way for the destruction of that world for the sake of utility and industrialization at the hands of an arrogant humanism.[6] Ecofeminists equate such practices with patriarchal and masculine epistemology,[7] which predates the Enlightenment by several thousand years.

The upshot is that in using the technological powers in our hands to turn the world to our use, we are destroying that world. No longer able to devise correctives for the proliferating secondary and tertiary effects of our instrumental interventions, we find that nature takes its revenge upon us in the form of environmental crisis.[8]

This critique of instrumental rationality can also be extended to abstractly rational argument in favor of *general* moral principles. In this context, feminists argue that most contemporary political theory, whether liberal, Marxist, or Frankfurt School, works from a model of *man* which is universal, uniform, ahistorical, and transcendent, excluding a model of *woman* which is contextual, relational, and particularistic.[9] Ecofeminists add that the traditional model of man is alienated from natural contexts too.[10]

One goal of environmental ethics is, of course, to generate solutions to the problems associated with our estrangement from the natural world. To what extent, then, are existing schemes crippled by their vestigial ties to exclusively instrumental rationality? Consider, first of all, deep ecology, which is claimed to be the most radically anti-anthropocentric (its critics would say misanthropic) ethic. When it comes to implementing this program, Devall and Sessions can suggest little more that "policies must be changed."[11] In other words, instrumentally rational actions (such as population control) are commended to the very agencies (governments and other organizations) whose rationality is elsewhere condemned for contributing to environmental decay. In their inattention to the side effects of their proposed strategies Devall and Sessions are likely to discover that their ends are subverted by their means.

Further examples of a lingering stress on instrumental reason are readily identifiable. In his classic argument for the rights of natural objects, Stone asks that these rights be embodied in law—a system of instrumental-analytic—rationality *par excellence*.[12] Lemons suggests that we take ideas promulgated by natural science, such as homeostasis and diversity, as the basis for an environmental ethic—and, implicitly, as the end for instrumental manipulations.[13]

A subtle extension of the dialectic of Enlightenment may come into play here. According to Horkheimer and Adorno, the dialectic of Enlightenment tells us that the more successful we become in securing the material conditions for human freedom (in part through control of the natural world), the more repressed we become as human subjects, unable to partake of freedom.[14] To overstate my proposed extension: the more assiduously we cultivate the ethical principles for benign but still instrumental action toward the environment, the less likely it becomes that we shall be able to reconcile ourselves to that environment in productive fashion. That is, nature will become still more firmly the "other" from which we are estranged, even if our instrumental manipulations of it are well motivated.

The challenge here then is to locate an epistemology less prone to the subversion of environmental ethics than the exclusively instrumental fixation associated with dominant (post-Enlightenment) conceptions of rationality. Another way of stating the same point is that we should seek what Habermas disparages as the "resurrection of nature."[15] On this account, nature was not simply disenchanted by the Enlightenment—it was killed. As a result, no longer could meanings and purposes be discerned in the nonhuman world. How then may they be retrieved?

III. Two Ways to Resurrect Nature

Although the idea that nature merits resurrection is indeed current in the field of environmental ethics, most of those who subscribe to this idea seek resurrection through spirituality, religion, feeling, and intuition. That is, they accept the dichotomy established by Enlightenment rationalists and seek a return to pre-Enlightenment—or even prehistoric—sensibilities.[16]

The idea that spirit is ultimately preferable to rationality is perhaps held most strongly by deep ecologists, although a host of other writers—including some critics of deep ecology—is equally enamored of spirit and suspicious of any kind reason. It is an easy step from condemnations of rationality to arguments for more holistic, intuitive, emotional, spiritual, or experiential "oneness" to mediate our relations with the natural world (and one another). Franciscan Christianity, Taoism, Buddhism, pagan religions, feminist spirituality, and American Indian beliefs all have their adherents and admirers.[17]

An advocacy of a particular spiritual position can be rooted in rejection of another spirituality, rather than in opposition to rationality. For example, Lynn White argues that because the source of environmental crisis is one kind of religion—specifically, the Judeo-Christian tradition that places man above nature—the solution must lie in adoption of a different kind of religion.[18] Gary Snyder makes a similar point in bemoaning the establishment of "male deities located off the planet."[19]

Nevertheless, even if a particular spirituality is the problem, it does not follow that a different spirituality has to be the solution. Nor does it follow that if a particular rationality is the problem, then spirituality is the solution. Although the right kind of spirituality may be one answer, I argue that the right kind of rationality is a better one. I draw on the rationality debates now cutting across a variety of disciplines to argue that a broadened notion of rationality can meet the concerns of ecological anti-rationalists.[20] I contend that provided our notions of rationality are expanded in the right direction, human dealings with the environment are indeed best governed by rational standards and that a regressive emphasis on spirit is therefore unnecessary. To be sure, because the rationality debates have for the most part missed the ecological dimension, some specifically green correctives must be brought to bear upon them. Thus, the kind of reason I argue for here is not only expanded beyond instrumental conceptions, but is also avowedly ecological.

IV. The Hazards of Spiritual Alternatives

Before turning to an examination of this kind of rationality, let me identify some of the shortcomings inherent in excessive reliance upon its spiritual alternatives. Clearly an ecologically sensitive spirituality is not automatically to be commended. For an extreme negative model, we need look no further than the Third Reich and Hitler's invitation to good Aryans to think with their blood rather than their brains. Along with Teutonic mythology, Naziism embodied a peculiar kind of reverence for (German) nature and fatherland. Today's German Greens are well aware of this history, and so avoid any association with ecological spirituality.[21]

Even if Naziism is dismissed as an irrelevant possibility involving only perversion and abuse of ecological spirituality, one can discern political dangers in the schemes of some contemporary ecological philosophers. For example, Devall and Sessions prescribe the true realization of the "self" in a larger communal "Self" of "organic wholeness" as an antidote to liberal individualism.[22] Even though the "Self" of Devall and Sessions is benign, extending beyond humanity to the natural world, willing immersion in a larger "Self" is also surely the essence of totalitarianism.[23]

Some advocates of an ecological spirituality are impressed by the functions of myth and ritual in preliterate societies; nevertheless, as Luke points out, myth and ritual in primal societies can also form the substance of attempts to control and manipulate nature and other persons—the very sins of which instrumental rationality is accused.[24]

Although there are important differences between an earth ceremony at a gathering of contemporary environmentalists and a Nuremburg rally, spirituality as such cannot speak to these differences and help us choose one over the other. Thus, ecological spirituality by itself provides no defense against authoritarianism. As Bookchin points out, ecological religious sensibilities have often coexisted with despotic social order (as in ancient Egypt).[25]

Even if one dismisses these authoritarian possibilities to embrace a more tolerant and pluralistic spirituality, there are two reasons why any such orientation remains inadequate. First, natural systems are complex; it is a familiar adage that "everything is connected to everything else" in ecosystems.[26] It is also the case that interventions in complex systems often have counterintuitive results, as actions ramify extensively through these systems. As a result, intuitions, good intentions, and sympathetic sensibilities are insufficient guides to action. Think, for example, of the well-intentioned fire-control policies long followed in the forests of the American West which interrupted the life cycles of species and the well-being of ecosystems that depend on periodic scorching. To take another example, one might out of a reverence for all things living remove only deadwood from a forest for fuel, thereby undermining the key habitat dead trees provide.

Now it might be argued here that an appropriate spirituality could somehow be combined with a suitably tamed instrumental rationality to effectively cope with complexity. However, often ecological systems are *so* complex that they defy the efforts of instrumental rationalists to model them.[27] In such cases, spirituality is not likely to be of much help either. I suggest below that a noninstrumental kind of reason can compensate for the deficiencies of instrumental rationality under complex conditions.

A second shortcoming of a spiritual approach is contingent on the conditions of our interactions with the natural world. One may assume that these conditions are in a state of some disequilibrium (otherwise, there would be little need to worry about environmental ethics, policies, and politics). Thus, even if a primarily spiritual orientation toward nature is adequate for maintaining an ecologically harmonious society, it contains no effective guidance about how to reach this happy state from our current plight (except perhaps through a massive exercise in spiritual empowerment). To put it crudely, there is no effective "theory of transition." Most of those who speak of ecological spirituality say little about this transition, let alone any practical political program.

Required here then is a noninstrumental capacity analogous to that of "resilience" in natural systems, which can be defined in terms of a capacity to return to a stable operating range from a disequilibrium state.[28] Natural systems can do this on their own without us. Moreover, if Lovelock is right about the ability of the planet's biota to sustain the physical conditions for all life—thereby constituting an entity he calls Gaia—these systems can also correct for many human excesses.[29] Nevertheless, larger stresses in systems with substantial human complicity require a human contribution to problem solving (as even Lovelock admits).

V. Communicative Reason

At this juncture we might seem in a bit of a quandary. On the one hand, instrumental rationality and abstract reasoning about values imply hierarchy and domination. On the other, spirituality is an inadequate alternative. Its inadequacy is implicitly confirmed by Spretnak, who qualifies her advocacy of green spirituality with a recognition that "holistic, or ecological, thinking is not a retreat from reason; it is an enlargement of it to more comprehensive and hence more efficient means of analysis."[30] Spretnak, of course, wishes to enlarge reason by incorporating spirituality, but, like other environmentalists who bemoan "dualistic thinking," she offers no hints as to how this might be done. In contrast, the alternative I propose is to expand reason in a different direction.

How then can an expanded, nonhierarchical conception of rationality point to what Whitebook calls a "non-regressive reconciliation with nature" that may allow us to escape from this impasse?[31] We may begin to chart this escape by noting that rationality is properly a property of community, and not just individuals, if for no other reason than that social isolates have no standards of judgement. As Dewey argues, "our intelligence is bound up . . . with the community of life of which we are a part."[32] We can describe a collective as *communicatively* rational to the extent that its interactions are egalitarian, uncoerced, competent, and free from delusion, deception, power, and strategy.[33] Communicative rationality is best thought of as a regulative ideal for human social practices, which can then be condemned to the extent of their violation of its precepts. No realizable blueprint is implied.

Most of those who recognize this kind of rationality believe it is embedded first and foremost in processes involving the creation of meaning—culture, socialization, friendship, and so forth. Nevertheless, communicative rationality may also be conducive to the resolution of complex problems, inasmuch as it promotes the free harmonization of actions by disparate individuals concerned with the different facets of such problems.[34] Thus, communicative reason may rest more easily in a complex world than either spirituality or instrumental rationality.

One might argue that the ideal discursive community of communicative rationality is presupposed even in discussions about ecological spirituality, for if one accepts that some spiritualities have more benign ecological implications than others—and surely this is unarguable—then one needs some means of sorting them out. These means cannot themselves be spiritual, since spirituality is internal to the schemes one is sifting. Within the Catholic schema, Catholics are right by revelation; within the pagan schema, pagans are right by revelation. Arguments across the boundaries of spiritual schemes, however, have to be reasoned arguments—of exactly the kind that proponents of such schemes deploy in the literature on environmental ethics. In deploying arguments, moreover, one is implicitly accepting the constitutive principles of a discursively rational community (however much one violates these principles in practice). My point here echoes Apel's analysis of scientific communities.[35] Apel points out that the practice of science presupposes a measure of communicative rationality within these communities. Just as scientists cannot deny their humanity, those who proclaim spirituality cannot, in this age of lost innocence, deny their rationality.

Communicative rationality as generally stated (e.g., by Habermas) is not, however, conducive to harmonious relationships with the natural world. A first defect arises from its transcendent, ahistorical leanings. In practice, all ecological contexts are different, and individuals are likely to interpret and experience them in diverse ways. This problem can be overcome by the explicit recognition of the ineliminable plurality in human discourse. In this way, communicative rationality becomes simply a *procedural* standard for human interaction, dictating no *substantive* resolution of disputes.[36]

A second defect cuts deeper. If communication is seen merely as a property of human dealings with each other, then its rationality may coexist easily with instrumental and dominating attitudes toward the nonhuman world. Indeed, Habermas proposes this coexistence as a *solution* to the problem posed by the dialectic of Enlightenment that will move critical theory beyond the impasse reached by the earlier work of Adorno and Horkheimer. Habermas tries to draw a clear line between the relationships we construct with the natural world and those we establish with one another. He avers that the only attitude toward the natural world which is fruitful in securing the material conditions for human existence is an instrumental one.[37] The domination of nature is a price that Habermas is willing to pay for fulfillment of the Enlightenment's promise of human emancipation: "the dignity of the subject . . . is attained at the price of denying all worth to nature."[38] To Habermas, there is ultimately no ontological distinction between inorganic and organic nature.[39] A lump of iron and an ecosystem should be treated in the same terms, as objects for manipulation. Only in our relationships with other persons can instrumental rationality be overcome and communicative rationality flourish; Habermas's goal here is to "prevent social relations becoming like our relations with the natural world."[40]

Habermas believes that we can only truly know that which we have ourselves created—language—and that nature will always remain estranged and separate. We cannot truly *know* anything about nature; we can only observe the results of our interventions in it. Challenged on the potentially destructive environmental implications of this dichotomy, Habermas replies that one should not confuse ethics with epistemology.[41] Thus, he believes that an environmental ethic can be grafted onto our instrumental relations with the natural world—although, given that Habermas believes that the only entities that bear value are those which can participate in discourse, this ethic has to be anthropocentric.[42] As a result, Habermas ends up just where the interesting problems in environmental ethics (and epistemology) begin. However, the best move here is not to reject communicative rationality, but to extend it.

VI. From Communicative to Ecological Rationality

How may communicative rationality be extended to incorporate procedural standards which are not obviously intrinsic to human discourse, but which are essential to good order in human interactions with the natural world? One place to begin might be with the establishment of ecological principles—or ecosystem analogues—such as diversity, homeostasis, flexibility, and resilience as critical standards in human discourse. In so doing, we would not submit to nature's authority, in the manner advocates of biocentrism (the doctrine that value is created by and in natural systems) sometimes seem to demand. Nor would we merely apply nature's standards to human communities (in the way Bookchin and Ophuls suggest).[43] Rather, individual ecological principles would always be applied, debated, redeemed, or rejected. In this sense, these principles would supplement the familiar standards intrinsic to the idea of communicative rationality (equality, noncoercion, truthfulness, etc.).

If we take away the dressing of communicative rationality, this first proposal is a bit facile, reducing as it does to advocacy of ecological principles in human debates. As such, it severs ethics from epistemology once again, though it grafts environmental ethics onto communicative, rather than instrumental, rationality. For their part, critical communications theorists would probably object that such a move is tantamount to the coercive imposition of an external, substantive, and transcendent judgment upon human discourse. One might equally well impose economic efficiency, political stability, or social harmony as a standard, for none of these principles is intrinsic to the idea of rational discourse, and so cannot be grounded in it.

How might one go about establishing the special claims of ecology upon human communication? One could start by arguing that intersubjective discourse presupposes some ecological—and not just linguistic—standards. Although it is easy to forget, our communications with one another can proceed only in and through the media made available by the natural world (in addition to our own medium of language). It is not just brute matter we are taking advantage of here, for, if Lovelock is right, the atmosphere in which we live, talk, hear, write, read, smell, and touch is composed and regulated by the planet's biota acting in concert.[44] This biota makes possible and maintains a physical environment fit for itself—and for us, and our communications. With this awareness in mind, we can no longer speak of communicative acts in a vacuum. Because any such act is made possible by this ecological system, it can be called to account in accordance with ecological standards. If indeed nature is a silent participant in every conversation, then perhaps it deserves a measure of the respect that we accord to human participants. If critical communications theorists argue that only entities capable of entering into communication can be assigned value, then there is a sense in which Gaia passes their test.

Assuming that the Gaia hypothesis holds, then we live *in* a highly differentiated, self-regulating global system whose "intelligence," which though not *conscious,* is of a complexity equal to that of any group of humans. Thus, "the Gaia hypothesis implies that the stable state of our planet includes man as a part of, or partner in, a very democratic entity."[45] Any special capabilities we do have—perhaps even, as Lovelock himself suggests, as Gaia's "nervous system and a brain"[46]—do not set us apart, but emphasizes our embeddedness.

Lovelock himself equivocates between two extremes on the implications of his hypothesis for the standing of Gaia's "intelligence." On the one hand, he develops a reductionist model sufficient to explain climatic stability in the face of wide fluctuations in the flow of solar radiation. This model is demonstrated in a hypothetical "Daisyworld" populated only by light and dark daisies whose relative numbers, and hence the planet's albedo, change in response to the intensity of radiation.[47] Somewhat surprisingly, in the same volume Lovelock endorses a mystical view which interprets Gaia in religious terms.[48]

If one eschews these two extremes, then the Gaia hypothesis indicates that there is agency (but not divinity) in the natural world. But let me stress that this hypothesis and its supporting evidence are not the only indications of such agency, which can also be found at lower levels of biological organizations. For example, in her discussion of the work of the celebrated geneticist Barbara McLintock, Keller argues that the key to McLintock's success is her "feeling for the organism," or, more precisely, for "the prodigious capacity of organisms to devise means for guaranteeing their own survival."[49] Thus, to McLintock, "the objects of her study have become subjects in their own right; they claim from her a kind of attention that most of us experience only in relation to other persons."[50]

To the biologist Charles Birch, this extension of subjectivity to nonhuman entities is the essence of "postmodern biology."[51] He treats "human experience as a high-level exemplification of entities in general, be they cells or atoms or electrons. All are subjects."[52] He argues that we should recognize the "self-determination exercised by natural entities in response to possibilities of their future."[53] Such an approach is also found in the work of Jane Goodall on chimpanzees and Donald Griffin on animal thinking.[54] Goodall and Griffin practice an essentially hermeneutic biology involving imaginative attempts to reconstruct the actions-in-context of other thinking beings.

Obviously there is a large gap between an "intelligent" Gaia and thinking organisms. In the early twentieth century this gap would have been handled by interpreting ecosystems as teleological entities seeking ever higher stages of ecological succession, culminating in climax. Today this superorganismic view of ecosystems is out of fashion in academic ecology, which has become thoroughly reductionistic and stochastic. Whether this epistemological commitment has more to do with academic ecology's desire for permission to worship in the temple of science than with the intrinsic superiority of the reductionist view remains an open question.

Regardless of its source, any recognition of agency in nature clearly undercuts the Cartesian subject-object dualism that legitimates the domination of nature[55]—just as a recognition of *human* agency undermines the instrumental manipulation that legitimates authoritarian politics. Nevertheless, agency in the natural world also makes the restriction of communicative rationality to purely human communities appear arbitrary. This world is not silent and passive, but *already* full of "values, purposes, and meanings," irrespective of what we ascribe to it.[56] As Abram argues, human perception can be reinterpreted in terms of reception of communication from the natural world.[57]

In this discussion of communicative possibilities encompassing human and natural systems I have taken for granted the communicative competence of humans and sought analogues in nature; nevertheless, this issue may also be approached from the opposite direction by contemplating what is natural in humans. Human nature is not just human; it is also nature. We can communicate not only because we are human, but also because we are natural. This precondition for communicative competence applies to humans, other primates, cetaceans, and insects alike. True, human communication mechanisms, language in particular, are more elaborate than those of most other species; however, greater continuity across human and nonhuman species is evident in nonlinguistic forms of communication, such as body movements or pheronomes.

If the idea of communicative interaction can indeed encompass the natural world, then so too can standards of communicative rationality. These standards, nevertheless, will not be the same as those enumerated above for speech among humans. So what standards are appropriate, and in what rational processes could such standards be embodied?

VII. Toward a Communicative Ecological Ethic

The specification of a communicative ethic for interactions encompassing the natural world is no small task, and what follows is intended to be suggestive rather than definitive. The task becomes somewhat easier upon noting that the objective here is a set of procedural criteria to regulate actions, rather than a full resolution of the content of actions.

Any attempt at substantive resolution here would involve flirting with instrumental rationality (which, when all is said and done, is often unavoidable). Such resolution may, however, be appropriate with reference to one universal principle: respect for the perceptual media furnished by nature. This principle in turn implies special respect for any "vital organs" that sustain these media (most especially, the life-sustaining composition of the atmosphere). According to Lovelock, these organs may well be the tropical forests, wetlands, and continental shelves (we would do well to find out if they are!).[58]

For the most part, though, substantive norms will have to be contingent on time, place, and particular human and ecological circumstances. It is also worth bearing in mind that perfection is impossible. Procedural criteria should function as critical standards from which some practices depart more than others.

An approach to the specification of such criteria can begin by noting the sense in which there can be equality in interactions with the natural world. Although equality in communicative competence of the sort that one can hypothesize within human communities is out of the question here, one can still postulate equality in the minimal terms of the very ability to communicate. This recognition rules out two extremes. The first is the idea that ecological processes should be engineered by human minds that essentially transcend the natural world. This first extreme finds its culmination in the notion that a "noosphere" could supplant the ecosphere.[59] The second extreme is based on the idea that "nature knows best,"[60] carrying with it implicit rejection of the idea that human problem-solving intelligence has any meaningful role to play in environmental affairs. To avoid these extremes we need a symbiotic intelligence in which both human minds and the self-organizing, self-regulating properties of natural systems play a part.

"Intelligence" in natural systems does not arise through the existence of any communications center; Gaia may have vital organs, but she has no brain. Rather, the feedback processes which organize, regulate, and maintain natural systems are of a diffuse and internal type—signals do not pass through any central thermostat analog.[61] Bearing in mind the principle of rough equality in communicative capability, we should be wary of highly centralized decision mechanisms—national environmental bureaucracies, multinational mining or logging corporations, international resource management agencies, and so forth—which could dominate, ignore, or suppress local ecological signals. The principle of rough equality suggests instead that diffuse feedback processes in the natural world should be matched by diffuse decision processes in human societies. This contention obviously provides further support to a presumption that "small is beautiful" in social organization—and, in practical political terms, to bioregionalism.

Obviously, though, not all of nature's feedback processes are localized. They can also be regional, even global. Think, for example, of ozone depletion or the greenhouse effect. The principle of rough equality does not limit the size and scope of political institutions in such cases. However, their designers should be careful to limit the purview of any such regional or global institutions to issues and problems which are themselves regional or global. Given the tendency of large organizations toward aggrandisement, the benefit of any doubt should probably go to the small-scale level.

Economic institutions, for their part, cannot escape size limitations so easily. Corporations whose reach is limited could not extend their operations to "pollution havens" in which they have no other interest. Similarly, the World Bank has no business making decisions for particular development projects based on universalistic, contextually inappropriate criteria. Such decisions have already led to numerous social and ecological disasters in the Third World, for example, in connection with the construction of large dams.[62]

What can we say about decision processes beyond questions of appropriate scale? Obviously there is much we do not know—and cannot know—about the workings of the natural world (and, for that matter, the human world). Thus, some kind of experimental practice in better living with the world seems to be appropriate. Yet experimentation in the image of science—manipulative, analytic, piecemeal, controlled, seeking generalizations across contexts—clearly violates the canons of communicative ethics. A

more appropriate experimental practice would interpret any particular interaction of human and natural systems in terms of a complex, nonreducible,
and unique entity. This kind of "holistic experimentation" (sketched in a
nonecological context by Mitroff and Blankenship) makes no attempt to control conditions and keep them constant, generalize results beyond the case at
hand, or distinguish between experimenters and subjects.[63] Nor does it impose any restrictions on the kinds of knowledge and perceptions admissible
in experimental design, evaluation, and redesign. The trick is, of course, to
extend participation in such experimentation to nonhuman entities.

This requirement returns us to the question of the perception of things
natural and its relationship to communication. If in fact we can equate perception with communication, then the contemporary gross failings in human
perception can be called to account by standards of communicative reason.
Perceptual failure pervades industrial societies, as people simply fail to recognize the effects of their actions on the natural world (not to mention other
people). Although these effects are sometimes visible, even to urban
dwellers, who cannot escape the effects of pollution, in other ways nature is
easy to ignore, especially by people who have no idea where and how their
food is grown, or what resources go into making the goods they buy.
Communicative ethics suggests improved perception.

Improvement could be sought at the level of social institutions. It is
clear that small-scale, autonomous societies really do have to pay a great deal
of attention to signals from their local environment. This necessity helps to
explain the ecological sensibilities found in many preliterate societies: those
without such orientations soon expire. These perceptual considerations obviously reinforce the argument for appropriate scale in social institutions—and
in holistic experimentation.

Perceptual capabilities can also be addressed at the level of individuals.
Again, it is possible to extend some critical theory notions here. In his most
recent attempts to ground his theoretical project, Habermas appeals to the
"reconstructive science" associated with figures such as Noam Chomsky,
Lawrence Kohlberg, and Jean Piaget.[64] The stages of individual moral and
cognitive development identified by Kohlberg and Piaget do, according to
Habermas, serve as a fixed and true model for social evolution. Higher levels
of individual development are characterized by increasing linguistic competence, by sensitivity to links with other individuals, by awareness of the interests of others—and, he adds, unfortunately, by recognition of the qualita-
tively different status of human and nonhuman entities.[65] Again, though,
Habermas has taken what are really just contingent empirical conjectures,
generalized them into timeless and nonfalsifiable truths, and frozen their
boundaries.[66] Thus, he rules out the possibility that sensitivity to interconnec-
tions with the natural environment might also enter individual development.[67]

Habermas' perspective may be limited by what bourgeois society currently allows and encourages in the way of individual development, which he mistakes for timeless truth. One can imagine moral development that proceeds further.

VIII. Conclusion

By now I hope I have demonstrated the promise of a communicative epistemology for environmental ethics which embraces the natural world in rational terms. There is no need here for mystical notions about spiritual communion with nature. Immersion in the world can be a thoroughly rational affair, provided we expand our notion of rationality in the appropriate directions. Reason too can be green. But clearly much remains to be done in the construction of a communicative ethics of rational interaction that embraces the natural world.

Notes

Dryzek, who teaches in the Department of Political Science, University of Oregon, is the author of *Rational Ecology: Environment and Political Economy* (New York: Basil Blackwell, 1987) and *Discursive Democracy: Politics, Policy, and Political Science,* (Cambridge: Cambridge University Press, 1990). An earlier version of this paper was presented at the conference "Upstream/Downstream: Issues in Environmental Ethics," held at Bowling Green State University, September 1988.

First published in *Environmental Ethics* 12, no. 3. Permission to reprint courtesy of *Environmental Ethics* and the author.

1. For a taxonomy of normative orientations toward environmental affairs, and a discussion of how these positions relate to political movements, see John S. Dryzek and James P. Lester, "Alternative Views of the Environmental Problematic," in James P. Lester, ed., *Environmental Politics and Policy: Theories and Evidence* (Durham, N.C.: Duke University Press, 1989).

2. Alasdair MacIntyre, "Does Applied Ethics Rest on a Mistake?" *The Monist* 67 (1984): 498–513.

3. Instrumental rationality may be defined in terms of the capacity to devise, select, and effect good means to clarified ends.

4. See, for example, Marti Kheel, "Ecofeminism and Deep Ecology: Reflections on Identity and Difference," unpublished manuscript, 1987.

5. Max Horkheimer and Theodore Adorno, *Dialectic of Enlightenment* (New York: Herder and Herder, 1972).

6. David Ehrenfeld, *The Arrogance of Humanism* (Oxford: Oxford University Press, 1978).

7. For example, Donald Davis, "Ecosophy: The Seduction of Sophia?" *Environmental Ethics* 8 (1986): 157–159.

8. C. Fred Alford, *Science and the Revenge of Nature: Marcuse and Habermas* (Gainesville: University Presses of Florida, 1985), p. 7.

9. See Stephen T. Leonard, *Critical Theory in Political Practice* (Princeton, N.J.: Princeton University Press, 1990).

10. For example, Kheel, "Ecofeminism and Deep Ecology," pp. 1–2.

11. Bill Devall and George Sessions, *Deep Ecology: Living as If Nature Mattered* (Salt Lake City: Peregrine Smith, 1985), pp. 70, 73.

12. Christopher D. Stone, "Should Trees Have Standing? Toward Legal Rights for Natural Objects," *Southern California Law Review* 45 (1972): 450–501.

13. John Lemons, "Cooperation and Stability as a Basis for Environmental Ethics," *Environmental Ethics* 3 (1981): 219–30.

14. Horkheimer and Adorno, *Dialectic of Enlightenment.*

15. Jurgen Habermas, *Knowledge and Human Interests* (Boston: Beacon Press, 1971), pp. 32–33. The reason Habermas disparages this resurrection is that he believes it could only occur in mystical form. Such romanticism may have been attractive to his Frankfurt School precursors, especially Adorno, Marcuse, and Horkheimer, but it has no place in Habermas' own rationalistic ambitions.

16. Starhawk, *Truth or Dare: Encounters with Power, Authority, and Mystery* (San Francisco: Harper and Row, 1987).

17. For suggestions, see Lynn White, Jr., "The Historical Roots of Our Ecologic Crisis," *Science* 155 (1967): 1203–07; Charlene Spretnak, *The Spiritual Dimension of Green Politics* (Santa Fe, N.M.: Bear and Co., 1986); Dolores LaChapelle, *Earth Wisdom* (San Diego: Guild of Tudors, 1978); Devall and Sessions, *Deep Ecology,* pp. 8, 90–91, 100–01; Warwick Fox, "On Guiding Stars to Deep Ecology: A Reply to Naess," *The Ecologist* 14 (1984): 203–04; Kheel, "Ecofeminism and Deep Ecology"; Arne Naess, "A Defense of the Deep Ecology Movement," *Environmental Ethics* 6 (1984): 266. Clearly, religions differ in their environmental implications, and so constitute fit objects for comparative scrutiny in the light of ecological concerns. See, for example, Eugene C. Hargrove, ed., *Religion and Environmental Crisis* (Athens: University of Georgia Press, 1986).

18. White, "Historical Roots," p. 1203.

19. Quoted in Spretnak, *Spiritual Dimension,* p. 33.

20. For a survey of these debates, see Richard J. Bernstein, *Beyond Objectivism and Relativism: Science, Hermeneutics, and Praxis* (Philadelphia: University of Pennsylvania Press, 1983).

21. Fritjof Capra and Charlene Spretnak, *Green Politics: The Global Promise* (New York: E. P. Dutton, 1984), pp. 53–56.

22. Devall and Sessions, *Deep Ecology,* p. 67.

23. See Murray Bookchin, "Social Ecology versus Deep Ecology: A Challenge for the Ecology Movement," *Green Perspectives* 4–5 (1987): 10–12.

24. Timothy W. Luke, "Deep Ecology and Distributive Justice," paper presented to the annual meeting of the Midwest Political Science Association, 1987, pp. 17–18.

25. Bookchin, "Social Ecology versus Deep Ecology," pp. 7–8.

26. Barry Commoner, *The Closing Circle* (New York: Bantam Books, 1972).

27. Garry D. Brewer, "Some Costs and Consequences of Large-Scale Social Systems Modeling," *Behavioral Sciences* 28 (1983): 166–185; John S. Dryzek, "Complexity and Rationality in Public Life," *Political Studies* 35 (1987): 424–42.

28. John S. Dryzek, *Rational Ecology: Environment and Political Economy* (Oxford and New York: Basil Blackwell, 1987), pp. 52–54.

29. James E. Lovelock, *Gaia: A New Look at Life on Earth* (Oxford: Oxford University Press, 1979).

30. Spretnak, *Spiritual Dimension,* p. 29.

31. Joel Whitebook, "The Problem of Nature in Habermas," *Telos* 40 (1979): 42.

32. John Dewey, *Human Nature and Conduct* (New York: Modern Library, 1922), p. 314.

33. Jurgen Habermas, *The Theory of Communicative Action I: Reason and the Rationalization of Society* (Boston: Beacon Press, 1984).

34. See Dryzek, "Complexity and Rationality."

35. Karl-Otto Apel, "The *A Priori* of Communication and the Foundation of the Humanities," *Man and World* 5 (1972): 3–37.

36. Bernstein, *Beyond Objectivism and Relativism,* pp. 191–94.

37. See, for example, Jurgen Habermas, "A Reply to My Critics," in John B. Thompson and David Held, eds., *Habermas: Critical Debates* (Cambridge, Mass.: MIT Press, 1982), pp. 243–45.

38. Whitebook, "The Problem of Nature," p. 53.

39. Russell Keat, *The Politics of Social Theory: Habermas, Freud and the Critique of Positivism* (Chicago: University of Chicago Press, 1981), pp. 88–92.

40. Alford, *Science and the Revenge of Nature*, p. 77.

41. Habermas, "A Reply to My Critics," pp. 241–42.

42. Whitebook, "The Nature Problem," p. 52.

43. Murray Bookchin, *Post-Scarcity Anarchism* (San Francisco: Ramparts, 1971), p. 80; William Ophuls, *Ecology and the Politics of Scarcity* (San Francisco: W. H. Freeman, 1977).

44. Lovelock, *Gaia.*

45. Ibid: p. 145.

46. Ibid: p. 147.

47. James Lovelock, *The Ages of Gaia: A Biography of Our Living Earth* (New York: Norton, 1988), pp. 45-61.

48. Lovelock, *Ages of Gaia,* p. 206.

49. Evelyn Fox Keller, *A Feeling for the Organism: The Life and Work of Barbara McLintock* (San Francisco: W. H. Freeman, 1983), p. 199.

50. Keller, *A Feeling for the Organism,* p. 200.

51. Charles Birch, "The Postmodern Challenge to Biology," in David Ray Griffin, ed., *The Reenchantment of Science: Postmodern Perspectives* (Albany: State University of New York Press, 1988), pp. 69–78. *Postmodern* used in this sense has no nihilistic or relativist connotations.

52. Ibid., p. 71.

53. Ibid., p. 75.

54. Jane Goodall, *The Chimpanzees of Gombe: Patterns of Behavior* (Cambridge, Mass.: Harvard University Press, 1986); Donald R. Griffin, *Animal Thinking* (Cambridge, Mass.: Harvard University Press, 1984).

55. David Abram, "The Perceptual Implications of Gaia," *The Ecologist* 15 (1985): 96.

56. Ibid., p. 88.

57. Ibid.

58. Lovelock, *Gaia,* pp. 129–31.

59. V. I. Vernadsky, "The Biosphere and the Noosphere," *American Scientist* 33 (1945): 1–12.

60. Commoner, *Closing Circle.*

61. Bernard C. Patten and Eugene P. Odum, "The Cybernetic Nature of Ecosystems," *American Naturalist* 118 (1981): 886–95.

62. Edward Goldsmith and Nicholas Hildyard, *The Social and Environmental Effects of Large Dams* (Camelford: Wadebridge Ecological Centre, 1985).

63. Ian Mitroff and L. Vaughan Blankenship, "On the Methodology of the Holistic Experiment: An Approach to the Conceptualization of Large-Scale Social Experiments," *Technological Forecasting and Social Change* 4 (1973): 339–53.

64. Habermas, *Theory of Communicative Action.*

65. Ibid., pp. 68–69.

66. See Alford, *Science and the Revenge of Nature,* p. 126.

67. An extension of Kohlberg along these lines is suggested by Brock B. Bernstein, "Ecology and Economics: Complex Systems in Changing Environments," *Annual Review of Ecology and Systematics* 12 (1981): 327.

Part II

Environmental Ethics,
Postmodern Politics,
and the Other

6

Radical Environmentalism and the Political Roots of Postmodernism: Differences That Make a Difference

Robert Frodeman

I. Introduction

The 1980s saw a shift in the political landscape, as environmental issues, once dismissed as a fringe movement of tree huggers, became the concern of millions of Americans. At the same time, there was a change within the environmental movement itself. There was a growing sense of crisis, a feeling that our ecological problems could not be resolved in a piecemeal fashion, and that ecological claims could no longer be viewed as simply another interest group clamoring for a share of the political spoils. Radical environmental groups such as Earth First! and Greenpeace rejected the incrementalist approach to environmental reform advocated by such organizations as Sierra Club. Making claims in the name of the truly *common good* (understood now to include nonhuman nature as well as humans), radical environmentalists felt that ecological needs should hold a special status in public debate.[1]

Radical environmentalists have articulated a set of intuitions sharply at odds with those that have guided our culture since the Enlightenment. At times they have shown a willingness to use tactics contrary to consensus politics (such as ecotage, the sabotaging of industrial equipment used to destroy nature) in order to press their claims. Their perspective is fundamentally at odds with the quantitative, analytical, and reductively economic rationality characteristic of modern culture—an outlook apparently acceptable to reform environmentalists. In contrast, radical environmentalists posit the fundamental relatedness and equality of all beings, and envision a naturalized self sharply opposed to classic liberalism's tradition of the autonomous and isolated individual for whom nature is mere material or property.

In its attempt to provide a philosophical elaboration of its position, radical environmentalism (also called ecosophy and deep ecology[2]) has at times emphasized its indebtedness to non-Western traditions of thought such as Daoism, Buddhism, and Native American cosmologies.[3] At other points, it has turned to Western sources in search of a minority tradition that gives hints of an ecological outlook. Thinkers as diverse as the pre-Socratics, Plato, Spinoza, the German idealists, Whitehead, and Heidegger have been interpreted as proto-environmentalists. In this paper, I focus upon a third candidate, seized upon by some in the environmental movement, the widespread (if diffuse) movement on the contemporary scene known as postmodernism.

Because *postmodernism,* like *radical environmentalism,* is a term with varying connotations, one must be wary of referring to postmodernism as if the term designates a unified program. In fact, postmodernism is a movement that celebrates its own schizophrenia, embracing pastiche and spontaneity and renouncing self-classification. Nonetheless, it is possible to identify a central set of terms common to most varieties of postmodernism.

Postmodernist thought shares radical environmentalism's sense of the oppressive and truncated nature of modern rationality, but it carries the critique of modernism much further by uncovering and attacking the hidden premises of modernism: particularly the belief in the metaphysics of presence (by which is meant the assumption of the absolute clarity of the self to itself) and the Cartesian focus upon the individual as the source of meaning. In addition, postmodernism rejects modernism's belief in quantification as the defining character of the real, as well as its acceptance of oppositional and exclusionary hierarchies (e.g., male/female, mind/body, fact/value), in which the first in each pair is utterly separate from and privileged over the second. Such values have too often been used to legitimate the rule of a given group or class, while excluding those who do not fulfill the requirements for membership in the dominant group. Radical environmentalism's interest in undermining the nature/culture distinction, in which culture is seen as opposite to and excluding nature, as well as its desire to overturn the privileged role given to the human species, meshes well with this perspective.

Similarly, radical environmentalists and postmodernists both see a connection between the domination of others and the domination of nature.[4] Postmodernism's anti-authoritarianism, which stresses the legitimacy and equality of all people regardless of class, race, gender, and sexual or religious orientation, seems to find its echo in radical environmentalism's emphasis upon ecocentric equality, according to which all life (meant in a very broad sense that embraces the entire Earth) is thought of as being in principle equal.

Postmodernism and radical environmentalism have thus seemed in the eyes of some as natural complements to one another. Postmodernism deepens radical environmentalism's criticism of the modernist project, especially in its focus upon the limits of quantitative rationality, as well as its criticism of hierarchical relations. For its part, radical environmentalism more fully and consistently carries out the egalitarian goals of postmodernism by its insistence upon ecocentric equality. The two perspectives appear to be destined for a long and fruitful relationship.

Nevertheless, I have concerns about the long-term prospects of this alliance. In this paper, I examine one of the crucial points at which radical environmentalism and postmodernism intersect: the emphasis upon equality, the respect for difference, and the avoidance of any type of dominating or subordinating relationship. This issue reveals an incoherence within most postmodernist thought, born of the unwillingness or incapacity to distinguish between claims true from an ontological or epistemological perspective and those appropriate to the exigencies of political life. The failure to distinguish which differences make a difference not only vitiates postmodernist thought, but also runs up against some of the fundamental assumptions of radical environmentalism.

II. Epistemology and Community

In "Nature and the Theorizing of Difference," Jim Cheney examines radical environmentalism, and particularly deep ecology, from the perspective of postmodernist and feminist thought. While in basic sympathy with radical environmentalism, Cheney is critical of deep ecology's "broader metaphysical framework" when it entails the overcoming of otherness.[5] He begins by reviewing feminist claims on the importance of respecting difference (that is, the awareness of the legitimacy of alternative perspectives and life styles). He then applies these claims to the recent ecological debate in order to show that deep ecology presupposes and is possessed by the authoritarian attitudes it explicitly tries to challenge. It is, thus, in need of the cleansing discipline of a postmodernist (particularly, ecofeminist) perspective.

Cheney cites Marilyn Frye to define the "theorizing of difference" as that type of non-totalizing or anti-totalitarian discourse that deep ecology has only partially achieved. This discourse denies the claim that all knowers are essentially alike, and hence are able to resolve differences by appeal to objective standards of reason. Specifically, Frye and Cheney reject the view that the "Non-congruence of observers' observations either is merely apparent or is due to observers' mistakes or errors which are themselves ultimately explainable, ultimately congruent with the rest of the world-picture."[6] Rather, different opinions on matters of substance are based on the different perspectives of each correspondent. Each person's history and specific place in the world (in terms of wealth, race, gender, and religious or sexual orientation) constitutes what counts as a proper question or answer to a given problem.

These various positions are essentially incommensurable, Cheney argues, and any attempt to find a privileged standpoint for fairly adjudicating between them is hopeless.

Cheney also rejects the claim that "if we were all similarly positioned we would all arrive at the same views." "The thought that all who are positioned alike will have the same knowledge or set of beliefs is either tautological and useless or questionable as to its truth."[7] Although he describes this objection as "non-postmodernist," Cheney's position is consistent with the postmodernist criticisms of modernism's prescriptive and univocal use of the concept of rationality, as well as the postmodern claim that language is so deeply implicated in our understanding of the world that "there is nothing outside the text," no object, transcendental or empirical, outside of language to provide solid ground and referent for language.[8] Different vocabularies define differing conceptual schemes, and there is no conceptual scheme outside the play of language. As a result, the thesis of the sameness of all knowers can only be "an ideological tool," "designed to coerce agreement, to socialize people to particular conceptions of rationality."[9] Truth is individualized: there is no longer "the truth," but only a potentially infinite number of truths corresponding to the equally infinite number of different places that people inhabit in the world. Given this truth (though we may wonder about the status of this claim, whether it is only true for Cheney in this historical epoch or somehow exceeds the limitations that apply to all other truths), it becomes clear that any position claiming priority over other positions is engaged in a rhetorical exercise in order to justify and enforce domination.

Frye and Cheney emphasize the need to respect otherness, letting differences exist without any pressure to compromise. Compromise entails repression of legitimate needs and claims; their goal is a society—and by extension, an ecology—in which no one's opinions or actions are repressed. Adopting and adapting an attitude found in Heidegger, each entity is to be given full latitude to develop the way that best expresses its own particular existence. Frye and Cheney thus share the view of the ecofeminist Karen Warren, who defines feminism as "the movement to end all forms of oppression" (in Cheney's own words, "the project of the elimination of all oppression").[10] Political philosophy's rational concern with the question of the proper limits to power is obliterated, as any coercive use of power is held to be illegitimate.

Cheney and Warren do acknowledge that there may be times when coercion or hierarchical thinking are necessary: ". . . for certain purposes such coercion is practical and, sometimes, perhaps, desirable."[11] But note their examples. Cheney's is "the instrumental use of language by a trained community of scientists for the purpose of manipulating physical reality." Similarly, Warren's example of a justifiable instance of hierarchical relations is the case of plant taxonomies.[12] Cheney does grant that "to a certain extent, of course, all cultures seem to function coercively."[13] However, these concessions are not developed, and evidently carry little weight for either thinker. Instead of an analysis of power, distinguishing between justifiable and unjustifiable hierarchies, we have sloganeering: Cheney claims that the "logic of domination" prevalent in our culture betrays a lack of interest in "the Other as Other."[14] There is no discussion of the possibility that the expression of one person's nature within a community could entail the suppression of another, forcing the community to define a hierarchy of values.

Nevertheless, consider for a moment the implications of their concessions. The fact that all cultures function coercively demands explanation, and (if possible) reconciliation with the goal of "respecting difference" and "ending all forms of oppression." Scientists are human, and the work of scientists is not hermetically sealed from the rest of society. Suppression within the scientific community—for example, of new research into avian mating that undercuts claims about the naturalness of monogamy—is suppression of humans per se. Furthermore, their seemingly innocuous examples of coercion and hierarchy (scientific research, plant taxonomies) suggest an indebtedness to the modernist conception of scientific knowledge as non-ideological, separate from power and politics—despite the rejection of this position by much recent philosophy of science, which holds that facts are always impregnated with value judgments.[15]

In fact, the ideal of an utterly noncoercive environment is incoherent, for it is both impossible and undesirable. It is impossible because coercion and hierarchy are a definitive part of life. Biological sustenance requires the incorporation of other bodies, the subordination of one life to another. Every organism plays both the role of predator and prey. Of course, some will argue that incorporation is a mere biological *factum,* unrelated to human or political relations. Nevertheless, it is on this point that radical environmentalism breaks with postmodernism's humanism, which places the human species outside nature's economy and reduces all other life forms to merely instrumental value. Dave Foreman, one of the founders of Earth First!, argues that a grizzly "has a life just as full of meaning and dignity to her as my life is to me," and derides attempts to find criteria demonstrating that one type of life has more value than the other.[16] Likewise, Arne Naess is explicit in insisting that "No single species of living being has more of this particular right to live and unfold than any other species."[17] Deep ecology's principle of ecocentric equality differs from an absolute respect for difference in that the former recognizes subordination and hierarchy as part of all life. Thus, Naess, while adhering to the general principle of biocentric equality, also acknowledges that "any realistic praxis necessitates some killing, exploitation, and suppression."[18] The general goal of equality between humans does not preclude the recognition that in particular circumstances one individual may have to be subordinated to another. Hierarchy and coercion are thus an inescapable part of life politically and personally as well as biologically: "Every morality is, as opposed to *laisser aller,* a bit of tyranny against 'nature' . . . what is essential and inestimable in every morality is that it constitutes a long compulsion."[19]

In *Gay Science,* Nietzsche claims that "Life is itself essentially appropriation, injury, overpowering of what is alien and weaker; suppression, hardness, imposition of one's forms, incorporation and at least, at its mildest, exploitation—but why should one always use those words in which a slanderous intent has been imprinted for ages?"[20] Although one-sided and harshly stated, the point is a useful counterbalance to those who tend to romanticize the web of life. Nietzsche also notes a problem inherent in this position: the slanderous sense of the available terms. The rehabilitation of at least one of these concepts (oppression, repression, domination, subordination, suppression, exploitation, coercion) will form part of the project of distinguishing between legitimate and illegitimate forms of power.

Cheney, Frye, and Warren also ignore the inherently hierarchical and restrictive nature of conceptualization. Strictly speaking, concepts always misrepresent the individual, for the very act of dividing a previously undifferentiated (social or physical) space results in the creation of centers of power that compete for control over particulars.[21] A conceptual account that groups and distinguishes particulars is an abstraction that does violence to those particulars by lumping together individuals that only more or less fit within the category in which they are placed, and by opposing them to other individuals that from another view are the same as they. These writers thus miss one of the central equations of postmodernism: the relation between knowledge and power.

Both Cheney and Warren try to distinguish between oppressive and non-oppressive conceptual frameworks. Cheney thinks that "the danger is that the theory . . . will not serve to *articulate* the new situation, that is, bring it to experiential and moral coherence, but rather will serve as a mechanism of *de facto* repression."[22] Warren identifies three features that characterize oppressive conceptual frameworks: (1) "value-hierarchical thinking," which places higher value on what is up than on what is down; (2) "value dualisms," which are oppositional and exclusionary rather than complementary and inclusionary; and (3) "the logic of domination," a structure of argumentation that leads to the justification of subordination.[23] However, she does not explain how a conceptual framework could function without the characteristics listed under (1) to (3). This silence is understandable, for every conceptual scheme structures and hierarchizes its material, as part of the tension intrinsic to the move from a particular to a general concept encompassing the particular. All conceptualization is value hierarchical, for all thinking presupposes values, and values are intrinsically hierarchical, establishing relations of super- and subordination. Concept formation requires the selection of the salient features of a given situation according to our needs. A given conceptual space can always be divided in a variety of ways; the choice of how to divide that space reflects the interests and values of the parties involved. Moreover, values are intrinsically hierarchical: every affirmation implies a negation; to highlight a given object is to cast the others in shadow. Nevertheless, these authors seem to understand the exercise of power as being somehow avoidable, as if power only proceeds from the top down, rather than being capillary and circulating, operative in all social spaces, the very means for structuring social spaces.[24]

The heart of their difficulties, however, does not lie in the distinction between oppressive and non-oppressive conceptual schemes. Rather, it lies in their failure to distinguish between different contexts. Both Cheney and Warren argue from an epistemological rather than a political or practical point of view—or rather refuse to distinguish between these two contexts. Although in the public realm, we are often able to distinguish between oppressive and non-oppressive schemas, this distinction breaks down when we move to an ontological or epistemological point of view. From an ontological point of view, *every* conceptual scheme is oppressive. The distinction between oppressive and non-oppressive schemes is political rather than epistemological—political in the sense that a community chooses a conceptual scheme that all in all seems fair relative to a given instance.

In the public realm, there is a clear consensus that equal opportunity in education and hiring is fair, that racist or sexist hiring practices are unacceptable. However, consensus wavers when we consider affirmative action. To tell historically oppressed minorities that they will now be given equal opportunity "if they make the grade" ignores the historical and embedded nature of their situation. At the same time, preferential hiring of women or minorities is unfair to the white male, who, *ex hypothesi,* did not contribute or participate in their oppression. In such cases, epistemological purity is impossible: both choices involve a degree of oppression. We simply choose the alternative that seems fairest, admitting that this choice (indeed, any choice) will place restrictions upon a given group.

Cheney, Frye, and Warren highlight a tendency prevalent within postmodernism: the unwillingness or inability to distinguish between contexts. This failure—to identify which differences make a difference—is not accidental, for it reflects (as Arendt argues) a breakdown of community and the divorce of private and public realms in contemporary society.[25] Postmodernism reflects, more than contributes to, this situation, in which the *res publica* has been reduced to the ersatz community created by advertising, opinion polls, television, and the mass media, which then confronts an essentially passive and passified individual. If the relation between the individual and modern society has become unbridgeable, it is understandable that postmodernism espouses positions in which its metaphysical insight is matched by a blindness to the political consequences.[26]

Thus, for all its acuity, postmodernism's critique of the history of metaphysics is in danger of missing the point. Although it is true that the belief in the sameness of all knowers cannot withstand the deconstructive analysis of postmodernism, we should view this belief, not as a metaphysical or epistemological first principle, but rather as a practical and political assumption necessitated by the requirements of living together as a community. It is these requirements, rather than the need for metaphysical certitude, that necessitate the search for foundations. The existence of community requires a ground or foundation of conversation and action, a set of principles that serve as a basis for compromise, and an impersonal standard that offers a fair basis for discipline or coercion. Wisdom lies in knowing the point at which relative distinctions become essential ones.

III. Ecology and Political Theory

Ironically, postmoderism's tendency to fail to distinguish between political and metaphysical contexts reflects its unconscious allegiance to modernist assumptions. Its often single-minded insistence on respecting difference—single-minded because it refuses to articulate a defensible sense of power and hierarchy—presupposes the modernist viewpoint that it claims to have transcended. Modernism is a political as well as a metaphysical and epistemological program. Postmodernism criticizes the epistemological basis of modernism while assuming the individualistic outlook that was the political correlate of modernist metaphysics. It is the ecological consequences of this political allegiance to Cartesian subjectivity that places postmodernism at odds with radical environmentalism.

John Locke drew out the social and political consequences of modernist physics and metaphysics. Following Descartes, he divides the cosmos into material and mental substances, concluding that the entire physical world—the Earth, plants and animals, and even our own bodies—consists of extended matter ruled by mechanical causation. Separate from this physical realm are mental substances possessing free will, entities that are self-subsistent and independent. How the two substances relate—how free will enters into the world of physical causation—is left a mystery.

Locke's political theory flows from his understanding of mental substance. His theory is based upon two premises: the natural rights of the individual and the contractual relation between the individual and government. Far from being, as Aristotle thought, a political animal, Locke presents humans as naturally independent of social relations. For Locke, each of us is born into perfect freedom. Because there is no shared space or natural relation between mental substances, all relations that do exist are conventional. In his state of nature, all men are "in a state of perfect freedom, to order their actions and dispose of their possessions, as they see fit . . . without asking leave . . . of any other men."[27] They remain in this state "till by their own consents they make themselves members of some politick society."[28] Crucially, the individual's ownership extends to one's labor power. Although the world has been given to all in common, private property results from mixing our labor with common things of the Earth. In this way, private property becomes a natural right.

Locke believed that men are quite able to satisfy their basic needs in the state of nature. It is only the precariousness of their hold upon their property, the likelihood of others dispossessing them of it—rather than any need for community—that causes them to enter into civil society. The Lockean state is thus based upon, and gains whatever sanctions it possesses from, individuals who have consented to give up some of their personal freedom in exchange for better security for their personal property. In Locke's words: "The great and chief end, therefore, of men uniting into commonwealths, and putting themselves under government, is the preservation of their property."[29]

It is clear today that the foundations of Locke's political theory—individualism and private property—presuppose very specific ecological conditions. Locke's theory depends upon the existence of a New World with an endless supply of space and resources ripe for colonization and plunder.[30] In making this assumption, Locke was a creature of his time, living in the midst of the unprecedented "boom" period begun with Columbus' discovery. Nature seemed infinite, both in terms of space and resources. It was inconceivable that the vast tracts of land in the Americas and elsewhere could be exhausted. Even a century later, in 1804, at the time of the Louisiana Purchase, Thomas Jefferson thought it would take 200 years just to settle the new land.

Today the inviolability of individual rights and private property has been undermined by population growth and advances in technology. The distinction between common and private property becomes problematic once the private acts of an individual or group of individuals, coupled with technology, are able to affect entire regions of the planet. The chemical company stores toxic materials on its own property that end up in the community water table. The burning of high-sulphur coal in Ohio creates acid rain that sterilizes lakes in Ontario. The cutting of forests in Amazonia raises global temperatures, melting ice caps and flooding coastal areas around the world. Situations such as these, common today and destined to become more so, undermine Lockean notions of private property and individualist-based theories of government. In *On Liberty,* Mill argues that individuals should be able to do as they please as long as their actions do not directly harm others. However, the distinction between direct and indirect harm, like Locke's theory, presupposes abundance and wide-open spaces, and becomes meaningless once population and technology redefine our relation to others and the world. The question is whether individualism can have the same meaning, or should remain an ideal, in a world with over 5 billion human beings.

For Aristotle, two constraints define the realm of politics. First, issues that can't be answered with certainty, but must be decided if people are to live together, are political issues. Second, politics is the space in which talk is necessary in order to persuade people to work for the common good. For Aristotle, it is self-evident that a community must share a common sense of good. It is a mistake to assume that consensus was somhow easier to achieve in Aristotle's time: ostracism was a severe, but effective means of eliminating representatives of competing and irreconcilable conceptions of the good.

With the discovery of the New World, the second of Aristotle's constraints was lifted: it became possible to go elsewhere if one's ideas of the good differed from others. This possibility of escape made it possible for the question of the good to be privatized within the community, thus making possible the political theory of John Locke. Today, however, these conditions no longer prevail. Because there are no more elsewheres—all the spaces are filled; all countries are settled—the question of the common good is reasserting itself with renewed force.

IV. Ecology and the Postmodernist Community

The importance of the category of ecology decisively separates political theorizing relevant for our time from that of Locke's. Before us lies a task comparable to that faced by the framers of the American Constitution: just as they created the political grammar of modernism, our task is the creation of a political framework expressing a new understanding of community appropriate to an age of ecological limit and technological prowess. While the contours of this future are unclear, it seems certain that the category of ecology will be fundamental. Our sense of community must widen to include the natural world.

But by what means are we to build this new sense of community? Postmodernism seems to be of little help, since its often uncritical embrace of the politics of difference assumes the continued existence of the ecological conditions of the seventeenth century. Radical environmentalism rejects postmodernism's individualist and subjectivist bias as it reveals itself in this ecologically (and politically) untenable apotheosis of difference. Too often, postmodernists still live in that America of the imagination in which compromise isn't necessary—believing that one can always move to the frontier. To the contrary, an uncompromising defense of difference can only lead to a situation akin to the Protestant proliferation of sects: the formation of communities of one.

It would be incorrect to say, however, that radical environmentalism and postmodernism are implacably hostile to one another or that postmodernism offers no resources for the creation of a new type of community. As noted earlier, radical environmentalism is "postmodern" in its opposition to the modernist understanding of nature as matter in motion, utterly separate from humans and merely of instrumental value. The two movements are, at their best, complementary. In fact, radical environmentalism could be viewed as the first fully "postmodern" Weltanschauung, thoroughly surpassing the modernist paradigm of the last three centuries. The goal of radical environmentalism—which can be described as the creation of an "ecological contract," the articulation of a post-Lockean conception of good—can be seen as the fulfillment of postmodernism.[31]

No critique is complete until it offers at least a sketch of what should replace the status quo. It is at this point that postmodernism too often has failed. Postmodernists have seldom offered a program for bettering society. The insistence upon respect for difference embodies only the negative goal of *freedom from* coercion. The refusal to define a goal or program has been a point of honor for postmodernists, who hold that challenges to the system are quickly incorporated into the status quo, thereby strengthening it. In contrast, although still in its infancy as a social movement, radical environmentalism is working to develop a conception of community in keeping with our new ecological awareness.

Some deep ecologists have focused upon a reinterpretation of the self as a basis of a new sense of community.[32] Rejecting the simplistic dichotomy of the individual versus the community, these thinkers challenge modernism's "Robinson Crusoe" sense of self in favor of a more expansive and encompassing type of identification. If the choice must be put in terms of the individual or the community, most radical environmentalists will favor the community or the ecosystem. In the words of one of the founders of Earth First!, "We're concerned about people, but it's Earth first."[33] However, this choice still assumes the Cartesian myth of the self known in inwardness, radically separate from both other humans and the natural world. Deep ecology offers an alternative myth: the idea of a more diffuse and protean sense of self. Rather than the narrow identification with our own ego or body, deep ecologists suggest that we can come to identify with all of nature.

For Naess, our ability to identify with others is based upon our recognition of a common spirit or telos in all life, our realization that all life shares a basic conatus or urge to persevere in its processes.[34] Each organism, unless it is hindered in some way, eventually achieves its full realization. Naess emphasizes that this process of self-realization has reached a new stage in humans, in that we are able consciously to appreciate that other beings share with us the desire for self-realization—and that this recognition entails the responsibility on our part to care for other living beings as we do for ourselves. It is through this process of self-realization, based on identification, that we begin to widen our sense of identification from self, family and friends, and community and nation to include the natural world surrounding us.

It is possible to interpret such a process of identification as the absorption of the natural world by humanity. Cheney criticizes this approach for its hegemonic impulses, arguing that the desire to identify with the world by expanding our sense of self is an engagement in "the containment of the Other, of difference, rather than genuine *recognition,* acknowledgement, and embracing of the Other."[35] What Cheney misses is that the expansion of self means the "othering" of self as well. It is unlikely that the self can remain unaffected by its identification with otherness; rather, when we look at the natural world and see self, the natural world invades us at the same time, as we come to experience the animal, vegetable, and mineral parts of ourselves. In the *Chuang Tze,* Tzu Li's response to the death of Tzu Lai is: "Great is the working of the Creator! Where is he going to lead you? Will he turn you into a rat's liver? An insect's arm?"[36] We are a combination of willow branches and igneous intrusions, reptiles and antelopes. Salt water runs in our veins. We are in symbiotic relation to the oxygen-producing plants of the world. Recognizing this continuity between ourselves and the natural world strengthens the bonds between the two, and allows us to transcend the question of the value of nature: as Naess has noted, "Care flows naturally if the 'self' is widened and deepened so that protection of free Nature is felt and conceived as protection of ourselves."[37] Emphasizing our commonality and continuity with the natural world, rather than the differences, allows us to reinterpret our sense of self-interest in terms of others, our community, and the natural world.

Notes

Frodeman teaches in the Department of Philosophy, Fort Lewis College, Durango, Colorado. Frodeman's interests include history of philosophy and continental philosophy. He thanks Jim Cheney for his helpful criticism of an earlier version of this paper.

First published in *Environmental Ethics* 14, no. 4. Permission to reprint courtesy of *Environmental Ethics* and the author.

1. Although some, it should be noted, have gone further, defending nonhuman nature exclusively. In this view, humanity, or at least industrial civilization, is the problem: humans, in the words of Dave Foreman, are a cancer within the natural world.

2. Even though there is considerable debate about the proper use of the term *deep ecology* (see Warwick Fox, *Toward a Transpersonal Ecology* [Boston: Shambhala, 1990], for a thorough discussion of this issue), the differences between ecosophy, deep ecology, and radical environmentalism are not germane to the argument of this essay. All share a commitment to ecocentrism and the view that nature is of more than simply instrumental value. My focus is on the delimitation of the general parameters of a possible rapprochement between radical environmentalism and postmodernism. Similarly, I am cognizant of the often sharp debate over the meaning of the term *postmodern*. See Jean-Francois Lyotard, *The Post-Modern Condition* (Minneapolis: University of Minnesota Press, 1984) and Arthur Kroker and David Cook, *The Post-Modern Scene* (New York: St. Martin's Press, 1986). Despite these difficulties, I believe that it is possible and useful to identify certain broad features common to most versions of postmodernist thought.

3. See Bill Devall and George Sessions, *Deep Ecology: Living as If Nature Mattered* (Salt Lake: Peregrine Smith, 1985).

4. See Carolyn Merchant, *The Death of Nature: Women, Ecology, and the Scientific Revolution* (New York: Harper and Row, 1980).

5. Jim Cheney, "Nature and the Theorizing of Difference," *Contemporary Philosophy* 13, no. 1 (1990): 3.

6. Ibid., p. 6. The quote is from Marilyn Frye, "The Possibility of Feminist Theory," in Deborah L. Rhode, ed., *Theoretical Perspectives on Sexual Differences* (New Haven, Conn.: Yale University Press, 1990).

7. Ibid.

8. Ibid. The quote is from Jacques Derrida, *Of Grammatology*, trans. Gayatri Chakravorty Spivak (Baltimore: Johns Hopkins University Press, 1976), p. 158.

9. Ibid.

10. Karen J. Warren, "The Power and the Promise of Ecological Feminism," *Environmental Ethics* 12 (1990): 132 (emphasis added); Cheney, "Nature and the Theorizing of Difference," p. 4.

11. Cheney, "Nature and the Theorizing of Difference," p. 6.

12. Ibid.; Warren, "The Power and the Promise," p. 128.

13. Cheney, "Nature and the Theorizing of Difference," p. 6

14. Ibid.

15. See Joseph Rouse, *Knowledge and Power: Toward a Political Philosophy of Science* (Ithaca, N.Y.: Cornell University Press, 1987) and Paul Feyerabend, *Against Method* (London: New Left Books, 1975).

16. Speech by Dave Foreman, Sante Fe, New Mexico, 25 June 1989. Quoted in Christopher Manes, *Green Rage* (New York: Little, Brown and Co., 1990), p. 72.

17. Arne Naess, *Ecology, Community and Lifestyle,* trans. and ed. David Rothenberg (New York: Cambridge University Press, 1989), p. 166.

18. Arne Naess, "The Shallow and the Deep, Long-Range Ecology Movement: A Summary," *Inquiry* 16 (1973): 95. Cited in Warwick Fox, "The Deep Ecology-Ecofeminism Debate and Its Parallels," *Environmental Ethics* 11 (1989): 7. See also Naess' *Ecology, Community and Lifestyle,* pp. 168, 174.

19. Friedrich Nietzsche, *Beyond Good and Evil,* trans. Walter Kaufman (New York: Vintage Books, 1966), p. 100.

20. Ibid., p. 203.

21. Cf. Michael Foucault, *The History of Sexuality,* vol. 1, trans. Robert Hurley (New York: Vintage Books, 1980).

22. Jim Cheney, "Postmodern Environmental Ethics: Ethics as Bioregional Narrative," *Environmental Ethics* 11 (1989): 120.

23. Warren, "The Power and the Promise," p. 128.

24. See Michael Foucault, "Two Lectures," in *Power/Knowledge: Selected Interviews and Other Writings, 1972–1977* (New York: Pantheon Books, 1980).

25. On the breakdown of the relation between the public and the private realms, see Hannah Arendt, *The Human Condition* (Chicago: University of Chicago Press, 1958).

26. Cheney has elsewhere written in a manner much closer to the position defended in this paper ("Postmodern Environmental Ethics" and personal correspondence). However, in the article considered here, one finds ample evidence substantiating my reading. Cheney calls for an environmental version of the politics of difference, but neglects to define the source of one's identity that makes the delineation of difference possible. If we try to tease this distinction out of Cheney's paper, we find the assumption that one is condemned to one's race and gender. Cheney capitalizes the phrase "Women of Color" as if it identifies a clear division of humanity. Similarly, he speaks of white feminists and white-male intellectuals as if they are essential categories of being. He does not mention that one could simply be speaking as a human on a given issue or that "cross-identification" is possible. He does not even discuss what stops the fragmentation of difference. For example, should the politics of difference recognize categories such as "lower middle class," "Italian-American," or "thirty-year-old woman"?

27. John Locke, *Two Treatises of Government* (New York: New American Library, 1963), p. 309.

28. Ibid., p. 318.

29. Ibid., p. 373.

30. Eugene C. Hargrove, *Foundations of Environmental Ethics* (Englewood Cliffs, N.J.: Prentice-Hall, 1989), makes a similar point. See pages 64–73, esp., p. 68.

31. See William Ophuls, *Ecology and the Politics of Scarcity* (San Francisco: W. H. Freeman, 1977), on the need for an "ecological contract."

32. Cf. Naess, *Ecology, Community and Lifestyle,* and Fox, *Toward a Transpersonal Ecology.*

33. Quoted in Manes, *Green Rage,* p. 73.

34. Naess, *Ecology, Community and Lifestyle,* p. 166.

35. Cheney, "Nature and the Theorizing of Difference," p. 3 (italics in the original).

36. Chuang Tzu, *Chuang Tzu: Basic Writings,* trans. Burton Watson (New York: Columbia University Press, 1964), chap. 6.

37. Arne Naess, "Self-Realisation: An Ecological Approach to Being in the World," Fourth Keith Roby Memorial Lecture in Community Science, Murdoch University, Western Australia, 12 March 1986. Cited in Fox, *Toward a Transpersonal Ecology,* p. 217.

7

The Incarceration of Wildness:
Wilderness Areas as Prisons

Thomas H. Birch

I. Bad Faith in Wilderness Preservation?

American preservationists cherish the belief that, as Roderick Nash has stated it,

> Wilderness allocation and management is truly a cultural contribution of the United States to the world. Although other nations have established programs to preserve and protect tracts of land, it is only in the United States that a program of broad scope has been implemented, largely because of the fortuitous combination of physical availability, environmental diversity, and cultural receptivity. Despite the continuing ambivalence of American society towards wilderness, the reserves should be regarded as one of the Nation's most significant contributions.[1]

While wilderness preservation is truly a significant contribution to world civilization, the question whether this contribution, as it is usually understood, is entirely positive ethically is more problematic. As wilderness preservation is generally understood and practiced by mainstream American tradition, and as it often appears to others, particularly those Third and Fourth World peoples who actually live on the most intimate terms with wild nature, it may well be just another stanza in the same old imperialist song of Western civilization.[2]

Nash himself seems close to noticing this problem when he says that "Civilization created wilderness," and when he points out that "Appreciation of wilderness began in the cities."[3] The urban centers of Western civilization are the centers of imperial power and global domination and oppression. Whatever comes from them, including classic liberalism, is therefore likely to be tainted by the values, ideology, and practices of imperialism, as the mainstream white man (and his emulators) seeks to discharge (impose) his "white man's burden," the burden of his "enlightenment," on all the others, of all sorts, on this planet.

In his most recent book, *The Rights of Nature,* Nash suggests that

> . . . liberty is the single most potent concept in the history of America. The product of both Europe's democratic revolutions and, following Frederick Jackson Turner's hypothesis, the North American frontier, liberalism explains our national origins, delineates our ongoing mission, and anchors our ethics. Natural rights is a cultural given in America, essentially beyond debate as an idea. The liberal's characteristic belief in the goodness and intrinsic value of the individual leads to an endorsement of freedom, political equality, toleration, and self-determination.[4]

This is an accurate statement of what mainstream Western man has taken to be his beneficent burden, as he has sought to bring civilization and liberty (as he conceives it) first to the peoples and the land of North America and then to the entire planet.

Having established the liberal tradition as his starting point, Nash proceeds to subsume or appropriate (reduce) radical or "new" environmentalism into this story: "Much of the new environmentalists' criticism of American tradition is warranted, but in adopting a subversive counter-cultural stance, they overlooked one important intellectual foundation for protecting nature that is quintessentially American: natural-rights philosophy, the old American ideal of liberty that they themselves were applying to nature."[5] Here Nash seems to be suggesting that the American ideals of liberty and natural rights have been overlooked in the new environmentalists' rhetoric but not in their action. Accordingly, Nash presents such diverse thinkers as Paul Shepard, Murray Bookchin, and the deep ecologists as best understood, not as subversive radicals who demand revolutionary changes in our environmental ethics and in our social structures, but as closet champions of the mainstream liberal tradition of natural rights, who would "extend" the benefits and protections of civilization to nature. Just as the once radical appearing abolitionist movement was an extension of our ethics to liberate blacks from exploitation by granting them rights, so the preservation of wilderness is essentially only a next step in the evolution of our liberal tradition, which now would allow even the freedom of self-determination for wild nature.

I suggest that belief in this liberal-tradition story involves self-deception—that it is a cloaking story to cover and legitimate conquest and oppression that needs substantial correction if we are to understand wilderness and the ethics of our relationship with it. Still, if this liberal-tradition story were truly put into practice, if nature were allowed self-determination, then it would be transformed into a radically different story for us to inhabit. That is, this old story does contain some germs for its own transcendence. As things stand, however, self-determination is not permitted for nature, even in legally established wilderness reserves, in spite of much rhetoric to the contrary. Instead, wild nature is *confined* to official wilderness reserves. Why? Probably, I argue, because it would be self-contradictory for imperial power to allow genuine self-determination for the others it would dominate, since doing so would be an abrogation of its power.

John Rodman has exposed the dangers and limitations of our liberal tradition with regard to the animal liberation movement.[6] I am concerned here to do much the same thing with wilderness preservation and the liberation of nature movement. The nub of the problem with granting or extending rights to others, a problem which becomes pronounced when nature is the intended beneficiary, is that it presupposes the existence and the maintenance of a position of power from which to do the granting. Granting rights to nature requires bringing nature into our human system of legal and moral rights, and this is still a (homocentric) system of hierarchy and domination. The liberal mission is to open participation in the system to more and more others of more and more sorts. They are to be enabled and permitted to join the ranks and enjoy the benefits of power; they are to be absorbed. But obviously a system of domination cannot grant full equality to *all* the dominated without self-destructing. To believe that we can grant genuine self-determination to nature, and let its wildness be wild, without dis-inhabiting our story of power and domination, even in its most generous liberal form, is bad faith.

Bad faith is compounded if we believe that the Turner hypothesis, as cited by Nash, can be invoked to support the story of our culture's mission to bring freedom to the wilds of America. The explanatory power of Turner's frontier hypothesis, which proposes that the frontier produced "a culture of individualism, self-reliance, and diffused power—the culture of American democracy," has now been discredited as far as the history of American culture is concerned. Donald Worster writes that it is "a theory that has no water, no aridity, no technical dominance in it."[7] Patricia Liberick holds that it is "ethnocentric and nationalistic" and that "the history of the West is a study of a place undergoing conquest and never fully escaping its consequences."[8] Once we have demythologized American history, we see that Turner's frontier hypothesis is only an instance of a central myth of Western culture, the story that civilization brings light and order to the wild darkness of savagery—the legitimizing story that cloaks conquest, colonization, and domination. We deceive ourselves if we think that wilderness preservation can be adequately understood in terms of this suspect mythology. To overcome this self-deception we must attend to the less savory side of our tradition, to imperialism and domination (the subtext of the liberal story as usually told).

It is therefore incumbent upon wilderness preservationists, especially those who are privileged to live in the centers of imperial power, to examine their position critically. Even though the establishment of wilderness reservations may well be the best gesture of respect toward nature that Western culture can offer at its present stage of ethical development, unless we Westerners see and acknowledge the shortcomings of this gesture we will languish in self-congratulatory bad faith. My aim here is to expose the bad faith that taints our mainstream justifications for wilderness preservation and to sting us out of it toward a more ethical relationship with wild nature, with wildness itself, and thereby with one another.

II. Bringing the Law to the Land

At the center of Western culture's bad faith in wilderness preservation are faulty presuppositions about otherness, about others of all sorts, both human and nonhuman, and consequently about the "practical necessities" of our relationship with others. In speaking of "practical necessities" I am raising questions about how others *must* be related to in the deepest sense of *must.*[9]

Problems arise when the other is understood in the usual Western, and imperialistic, manner: as the enemy. In this sense, mainstream Western culture views the oppositional opportunities that otherness affords as adversarial. It presupposes that opposition is fundamentally conflictive, rather than complementary, or communal, or Taoist, or ecosystemic. At best, others are to be "tolerated," which is close to pitying them for their unfortunate inferiority. The central presupposition is thus Hobbist: that we exist fundamentally in a state of war with any and all others. This is perhaps the most central tenet of our guiding mythology, or legitimizing story, about the necessary manner of relationship with others. Thus, in practice, others are to be suppressed or, when need be, eradicated. This mythology is typical of, but not, of course, limited to mainstream Western culture. William Kittredge has given us a powerful summary of Western culture's leading story: "It is important to realize that the primary mythology of the American West is also the primary mythology of our nation and part of a much older world mythology, that of law-bringing. Which means it is a mythology of conquest. . . . Most rudimentarily, our story of law-bringing is a story of takeover and dominance, ruling and controlling, especially by strength."[10] In the case of wildland preservation, bad faith arises when we believe that the simple creation of legal entities such as wilderness areas (a land-use allocation or "disposition" category) can satisfy the practical necessities of relationship with wild land, and with wildness itself. To create legal entities such as wilderness areas is to attempt *to bring the law to wildness,* to bring the law to the essence of otherness, to impose civic law on nature. And this is *all* that it is as long as the customary story is still presupposed, even though it does reform the system of legal institutions. But this is precisely the same sort of reform as the incarceration of Native Americans (paradigm "others") on reservations, even with the putatively well-intended aim of making them over into "productive citizens," in place of the former practice of slaughtering them. Mere reform that is bound by the terms of the prevailing story not only fails to liberate us from the story, but also tends to consolidate its tyranny over us. The reform that appears to be a step in the right ethical direction backfires and turns out to increase the bad faith we have about the ethical quality of what is done. Finding the practical necessities of relationship with nature as other requires breaking the grip of our culture's imperialistic story. It further requires preserving wild land *in order* to help break the grip of this story. It is finally a matter of ethically resolving what Kittredge calls the struggle "to find a new story to inhabit."[11] Then, but only then, can bad faith be left behind.

As things stand for Western culture, committed as it is to the completion of an *imperium* over nature, wilderness reservations are "lockups."[12] The popular terminology of the opponents of wilderness areas about "locking up" wildland is accurate and insightful. The otherness of wildland is objectified into human resource, or value, categories and allocated by law to specific uses (thus bringing law to the land). Of course, as preservationists have often pointed out, allocations of land to specific hard uses such as intensive timber management, strip mining, motorized recreation, etc., are also "lockups," but the attempt to lock out exploiters by locking up wildland turns out, when properly understood, to be just another move in the imperial resource allocation game. This, in fact, is the language of the Wilderness Act of 1964, which states that its purpose is "to *secure* for the American people of present and future generations the *benefits* of an *enduring resource* of wilderness."[13] Wilderness areas in the United States are meant to serve four of the five main multiple uses for public lands: watershed, wildlife, grazing, and recreation. Only timber harvesting is excluded. Mining is often permitted.[14]

But what about the wildness itself? How could wildness be brought under the rule of law? By definition wildness is intractable to definition, is indefinite, and, although it is at the heart of finding utility values in the first place, wildness itself cannot plausibly be assigned any utility value because it spawns much, very much, that is *useless,* and much that is plain disutility. It is for this reason that it is so puzzling, to the point of unintelligibility, to try to construe wildness (or wilderness) as a resource, though we often hear wilderness called a resource. Since wildness is the source of resources, any attempt to construe it as a resource in terms of the rhetoric of resources re-duces it to some set of resources.[15] Wildness itself, to the mind of the law-bringing imperium, is lawless; it is the paradigm of the unintelligible, unre-pentant, incorrigible outlaw. How then is the imperium to deal with it?

All the usual attempts to subdue wildness by destroying its manifesta-tions fail, although wildness may be driven into hiding for awhile, or, more ac-curately, may be lost sight of for awhile. Although the forest and the bison and the Indian may be exterminated, this does not affect wildness itself. In the case of wildness itself, there is nothing there to aim at and shoot. As what we might call the "soul" of otherness, wildness is no usual sort of other. To take the manifestations of wildness for the thing itself is to commit a category mistake. Wildness is still very much there and will not go away. How then is the im-perium to deal with it, given that the usual strategies of conquest cannot work? Wildness cannot be ostracized, or exterminated, or chastened into discipline through punishment, reward, or even behavior modification techniques. Yet according to the dictates of the imperium, which claims total control, wildness must be, or at least must seem to be, brought into the system, brought under the rule of law. While the older ("conservative") factotums of the imperium still pursue the strategy of obliterating wildness by destroying its manifesta-tions, the modern ("liberal") reformist factotums see the futility of the older strategy and therefore follow a more subtle strategy of "cooptation," or appro-priation, through making a place for wildness within the imperial order and putting wildness in this place. The place that is made is the prison, or the asylum. When this place is made and wildness is incarcerated in it, the im-perium is completed. Consider Foucault's observations: "The carceral net-work does not cast the unassimilable into a confused hell; there is no outside. It takes back with one hand what it seems to exclude with the other. It saves everything, including what it punishes. It is unwilling to waste even what it has decided to disqualify."[16] In this way, designated wilderness areas become prisons, in which the imperium incarcerates unassimilable wildness in order to complete itself, to finalize its reign. This is what is meant when it is said that there is no wilderness anymore in the contemporary world, in the technolog-ical imperium. There is, or will be soon, only a network of wilderness reserva-tions in which wildness has been locked up.

To press the use of prison terminology, we may say that just as the "lockup" occurs at the end of the prison day, so wildness is locked up at the twilight time of modernism. To press prison terminology a bit more, we may say also that when wildness as prisoner "misbehaves" (by being its sponta-neous self) the imperium "locks it down." A "lockdown" involves confining prisoners to their cells, revoking privileges, conducting searches, etc., to root out and correct the maleficence.[17]

Wilderness reservations are not intended or tolerated as places where nature is allowed to get out of control, even though a degree of aberrant behavior is permitted, just as a degree of it is permitted within the edifices of the penal system for humans. Wilderness reservations are not meant to be voids in the fabric of domination where "anarchy" is permitted where nature is actually liberated. Not at all. The rule of law is presupposed as supreme. Just as wilderness reservations are created by law, so too can they be abolished by law. The threat of annihilation is always maintained. Just as a certain inmate, say a tree fungus, may be confined to the wilderness reservations by law, so too can it be exterminated by law, even within the reservation. The imperium does not, and cannot, abrogate these "rights," although it has arrogated them in the first place.

III. Otherness as Wildness

At the center of the problem of Western culture's incarceration of wildness is its prevailing (mis)understanding of otherness as adversarial, as recalcitrant toward the law, as therefore irrational, criminal, outlaw, even criminally insane (like the grizzly bear). This understanding of the other is a part and product of Western culture's imperialistic mythology of law bringing. It is the meaning of otherness that the story of the imperium has created. It is an enforced misunderstanding, myth or story. Accordingly, texts such as Joseph Conrad's *Heart of Darkness* and E. M. Forster's *A Passage to India* have been incorporated into our literary canon and are taught in our educational institutions, as part of what is called the process of "the indoctrination of the young" by ruling elites,[18] or as what we may more politely call the inculcation and perpetuation of the mythology of Western culture.

If we are to understand what the creation of legally designated wilderness reservations amounts to ethically, then we must disentangle the threads of Western culture's mythology from the realities of otherness. Let us begin by emphasizing that the essence of otherness is wildness. If any other is to preserve its (his, her) identity as other, as other in relation to another person, society, species, or whatever, then it must at bottom resist accepting any *final* identity altogether. An other cannot *essentially* be what it is objectified, defined, analyzed, legislated, or understood to be if it is to be and remain an other. The maintenance of otherness requires the maintenance of a radical openness, or the maintenance of the sort of unconditioned freedom that permits sheer spontaneity and continuous participation in the emergence of novelty.

The need for others to preserve this sort of freedom is especially pronounced in encounters with imperial power (even in its putatively beneficent liberal form), because imperial power seeks to define and fix identities in order to internalize others into its own system of domination—domination through objectification. But the maintenance of this sort of freedom is also necessary for the dynamics of nonconflictive, complementary relationship with otherness. Unfinalized, contingent, or working identities are, of course, also indispensable, but any *finalization* of identities is an anathema that destroys otherness.

A finalization of the identification of the other is a (self-deceived) absorption or ingestion of the other into the subjectivity of the self, or, on the social level, into the "system." Such an absorption is also a finalization of self or of system definition that takes self or system out of the world into a state of alienation. Self-becoming in and out of dialectical response to others and to other-becoming is then no longer possible. The ultimate end of the imperial project is realized at the point of total finalization. This is why wildness, which contradicts any finalization in identification, is at the heart of otherness, as well, of course, as at the heart of any *living* self or society.

IV. The Voice and Residence of the Imperial Other

Perhaps the most strikingly articulate voice of the other to emerge within Western culture is that of Jean Genet. Although his writings are fairly well known, they are not part of our literary canon. They are far too unsettling, insightful, and impolite. A foundling, an illegitimate child, a bastard (note *why* this is a term of derogation), Genet was illegal and unlawful from before his birth, and he became a thief, a homosexual, a prostitute, a convict, and as an author, a celebrant of criminality and of all that imperial society finds intolerable and disgusting. As a celebrant of the wild underside of Western society, Genet is a devastating critic of the entire system of the imperium. He portrays as most beautiful what imperial culture takes as most ugly and unacceptable. Sartre proposes that Genet's original illegality destined him to become an other to the imperium:

> Genet has neither mother nor heritage—how could he be innocent? By virtue of his mere existence he disturbs the natural order and the social order. . . .
>
> . . . The collectivity doomed him to Evil. They were waiting for him. There was going to be a vacancy: some old convict lay dying on Devil's Island; there has to be new blood among the wicked too. Thus, all the rungs of the ladder which he has to descend have been prepared in advance. Even before he emerged from his mother's womb, they had already reserved beds for him in all the prisons of Europe and places for him in all the shipments of criminals. He had only to go to the trouble of being born; the gentle, inexorable hands of the Law will conduct him from the National Foundling Society to the penal colony.[19]

In strict obedience to its own logic, which will be explored more fully below, the imperium creates a place for its own other, which it must have and therefore must create and maintain.[20] Consider Genet's own reflections about the prison and the palace, the two most illustrative edifices of imperial power:

> They are the two buildings constructed with the most faith, those which give the greatest certainty of being what they are—which are what they are meant to be, and which they remain. The masonry, the materials, the proportions and the architecture are in harmony with a moral unity which makes these dwellings indestructible so long as the social form of which they are the symbol endures. . . . They are also similar in that these two structures are one the root and the other the crest of a living system circulating between these two poles which contain it, compress it and which are sheer force.[21]

In this passage, we find the voice of the other, the other speaking both as an artifact of the imperium, defined and produced by the imperium, and speaking as himself. Note that the imperium does not recognize that the other has anything at all to say, and certainly nothing to say on matters of importance. With regard to wildland the situation is much worse, for such land, because it is mute, cannot speak out like Genet from its category of incarceration and is therefore a perfect candidate for oppression as paradigm other. In other cases, the other is meant to be silent. In Joseph Conrad's *Heart of Darkness,* for example, Africans virtually do not speak at all, Marlow finds the wilderness inarticulate, "dumb," a "thing that couldn't talk and perhaps was deaf as well," and Kurtz turns out to be merely "A voice. He was little more than a voice. And I heard—him—it—this—voice—other voices—all of them were so little more than voices—and the memory of that time itself lingers around me, impalpable, like a dying vibration of one immense jabber, silly, atrocious, sordid, savage, or simply mean, without any kind of sense."[22]
Similarly, consider the "terrifying echo" of the Marabar caves, of E. M. Forster's other, the essential India under the British raj:

> The echo in Marabar cave . . . is entirely devoid of distinction. Whatever is said, the same monotonous noise replies, and quivers up and down the walls until it is absorbed into the roof. "Boum" is the sound as far as the human alphabet can express it, or "bou-oum," or "ou-boum," utterly dull. . . . And if several people talk at once, and overlapping howling noise begins, echoes generate echoes, and the cave is stuffed with a snake composed of small snakes, which writhe independently.[23]

To Forster's kind and liberal Mrs. Moore this echo had "managed to murmur, 'Pathos, piety, courage—they exist, but are identical, and so is filth. Everything exists, nothing has value.'"[24] So goes our culture's story about the wild essence of the other. For the imperium, the other, and wildness, has nothing sensible to say, and is intolerable when it sometimes noisily, sometimes silently is said to say, "Nothing, Nothing!" It is this same "Nothing" that drives Sartre's Antoine Roquentin to nausea (in *Nausea*), and which for the imperium legitimates law bringing as the establishment of "Meaning," by whatever means are necessary, *ergo,* force and violence.

Genet, however, confronts the imperium with an undeniably articulate voice. Now that Third World and minority literature is beginning to achieve some notice and acceptance in the West, Genet is no longer so alone, although none of this literature has been incorporated into the Western canon. Genet's language equals or even surpasses Proust in its elegance. The highest style, often with what the imperium considers the lowest content, stops and exposes the imperial mind square in the tracks of its bad faith. The voice of the other speaks more beautifully of what the imperium despises than the imperium itself can speak of what it prizes. Genet is intentionally the *revolting* other in both senses of the word, both nauseating and rebellious. In response to the imperium Genet is that "corrosive spirit" (his phrase) of denunciation and revolt that comes out of hiding, refuses to go away, and shows the story of our culture as false, and thereby refutes it.

In concluding her convincing account of *Heart of Darkness* and *A Passage to India* as legitimations of imperialist ideology, Mary Layoun writes:

> Nowhere is the value or meaning-making machinery of the Subject/ Colonizer/Text/Ideology brought more into question than when faced with the "reality," or the textual representation of that "reality," of what Jean-Paul Sartre, in a slightly different context, calls "the glance of the Other"—the Other as primeval and savage, as repressed desire, as the unremitting landscape, as the recalcitrant Native, as an incomprehensible language—that not just the "dark continent" or an elusive India are called into question but the white continent and its production of meaning and value in narratives and outside of them.[25]

If an apology for imperialist ideology is to be at all plausible, then the reality of the other must be represented, and the more this is achieved by attempts to legitimize our false story of the need for law bringing, the more transparently false such attempts become. These legitimations therefore tend toward self-refutation, or at least contain the seeds of their own self-destruction. The glance of the other flashes right through the texts.

If the "glance" of the other shines forth from the texts of Conrad and Forster and calls our culture's mythology into question, then Genet's texts are the *glare* of the other, a glare that starkly illuminates our culture's oppressive structures and practices. In response to the oppression of the imperium Genet adamantly refuses reconstruction or assimilation: "If I had to live . . . in your world, which, nevertheless, does welcome me, it would be the death of me."[26] His aspiration is to ostracism, to the "outside," or, more exactly, to the most marginal, peripheral, the nearest to an "outside" that the imperium permits, which it declares to be outside but which is in reality still very much inside the imperium. He aspires to Guiana, the penal colony, in comparison with which the prisons or reformatories constructed within the centers of power are an obliteration of his otherness:

> I aspire to Guiana. No longer to that geographical place now depopulated and emasculated, but to the proximity, the promiscuity, not in space but in consciousness, of the sublime models, of the great archetypes of misfortune. Guiana is kindly. . . . It suggests and imposes the image of a maternal breast, charged, in like manner, with a reassuring power, from which rises a slightly nauseating odor, offering me a shameful peace. I call the Virgin Mother and Guiana the Comforters of the Afflicted.[27]

Genet sees that "The end of the penal colony prevents us from attaining with our living minds the mythical underground regions." The "destruction of the colony corresponds to a kind of punishment of punishment: I am castrated, I am shorn of my infamy."[28] The Network of imperial control is completed, and there is no place left where the other can be itself.

Guiana, like roadless and undisposed wildland, was decommissioned because it gave comfort to the other. It made escape possible. As Foucault has pointed out, now even the "criminality" of the other is utilized. Nothing is wasted, not even waste itself. Accordingly, what was once the wasteland of wilderness, the "outside," is brought inside the imperium as legally designated wilderness reserves, thus making a proper place for wildness in the universal system of universal control.

Genet's intractability to assimilation into this system does not permit the usual sorts of rebellion. He has no concern for justice, or for some better system of laws, or even for "morality." He has no concern for any "liberal" reshuffling of the categories of domination. A successful revolt and revolution that is confined by Western culture's presuppositions about otherness would at best amount to reform, to nothing more than some shift in the arrangements of power, as from conservative to liberal, or capitalist to socialist. Genet's revolt cuts far deeper and demands the recognition and respect and liberation of otherness itself. Because the imperium names the other, the other must find a way to insist on its intrinsic namelessness:

> Erotic play discloses a nameless world which is revealed by the nocturnal language of lovers. Such language is not written down. It is whispered into the ear at night in a hoarse voice. At dawn it is forgotten. Repudiating the virtues of your world, criminals hopelessly agree to organize a forbidden universe. . . . Criminals are remote from you—as in love, they turn away and turn me away from the world and its laws. . . . My adventure, never governed by rebellion or feeling of injustice, will be merely one long mating, burdened and complicated by a heavy, strange, erotic ceremonial (figurative ceremonies leading to jail and anticipating it).[29]

Genet's path becomes the erotic, that essential element of wildness that the imperium finds most problematic. Recall Conrad's "wild and gorgeous apparition of a woman" and the erotic alienation of Forster's Adela. The erotic side of love remains intractable to reconstruction into anything abstractly and putatively agapic that can be, and is, abused to legitimate oppression for the other's "own good," to relieve the white man of his burden. Because the erotic side of love is so troublesome for the imperium, it is quite properly the territory of the other, and is therefore the place in which Genet feels compelled to take up residence. Both the imperium itself and its other agree that the erotic is a place for the other. The erotic has not yet succumbed to domination, in spite of the imperial attempt to "lock it up" into trivialization, perversion, and sterility (or "simulation," as I argue in the next section), to cast it as evil, and even to use it as an instrument of terror. AIDS, for example, becomes a grizzly bear lurking in the wild otherness of the erotic (and do note how extraordinarily erotic we feel the bear to be).

Like Sid Vicious, Genet sees no alternative to being cast and casting himself as evil, thereby allowing the imperium to define him as *its sort* of other. Although his deepest desire is to deconstruct the imperium, Genet is trapped in the terms of the debate with any opposition that the imperium sets and controls. Thus Genet focuses his love on the criminal, with the liberation of the other as his goal, so far as this is at all possible in the face of, and in spite of, the imperium's definition, and in the only terms remaining for the other to claim—a liberation of the other into its own eroticism and into its own beauty: ". . . *there is a close relationship between flowers and convicts. The fragility and delicacy of the former are of the same nature as the brutal insensitivity of the latter. Should I have to portray a convict—or a criminal—I shall so bedeck him with flowers that, as he disappears beneath them, he will himself become a flower, a gigantic new one.*"[30]

Although Genet strives for liberation mainly through a kind of secular beatification *within* the given framework of the law-bringing imperium, his real liberation requires abolishing the imperium. What is required is a different world, a world in which the imperial order and the imperial other no longer exist, a world in which others can be themselves and not products defined by the imperial order, a world in which the wildness of others of all sorts is respected in the only way this can really be done—by not trying to subject their wildness to the totalizing rule of law, for the bringing of law to wildness, or to the wildness of others, is ineluctably imposition and domination by force. What Western culture needs is an entirely different story about wildness and otherness, a story that does not produce the sort of "criminal" otherness that is Genet's only residence and refuge, and that, given the terms of the prevailing story, is the only fit condition for any other, so defined, to occupy and to celebrate.

V. Wilderness Areas as "Simulations" of Wildness, and the Risk of the Real

Jean Baudrillard's brilliant and alarming analysis of modern Western culture starkly illuminates the uses to which imperial culture puts its wild others, both human and nonhuman. Baudrillard's analysis also explains the imperium's need to manufacture and maintain an adversarial sort of other to serve these uses. Briefly, these uses are to provide meaning and legitimation for the institution of imperial power and to enforce its reign with the threat of terror and chaos. For Baudrillard, modern Western culture is headed toward, and to a great extent has already reached, a condition of "hyperreality," and has taken up residence in a world of "simulation," a simulated world of "simulacra," with no remaining contact with reality, including ecological reality. In one of Baudrillard's more noted statements, "The very definition of the real has become: *that of which it is possible to give an equivalent reproduction. . . .* The real is not only what can be reproduced, *but that which is always already reproduced.* The hyperreal . . . which is entirely in simulation."[31]

In order to solidify its reign, to realize its goal of total control, power must create its own world, defined in its own terms, by means of models that are simulations of realities (of all sorts). Total control of such, and only such, simulacra is possible because they are reproducible and therefore fungible. Should any one of them stray from the grip of control, it can be eradicated and replaced with another. Appropriation into this throwaway world involves throwing away the former, and other, reality in favor of a simulation that is illusory: "We live everywhere already in an 'aesthetic' hallucination of reality."[32] Nevertheless, imperial power cannot afford to throw reality away entirely, because it needs some reality or semblance of reality to save its own meaningfulness and legitimacy.

Legally designated wilderness reserves thus become simulacra insofar as it is possible for the imperium to simulate wildness. The pressure on the imperium is to institute simulations of wildness in order to appropriate wildness into the imperium under the rubric of the model. Simulacra are produced according to the dictates of models, and we come to inhabit a modelling of reality that is purported to be all the reality there is. Otherness is incarcerated in simulacra, in models of otherness. But why must the imperium go to the trouble of preserving wild otherness, even if only as simulacra, rather than totally destroying this adversarial opposition and then forgetting about it altogether? Why does the imperium need to create and preserve its Genets and its wilderness preserves? At bottom, it is a matter of the imperium's need to preserve its own meaningfulness, to protect itself from "vanishing into the play of signs":

> Power . . . for some time now produces nothing but signs of its resemblance. And at the same time, another figure of power comes into play: that of a collective demand for *signs* of power—a holy union which forms around the disappearance of power. . . . When it has totally disappeared, logically we will be under the total spell of power—a haunting memory already foreshadowed everywhere, manifesting at one and the same time the compulsion to get rid of it (nobody wants it anymore, everybody unloads it on others) and the apprehensive pining over its loss. . . .[33]

The whole point, purpose, and meaning of imperial power, and its most basic legitimation, is to give humans control over otherness. Once this is totally achieved, or perceived to be achieved, the game is over, and continuing to play it is meaningless. This holds true as much in the case of the manufactured hyperreality, which generates what is really an illusion or "hallucination" of total control, as it does for the real thing (which could be achieved only by some imperial eighteenth-century God the Father). The imperium must therefore attempt to keep its game, itself, alive by preserving its "reality principle," but preferably to the greatest extent possible by simulating this too. Thus, we are given Disneyland and the fantasy fare of television:

> Disneyland is there to conceal the fact that it is the "real" country, all of "real" America, which *is* Disneyland (just as prisons are there to conceal the fact that it is the social in its entirety, in its banal omnipresence, which is carceral). Disneyland is presented as imaginary in order to make us believe that the rest is real, when in fact all of Los Angeles

and the America surrounding it are no longer real, but of the order of the hyperreal and of simulation. It is no longer a question of a false representation of reality (ideology), but of concealing the fact that the real is no longer real, and thus of saving the reality principle.[34]

This Disneyland sort of simulation of fantasy is not, however, by itself, enough to meet the threat to the meaningfulness of power that is constituted by power's own success in simulation, and is not by itself enough to rejuvenate hyperreality or the imperial game. Thus, "When it is threatened today by simulation (the threat of vanishing in the play of signs), *power risks the real, risks crisis, it gambles on remanufacturing artificial, social, economic, political stakes. This is a question of life or death for it. But it is too late."[35] Consequently, we are presented periodically with "scandals" such as Watergate and Irangate, and in the United States with election contests between Democrats and Republicans. According to Baudrillard, Watergate was "a trap set by the system to catch its adversaries—a simulation of scandal to regenerative ends."[36]

Still, even though such scandals are meant to be controlled simulations, there is some risk of generating real challenge or resistance to power. When it comes to the wild others, like Genet and wild land, which must continue to exist or be posited as existing in contrast and opposition to imperial power if power is to save its reality principle, the risk of the real is somewhat amplified. In order to do the job of preserving its reality principle, and in spite of its need to simulate or define the other according to its own models, the imperium must leave at least enough otherness intact to *maintain the glance of the other*. It does not seem possible to simulate this otherness entirely while at the same time also preserving the needed significance of its glance. The other must be able to cast its glance at the imperial enterprise to preserve the meaning of that enterprise, to legitimate its purpose of bringing law and order to wild chaos, and to threaten those who might question its good intentions and overall beneficence. There must remain at least some vestiges of wildness to be kept at bay.

The risk of the real is that in seeing the glance of the other, in reading Genet, in attending to wilderness, one sees, or is likely to see, that the other is more than, other than, independent of, the definitions, models, and simulations that the imperium proposes as exhaustive of it. On reading Genet, one sees that, even though perhaps he cannot quite accept it, because he has acquiesced to the imperium's model of what he is, there is far more to him as a human being than the imperium would have it. One sees his real otherness shining through and overwhelming all the imposed categorizations of him. To scratch the surface, one sees a thoroughly sensitive, loving, ethical human being who is perhaps justified in his forms of resistance to what the imperium has done to him—even though we might hope to find different forms of resistance for ourselves. Likewise, in coming to know wilderness, we see beneath its glance as this has been construed for and purveyed to us. When we see the real otherness that is there beneath the imperium's version of it, beneath all the usual categories of use and value, then we see an otherness that can never be fully described, understood, or appropriated, and the entire edifice of the imperium is called into question to such a degree that it becomes practically necessary to resist and deconstruct it, because it so epitomizes bad faith and delusion.[37]

VI. The Ground of Subversion

When Roderick Nash argues that "Civilization created wilderness," he quotes Luther Standing Bear: "We did not think of the great open plains, the beautiful rolling hills and the winding streams with tangled growth as 'wild.' Only to the white man was nature a 'wilderness' and . . . the land 'infested' with 'wild' animals and 'savage' people. . . . There was no wilderness; since nature was not dangerous but hospitable; not forbidding but friendly."[38] The real point, which is not the point that Nash is trying to make out of what Luther Standing Bear has said, is that the wilderness, and now the wilderness reservations that the white imperium has created in obedience to its traditional story of law bringing, is an adversarial other to be subdued and controlled. In response I would argue that the other does not *have to be* an adversary or a simulation of an adversary. Certainly it is not an adversary for Luther Standing Bear. He sees the land in terms of a different story, a story which holds that the fundamental human relationship with nature, and with wildness itself, is participatory, cooperative, and complementary, rather than conflictive. At times, of course, and also in the terms of the other story, there is conflict, but normally wild nature sustains, sponsors, empowers, and makes human existence possible. Nature is wild, always wild, in the sense that it is not subject to human control. In this sense, humans are participants in a wildness that is far larger and more powerful than they can ever be, and to which human law bringing is so radically inappropriate as to be simply absurd. This is the sort of understanding of wilderness and its relationship with culture that we need to retrieve and reconstruct in postmodern society in response to the imperium's desire for total dominion.

It seems fair to take the RARE II (Roadless Area Review and Evaluation, second try) process in the United States as typical of and precedent setting for Western civilization's approach to wildland. The United States is, at the moment, the most powerful center of the imperium of Western culture, and the example of RARE II will be followed on the global level. Note that RARE II was implemented by the relatively liberal Carter administration and was intended as reform of RARE I, to correct its mistakes. The purpose of the RARE process was to search out and evaluate the utilities of all remaining wildland in the national forests with the goal of determining its allocation or disposition, thereby giving it definition, bringing meaning into its nothingness, so that nothing remains unmanaged waste outside of the imperium. RARE II typifies the final step in the imperium's appropriation of wild nature, its most powerful enemy. The RARE process should be seen as a "search and destroy" mission to discover and appropriate or exterminate the last vestiges of wild land in America, to complete the imperium. The acronym for the key instrument of wilderness evaluation in the field was WARS (Wilderness Attribute Rating System). As in the case of a racist joke, the subtext, or presupposition, of this cynical attempt at humor is near the surface and easily seen.[39]

The RARE II process thus marks the completion of the imperium's imposition of its network of control, bringing all wildland under management for some set of utilities. Whereas in the past there were wildland Guianas, which were ignored and to which wildness and wild nature were either let go or ostracized from civilization, places that were *outside* the system of management, but places where wildness could to some extent flower in its own integrities, with RARE II there are only legally designated wilderness areas or reservations in which wild nature, the ultimate other, has been locked into specific management schemata. Whereas, once upon a time, for example in the time of Homer, Western culture was a cluster of tenuously connected islands surrounded by a sea of wildness, civilization now surrounds (or so goes the deluded story) the last islands of wildness, and puts everything to use, wasting nothing. Even Genet is published—just as one of the recognized reasons for official wilderness is to benefit those "oddballs" who thrive on it, or even to permit the furtherance of their "self-realization." Wilderness and wildness are placed on the supermarket shelf of values along with everything else, and everything is enclosed *inside* the supermarket.

Yet there is a contradiction in the imperium's attempt to appropriate wildness, for, as we have seen above, it is not possible practically for the imperium to silence the subversive voice of the other completely or to stifle its glance. For the imperium, the problem with appropriating wildness by incarcerating it in the prisons of wilderness reservations is that the wildness is still there, and it is still wild, and it does "speak" to us. Genet writes, and he insists on his integrity, no matter that it is tainted by the categories that the imperium has inflicted on it. The prisons and asylums are still rich with other minds. When wildness speaks, it always says more than what the imperium would train it to say or train us to hear because wildness stays adamant in its own integrity, as other in its own unconditioned freedom. Thus, managing wildness is contradictory, even though managing official wilderness areas and prisons is not. There is an insurmountable tension in the notion of managing wildness, and of managing land *for* wildness. How much wildfire, how much insect evolution, for example, is to be permitted? We *cannot* know. Wildness is logically intractable to systemization. There can be no natural laws of wildness.

What follows is that making a place for wildness within the system of the imperium creates, institutionalizes, and even legalizes, a basis, literally a ground, for the subversion of the imperial system just as prisons and reformatories succeed mainly in generating better "criminals." If it does nothing more than open a path for our gaze to fasten with the stars, with the wildness of the universe in which we inhabit our mote of dust, a wilderness reservation can still give the lie to the imperial story of Western civilization. No matter how the imperium deals with wild nature, whether by extermination or incarceration and the logically impossible fiction of total management, wild otherness will continue to show up the belief in our culture's most formative myth of law bringing for the bad faith it is.

Yet, even so, the establishment of wilderness reserves is not enough to counter the imperium's assault on wildness. First, the battle to save wildland through legal preservation, like scandals or simulated scandals, can be a trap that only serves to further power. In the terms of the struggle as set by the imperium, the imperium wins whether a tract of land is classified as legal wilderness or not, because the imperium has been allowed to get away with setting the terms of the debate. The energies of the champions of wildness are appropriated and exhausted by the legal battles for preservation. If an area of wildland is classified as official wilderness, the imperium wins the other it needs; if it is not preserved, the imperium wins something else it needs. The real issue, the preservation of wildness and of knowing human participation in wildness, is very easily lost in the fogs of legal-political controversy, at least in the forms that imperial society permits. But, secondly, we should never forget that the imperium has the power to manage, invade, declassify, abolish, desanctify the legal wildland entities it has created, and the creation of such entities on its terms does little to diminish this power. Because it probably tends to strengthen this power, it is imperative to dig out and clarify what is basically at stake and what underlies the task of preserving wilderness in order to see how such efforts should contribute to the fundamental task of saving wildness and resisting the imperium.

VII. Toward Residence in Sacred Space

Thinking of legally designated wilderness reserves as "sacred spaces" is not by itself enough to rescue official wilderness spaces from the totalizing grip of imperial power. Although there has always been a place for the sacred in the imperial order, in Western culture secular power has long ago triumphed over the church. As far as the imperium is concerned, the sacred, the mystical, and so forth are just the other side of the coin of criminal wild otherness.[40] Wilderness, like religion and morality, is fine for weekends and holidays, but during the working week it may in no way inform business as usual. Thus, the imperium incarcerates its sacred other in churches, convents, and ministries, but if its functionaries (like the Berrigans) take their sacred obligations out of the assigned area and, say, into the streets, they are imprisoned, or otherwise neutralized. It is perfectly fine with the imperium if, on weekends and holidays, some of its citizens wish to follow John Muir to the temples of the wilderness areas, rather than the usual churches—and this will probably hold for American Indian religions as well.[41] By making room for sacred space, the imperium confirms its tolerance, generosity, its rectitude, its beneficence, and it does so without having to abrogate *its* other (thus maintaining its bad faith). However, actually to inhabit, to live in, sacred space is an anathema, absolutely incompatible with the imperium: "The idea that holiness inheres in the place where one lives is alien to the European tradition, for in that tradition sacred space is sundered, set aside, a place one goes only to worship. But to live in sacred space is the most forceful affirmation of the sacredness of the whole earth."[42] For the imperium, only that which is other can be sacred, because all of the usual world, the mundane and the not-so-mundane, is taken to be profane, secular, objective. The imperium is committed to cordoning off sacred space, to separating it as other, effectively keeping it out of the center of our practical lives, and keeping us out of it and thus safe from its subversive effect. Wildness as wilderness land is incarcerated as sacred space. This is perhaps one of the main uses to which the imperial order puts wilderness. It consigns sacred space to the museum of holy relics, as one of the prime manifestations of the wildness it is compelled to incarcerate in order to demonstrate its total triumph.

The point, then, is that even the preservation of wilderness as sacred space must be conceived and practiced as part of a larger strategy that aims to make all land into, or back into, sacred space, and thereby to move humanity into a conscious reinhabitation of wildness. As Gary Snyder has pointed out: "Inspiration, exaltation, insight do not end . . . when one steps outside the doors of the church. The wilderness as a temple is only a beginning. That is: one should not . . . leave the political world behind to be in a state of heightened insight . . . [but] be able to come back into the present world to see all the land about us, agricultural, suburban, urban, as part of the same giant realm of processes and beings—never totally ruined, never completely unnatural."[43]

Wilderness reserves should be understood as simply the largest and most pure entities in a continuum of sacred space that should also include, for example, wilderness restoration areas of all sizes, mini-wildernesses, pocket-wildernesses in every schoolyard, old roadbeds, wild plots in suburban yards, flower boxes in urban windows, cracks in the pavement, field, farm, home, and workplace, all the ubiquitous "margins." As Wendell Berry puts it: ". . . lanes, streamsides, wooded fence rows . . . freeholds of wildness . . . enact, within the bounds of human domesticity itself, a human courtesy toward the wild that is one of the best safeguards of designated tracts of true wilderness. This is the landscape of harmony . . . democratic and free."[44]

Wilderness reserves make an indispensable contribution to establishing and inhabiting Berry's "landscape of harmony" writ large, which is how we should write it, a landscape that is thoroughly predicated upon and infused with wildness. The larger wilderness reserves, where the essence of otherness as wildness is most powerfully evident, continuously freshen, enliven, and empower this infusion of wildness, on the analogy of water from mountain watershed sources. The ideal goal, however, is a landscape that is self-sustaining and everywhere self-sufficient in wildness. Enough margins in some locales (perhaps including some Third World locales) could bring this about, or serve as the starting point toward reaching the goal of a larger harmony.

Because the landscape of harmony is an inhabited harmony with otherness and with others, respected in their own integrities, and thus a landscape, a "land" in Leopold's sense, and a form of human life that cooperates with others as complementary to us, it constitutes hope for an implacable counter-force to the momentum of totalizing imperial power. Furthermore, to a great extent, the margins still exist, although we seldom notice them and neglect them. To achieve Berry's landscape of harmony we must, as it were, demarginalize the margins, including the legal wilderness reserves, and come to see and practice their continuing and sustaining primacy to all that we humans can value and construct. Then we can take up residence in wildness, where Luther Standing Bear lived, reinhabiting it now, of course, with different appropriate technologies and social forms. Then we can recover our endangered knowledge of reality and disempower the bad faith that the imperium puts upon us.

VIII. The Justification of Legal Wildland Entities

Wilderness reservations are best viewed as holes and cracks, as "free spaces" or "liberated zones," in the fabric of domination and self-deception that fuels and shapes our mainstream contemporary culture. Working to preserve wild nature, in wilderness reservations, or anywhere, is primarily, at this historical moment, an essential holding action, to stop the complete triumph of the bad faith of our culture, especially in regard to ecological reality, and to save us from ineluctably destructive self-deception. Although the culture may deceive itself and believe that wilderness reservations are successful appropriations of the wild and/or sacred and ethical opposition, in fact, their existence, properly understood, helps preserve and foster the possibility of liberation from our imperialist tradition. This subversive potential is what justifies their establishment.

From the ethical standpoint, the purpose and the only justification of laws is to help us fulfill our obligations, or to meet the practical necessities that are incumbent upon us. If legally created wilderness areas do, or can be made to serve the subversive role I have pointed out, then the laws that create them are thereby ethically justified. Then wilderness reservations serve as a crucial counterfriction to the machine of total domination, slowing it down and creating a window through which a postmodern landscape of harmony may be found. But insofar as wilderness reservations, as they are so often (mis)understood, only serve the completion of the imperium, they are not justifiable. Wilderness must be preserved for the right reasons—to help save the possibility and foster the practice of conscious, active, continuing human participation in wildness, as well as to preserve others for their own sakes. The institution of legally designated wilderness reserves does make an essential contribution toward meeting this larger necessity. However, it is crucial to remember that, important as they are, legal wildland entities are not always and everywhere either the ethically sound or most effective means for meeting this larger necessity, especially if they are imperialistically understood and exported and colonially imposed, either domestically or internationally. I have suggested above what some of the other means may be. But on this question there is very much culturally and economically imaginative and sensitive work waiting to be done.

Of course, all of this looks to the possibility of a more ideal time, to a vision toward which we can struggle, when our practice of respect for nature has become so refined that preservationist laws would no longer be needed, a time when we have moved out of the imperium and taken up residence in wildness. The realization of this vision would mean recovering the sort of relation between humans and others, including human others, that Luther Standing Bear, for instance, sees as basic. It would mean realizing in contemporary practice what Leslie Marmon Silko has called "the requisite balance between human and *other*."[45] Others would then be seen and lived with as complementary to us, as we all live together in the wild and continuous composition of the world.

Notes

Birch teaches in the Department of Philosophy, University of Montana, Missoula. Birch's professional concerns include ethics, environmental ethics, and the philosophy of ecology. As an environmental activist, he has served as a member-at-large on the Sierra Club's National Wilderness Committee and participated in many local groups and controversies. For their encouragement and for their many helpful comments and suggestions, all of which have been taken seriously, and many of which have been taken, he wishes to thank Fred McGlynn, Jim Aton, Jim Cheney, Donald Worster (at his 1988 NEH Summer Seminar on "The American West: Environment and History"), Richard A. Watson, and Holmes Rolston, III.

First published in *Environmental Ethics* 12, no. 1. Permission to reprint courtesy of *Environmental Ethics* and the author.

1. Roderick Nash, "International Concepts of Wilderness Preservation," in Hendee, Stankey, and Lucas, *Wilderness Management,* Miscellaneous Publication no. 1365 (Washington, D.C.: U.S. Forest Service, 1977), p. 58.

2. For a forceful account of how First World wilderness preservation can appear to Third World peoples see Ramachandra Guha, "Radical American Environmentalism and Wilderness Preservation: A Third World Critique," *Environmental Ethics* 2 (1989): 71–83. There are obvious analogies (which cannot be pressed too far) between Third World countries and western American states, like Idaho and Montana, that are rich in wildland areas subject to "lockup" into the wilderness preservation system by colonial and neocolonial powers. Of course, these areas are also subject to lockup into other uses.

3. Roderick Nash, *Wilderness and the American Mind,* 3d ed. (New Haven, Conn.: Yale University Press, 1982), pp. xiii, 44.

4. Roderick Nash, *The Rights of Nature* (Madison: University of Wisconsin Press, 1989), p. 10.

5. Ibid., p. 11.

6. See John Rodman, "The Liberation of Nature?" *Inquiry* 20 (1977): 83–145; and "Four Forms of Ecological Consciousness Reconsidered," in Donald Scherer and Tom Attig, eds., *Ethics and the Environment* (Englewood Cliffs, N.J.: Prentice-Hall, 1983), pp. 89–92.

7. Donald Worster, *Rivers of Empire* (New York: Pantheon Books, 1985), p. 11.

8. Patricia Nelson Liberick, *The Legacy of Conquest* (New York: W. W. Norton and Company, 1987), pp. 21, 26.

9. I am using the expression "practical necessities" in the sense offered by Bernard Williams: "When a deliberative conclusion embodies a consideration that has the highest deliberative priority and is also of the greatest importance (at least to the agent), it may take a special form and become a conclusion not merely that one should do a certain thing, but that one *must,* and that one cannot do anything else. We may call this a conclusion of practical necessity. . . . a 'must' that is unconditional and *goes all the way down.*" Bernard Williams, *Ethics and the Limits of Philosophy* (Cambridge, Mass.: Harvard University Press, 1985), pp. 197–98.

10. William Kittredge, *Owning It All* (Saint Paul, Minn.: Graywolf Press, 1987), pp. 156–57.

11. Ibid., p. 64.

12. I am using the term *imperium* in the sense given by the *Oxford English Dictionary:* "command; absolute power; supreme or imperial power: Empire."

13. Section 2(a) of the Wilderness Act of 1964; emphasis added.

14. See Section 4(a)1 of the Wilderness Act of 1964, where consistency with the Multiple-Use Sustained-Yield Act is stipulated. The Wilderness Act permits the mining of claims established until 1984 for lands covered by the act. Roughly speaking, the legality of mining for other designated wilderness land has been decided on a case by case basis. For an excellent account of wilderness values, see Holmes Rolston, III, *Philosophy Gone Wild* (Buffalo: Prometheus Books, 1986), pp. 180–205. Note further that the Wilderness Act, at Section 4(d)f, explicitly reserves the right to further resource uses within designated wilderness areas: ". . . prospecting for water resources, water-conservation works, power projects, transmission lines, and other facilities needed in the public interest, including road construction and maintenance. . . ."

15. For a sound discussion of wilderness as the source of resources, and not a resource itself, see Holmes Rolston III, "Values Gone Wild," in *Philosophy Gone Wild,* pp. 118–42.

16. Michel Foucault, *Discipline and Punish* (New York: Vintage Books, 1979), p. 301. Also see Foucault's *Madness and Civilization* (New York: Vintage Books, 1973).

17. See the Wilderness Act at Section 4(d)1: ". . . such measures may be taken as may be necessary in the control of fire, insects and diseases, subject to such conditions as the Secretary deems desirable." For an interpretation of the Wilderness Act, see Hendee et al., *Wilderness Management,* p. 82. Note the current halt and reconsideration of the let-burn policy for wilderness fire management, as the result of the huge Yellowstone and Canyon Creek (Scapegoat Wilderness Area) fires in the summer of 1988.

18. See Noam Chomsky, *The Culture of Terrorism* (Boston: South End Press, 1988), p. 32. Chomsky quotes the first major publication of the Trilateral Commission as saying that our educational institutions are responsible for "the indoctrination of the young."

19. Jean-Paul Sartre, *Saint Genet: Actor and Martyr* (New York: Pantheon Books, 1963), pp. 7, 31.

20. Although there is probably some real criminality in all human cultures, in the sense of the monstrous, or criminal insanity, a huge amount of what imperial society sees as criminal is created by its own laws and social structures. Thus in the U.S. (where the per capita prison population approaches that of South Africa, the world's

highest) most incarcerated "criminals" are there for economic crimes, for example, stealing tires. Very few are monsters. The strategy of an oppressive culture is to enlarge the category of the really criminal, the monstrous, to include the "criminality" it has fabricated.

21. Jean Genet, *The Thief's Journal* (New York: Bantam Books, 1965), pp. 76–77. The prison to which Genet alludes, Fontevrault, was once in fact a palace.

22. Joseph Conrad, *Heart of Darkness,* ed. Robert Kimbrough (New York: W. W. Norton, 1988), pp. 29, 48–49.

23. E. M. Forster, *A Passage to India* (New York: Harcourt, Brace, 1924), pp. 147–48.

24. Ibid., p. 149.

25. Mary Layoun, "Production of Narrative Value: The Colonial Paradigm," *North Dakota Quarterly* 55 (1987): 202–03. I have replaced "represented" in Layoun's published text with "repressed" from her original manuscript.

26. Genet, *Thief's Journal,* p. 232.

27. Ibid., p. 230.

28. Ibid., p. 5.

29. Ibid., p. 4.

30. Ibid., p. 3.

31. Jean Baudrillard, *Simulations* (New York: Semiotext[e], 1983), pp. 146 and 147.

32. Ibid., pp. 147–48.

33. Ibid., pp. 44–45.

34. Ibid., p. 25.

35. Ibid., p. 44; emphasis added.

36. Ibid., p. 30. Also see Chomsky, *The Culture of Terrorism,* chap. 4, "The Limits of Scandal." Chomsky argues convincingly that, in the course of treating scandals, the power structure is always careful to avoid asking the real questions, such as, "What moral right do we have to create and finance a proxy army to terrorize Nicaragua?"

37. This is an opportune point to notice just how natural, appropriate, and even plausible it is for Roderick Nash, in his chapter on "The International Perspective" in *Wilderness and the American Mind,* to subsume wild nature and wilderness reservations into the rhetoric of international export-import commercialism. In this vein, he suggests that "national parks and wilderness systems might be thought of as institu-

tional 'containers' that developed nations send to underdeveloped ones for the purpose of 'packaging' a fragile resource" (p. 344). Such a packaging in containers, defined by *its* model of the wild other, and the experience of it (the "wilderness experience"), *is* precisely what the imperium tries to achieve.

38. Ibid., p. xiii.

39. In the same vein, the acronym for the latest wilderness management practices is LAC (Limits of Acceptable Change).

40. See Guha, "Radical American Environmentalism and Wilderness Preservation," for development of this point. The imperium is thoroughly "Orientalist," in Edward Said's sense. See his *Orientalism* (New York: Pantheon Books, 1978). Its other is thus either criminal and diabolical or mystically enlightened, like the noble savage or the guru of the East, but irrational and benighted in either case.

41. Eventually either the recent negative Supreme Court decision on Indian religious rights to preserve sacred lands (*Lyng* v. *Northwest Indian Cemetery Protective Association*) will be somehow softened by the courts or Congress will (slightly) strengthen the American Indian Religious Freedom Act. The logic of imperial power requires this sort of liberality. Of course, the imperium could never afford the liberality of classifying all land as sacred in any meaningful sense. But some designated and narrowly defined sacred areas will be allowed, or, to use the language of rights, "granted."

42. J. Donald Hughes and Jim Swan, "How Much of the Earth Is Sacred Space?" *Environmental Review* 10 (1986): 256.

43. Gary Snyder, "Good, Wild, Sacred," in Wes Jackson et al., eds., *Meeting the Expectations of the Land* (San Francisco: North Point Press, 1984), p. 205.

44. Wendell Berry, "Preserving Wildness," in *Home Economics* (San Francisco: North Point Press, 1987), p. 151. The antithesis of the "landscape of harmony" is that of industrial monoculture—the landscape of the imperium.

45. Leslie Marmon Silko, "Landscape History, and the Pueblo Imagination," *Antaeus* 57 (1986): 92. The "balance" we need to find is that which Silko says the Pueblo people had to find, and did, in order to become a culture. It is not the balance of cost-benefit analysis, but that of the dance, which requires loving, graceful integration of self and society within the wild whole of an otherness we revere.

8

The Call of the Wild:
The Struggle Against Domination and the Technological Fix of Nature

Eric Katz

I

During the summer I live with my family on Fire Island, a barrier beach off the coast of Long Island. Most mornings, if I wake up early, I can look out my window and watch white-tailed deer munching their breakfast of flowers and leaves from the trees surrounding my house. The deer are rather tame; they have become accustomed to the transient human population that invades the island each summer. A few years ago, if they had heard me walking onto the deck, they would have jumped and run off into the thicker underbrush. Now, if they hear me, they might look up to see if I have a carrot; more likely still, they will simply ignore me and continue foraging. My experiences with these deer are the closest encounters I have with what I like to call the "wild."

Using the adjective *wild* to describe these deer is obviously a distortion of terminology. These are animals that live in and around a fairly dense human community; they consume, much to the dismay of many residents, the cultivated gardens of flowers and vegetables; they seek handouts from passing humans—my daughters often feed them breadsticks and pretzels. Yet, seeing them is different than my experience with any other animal, surely different than seeing white-tailed deer in the zoo, on a petting farm, or in a nature documentary film on television. The mornings when I find them in my yard are something special. If I walk close to one, unaware, at night, my heart beats faster. These animals are my connection to "wild nature." Despite their acceptance of the human presence, they embody something untouched and beyond humanity. They are a deep and forceful *symbol* of the wild "other." The world—my world—would be a poorer place if they were not there.

In this essay, I explore this "call of the wild"—our *attraction to value* that exists in a natural world outside of human control. To understand this value, we must understand the relationship between technology and the natural world, the ways in which humanity attempts to "fix" and mold nature to suit human purposes. Thomas Birch has described this project as the "control of otherness,"[1] a form of domination that includes the control of nature and all such outsiders of human society. Here I bring together several ideas about the philosophy of technology and the nature of artifacts, and combine them with themes raised by Birch. I argue that value exists in nature to the extent it avoids the domination of human technological practice. Technology can satisfy human wants by creating the artifactual products we desire, but it cannot supply, replace, or restore the "wild."

II

One promise of the technological enterprise is the creation of "new worlds." This optimistic view of the ability of technology to improve the human condition is based on the belief that humanity has the power to alter the physical structure of the world. Consider the words of Emmanuel Mesthene: "We . . . have enough . . . power actually at hand to create new possibilities almost at will. By massive physical changes deliberately induced, we can literally pry new alternatives out of nature. The ancient tyranny of matter has been broken, and we know it. . . . We can change it and shape it to suit our purposes."[2] No longer limited by the physical necessities of the "given" natural world, our technological power enables us to create a new world of our dreams and desires. Nature can be controlled; its limitations overcome; humanity can achieve its highest potential. For Mesthene, "our technical prowess literally bursts with the promise of new freedom, enhanced human dignity, and unfettered aspiration."[3]

I admit to being mesmerized by the resonances of meaning in the concept of the "new world." The technological promise of a new dignity and freedom, a limitless opportunity, an unchained power, sounds suspiciously like the promise envisioned in the new political and social conditions of the New World of the European discovery, our homeland, the Americas. But the "new world" of the European discovery was not, in fact, a *new* world; indeed, it was a very *old* world, the world of a wild untamed nature, with a minimal human presence that was itself quite old. The freedom, dignity, and benefits of the new human population were achieved, to some degree, at the expense of the older natural world. For the new world to be useful to humanity, it had to be developed and cultivated.[4] The New World had to cease being wild.[5]

The comparison between the taming of the American wilderness and the technological control of brute physical matter is disturbing. I do not believe that the technological control of nature is a desirable end of human activity. The control of nature is a dream, an illusion, a hallucination. It involves the replacement of the wild natural environment with a human artifactual environment. It creates a fundamental change in the value of the world. This change in value, in turn, forces a reexamination of the ethical relationship between humanity and the natural environment.

III

It is a commonplace to refer to the improvements of technology as a "technological fix." It is supposed that the advanced technology of the contemporary world can "fix" nature. The term *fix* is used here in two complementary ways: it implies either that something is broken or that it can be improved. Thus, the technological fix of nature means that natural processes can be "improved" to maximize human satisfaction and good; alternatively, damage to the environment can be repaired by the technological reconstruction of degraded ecological systems. Humans use nature to create benefits for humanity, and we can restore natural environments after they have been damaged by use. The only new aspect of this technological activity is its increased scope and power. The practical control of natural processes has increased to such an extent that we no longer acknowledge the impossibility of doing anything; nature can be improved and restored to any extent that we wish.

Both processes—the improvement-use and the restoration of nature—lead to serious questions about value and moral obligation. The idea that nature ought to be used (and improved, if necessary) for human benefit is the fundamental assumption of "resource environmentalism"—arguably the mainstream of the American conservation movement. Under this doctrine, environmental policies are designed to maximize human satisfactions or minimize human harms. The pollution of the atmosphere is a problem because of the health hazards to human beings. The extinction of a species is a problem because the extinct species may be useful to humans, or the resulting instability in the ecosystem may be harmful. The greenhouse effect is a problem because the changes in climate may have dramatic impacts on agriculture and coastal geography. With all environmental problems, the effects on humanity are the primary concern.[6]

These "human interest" resource arguments for environmental protection have been criticized by thinkers in several disciplines concerned with environmental philosophy and environmental ethics. A full inventory of the arguments against so-called "anthropocentric" environmental ethics is clearly beyond the scope of this discussion.[7] Here I focus on one particular implication of the anthropocentric resource view, i.e., the creation of an artificial world that more adequately meets the demands of human welfare. As Martin Krieger has written: "Artificial prairies and wildernesses have been created, and there is no reason to believe that these artificial environments need be unsatisfactory for those who experience them. . . . What's wrong with plastic trees? My guess is that there is very little wrong with them. Much more can be done with plastic trees and the like to give most people the feeling that they are experiencing nature."[8] Krieger thus argues for "responsible interventions" to manage, manipulate, and control natural environments for the promotion of human good. "A summmum bonum of preserving trees has no place in an ethic of social justice."[9] Because human social justice, the production and distribution of human goods, is the primary policy goal, the manipulation of natural processes and the creation of artificial environments is an acceptable (and probably required) human activity.

Krieger's vision of a "user-friendly" plasticized human environment is chilling; it is not a world view that has many advocates. Nevertheless, the point of his argument is that a primary concern for the human uses of the natural environment leads inevitably to a policy of human intervention and manipulation in nature, and the subsequent creation of artificial environments. If humanity is planning to "fix" the natural environment, to use it and improve it to meet human needs, wants, and interests, the conclusion of the process is a technologically created "new" world of our own design. "Wild" nature will no longer exist, merely the controlled nature that offers pleasant experiences.

The restoration of nature, the policy of repairing damaged ecosystems and habitats, leads to similar results. The central issue is the *value* of the restored environments. If a restored environment is an adequate replacement for the previously existing natural environment, then humans can use, degrade, destroy, and replace natural entities and habitats with no moral consequences whatsoever. The value in the original natural entity does not require preservation.

The value of the restored environment, however, is questionable. Robert Elliot has argued that even a technologically perfect reproduction of a natural area is not equivalent to the original.[10] Elliot uses the analogy of an art forgery, in which even a perfect copy loses the value of the original artwork. What is missing in the forgery is the causal history of the original, the fact that a particular human artist created a specific work in a specific historical period. Although the copy may be as superficially pleasing as the original, the knowledge that it is not the work created by the artist distorts and disvalues our experience. Similarly, we value a natural area because of its "special kind of continuity with the past." This history, Eugene Hargrove argues, provides the authenticity of nature. He writes: "Nature is not simply a collection of natural objects; it is a process that progressively transforms those objects. . . . When we admire nature, we also admire that history."[11] Thus, a restored nature is a fake nature; it is an artificial human creation, not the product of a historical natural process.

The technological "fix" of repairing a damaged and degraded nature is an illusion and a falsehood; elsewhere, I have called it "the big lie."[12] As with all technology, the product of nature restoration is a human artifact, not the end result of a historically based natural process. Artifacts, of course, can have positive or negative value. However, what makes the value in the artifactually restored natural environment questionable is its ostensible claim to be the original.

Both forms of technological intervention in the natural world thus lead to the same result: the establishment of an artifactual world rather than a natural one. When our policy is to use nature to our best advantage, we end up with a series of so-called "responsible interventions" that manipulate natural processes to create the most pleasant human experiences possible. When our policy is to restore and repair a degraded natural environment, we end up with an unauthentic copy of the original. The technological "fix" of nature merely produces artifacts for the satisfaction of human interests.

IV

The issue of *value* now has a sharper focus. We can ask, "What is the value of artifacts and what are the moral obligations that derive from that value?" More precisely, "How is the value of the artifacts, and the derivative moral obligations, different from the value and moral obligations concerning 'wild' nature?" Framed in this manner, the answer to the problem is clear: artifacts differ from natural entities in their anthropocentric and instrumental origins. Artifacts are products of the larger human project of the domination of the natural world.

The concepts of function and purpose are central to an understanding of artifacts.[13] Artifacts, unlike natural objects, are created for a specific purpose. They are essentially anthropocentric instruments, tools or objects, that serve a function in human life. The existence of artifacts is centered on human life. It is impossible to imagine an artifact that is not designed to meet a human purpose, for without a foreseen use the object would not have been created.

The anthropocentric instrumentality of artifacts is completely different from the essential characteristics of natural entities, species, and ecosystems. Living natural entities and systems of entities evolve to fill ecological niches in the biosphere; they are not designed to meet human needs or interests. Andrew Brennan thus argues that natural entities have no "intrinsic functions": they are not created for a particular purpose; they have no set manner of use. We may speak as if natural individuals (e.g., predators) have roles to play in ecosystemic well-being (the maintenance of optimum population levels), but this talk is either metaphorical or fallacious. No one created or designed the mountain lion as a regulator of the deer population.[14]

From a moral point of view, the difference between purposely designed artifacts and evolving natural entities is not generally problematic. The anthropocentric instrumentality of artifacts is not a serious moral concern, for most artifacts are designed for use in human social and cultural contexts. Nevertheless, the human intervention into "wild" nature is a different process entirely. Hargrove notes how human intervention alters the aesthetic evaluation of nature: "To attempt to manipulate nature, even for aesthetic reasons, alters nature adversely from an aesthetic standpoint. Historically, manipulation of nature, even to improve it, has been considered subjugation or domination."[15] This domination resulting from human intervention can be generalized beyond aesthetic valuations; it leads to more than just a loss of beauty. The management of nature results in the imposition of our anthropocentric purposes on areas that exist outside human society. We intervene in nature to create so-called natural objects and environments based on models of human desires, interests, and satisfactions. In doing so, we engage in the project of the human domination of nature: the reconstruction of the natural world in our own image, to suit our purposes.

Need we ask why domination is a moral issue? In the context of human social and political thought, domination is the evil that restricts, denies, or distorts individual (and social) freedom and autonomy. In the context of environmental philosophy, domination is the anthropocentric alteration of natural processes. The entities and systems that comprise nature are not permitted to be free, to pursue their own independent and unplanned course of development. Even Hargrove, who emphasizes the aesthetic value of nature, judges this loss of freedom the crucial evil of domination: it "reduces [nature's] ability to be creative."[16] Wherever it exists, in nature or in human culture, the process of domination attacks the preeminent value of self-realization.

Is the analysis of domination appropriate here? Does it make sense to say that we can deny the autonomy, the self-realization, of natural nonhuman entities? The central assumption of this analysis is that natural entities and systems have a value in their own right, a value that transcends the instrumentality of human concerns, projects, and interests. Nature is not merely the physical matter that is the *object* of technological practice and alteration; it is also a *subject,* with its own process and history of development independent of human intervention and activity. Nature thus has a value that can be subverted and destroyed by the process of human domination. In this way, human domination, alteration, and management are issues of moral concern.

V

But does the "wild" have a moral claim on humanity? The answer to this question determines the moral status of the human domination of nature. Does the wilderness, the world of nature untouched by the technological alteration of humanity, possess a moral value worth preserving? Is the creation of a technological "new world" morally harmful? Does it destroy the value of the original New World of the European discovery of America, the untamed and "wild" wilderness? How do we discern a method for answering these questions?

It is at this point that my thoughts return to my encounters with the white-tailed deer on Fire Island. They are not truly wild, for they are no longer afraid of the human presence on the island. They seem to realize that the summer residents are not hunters. These humans come with pretzels, not rifles. Nevertheless, there are some human residents who are deeply disturbed by the existence of the deer. The deer carry ticks that are part of the life cycle of Lyme disease. They eat the flowers and vegetables of well-tended gardens. They are unpredictable, and they can knock a person down. A considerable portion of the human community thus wants the deer hunted and removed from the island.

Just the thought of losing these deer disturbs me—and until recently I did not understand why. In my lucid rational moments, I realize that they are not "wild," that they have prospered on Fire Island due to an unnatural absence of predators; their population could be decreased with no appreciable harm to the herd or the remaining natural ecosystem of the barrier beach. Nevertheless, they are the vestiges of a truly wild natural community; they are reminders that the forces of domination and subjugation do not always succeed.

Birch describes the process of wilderness preservation as "incarceration" by "the technological imperium"—i.e., by the primary social-political force of the contemporary world.[17] The entire process of creating and maintaining wilderness reservations by human law is contradictory, for the wildness is destroyed by the power of the human-technological system: "Wilderness reservations are not meant to be voids in the fabric of domination where anarchy is permitted, where nature is actually liberated. Not at all. The rule of law is presupposed as supreme. Just as wilderness reservations are created by law, so too they can be abolished by law. The threat of annihilation is always maintained."[18] The domination of natural wildness is just one example of the system of power. "The whole point, purpose, and meaning of imperial power, and its most basic legitimation, is to give humans control over otherness."[19]

It is here that Birch sees the contradiction in the imperial technological domination of wild nature. "The wildness is still there, and it is still wild," and it maintains its own integrity.[20] The wildness, the otherness of nature, remains, I suggest, because the forces of the imperial power require its existence. If there is no "other" recognized as the victim of domination, then the power of the imperium is empty. There would be nothing upon which to exercise power. But maintaining the existence of the wild other, even in the diminished capacity of wilderness reservations managed by the government, lays the seeds for the subversion of the imperial domination of technology.

Birch thus recommends that we view wilderness, wherever it can be found, as a "sacred space" acting as "an implacable counterforce to the momentum of totalizing power." Wilderness appears anywhere: "old roadbeds, wild plots in suburban yards, flower boxes in urban windows, cracks in the pavement. . . ."[21] And it appears, in my life, in the presence of the white-tailed deer of Fire Island. My commitment to the preservation of the deer in my community is part of my resistance to the total domination of the technological world.

This resistance is based on yet a deeper moral commitment: the deer themselves are members of my moral and natural community. The deer and I are partners in the continuous struggle for the preservation of autonomy, freedom, and integrity. This shared partnership creates obligations on the part of humanity for the preservation and protection of the natural world. This is the *call of the wild*—the moral claim of the natural world.

We are all impressed by the power and breadth of human technological achievements. Why is it not possible to extend this power further, until we control and dominate the entire natural universe? This insidious dream of domination can only end by respecting freedom and self-determination, wherever it exists, and by recognizing the true extent of the moral community in the natural world.

Notes

Katz teaches at the Center for Technology Studies, in the Science, Technology, and Society Program, New Jersey Institute of Technology. He recently completed his second annotated bibliography of the field of environmental ethics, *Research in Philosophy and Technology* 12 (1992): 287–324. An earlier version of this paper was presented at the Second Interamerican Conference of Philosophy and Technology, University of Puerto Rico, Mayaguez, March 4, 1991.

First published in *Environmental Ethics* 14, no. 3. Permission to reprint courtesy of *Environmental Ethics* and the author.

1. Thomas H. Birch, "The Incarceration of Wildness: Wilderness Areas as Prisons," *Environmental Ethics* 12 (1990): 18 [Chapter 7 in this book].

2. Emmanuel G. Mesthene, "Technology and Wisdom," in *Philosophy and Technology: Readings in the Philosophical Problems of Technology,* ed. Carl Mitcham and Robert Mackey (New York: The Free Press, 1983), p. 110.

3. Ibid., p. 111.

4. One of the best examples of this attitude from a historical source contemporaneous with the period of European expansion is the discussion of property by John Locke, *Second Treatise on Government,* ch. 5, especially, secs. 40–43. Locke specifically mentions the lack of value in American land because of the absence of labor and cultivation.

5. For my purposes, it is irrelevant to raise the question, whether North America ever really was wild. It existed then, and now, as a *symbol* of nature uncontrolled by human civilization. Of course, it may have been altered and modified through fire and hunting by Native American populations. Such practices, however, do not change its *significance* as wild and untamed. First, the control of the natural world by Native Americans was definitely limited compared to the new European attempt of total cultivation. Second, the issue here is *not* the purity of the wild in frontier America, but rather the ethical significance of the Western belief that value only arises in nature with human intervention and modification. To discuss that issue, the New World of the Western discovery is useful, because it was relatively uncontrolled and uncultivated, i.e., wild.

6. There are sound political and motivational reasons for arguments that outline the threat to human interests caused by environmental degradation. These arguments have been the rallying cry of popular conservationists from Rachel Carson, *Silent Spring* (New York: Houghton Mifflin, 1962), to Barry Commoner, *The Closing Circle: Nature, Man, and Technology* (New York: Alfred A. Knopf, 1971), to Bill McKibben, *The End of Nature* (New York: Random House, 1989). My philosophical criticisms of these views do not diminish my respect for the positive social and political changes these works have inspired.

7. A complete listing of the relevant literature is impossible. One of the best early works is David Ehrenfeld, *The Arrogance of Humanism* (New York: Oxford University Press, 1978). Other major representative works of nonanthropocentric strands in environmental ethics are Holmes Rolston, III, *Environmental Ethics: Duties to and Values in the Natural World* (Philadelphia: Temple University Press, 1988), J. Baird Callicott, *In Defense of the Land Ethic* (Albany: SUNY Press, 1989), Paul Taylor, *Respect for Nature: A Theory of Environmental Ethics* (Princeton, N.J.: Princeton University Press, 1986), Arne Naess, *Ecology, Community and Lifestyle,* trans. and ed. David Rothenberg (Cambridge: Cambridge University Press, 1989). For a discussion of enlightened anthropocentric views, see Bryan G. Norton, *Why Preserve Natural Variety?* (Princeton, N.J.: Princeton University Press, 1987), Eugene C. Hargrove, *The Foundations of Environmental Ethics* (Englewood Cliffs, N.J.: Prentice-Hall, 1989), and Mark Sagoff, *The Economy of the Earth: Philosophy, Law, and the Environment* (Cambridge: Cambridge University Press, 1988).

8. Martin H. Krieger, "What's Wrong with Plastic Trees?" *Science* 179 (1973): 453.

9. Ibid.

10. Robert Elliot, "Faking Nature," *Inquiry* 25 (1982): 81–93, specifically, p. 86.

11. Hargrove, *The Foundations of Environmental Ethics*, p. 195.

12. Eric Katz, "The Big Lie: Human Restoration of Nature," *Research in Philosophy and Technology* 12 (1992): 231–41.

13. The argument of this section is based on Katz, "The Big Lie." For a further discussion, see Michael Losonsky, "The Nature of Artifacts," *Philosophy* 65 (1990): 81–88.

14. Andrew Brennan, "The Moral Standing of Natural Objects," *Environmental Ethics* 6 (1984): 41–44.

15. Hargrove, *The Foundations of Environmental Ethics*, p. 195.

16. Ibid.

17. Birch, "The Incarceration of Wildness," p. 10.

18. Ibid.

19. Ibid., p. 18.

20. Ibid., pp. 21–22.

21. Ibid., pp. 24–25.

9

Rethinking Resistance: Environmentalism, Literature, and Poststructural Theory

Peter Quigley

Recent world events have marshalled the growing likelihood of a homogenous global capitalist power structure. Resistance movements, including the ecology movement, find themselves in disarray and in danger of becoming ineffective. In the same way that the "self" has become a problematic base for liberal humanism, so "nature" is in need of critical examination. Therefore, it is important to reconsider the practice of cultural criticism by reexamining the theoretical basis for opposing power. Because traditional and contemporary postures of ecological resistance share too many features with the power structure they wish to oppose, they could benefit from a thorough reconsideration in light of poststructural philosophy, which provides the basis for a sweeping resistance movement. In addition, new ways to evaluate social action and cultural artifacts emerge from such an investigation.

If there is going to be any new form of resistance on the horizon that is capable of challenging the dominance of capitalist hegemony, one that can align a cross section of participants, environmentalism (along with feminism) promises to be at the center of such contestatory activity. Although recent events in the East Bloc have prompted euphoric conservatives to claim that the end of history and resistance are upon us,[1] it seems clear that a battle between capitalist, industrial, and environmental interests will continue. However, if those in environmentalism are going to play a crucial political role, some of them will have to engage the theoretical dimensions of resistance. One can already see some of this activity within journals and books—for example, *Environmental Ethics* and Devall and Sessions's *Deep Ecology*. In addition, such theorists as Tom Regan and Peter Singer have been struggling with refining a position concerning animal rights.[2]

Concerned primarily with language, subjectivity, knowledge, and power, poststructural thought retheorizes and largely rejects a system of epistemological and metaphysical premises that are said to have been the foundation of Western society. Plato's theory of forms serves as a useful illustration. In an attempt to unify and systematize reality, to solve the problem of "the many and the one," Plato places all reality under the heading of the supreme Good. Plato's theories and absolutism did not occur in a disinterested vacuum, of course, but were directed against the relativism of the Sophists.

This hierarchical pyramid, culminating in a supreme value, also contains a metaphysical dualism. Like the Christian theory that followed, Plato posited a transcendent world of perfection along with a fallen or lesser world of apparent reality.[3] A transcendent realm of ideals allows for a referential theory of representation and a unifying process. For example, the particular is subsumed under the general: we are able to recognize particular acts of justice because we ("reasonable" folks anyway) have reference to the ideal of justice. In this referential system of reality, signs, i.e., actions and language, can be judged (by authorities) to the degree to which they correctly reflect the absolute.

In the field of literary interpretation, the notion of ultimate premises has been translated into an aesthetic elitism, a belief in a purely disinterested aesthetic response, and the establishment of the cult of the perceptive: those who can "get" or intuit the "essence" of a text. One could, in the past, make a case for Hemingway's characters being "true to life." With the advent of poststructural thinking, one asks, "Whose interests does it advance to promote (i.e., revere instead of interrogate) Hemingway's characterization of the world?" One assumes that there is not one reality that one author gets closer to than another. In the same way that there is no one world to depict, there is no one text; there is no determinate meaning in Hemingway's writing.

Terry Eagleton has recently commented that the judgments we advance concerning the meaning of pieces of literature "have a close relation to social ideologies. They refer in the end not simply to private taste, but to the assumptions by which certain social groups exercise and maintain power over others."[4] By assuming the existence of static universals or absolutes, the poem is said to possess an essence, a supersensible shape, and a determined meaning that may be apprehended. In this way, the poem achieves an ontological status since the essence is embodied and contained within the physical structure of the artifact. It becomes a "spatial figure rather than a temporal process."[5] This approach, however, absolutely disregards the sociohistorical conditioning of perception and attempts to naturalize a transhistorical aesthetic and humanistic essence. Literature, which has so often claimed to deal with the realm of feeling and experience, has seldom designated whose feeling and whose experience.

Jacques Derrida's work has been particularly focused on such systems. He is concerned with challenging the conception of knowledge that "governs structure while escaping structurality."[6] The poststructural assumption is that the premises held out of the structure—that govern structure—have no eternal truth, are not the transcendent essences that writers have claimed, but rather are arbitrary signifiers arrested from the chain of signifiers and privileged, or made to seem "natural," by a power group. This act of centering and freezing is an act of violence as it forces a structure and a hierarchy on society by insisting on a fixed center—Truth—and denying the play of the structure. Designed to benefit a particular segment within society, such principles generally register an anthropocentric, "for us," rendering of the world. Deconstruction demonstrates the arbitrary nature of this centering and forces the dismantling of the structure.[7]

What does all of this mean for resistance movements? Resistance movements, whether traditional Marxism or those emanating out of liberal humanism, are characterized by the same kind of belief in primary essences, or what Derrida calls logocentricity.[8] Both Marxism and liberal humanism have posited a suppressed or alienated nature that is in need of liberation. Marx imagines the truth of the worker's situation, the contact with the physical world, being distorted by a predatory, capitalist ideological apparatus. As Paul Smith states, "What is sketched out in Marx's work is a putative and utopian passage from the 'dominated subject' to 'fulfilled individual.'"[9] Similarly, liberal humanism has posited an intuitive, spontaneous, unquantifiable, and intangible individual that has suffered under the rule of the "outer" world, often depicted as a rational and mechanical technocracy.[10] In the West, this imagined space of resistance is filled by references to a vague set of spiritual premises—i.e., the spontaneous, the unique, etc.—that are difficult to translate into social practice. In other words, the spontaneous is easily co-opted by the style market; it ends up affirming a value within the structure it opposes.

Regarding the ineffectiveness of humanistic discourses to challenge power structures, John Carlos Rowe has credited Derrida with "flushing out of hiding those forces of the dominant ideology which have taken cover in the 'abstract,' 'impotent' discourses fixed on the supersensible. . . . In this way, Derrida helps demonstrate how the very 'powerlessness' of such humanistic discourses is in fact their most powerful resource, the means by which they serve the dominant ideology by protecting its founding concepts."[11]

Both Marxism and liberal humanism, then, are characterized by the same feature of logocentricity; they both refer to a pre-ideological essence, something that has not been distorted or shaped, something that is not represented but present: a "natural" basis for reality. Poststructuralism denies this metaphysical depth model, the attempt to posit a determined meaning or fixed origin, and suggests that ideology—or biased representation—is a permanent feature.

The problem here is not merely a philosophical but also a political one. The tendency to posit transcendent principles, whether for resistance or power structures, establishes, as Michael Ryan has stated, "a point of authority (an agency), a hierarchical command structure, and a police force."[12] This tendency asserts certainty and closes down open-ended play.[13] Deconstruction posits that the pressing for certainty and power is the history of Western metaphysics, what Paul Smith has recently referred to as "the romance of decisive mastery."[14] Abdicating a belief in progress toward truth, deconstruction finds knowledge to be a thinly veiled will toward mastery. Knowledge is then seen, not as disinterested understanding, but as biased organization and domination.

The difficulty for resistance movements can be demonstrated by an examination of a discussion in feminism. In her brilliant work, *The Lay of the Land,* Annette Kolodny examines the tendency of a male-centered culture to depict the land as feminine. She focuses on two structural narratives that emerge out of the initial, feminine characterization: earth as mother; earth as lover. Cultural complexity occurs when the "son" engages in opening the frontier in the role of the penetrating lover.

Such a structuralist discussion is helpful in that it moves away from eternal truths and looks at how a structure functions in accordance with its own set of rules: such structure is not recognized; rather, it is lived, giving it the feeling of being natural. In this case, Kolodny's examination exposes the male center as arbitrary and destructive. Exposing this male logic of appropriation, of course, is helpful. However, instead of challenging the entire structure, Kolodny works within the code. In an attempt to temper behavior generated by the sexual dimension of the paradigm, Kolodny privileges the earth-as-mother metaphor as opposed to earth-as-lover. As a result, she favors those moments in literature when writers conceive of a "nonexploitative relationship with a receptive and giving natural world."[15] In other words, she favors the depiction of earth as mother since it suggests a more nurturing and passive relationship. This relationship is then opposed to "a patriarchal social organization within which separate male-centered families compete, [where] all movement into unsettled areas inevitably implies conquest and mastery."[16] Correctly seeing that humans create these relations and that such relations are constructed within language, Kolodny wants to correct the situation by choosing a better metaphor. However, working within the paradigm that has been constituted by the power structure does not solve the problem.

Although Kolodny problematizes the metaphorical implications of wanting to be nonexploitive children, many current feminists and environmentalists work within this paradigm. As John Carlos Rowe has stated, those working with deconstruction as a contestatory practice can never forget "the extent to which the 'margin' is always already constituted by its exclusion, by a powerful act of cultural repression."[17] Instead of championing the repressed as a lost, true, utopian essence, Chantal Mouffe imagines a radical posture characterized by the absence of power. The result is a society in which democracy is equated with an empty space, in which no "identity is ever definitively established, there always being a certain degree of openness and ambiguity."[18] Laura Kipnis applies this perspective to feminism by stating that poststructural feminists need to see that "the site of political attention and engagement [is] a 'space' rather than a sex."[19] Patrick Murphy focuses this concern directly on ecofeminism when he suggests that environmentalism's tendency to associate the planet with the feminine "fails to encourage . . . change by inadvertently reinforcing current hierarchical sociogender stereotypes. . . . Any sex-typing that occurs within a society heavily laden with patriarchal values cannot expect to avoid reinforcing the gender biases that constitute part of the ideological paradigm."[20] It is not just that the oppositional element is often rife with subordination and, therefore, is unlikely to have contestatory potential, but also that the tendency of oppositional movements to assert a new set of ontological priorities reenacts the violence of the initial power structure.

I do not deny that a suppressed voice is in need of attention. There is no question that the epistemology of the oppressed is important. Because this voice is systematically suppressed, pushed to the margin and inscribed with inability or lack, it is useful for outlining the contours of the dominant hegemony.[21] Dominant structures, like patriarchy, work when they are thought of as natural, as the way things are. As Daniel Cottom has stated: "The most distinctive aspect of this power is that it cannot be recognized by those who are governed by it."[22] Thus, an examination of the site of discourse can expose the figurative nature of authority. The dominant voice wishes to appear as the only voice. As Rowe has stated, the "coin of the realm [attempts] to erase its figure; social convention works to obliterate its figurative origins, in order to masquerade as a signifier for some transcendental signified."[23] In other words, qualitative difference is enforced by means of an arbitrary centering. As Luce Irigaray suggests, sexual difference in social and economic life has been subject to such an arbitrary hierarchical rendering. As she puts it, the reality of "Heterosexuality is nothing but the assignment of economic roles."[24] Thus, because male and female do not refer to essences but gain reality by their differences from one another, foregrounding one term is always at the expense of the other and requires a powerful act of displacement and violence.[25]

As a result, an examination of the mechanisms of power is important; and attention to the suppressed voice is crucial. However, the tendency for resistance movements to suggest that the suppressed voice (female, worker, nature) offers a real and alternative essence, or that it should serve as the basis for a new society or a new age is my concern. As Rowe warns, it is important to recall that the qualities associated with the suppressed voice are produced by the manipulations of the dominant structure.

The problem for environmentalism is that current oppositional rhetoric seems firmly implicated in logocentricity. The positing of unseen, supersensible realities is not only vague and ultimately ineffective sociology, but it is also elitist.

Theodore Roszak's *Person/Planet* summarizes the oppositional structure most prevalent since the 1960s. His text asserts that the needs of the planet are the needs of the person. He posits an eternal essence and suggests that this essence is shared by the unique personality and spirit of nature. In a Socratic appeal to the reader, Roszak exhorts the reader to remember a primary reality, a pre-ideological reality, which has been sublimated by the power system: ". . . this right you feel so certain is yours, this right to have your uniqueness respected, perhaps even cultivated, is not at all an extension of traditional values like civil liberty, equality, social democracy. . . . It springs independently from another, far more mysterious source."[26] *Springs,* indeed. Roszak not only naturalizes the unique subjectivity of a pre-ideological individual, but he also links the resistant urges of the individual with the voice of an endangered planet. The "essential you somewhere inside, behind all the world's imposed identities"[27] is the vague, and finally complicit, basis that is to serve as a subversive politics. According to Roszak, "there is a planetary dimension to the spreading personalist sensibility which links the search for an authentic identity to the well-being of the global environment."[28] Roszak also claims that the emergence of feminism is no accident, suggesting that it is the alternative voice, the voice of the Earth, speaking through human agency. During the same period that Roszak was formulating and summarizing the position of 1960s' resistance, Herbert Marcuse also championed "a kind a radical and instinctive, but imperfectly remembered core of resistance . . . a kind of pre-Freudian 'subject' whose instinctual constitution is considered to promise a nonconflictual state or a civilization without repression."[29]

The problem with such a view of resistance is that this structure partakes of what it opposes. The positing and centering of a unique and transcendent being that is linked to a natural realm is the structure employed by power systems; more immediately, it is also the basis for a free market society. The illusion of a free and unencumbered individual is currently at the center of power.[30] The use of it as an imagined force of resistance demonstrates the degree of its dominance. As Kipnis has suggested, the individual is a "category that operated precisely from a blindness to its own determinations, whose greatest desire was to turn itself into an effect of nature."[31] Proposing a better metaphor, a better version of the free and unencumbered individual, misses the point; to echo Rowe, this approach allows the forces of the dominant ideology to take cover within the system of resistance. Instead of challenging the categories of knowledge that drive the power structure, Roszak actually reinforces the system by overlapping its fundamental priorities. The unique individual, for example, just as easily serves the rhetoric of the eccentric lives of the rich and famous as it does a New Age counterculture. As Terry Eagleton has recently stated, the liberal humanist tradition "grossly overestimated [its] transformative power. . . . Liberal humanism is a suburban moral ideology, limited in practice to largely interpersonal matters."[32] Anthropocentrism, the humanizing of reality, is still active. Only by an act of destruction of the human will to mastery, mastery disguised as the disinterested desire to know, organize, or even admire, will the appropriating activity be aborted.[33]

Nietzsche addresses this issue in *Beyond Good and Evil* where he writes that "while you rapturously pose as deriving your law from nature, you want something quite the reverse of that, you strange actors and self-deceivers? Your pride wants to prescribe your morality, your ideal, to nature, yes to nature itself, and incorporate them in it; you . . . would like to make all existence exist only after your own image. . . . But this is an old and never ending story."[34] Similarly, Langdon Winner states that the "writings of Hobbes, Locke, and Rousseau clearly demonstrate [that] discussions of 'natural law,' 'human nature,' and 'state of nature' are the occasions for the most extravagant theoretical fictions."[35] Winner goes on to suggest that most contemporary ecology movements don't realize that their vision of nature is

. . . itself a human creation, an abstract representation of certain kinds of phenomena. . . . The reflection of social conditions, issues, policies, and utopias in ideas of the natural is something more easily recognized in earlier periods than in our own. "Nature, red in tooth and claw" where only the fittest survive now seems to us a bizarre distortion from the era of nineteenth-century imperialism and robber baron capitalism. But there may come a time when our own attempts to live according to ecological principles will seem equally misguided. . . . Nature will justify anything. Its text contains opportunities for myriad interpretations.[36]

By fetishizing, or giving permanent ontological status to that which has been attacked by logocentric power, one runs the risk of repeating the transgressions of power. Thus, making references to mystical essences that serve as premises to establish a new and harmonious world may not be as effective as questioning the possibility and nature of knowledge. The history of attributing wonder and beauty to women, for instance, has proven to be a history of exploitation, not respect or self-determination.

Environmentalists often generate such an idealist point of departure. Catherine Ingram, for instance, recently lamented humanity's attempt to "control all that is wild in nature."[37] As with Kolodny, the diagnosis seems correct, but the cure is an imagined pre-ideological state of innocence. She suggests that we have forgotten a wisdom of the wild; we have forgotten our own spontaneity and intuitiveness. Nostalgia for a golden age of true, as opposed to ideological or false, existence is a typical environmental posture of resistance, and one that has limited contestatory abilities. In this way, environmentalism clearly links itself with a 1960s' style of resistance. It is the same structure depicted in Joni Mitchell's "Woodstock," a song that formed the centerpiece for 1960s' ideology: "We are stardust / We are golden / And we've got to get ourselves / Back to the garden." All that seems necessary is a release of repressed libidinal joy and innocence, a repressed core of edenic harmony.[38] Ironically enough, social visions based on such premises about the natural have the familiar ring of the confident voice of authority. As Winner reports, environmentalists are prone to replacing "traditional notions of liberty" with "coercive authority. . . . [Ophuls] recommends the creation of a class of 'ecological guardians' to handle the difficult policy decisions necessary to salvage a livable world."[39]

In addition, Leo Marx, while critiquing (correctly, I think) the heritage of a "man-centered attitude toward the environment fostered by a Judeo-Christian thought,"[40] nevertheless, calls for a "world government."[41] He finds that we have reached a level of technological advancement with "the capacity to supply everyone with an adequate standard of living."[42] Given the abuse of power demonstrated by Eastern Bloc countries, Marx's depiction of a benign central committee deciding what "adequate" means is less than desirable.

Marx also establishes logocentric first principles by stating that when life is natural, it is more "free, spontaneous, authentic." He goes to say that "the natural in psychic experience refers to activities of mind which are inborn or somehow primary. Whatever we call them, intuitive, unconscious, or preconscious, the significant fact is that they do not have to be learned or deliberately acquired." The pre-ideological and natural world is, typically, found to be repressed by an "expansionist society" that is "dangerously imbalanced on the side of . . . rational faculties."[43] The positing of a "natural" as opposed to a false reality is clear.

Finally, it seems that nowhere is the adoption of the principle of authority of the dominant structure more clear than in the use of violence.[44] Roderick Nash has recently observed that "American liberalism offered environmental radicals a way to justify violence."[45] The association of the self and nature in a mystical alliance allows for current environmentalists to suggest, as Dave Foreman of Earth First! does, that a river or wilderness defends itself by "operating through you."[46] As usual, this position is characterized by a belief in platonic constants, universal truth that can be represented in action. In the liberal humanist tradition, an individual is seen to gain "'moral maturity' when individuals are aware of 'universal truths' opposed to 'unjust laws.'"[47] Linking ourselves with fellow inhabitants of the planet (the way Derrida links signifiers in a chain) may be fruitful for challenging the hierarchical assumptions of our relations with living and nonliving things, but not as a basis for the cosmic administration of violence.

Jim Cheney's recent article, "Postmodern Environmental Ethics,"[48] which attempts to see environmental narrative (local and material) as freeing itself from totalization (humanization, universalization, and abstraction) proves promising and troublesome. Drawing on Native American myth, Cheney wishes to introduce the possibility of local, bioregional narratives that incorporate land and people in a balanced and healthy fashion. Most helpful is his notion of a horizontal as opposed to a vertical relationship between human and nonhuman agents, thus diminishing an essentialized and foregrounded self. In addition, his attention to the language of regional experience helps work against a monovoice. Cheney's project is admirable in that he wishes to see us "come into our own in nonrepressive ways."[49] However, there remain difficulties within his theory of representation and, most crucially, in his, admitted, lack of a theory of power, or "social negotiation."[50] Just as Kolodny ignored the issue regarding *who* chooses a "better metaphor," as well as the issue surrounding the appropriating quality of *any* metaphor, Cheney seems to run by these crucial issues toward a wisdom of the wild similar to Ingram. His approach is especially reminiscent of Kolodny when he states that science provides the "wrong kind of myth."[51] Cheney's paper is an important piece, however, because it is working at the heart of the current epistemological difficulty of reference and affirmation.

Cheney wishes to advance the insights of poststructuralism without letting go of cherished concepts such as "nature" and "experience." Cheney is correct when he points to poststructural language as language that does not "pretend to be giving the 'one true story.'" However, Cheney sustains logocentric principles by suggesting that a certain kind of language—local or bioregional—is an effect of nature. In addition, logocentric language such as "being," "truth," "moral imperative," "instruction," the world "expressing" and "disclosing" itself, problematizes a promising project.

Cheney makes room for cherished grounding as he attempts to wrestle against the poststructural claim concerning the entrapping quality of language; he says that "Language does not trap us in a world of words, but is the way in which the world is present to us."[52] Wouldn't it be more accurate to say that language is the way we have represented the world? Cheney romantically conceives of a language that is a "gift in which things come to presence."[53] There seems to be an innocent spontaneity here that is problematic.

Although Cheney agrees with poststructuralism that our experience is all sign, all human-centered language, one expects a more thorough application of these principles. What one expects to get is the world according to us, a human-centered "writing" of the world that is always ideological: i.e., always interested as opposed to disinterested and, therefore, always in need of a "counter-reading" that decenters the power of the text.[54]

What, then, does Cheney mean when he says that language is the way "in which the world is *present* to us"? Cheney's use of the term *present* resonates with the possibility of *presence* as opposed to the poststructuralist sense of a mediated *represented* reality. The world is not present to us; it is mediated by us through cultural and electrochemical filters. The world does not "disclose itself" (like a mistress?), or "speak through us" in a "primordial language" in which we then employ a kind of privileged "listening."[55]

The acts of writing and reading the world become confusing here. By suggesting that the world becomes present to us, Cheney seems to be suggesting that the Earth has a (determinate?) language that we can listen to. When Cheney describes the "percolation" of ideas "upward"[56] he suggests a base, a primordial and natural point of departure—the world expressing itself. Although Cheney would bristle at this accusation and declare that he is "not offering an *anti*postmodernist account,"[57] his description of the genesis of bioregional narrative allows for such a reading.

This "other" percolating language seems to be implied in moments when Cheney suggests that a wolf is an "expression"[58] on the part of the world. Although Cheney states that he is not positing "one true account of each situation,"[59] he nevertheless seems to suggest a language source other than the human brain. He does so, for instance, when he suggests that bioregional language exhibits "nature's role"[60] in its construction. But what is "nature's role"? Who decides how to recognize this role? Isn't Cheney suggesting an unmediated conception of nature? It is true that the totalizing and abstract nature of scientific and theoretical language, a "colonizing discourse" that attempts to "assimilate the world to it"[61] is in need of critique. Moreover, it is certain that the language (e.g., Native American) that has been invaded and/or repressed is definitely in need of foregrounding. However, to conclude that "Contextual discourse reverses this [totalization] . . . [and] assimilates language to the situation"[62] suggests that there is a present situation, one that can be mastered, represented, with language. How bioregional language "arises in such a way"[63] as to be free of its own distortions remains unclear.

If Cheney means by "the world is present" that we can see our textual construction of a world, a construction that is thoroughly a "for us" epistemology, and in this way understand (make *present* to ourselves) our ideologically fueled actions in the world, then I agree. However, his language, especially associated with nature, pushes toward romanticism and resolution, ignoring the way in which we entrap ourselves (and others), the way in which we attempt to give an innocent and disinterested rendering of nature—in the myths of Native Americans or in myths of science. He applauds these human-created myths without proper consideration for (a) the way in which myths come about through intertextual influence as opposed to a direct influence from the Earth, and (b) the way in which these myths were designed for survival, and, therefore, the way in which they render the world for us. It is true that these myths may be more tolerable than western European images in the way in which the fish and deer are given a story, the way that they become active subjects. They, nevertheless, are structuring narratives that organize the world in a way that is finally driven by a "for us" epistemology. These narratives, therefore, become "instructional," and with this transformation, they also become *the way* to see the world: they become tradition and authority, albeit locally applied.

Although admitting that there is reality construction, Cheney insists on the possibility of a writing that exhibits a "faithfulness to experiential embedment in the world."[64] How this privileged experience gets into our inescapably human-biased myths is problematic. Is it simply the mentioning of nonhuman entities? If our "reading" of the world is thoroughly constructed and if reference to a base is illusory, then what is it that we could possibly be faithful to, and how would we measure such faithfulness?

It is here that Cheney seems to unveil his ground.[65] He downplays the figurative and especially the appropriating quality of narrative, or "mythic thinking,"[66] and seems to suggest that language with relations to nature as opposed to the city is free from closure and the essentialized self and, therefore, defines our existence in a more accurate and "moral" fashion. There is no ground from which to make such a judgment, however, unless one is supplied. To this end, Cheney suggests that a language that grows (properly) out of experience is not a mere projection, but rather contains "the clues to the meaning of life" and "spiritual significance."[67]

Cheney's ground for narrative, which is alternately expressed as experience or nature, is quite clearly stated as the "geography of our lives."[68] Narratives that portray the "real" geography of our lives suggest an ahistorical grounding, a direct relation with the "world" as a cause for narrative instead of as an intertextual relation as a generating force—that is, in terms of texts that influence and are influenced by other texts.[69] Abandoning the modernist self and acknowledging the existence of texts do not solve the problem of the appropriating quality of language. Although myth forged in the forest may be useful for unsettling myth forged in the city, such myth is no less humanist. Although including the land in narrative is a significant feature, doing so does not make the language less appropriating.[70]

As is typical in gestures of resistance, even though Cheney correctly critiques the power structure, he attributes too much significance to language that is opposed to this particular manifestation of power. In sum, there is no need to privilege this language by unduly ascribing a superior reality to it. This localized language does not contain truth, but its existence and form testify to the power of dominant discourse. The texts of interest to Cheney have significance because of their usefulness to Cheney in relation to (totalizing) texts that he opposes. To suggest that they have a stable meaning outside of our use or their relation to power structures is problematic.[71] The stories that come from the margin are politically important; their "difference" is needed to outline the features of the dominant monovoice. These different voices are not marginal because they express esoteric secrets or have rare Himalayan value—and certainly not because they possess an inherent "moral imperative"—but because they are abused by power. Although they do not contain a new vision of society and of knowledge, they demonstrate a need for it.

My main point is that traditional environmental postures, and even Cheney's insightful view of a particularized environmental epistemology, have not come to terms with the sweeping critique of human desire and presence of which poststructural thought is capable. Solving our problem with the relation to the environment is not to be settled by references to vague or ultimate principles whereby we establish yet another hierarchical power arrangement. Power must be challenged, but, as Michael Ryan has put it, it must be challenged without authority. According to Ryan, "the elimination of domination cannot occur without the transformation of the categories of the thought processes that sustain and promote domination. Neither one before or above the others, but all together different yet articulated."[72]

Romanticism's complicity[73] with the dominant structure can be traced from the nineteenth century to current environmental theory. The critique of anthropocentricism seems already to be tainted with a logocentric structure of its own. Poststructuralism offers a point of departure that jettisons that epistemological privilege of the human and, therefore, short circuits a movement toward hierarchy and authority. Perhaps instead of the search for nature, one might be initially satisfied with a clearing of a space, a deconstructive clearing of humanism which might allow for, to repeat Ryan, "the transformation of the . . . thought processes that sustain and promote domination."

Notes

Quigley teaches in the Humanities and Social Science Department of Embry-Riddle Aeronautical University. Quigley's professional interests include critical theory, environmentalism, nineteenth-century American literature, and feminism. His specific interests relate to the current debate regarding representation and the grounds for resistance. A version of this paper was presented at the Fourteenth Annual Colloquium on Literature and Film: The Relationship Between Man and the Environment at West Virginia University, October 1989. The author wishes to thank the following people for comments and criticism: Pat Murphy, Tom Pagliasotti, Polly Webber, the anonymous referees, and especially Jim Cheney for a spirited review.

First published in *Environmental Ethics* 14, no. 4. Permission to reprint courtesy of *Environmental Ethics* and the author.

1. See "It's a Small World After All," in *The New Republic,* (September 18 and 25, 1989), pp. 7–10. The piece discusses, among other things, the controversial article by Francis Fukuyama, "The End of History," published in the *National Interest.*

2. Bill Devall and George Sessions, *Deep Ecology* (Salt Lake City: Gibbs M. Smith, 1985). For the history of the animal rights debate, see, for instance, Tom Regan, *All That Dwell Therein* (Berkeley: University of California Press, 1982).

3. This world is the material world. It also is a world of signs or language that can be read correctly or incorrectly depending upon one's access to the transcendent realm. One of the aims of deconstruction is to free the material signifiers from the yoke and tyranny of a transcendent absolute. This deconstruction then is not only an attack on elitist tyranny based on unseen presences, but is also a thorough materialization of existence. However, this materiality is always mediated by human desire in the form of language. We always render the world in one way or another; there is no absolute ground for ever achieving a position to see the "thing as it is."

4. Terry Eagleton, *Literary Theory* (Minneapolis: University of Minnesota Press, 1983), p. 16.

5. Ibid., p. 48.

6. Jacques Derrida, "Structure, Sign and Play in the Discourse of the Human Sciences," in Richard Mackey and Eugenio Donato, eds., *The Languages of Criticism and the Sciences of Man* (Baltimore: Johns Hopkins University Press, 1970), p. 248.

7. The objections to poststructuralism are numerous and well known. Some suggest that poststructuralism is in itself a privileged discourse (see Eagleton, *Literary Theory,* chapter on "Poststructuralism"); others suggest that it represents a neo-conservativism that paralyzes the basis for political opposition (Frank Lentricchia, *Criticism and Social Change* [Chicago: University of Chicago Press, 1985], pp. 50–51; also Gerald Graff, "The Pseudo-Politics of Interpretation," in W. J. T. Mitchell, ed., *The Politics of Interpretation* [Chicago: University of Chicago Press, 1983], pp. 153–54; and John Ellis, *Against Deconstruction* [Princeton, N.J.: Princeton University Press, 1989], p. 74). Still others, for example, Frederic Jameson in "Postmodernism, or the Cultural Logic of Late Capitalism," *New Left Review,* July/August 1984, pp. 53–92, suggest that poststructuralism attempts to evade history and needs to be historicized. In other words, Jameson wants to include poststructuralism within the purview of history instead of the other way around. In all of these

cases, poststructuralism is accused of freezing movement and establishing an authority of its own. The issue of privilege seems to be at the center of the complaint. Poststructuralism maintains that there is no knowledge, but only power—disguised as ideas—that serves the interests of some at the expense of others. The objection to this pronouncement is that poststructuralism is giving us the knowledge that there is no knowledge. By doing so, poststructuralism contradicts itself and, in addition, establishes itself as just the kind of privileged, totalizing discourse it opposes. The question of finality and closure is not an easy one to dispense with for sure. There is a kind of finality in saying that there is no finality, a kind of closure in saying that there is nothing but openness. Derrida and other poststructuralists, especially those with radical sociopolitical agendas, will want to say, however, that poststructuralism is not a theory, not an essence or stable body of thought, but a corrosive method of undoing that points beyond binary oppositions, that keeps things freed up, clearing the ground for a new paradigm that is as yet unthought. (Some, a certain stripe of Foucaulteans, object at this point that poststructuralism becomes utopian.) The point, then, is that there is nothing inherently conservative about poststructuralism, as can be witnessed by the use made of it by theorists such as Michael Ryan in *Marxism and Deconstruction* (Baltimore: Johns Hopkins University Press, 1982). See also Dominick LaCapra, *Soundings in Critical Theory* (Ithaca, N.Y.: Cornell University Press, 1989), where he states that deconstruction possesses no inherent political agenda but allows for multiple possibilities for political action (p. 131). This problem of privilege is not dissimilar to the challenge faced by Buddhism, which attempts to communicate a reality (or perhaps I should say the lack of one) that is not "reasonable," nor in any way apprehensible within the categories of mind. It should be added that, unlike Kant, the Buddhist is not suggesting a transcendental reality that lurks just beyond our finite capabilities. The sense is that there is "nothing," but not in a dialectical opposition to "something." This radical decentering of easy aphorisms regarding our "place" and "being" in the scheme of things presents the tendency to create an "object" of knowledge as a phenomenon of the human mind: the universe is under no compulsion to comply. Robert Magliola, *Derrida on the Mend* (West Lafayette, Ind.: Purdue University Press, 1984), has made the connection between Buddhist and deconstructive thought. Magliola states that deconstruction destroys, like the ancient Buddhist dialectician Nagarjuna, the notion of identity and evades the problem of binary opposition using "the same . . . strategy, and . . . arguments as Derrida" (p. 88). See also Peter Quigley "The Ground of Resistance; Nature and Power in Emerson, Melville, Jeffers, and Snyder," unpublished Ph.D. dissertation (Indiana University of Pennsylvania, 1990), pp. 221–69. The question is whether deconstruction accomplishes its undoing without establishing itself as an authoritative presence. Critics obviously disagree.

8. Particularly demonstrative of Marxist aesthetic theory is Georg Lukács' theory of the relationship between representation and history. See Geoffrey Thurley, *Counter-Modernism in Current Critical Theory* (New York: St. Martin's Press, 1983), pp. 202–03, for a discussion of this issue.

9. Paul Smith, *Discerning the Subject* (Minneapolis: University of Minnesota Press, 1988), p. 7.

10. See Eagleton, *Literary Theory*. He depicts this situation as one in which "the further we move from the rich inwardness of the personal life, of which literature is the supreme exemplar, the more drab, mechanical, and impersonal existence becomes" (pp. 196–97). It is important to note that poststructuralism's sense of play may seem similar to humanism's sense of the spontaneous. The difference, however, remains in the contrasting theories of self and the radicalness of the play. For humanism, spontaneity is an expression of the unique shape of the creative individual; the individual is considered a coherent and unified source of meaning.

11. John Carlos Rowe, "Surplus Economies: Deconstruction, Ideology, and the Humanities," in Murray Krieger, ed., *The Aims of Representation* (New York: Columbia University Press, 1987), p. 152.

12. Michael Ryan, *Marxism and Deconstruction* (Baltimore: Johns Hopkins University Press, 1982), p. 125.

13. Play is not to be understood in the sense of irresponsibility, but in the sense of dissent from the seriousness of those who claim to possess the truth that can be structured and enforced.

14. Smith, *Discerning the Subject*, p. 46.

15. Annette Kolodny, *The Lay of the Land* (Chapel Hill: University of North Carolina Press, 1975), p. 77.

16. Ibid., p. 133.

17. Rowe, "Surplus," p. 155.

18. Chantal Mouffe, "Radical Democracy: Modern or Postmodern?" in Andrew Ross, ed., *Universal Abandon? The Politics of Postmodernism* (Minneapolis: University of Minnesota Press, 1988), pp. 33–34.

19. Laura Kipnis, "Feminism: The Political Conscience of Postmodernism?" in Ross, ed., *Universal Abandon*, p. 159.

20. Patrick Murphy, "Sex-Typing the Planet: Gaia Imagery and the Problem of Subverting Patriarchy," *Environmental Ethics* 10 (1988): 106.

21. See V. N. Volosinov, *Marxism and the Philosophy of Language* (New York: Seminar Press, 1973), pp. 72–85, for a discussion of the sociological nature of language and comments on monologic language as opposed to utterance.

22. Daniel Cottom, *Text and Culture: The Politics of Interpretation* (Minneapolis: University of Minnesota Press, 1989), p. 72.

23. Rowe, "Surplus," p. 134.

24. In John Carlos Rowe, " To Live Outside the Law You Must Be Honest : The Authority of the Margin in Contemporary Theory," *Cultural Critique* 1 (Winter 1985–86): 44.

25. Language, from the poststructural point of view, does not refer to or contain transcendent concepts. The traditional view of writing is that it is part of the fallen world which refers to, points to, a higher realm of universals that are stable and intact. In contrast, language, from the poststructural point of view, is a system of signs. A word becomes significant, not because it refers to a higher realm or because it embodies or contains the essence of what it refers to, but because it simply is different from other signs that sound similar. The word *cat* becomes identifiable because of what it is not. It is not *pat* or *hat*. Its reality is gained because of its place in the system of signifiers, not because it contains an identity. Politically this view of language has taken at least two directions: (1) since assertion becomes possible only because of the denial of the "other," political problems arise when this denial takes the form of hegemonic dominance. Liberation of the suppressed voice begins from this point of departure. (2) The indeterminate quality of language makes an authoritative definition of meaning a suppression of desire, of the multiplicity of meaning.

26. Theodore Roszak, *Person/Planet: The Creative Disintegration of Industrial Society* (New York: Doubleday Books, 1979), p. 7.

27. Ibid., p. 8.

28. Ibid., p. xxx.

29. Smith, *Discerning the Subject,* p. 61.

30. Kipnis calls the recent attention to the self in American culture "hypervisibility." She states that the appearance of strong representatives of a coherent self—such as Rambo and Reagan—are due to the "loss of its legitimate function." Such radical assertions of stability are, she says, "compensating fantasies" ("Feminism," p. 158). Jameson summarizes the debate within poststructural circles on the constitution of the subject. He states that postmodernism replaces the various "depth models with surface . . . or multiple surfaces" ("Postmodernism," p. 62). He goes on to say that the more traditional view suggests that a once centered subject "has today in the world of organizational bureaucracy dissolved," while "the more radical poststructural position" states that "such a subject never existed in the first place but constituted something like an ideological mirage" ("Postmodernism," p. 63).

31. Ibid., p. 157.

32. Eagleton, *Literary Theory,* p. 207.

33. Here we run into another paradox in poststructural theory. Is "destroying the will to master" a kind of mastery or will?

34. Frederick Nietzsche, *Beyond Good and Evil* (Baltimore: Penguin Books, 1973), p. 21.

35. Langdon Winner, *The Whale and the Reactor: A Search for Limits in an Age of High Technology* (Chicago: University of Chicago Press, 1986), pp. 122–23.

36. Ibid., pp. 136–37.

37. Catherine Ingram, "Call of the Wild," *Utne Reader* 34 (1989): 103.

38. I regret that at this point I seem to be joining in with the trendy theoretical posture of 1960s bashing; I do not mean to suggest that the 1960s did not provide the opportunity to further work in the area of resistance. I am only suggesting that even a decade like the 1960s that foregrounded resistance is subject to absorption by and complicity with the principles of a dominant hegemony.

39. Winner, *The Whale,* p. 130.

40. Leo Marx, "American Institutions and Ecological Ideals," *Science* 170 (1970): 948.

41. Ibid., p. 945.

42. Ibid., p. 949.

43. Ibid., p. 950.

44. This is a particularly difficult issue. Nowhere does poststructural theory draw the criticism of political irresponsibility more clearly from political activists, especially committed environmentalists, than here. Michael Ryan has handled the question of action within a poststructural context rather well. He suggests that it is impossible to always behave in a way that is clean of the pattern of domination. Therefore, one must make provisional choices; one must act knowing that the action is not a move toward an answer, a settling of the question, but just the reverse, an unsettling of power.

45. Roderick Nash, *Wilderness and the American Mind* (New Haven, Conn.: Yale University Press, 1967), p. 197.

46. Ibid., p. 196.

47. Ibid., p. 197.

48. Jim Cheney, "Postmodern Environmental Ethics: Ethics as Bioregional Narrative," *Environmental Ethics* 11 (1989): 117–34 [Chapter 1 in this book].

49. Ibid., p. 121.

50. Ibid., p. 134.

51. Ibid., p. 132.

52. Ibid., p. 119.

53. Ibid., p. 119.

54. The course of action suggested by deconstruction is to relentlessly tear down this structure, not simply change the metaphor.

55. Cheney, "Postmodern Environmental Ethics," p. 119.

56. Ibid., p. 121.

57. Ibid., p. 121.

58. Ibid., p. 119.

59. Ibid., p. 121, n. 8.

60. Ibid., p. 133. "Nature's role" becomes a particularly difficult concept in Cheney's text when one considers that earlier he states that to get the kind of society he hopes for "nature must be transformed in image to perform this function" (p. 132). It appears as though nature takes on two roles in Cheney's text; it is autonomous and constructed, simultaneously. In addition, the power issue in relation to such figuration, or transformation, remains problematic.

61. Ibid., p. 120.

62. Ibid.

63. Ibid., p. 121, n. 8.

64. Ibid., p. 119.

65. Ibid., p. 119.

66. Ibid., p. 123.

67. Ibid., p. 132. Cheney, by allowing detotalized specificity to contain life's clues and meaning, seems to be working within the framework of a structural absolutist as opposed to a relativist. Joseph Campbell, for instance, explores the particular languages of cultures. He, however, tends to reduce this particularity by suggesting a spiritual base.

68. Ibid., p. 126.

69. Gary Snyder's use of Hopi myth, for example, is more interesting and useful for what it says about white, male, technological dominant mythology than for what it communicates about the "essence" of Hopi life. *Riprap and Cold Mountain Poems* (Berkeley, Calif.: North Point Press, 1990).

70. Here I am thinking of Snyder's difficulties with the feminization of the planet. His characterization of the planet as female creates enormous problems as it partakes of patriarchal elements. Such a text could have provisional success, but would also carry seeds of domination. In addition to foregrounding repressed texts, I find Snyder most helpful when he works against constituting tendencies and produces images that erase intellection: for instance, when he privileges gestures "Like a small creek off a high ledge / Gone in the dry air" (*ibid.,* p. 6). Robinson Jeffers often employs similar techniques when, as in "The Place for No Story" or "Love the Wild Swan," he deconstructs his own act of artistic appropriation.

71. In current critical theory there is much discussion about how texts "mean." More traditional views concentrate on what a particular text "says." Poststructuralism calls into question the possibility of a determinate reading, an essence, and tends to

see texts gaining their meaning from (a) the existence of other texts, their conscious or unconscious relation to other texts and (b) the time, place, and person doing the reading. Lack of clarification on this issue is the source of much of my difficulty with Cheney's article. Cheney does say in a note, while defending himself against epistemological foundationalism, that he privileges bioregional discourse because of its relation to totalizing discourses. He also states that a voice is to be privileged "to the extent that it spot[s] distortions, mystifications, and colonizing and totalizing tendencies within other discourses" (p. 118). In a response to this paper, Cheney states that my view of intertextual significance is a distortion of his use of texts. He protests that the texts he looks at in his article are not always displaced and repressed and "are not completely so even now," apparently, so as to discount the theory of textual significance and to posit the possibility of a static moment of intentional and determinate meaning. The first dilemma here is that just because a text is localized doesn't mean it "spots" anything. Another text (Cheney's) is needed to do that spotting. In addition, although Cheney suggests a relation between local texts and totalizing texts, intertextual significance seems to be abandoned in his article. In the article, Cheney insists on understanding bioregional texts, not in terms of intertextual relations, but in order to advance a certain image of materiality ("nature must be transformed in image" [p. 132]) that somehow percolates into a regional view. My continuing complaint is that his description of the "world presenting itself" leaves him open to the accusation of epistemological foundationalism; the lack of a theory of power tends to add to this reading.

72. Ryan, *Marxism,* p. 212.

73. Both Bruce Greenfield, "Thoreau's Discovery of America: A Nineteenth-Century First Contact" *ESQ* 32, no. 2 (1986): 85, and Richard Slotkin, *The Fatal Environment* (Middletown, Conn.: Wesleyan University Press, 1985), p. 52, discuss the agrarian myth as a means for excluding the Indians. Even current works that demonstrate an understanding of Romanticism's intersubjectivity posit a primal window onto nature. Bob Steuding, *Gary Snyder* (Boston: Twayne, 1976), states that the Romantics "asked many valid questions but were unable to decode the answers they received because of clinging Judaeo-Christian bias" (p. 38). True enough; however, he goes on to suggest that Snyder and others have saved themselves from such delusion and really *see* nature. Again this claim suggests a primal unmediated contact.

10

Traditional American Indian and Western European Attitudes Toward Nature: An Overview

J. Baird Callicott

I

In this paper I sketch (in broadest outline) the picture of nature endemic to two very different intellectual traditions: the familiar, globally dominant Western European civilization, on the one hand, and the presently beleaguered tribal cultures of the American Indians, on the other. I argue that the world view typical of American Indian peoples has included and supported an environmental ethic, while that of Europeans has encouraged human alienation from the natural environment and an exploitative practical relationship with it. I thus represent a romantic point of view; I argue that the North American "savages" were indeed more noble than "civilized" Europeans, at least in their outlook toward nature.

I do not enter into this discussion unaware of the difficulties and limitations which present themselves at the very outset. In the first place, there is no one thing that can be called *the* American Indian belief system. The aboriginal peoples of the North American continent lived in environments quite different from one another and had culturally adapted to these environments in quite different ways. For each tribe there was a cycle of myths and a set of ceremonies, and from these materials one might abstract *for each* a particular view of nature. However, recognition of the diversity and variety of American Indian cultures should not obscure a complementary unity to be found among them. Despite great internal differences there were common characteristics which culturally united American Indian peoples. Joseph Epes Brown claims that this common binding thread is found in beliefs and attitudes held by the people in the quality of their relationships to the natural environment. All American Indian peoples possessed what has been called a metaphysics of nature; all manifest a reverence for the myriad forms and forces of the natural world specific to their immediate environment; and for all, their rich complexes of rites and ceremonies are expressed in terms which have reference to or utilize the forms of the natural world.[1]

Writing from a self-declared antiromantic perspective, Calvin Martin has more recently confirmed Brown's conjecture:

What we are dealing with are two issues: the ideology of Indian land-use and the practical results of that ideology. Actually, there was a great diversity of ideologies, reflecting distinct culture and ecological contexts. It is thus more than a little artificial to identify a single, monolithic ideology, as though all Native Americans were traditionally inspired by a universal ethos. Still, there were certain elements which many if not all these ideologies seemed to share, the most outstanding being a genuine respect for the welfare of other life-forms.[2]

A second obvious difficulty bedeviling any discussion of American Indian views of nature is our limited ability to reconstruct accurately the abstract culture of New World peoples prior to their contact with (and influence from) Europeans. Documentary records of pre-contact Indian thought simply do not exist. American Indian metaphysics existed embedded in oral traditions. Left alone an oral culture may be very tenacious and persistent. If radically stressed, it may prove to be very fragile and liable to total extinction. Hence, *contemporary* accounts by contemporary American Indians of *traditional* American Indian philosophy are vulnerable to the charge of inauthenticity, since for several generations American Indian cultures, cultures preserved in the living memory of their members, have been both ubiquitously and violently disturbed by transplanted European civilization.

We ought, therefore, perhaps to rely where possible upon the earliest written observations of Europeans concerning American Indian belief. The accounts of the North American "savage" by sixteenth-, seventeenth-, and eighteenth-century Europeans, however, are invariably distorted by ethnocentrism, which to the cosmopolitan twentieth-century student appears so hopelessly abject as to be more entertaining than illuminating. The written observations of Europeans who first encountered American Indian cultures provide rather an instructive record of the implicit European metaphysics. Since Indians were not loyal to the Christian religion, it was assumed that they had to be mindfully servants of Satan, and that the spirits about which they talked and the powers which their shamans attempted to direct had to be so many demons from Hell. Concerning the Feast of the Dead among the Huron, Brebeuf wrote in 1636 that "nothing has ever better pictured for me the confusion among the damned."[3] His account, incidentally, is very informative and detailed concerning the physical requirements and artifacts of this ceremony, but the rigidity of his own system of belief makes it impossible for him to enter sympathetically that of the Huron.

Reconstructing the traditional Indian attitude toward nature is, therefore, to some extent a speculative matter. On the other hand, we must not abandon the inquiry as utterly hopeless. Post-contact American Indians do tell of their traditions and their conceptual heritage. Among the best of these nostalgic memoirs is Neihardt's classic, *Black Elk Speaks,* one of the most important and authentic resources available for the reconstruction of an American Indian attitude toward nature. The explorers', missionaries', and fur traders' accounts of woodland Indian attitudes are also useful, despite their ethnocentrism, since we may correct for the distortion of their biases and prejudices. Using these two sorts of sources, first contact European records and transcribed personal recollections of tribal beliefs by spiritually favored Indians, plus disciplined and methodical modern ethnographic reports, we may achieve a fairly reliable reconstruction of traditional Indian attitudes toward nature.

II

On the European side of the ledger, at first glance, an analogous pluralism appears to confound any generalizations. How different are the lands, the languages, the life styles of, say, the Swedes and the Spanish, or the Slavic and Gaelic peoples. If anything, Europeans appear to be a more ethnically diverse, motley collection of folks than Indians. Europeans, however, have enjoyed a collective intellectual *history* which the Indians, for better or worse, have not. Moreover, for many centuries a common learned language was shared by scholars of every civilized European country. This alone constitutes an enormously unifying force. The intellectual history of Europe has been, to be sure, dialectical and disputatious, but the pendulum of opinion has swung between well-defined limits and certain universally accepted assumptions have prevailed.

As the European style of thought was set by the Greeks of classical antiquity, I begin with them. I treat modern science, i.e., modern European natural philosophy, as a continuation and extrapolation of certain concepts originating with the fifth- and fourth-century Greeks. Greek ideas about nature were remarkably rich and varied, but only some of these ideas, for historical reasons which cannot be explored in this discussion, inspired and informed modern natural philosophy. They became institutionalized in the modern Western world view. It is upon them, accordingly, that I especially focus.

Mythopoeic Greek cosmology had curious affinities with some of the central cosmological concepts of the American Indians. Sky and Earth (Uranus and Gaia) are represented by Hesiod in the *Theogony* as male and female parents (Father and Mother) of the first generation of gods and either directly or indirectly of all natural beings. Some Ionian Greeks in the city of Miletus apparently became disenchanted with traditional Greek mythology and embarked upon speculations of their own. Everything, they said, is water or air. Things change because of the struggle of the Hot with the Cold and the Wet with the Dry. The implicit question—what is the nature of that out of which all things come and into which all things are resolved?—proved to be both fascinating and fruitful. After about 150 years of uninterrupted controversy, Leucippus and Democritus, with characteristic Ionian simplicity and force, brought this line of thought to a brilliant culmination in the atomic theory of matter. The atom was conceived by them to be an indestructible and internally changeless particle, "so small as to escape sensation." There are infinitely many of these. They have substance, that is they are solid or "full," and possess shape and relative size. All other qualities of things normally disclosed by perception exist, according to Democritus, only by "convention," not by "nature." In the terms of later philosophical jargon, characteristics of things such as flavor, odor, color, and sound were regarded as *secondary* qualities, the subjective effects of the primary qualities on the sensory patient. Complementary to the concept of the atom is the concept of the *void*— free, homogeneous, isotropic space. The atoms move haphazardly about in this space. Macroscopic objects are assemblages of atoms; they are wholes exactly equal to the sum of their parts. These undergo generation and destruction, which were conceived as the association and dissociation of the atomic parts. The atomists claimed to reduce all the phenomena of nature to this simple dichotomy: the "full" and the "empty," "thing" and "no-thing," the atom and space.

Thomas Kuhn succinctly comments that "early in the seventeenth century atomism experienced an immense revival. . . . Atomism was firmly merged with Copernicanism as a fundamental tenet of the 'new philosophy' which directed the scientific imagination."[4] The consolidated Newtonian world view included as one of its cornerstones the atomists' concept of free space, thinly occupied by moving particles or "corpuscles," as the early moderns called them. It was one of Newton's greatest achievements to supply a quantitative model of the regular motion of the putative material particles. These famous "laws of motion" made it possible to represent phenomena not only materially, but also mechanically.

That the *order* of nature can be successfully disclosed only by means of a quantitative description, a rational account in the most literal sense of that word, is itself, of course, an idea which originated in sixth-century Greece with Pythagoras. Pythagoras' insight had such tremendous scientific potential that it led Plato to eulogize it as Promethean, a veritable theft from the gods of the key to the secrets of the cosmos. It was cultivated and developed by the subsequent Pythagorean school and by Plato himself in the *Timaeus,* a work which enjoyed enormous popularity during the Renaissance. Modern philosophy of nature might be oversimply, but, nonetheless, not incorrectly portrayed as a merger of the Pythagorean intuition that the structure of the world order is determined according to ratio, to quantitative proportions, and the Democritean ontology of void space (so very amenable to geometrical analysis) and material particles. The intellectual elegance and predictive power of the Newtonian natural philosophy resulted, as Kuhn suggests, in it becoming virtually institutionalized in the nascent European scientific community. Its actual and potential application to practical matters, to problems of engineering and tinkering, also made it a popular, working picture of nature, gladly and roundly embraced by all Europeans participating in enlightenment.

Paul Santmire characterized the modern European attitude toward nature as it took root in the American soil in the nineteenth century as follows:

Nature is analogous to a machine; or in the more popular version nature *is* a machine. Nature is composed of hard, irreducible particles which have neither color nor smell nor taste. . . . Beauty and value in nature are in the eye of the beholder. Nature is the dead *res extensa,* perceived by the mind, which observes nature from a position of objective detachment. Nature in itself is basically a self-sufficient, self-enclosed complex of merely physical forces acting on colorless, tasteless, and odorless particles of hard, dead matter. That is the mechanical view of nature as it was popularly accepted in the circles of the educated [white Americans] in the nineteenth century.[5]

Santmire's comments bring to our attention a complementary feature of the European world view of particular interest to our overall discussion. If no qualms were felt about picturing rivers and mountains, trees, and (among the legions of Cartesians) even animals as inert, material, mechanical "objects," the line was drawn at the human mind. Democritus and later Hobbes had attempted a thoroughgoing and self-consistent materialism, but this intrusion of matter into the very soul of man did not catch on—everything else, maybe, but not the human ego.

The conception of the soul as not only separate and distinct from the body, but as essentially alien to it (i.e., of an entirely different, antagonistic nature) was also first introduced into Western thought by Pythagoras. Pythagoras conceived the soul to be a fallen divinity, incarcerated in the physical world as retribution for some unspecified sin. The goal in life for the Pythagoreans was to earn the release of the soul from the physical world upon death and to reunite the soul with its proper (divine) companions. The Pythagoreans accomplished this by several methods: asceticism, ritual purification, and intellectual exercise, particularly in mathematics. This led Plato, who was more than passingly influenced by Pythagoras, to (half) joke in the *Phaedo* that philosophy is the study of death, an exercise in the disentanglement of the soul from the body. The Pythagoreans and Plato indeed inverted the concepts of life and death. In the *Cratylus,* for example, Plato alleges that the word *body* (*sôma*) was derived from *tomb* (*sêma*). The body is thus the tomb of the soul as well as its place of imprisonment.

The Pythagorean/Platonic concept of the soul as immortal and otherworldly, essentially foreign to the hostile physical world, has profoundly influenced the European attitude toward nature. It was not only revived in a particularly extreme form by Descartes in the seventeenth century, but it became popularized much earlier in Pauline Christianity. The essential self, the part of a person by means of which he or she perceives and thinks, and in which resides virtue or vice, is not of this world and has more in common with god(s) than with nature. If the natural world is the place of trial and temptation for the soul, if the body is the prison and the tomb of the soul, then nature must be despised as the source of all misery and corruption, a place of fear and loathing: "a joyless place where murder and vengeance dwell, and swarms of other fates—wasting diseases, putrefactions and fluxes—roam in darkness over the meadow of doom."[6]

So what attitude overall to nature does modern classical European natural philosophy convey? In sum, nature is an inert, material, and mechanical continuum exhaustively described by means of the arid formulae of pure mathematics. In relation to nature the human person is a lonely exile sojourning in a strange and hostile world, alien not only to his physical environment, but to his own body, both of which he is encouraged to fear and attempt to conquer. Add to this Cartesian picture the Judaic themes forthrightly set out in *Genesis* (which Lynn White Jr., Ian McHarg, and others have so thoroughly criticized)—themes of dominion of man over nature, of its subjugation and domestication, of the *imago dei,* and so on—and we have a very volatile mixture of ingredients set to explode in an all-out war on nature, a war which in the twentieth century has very nearly been won. To the victors, of course, belong the spoils!

This world view might have been ameliorated by Greek biological theory beginning with Plato and reaching fruition with Aristotle, but unfortunately it too proved to be atomistic and ecologically blind. Plato accounted for the existence of kinds of individuals, i.e., species, by means of his theory of ideas. Each individual or specimen "participated," according to Plato, in a certain essence or form and it derived its specific characteristics from the form in which it participates. The impression of the natural world conveyed by the theory of ideas is that the various species are determined by the static logical-mathematical order of the formal domain and then the individual organisms, each with its preordained essence, are loosed into the physical arena to interact clumsily, catch-as-catch-can. Nature is thus perceived, like a roomful of furniture, as a collection, a mere aggregate of individuals of various types, relating to one another in an accidental and altogether external fashion. This picture of the world is an "atomism" of a most subtle and insidious sort. It breaks a highly integrated functional system into separate, discrete, and functionally unrelated sets of particulars. Pragmatically, approaching the world through this model—which we might call "conceptual" in contradistinction to "material" atomism—it is possible radically to rearrange parts of the landscape without the least concern for upsetting its functional integrity and organic unity. Certain species may be replaced by others (e.g., predator extermination) without consequence, theoretically, for the function of the whole.

Aristotle recoiled, of course, from the otherworldliness of Plato's philosophy, both from his theory of the soul and his theory of ideas. Aristotle, moreover, was a sensitive empirical biologist and did almost as much to advance biology as a science as Pythagoras did for mathematics and harmonics. Aristotle's subsequent influence on biological thought has been immense. Biology today still bears the personal stamp of his genius, especially in the system of classification (as modified and refined by Linnaeus) of organisms according to species, genus, family, order, class, phylum, and kingdom. This hierarchy of universals was not real or actual, according to Aristotle (to his everlasting credit); only individual organisms fully existed. However, Aristotle's taxonomical hierarchy (in isolation from evolutionary and ecological theory) resulted in a view of living nature which was, if that is possible, more ecologically blind than Plato's. Relations among things again are, in Aristotle's biological theory, accidental and inessential. A thing's essence is determined by its logical relations within the taxonomical schema rather than, as in ecological theory, by its working relations with other things in its environment—its trophic niche, its thermal and chemical requirements, and so on. As Aldo Leopold expresses this point with characteristic bluntness: "The species of a layer [in the biotic pyramid] are alike not in where they came from or in what they look like, but rather in what they eat."[7] Evolutionary and ecological theory suggest, metaphysically, that the essences of things, the specific characteristics of species, are a function of their relations with other things. To convey a very un-Aristotelian thought in an

Aristotelian manner of speech, relations are "prior" to the things related, and systemic wholes are "prior" to their component parts. A taxonomical view of the biotic world untransformed by evolutionary and ecological theory has the same ecologically misrepresentative feature as Plato's theory of forms: nature is seen as an aggregate of individuals, divided into various types, which have no functional connection with one another. And the *practical* consequences are the same. The biotic mantle may be dealt with in a heavy-handed fashion, rearranged to suit one's fancy without danger of dysfunctions. If anything, Aristotle's taxonomical representation of nature has had a more insidious influence upon the Western mind than Plato's real universals, since the latter could be dismissed, as often they were, as abstracted Olympians in a charming and noble philosophical romance, while metaphysical taxonomy went unchallenged as "empirical" and "scientific."

We should also not forget another Aristotelian legacy, the natural *hierarchy,* according to which the world is arranged into "lower" and "higher" forms. Aristotle's teleology required that the lower forms exist for the sake of the higher forms. Since human beings are placed at the top of the pyramid, everything else exists for the sake of them. The practical tendencies of this idea are too obvious to require further elaboration.

III

The late John Fire Lame Deer, a reflective Sioux Indian, comments, straight to the point, in his biographical and philosophical narrative, *Lame Deer: Seeker of Visions,* that although the whites (i.e., members of the European cultural tradition) imagine earth, rocks, water, and wind to be dead, they nevertheless "are very much alive."[8] In the previous section I tried to explain in what sense nature, as the *res extensa,* is conceived as "dead" in the mainstream of European natural thought. To say that rocks and rivers are dead is perhaps misleading since what is now dead once was alive. Rather in the usual European view of things such objects are considered inert. But what does Lame Deer mean when he says that they are "very much alive"?

He doesn't explain this provocative assertion as discursively as one might wish, but he provides examples, dozens of examples, of what he calls the "power" in various natural entities. According to Lame Deer, "Every man needs a stone. . . . You ask stones for aid to find things which are lost or missing. Stones can give warning of an enemy, of approaching misfortune."[9] Butterflies, coyotes, grasshoppers, eagles, owls, deer, especially elk and bear all talk and possess and convey power. "You have to listen to all these creatures, listen with your mind. They have secrets to tell."[10]

It would seem that for Lame Deer the "aliveness" of natural entities (including stones which to most Europeans are merely "material objects" and epitomize lifelessness) means that they have a share in the same consciousness that we human beings enjoy. Granted, animals and plants (if not stones and rivers) are recognized to be "alive" by conventional European conceptualization, but they lack awareness in a mode and degree comparable to human awareness. Among the Cartesians, as I mentioned earlier, even animal behavior was regarded as altogether automatic, resembling in every way the behavior of a machine. A somewhat more liberal and enlightened view allows that animals have a dim sort of consciousness, but get around largely by "instinct," a concept altogether lacking a clear definition and one very nearly as obscure as the notorious occult qualities (the "soporific virtues," and so on) of the Schoolmen. Of course, plants are regarded as, although alive, totally lacking in sentience. In any case, we hear that only human beings possess *self*-consciousness, that is, are aware that they are aware and can thus distinguish between themselves and everything else!

Every sophomore student of philosophy has learned, or should have, that solipsism is a redoubtable philosophical position; and corollary to that, that every characterization of other minds—human as well as nonhuman—is a matter of conjecture. The Indian attitude, as represented by Lame Deer, apparently was based upon the consideration that since human beings have a physical body *and* an associated consciousness (conceptually hypostatized or reified as "spirit"), all other bodily things, animals, plants, and, yes, even stones, were also similar in this respect. Indeed, this strikes me as an eminently reasonable assumption. I can no more directly perceive another human being's consciousness than I can that of an animal or plant. I *assume* that another human being is conscious since he or she is perceptibly very like me (in other respects) and I am conscious. To anyone not hopelessly prejudiced by the metaphysical *apartheid* policy of Christianity and Western thought generally, human beings closely resemble in anatomy, physiology, and behavior other forms of life. The variety of organic forms themselves are clearly closely related and the organic world, in turn, is continuous with the whole of nature. Virtually all things might be supposed, without the least strain upon credence, like ourselves, to be "alive," i.e., conscious, aware, or possessed of spirit.

Lame Deer offers a brief, but most revealing and suggestive metaphysical explanation:

> Nothing is so small and unimportant but it has a spirit given it by Wakan Tanka. Tunkan is what you might call a stone god, but he is also a part of the Great Spirit. The gods are separate beings, but they are all united in Wakan Tanka. It is hard to understand—something like the Holy Trinity. You can't explain it except by going back to the "circles within circles" idea, the spirit splitting itself up into stones, trees, tiny insects even, making them all *wakan* by his ever-presence. And in

turn all these myriad of things which makes up the universe flowing back to their source, united in one Grandfather Spirit.[11]

This Lakota pantheism presents a conception of the world which is, to be sure, dualistic, but it is important to emphasize that, unlike the Pythagorean-Platonic-Cartesian tradition, it is not an *antagonistic* dualism in which body and spirit are conceived in contrary terms and pitted against one another in a moral struggle. Further, and most importantly for my subsequent remarks, the pervasiveness of spirit in nature, a spirit *in* everything which is a splinter of the Great Spirit, facilitates a perception of the human and natural realms as unified and akin.

Consider, complementary to this pan-psychism, the basics of Siouan cosmogony. Black Elk rhetorically asks, "Is not the sky a father and the earth a mother, and are not all living things with feet or wings or roots their children?"[12] Accordingly, Black Elk prays, "Give me the strength to walk the soft earth, a relative to all that is!"[13] He speaks of the great natural kingdom as, simply, "green things," "the wings of the air, the four-leggeds," and "the two-legged."[14] Not only does everything have a spirit, in the last analysis all things are related together as members of one universal family, born of one father, the sky, the Great Spirit, and one mother, the Earth herself.

More is popularly known about the Sioux metaphysical vision than about those of most other American Indian peoples. The concept of the Great Spirit and of the Earth Mother and the family-like relatedness of all creatures seems, however, to have been very nearly a universal American Indian idea, and likewise the concept of a spiritual dimension or aspect to all natural things. N. Scott Momaday remarked, "'The earth is our mother. The sky is our father.' This concept of nature, which is at the center of the Native American world view, is similar to us all. But it may well be that we do not understand entirely what the concept is in its ethical and philosophical implications."[15] And Ruth Underhill has written that "for the old time Indian, the world did not consist of inanimate materials. . . . It was alive, and everything in it could help or harm him."[16]

Concerning the Ojibwa Indians, who speak an Algonquian language and at the time of first contact maintained only hostile relations with the Sioux, Diamond Jenness reports:

> Thus, the Parry Island Ojibwa interprets his own being; and exactly the same interpretation he applies to everything around him. Not only men, but animals, trees, even rocks and water are tripartite, possessing bodies, souls, and shadows. They all have a life like the life in human beings, even if they have all been gifted with different powers and attributes. Consider the animals which most closely resemble human be-

ings; they see and hear as we do, and clearly they reason about what they observe. The tree must have a life somewhat like our own, although it lacks the power of locomotion. . . . Water runs; it too must possess life, it too must have a soul and a shadow. Then observe how certain minerals cause the neighboring rocks to decompose and become loose and friable; evidently rocks too have power, and power means life, and life involves a soul and shadow. All things then have souls and shadows. And all things die. But their souls are reincarnated again, and what were dead return to life.[17]

Irving Hallowell has noted an especially significant consequence of the pan-spiritualism among the Ojibwa: "Not only animate properties," he writes, "but even 'person' attributes may be projected upon objects which to us clearly belong to a physical inanimate category."[18] Central to the concept of a person is the possibility of entering into social relations. Nonhuman persons may be spoken with, may be honored or insulted, may become allies or adversaries, no less than human persons.

The French fur traders and missionaries of the seventeenth century in the Great Lakes region were singularly impressed by the devotion of the savages with whom they lived to dreams. In 1648, Ragueneau speaking of the Huron, according to Kinietz, first suggested that dreams were "the language of the souls."[19] This expression lacks precision, but I think it goes very much to core of the phenomenon. Through dreams and most dramatically through visions, one came into direct contact with the spirits of both human and nonhuman persons, as it were, naked of bodily vestments. In words somewhat reminiscent of Ragueneau's, Hallowell comments, "it is in dreams that the individual comes into direct communication with the *atiso'kanak,* the powerful 'persons' of the other-than-human class."[20] Given the animistic or pan-spiritualistic world view of the Indians, acute sensitivity and pragmatic response to dreaming makes perfectly good sense.

Dreams and waking experiences are sharply discriminated, but the theater of action disclosed in dreams and visions is continuous with and often the same as the ordinary world. In contrast to the psychologized contemporary Western view in which dreams are images of sorts (like afterimages) existing only "in the mind," the American Indian while dreaming experiences reality, often the same reality as in waking experience, in another form of consciousness, as it were, by means of another sensory modality.

As one lies asleep and experiences people and other animals, places and so on, it is natural to suppose that one's spirit becomes temporarily dissociated from the body and moves about encountering other spirits. Or, as Hallowell says, "when a human being is asleep and dreaming his *otcatcakwin* (vital part, soul), which is the core of the self, may become detached from the body (*miyo*). Viewed by another human being, a person's body may be easily located and observed in space. But his vital part may be somewhere else."[21] Dreaming indeed may be one element in the art of American Indian sorcery ("bear walking" among the Ojibwa). If the state of consciousness in dreams may be seized and controlled, and the phenomenal content of dreams volitionally directed, then the sorcerer may go where he wishes to spy upon his enemies or perhaps affect them in some malevolent way. It follows that dreams should have a higher degree of "truth" than ordinary waking experiences, since in the dream experience the person and everyone he meets is present in spirit, in essential self. This, notice, is precisely contrary to the European assumption that dreams are "false" or illusory and altogether private or subjective. E.g., in the second meditation Descartes, casting around for an example of the highest absurdity, says that it is, "as though I were to say 'I am awake now, and discern some truth; but I do not see it clearly enough; so I will set about going to sleep, so that my dreams may give me a truer and clearer picture of the fact.'" Yet this, in all seriousness, is precisely what the Indian does. The following episode from Hallowell's discussion may serve as illustration. A boy claimed that during a thunderstorm he saw a thunderbird. His elders were skeptical, since to see a thunderbird in such fashion, i.e., with the waking eye, was almost unheard of. He was believed, however, when a man who had dreamed of the thunderbird was consulted and the boy's description was "*verified!*"[22]

The Ojibwa, the Sioux, and if we may safely generalize, most American Indians, lived in a world which was peopled not only by human persons, but by persons and personalities associated with all natural phenomena. In one's practical dealings in such a world it is necessary to one's well-being and that of one's family and tribe to maintain good social relations not only with proximate human persons, one's immediate tribal neighbors, but also with the nonhuman persons abounding in the immediate environment. For example, Hallowell reports that among the Ojibwa "when bears were sought out in their dens in the spring they were addressed, asked to come out so that they could be killed, and an apology was offered to them."[23]

In characterizing the American Indian attitude toward nature with an eye to its eventual comparison to ecological attitudes and conservation values and precepts I have tried to limit the discussion to concepts so fundamental and pervasive as to be capable of generalization. In sum, I have claimed that the typical traditional American Indian attitude was to regard all features of the environment as enspirited. These entities possessed a consciousness, reason, and volition, no less intense and complete than a human being's. The Earth itself, the sky, the winds, rocks, streams, trees, insects, birds, and all other animals therefore had personalities and were thus as fully persons as other human beings. In dreams and visions the spirits of things were directly encountered and could become powerful allies to the dreamer or visionary. We may therefore say that the Indian's social circle, his community, included all the nonhuman natural entities in his locale as well as his fellow clansmen and tribesmen.

Now a most significant conceptual connection obtains in all cultures between the concept of a person, on the one hand, and certain behavioral restraints, on the other. Toward persons it is necessary, whether for genuinely ethical or purely prudential reasons, to act in a careful and circumspect manner. Among the Ojibwa, for example, according to Hallowell, "a moral distinction is drawn between the kind of conduct demanded by the primary necessities of securing a livelihood, or defending oneself against aggression, and unnecessary acts of cruelty. The moral values implied document the consistency of the principle of *mutual obligations* which is inherent in all interactions with 'persons' throughout the Ojibwa world."[24]

The implicit overall metaphysics of American Indian cultures locates human beings in a larger *social,* as well as physical, environment. People belong not only to a human community, but to a community of all nature as well. Existence in this larger society, just as existence in a family and tribal context, place people in an environment in which reciprocal responsibilities and mutual obligations are taken for granted and assumed without question or reflection. Moreover, a person's basic cosmological representations in moments of meditation or cosmic reflection place him or her in a world all parts of which are united through ties of kinship. All creatures, be they elemental, green, finned, winged, or legged, are children of one father and one mother. One blood flows through all; one spirit has divided itself and enlivened all things with a consciousness that is essentially the same. The world around, though immense and overwhelmingly diversified and complex, is bound together through bonds of kinship, mutuality, and reciprocity. It is a world in which a person might feel at home, a relative to all that is, comfortable and secure, as one feels as a child in the midst of a large family. As Brown reports:

But very early in life the child began to realize that wisdom was all about and everywhere and that there were many things to know. There was no such thing as emptiness in the world. Even in the sky there were no vacant places. Everywhere there was life, visible and invisible, and every object gave us great interest to life. Even without human companionship one was never alone. The world teemed with life and wisdom, there was no complete solitude for the Lakota (Luther Standing Bear).[25]

IV

I turn now to the claim made at the beginning of this discussion, viz., that in its practical consequences the American Indian view of nature is on the whole more productive of a cooperative symbiosis of people with their environment than is the view of nature predominant in the Western European tradition.

Respecting the latter, Ian McHarg writes that "it requires little effort to mobilize a sweeping indictment of the physical environment which is [Western] man's creation [and] it takes little more to identify the source of the value system which is the culprit."[26] According to McHarg, the culprit is "the Judeo-Christian-Humanist view which is so unknowing of nature and of man, which has bred and sustained his simple-minded anthropocentricism."[27]

Popular ecologists and environmentalists (perhaps most notably, Rachel Carson and Barry Commoner, along with McHarg and Lynn White, Jr.) have with almost loving attention recited a litany of environmental ills, spoken of "chlorinated hydrocarbons," "phosphate detergents," "nuclear tinkering," and "the gratified bulldozer" in language once reserved for detailing the precincts of Hell and abominating its seductive Prince. Given the frequency with which we are reminded of the symptoms of strain in the global biosphere and the apocalyptic rhetoric in which they are usually cast I may be excused if I omit this particular step from the present argument. Let us stipulate that modern technological civilization (European in its origins) has been neither restrained nor especially delicate in manipulating the natural world.

With somewhat more humor than other advocates of environmental reform Aldo Leopold characterized the modern Western approach to nature thus: "By and large our present problem is one of attitudes and implements. We are remodeling the Alhambra with a steam shovel, and we are proud of our yardage. We shall hardly relinquish the shovel, which after all has many good points, but we are in need of gentler and more objective criteria for its successful use."[28] So far as the historical roots of the environmental crisis are concerned, I have here suggested that the much maligned attitudes arising out of the Judeo-Christian tradition have not been so potent a force in the work of remodeling as the tradition of Western natural philosophy originating among the ancient Greeks and consolidated in modern scientific thought. At least the latter has been as formative of the cultural milieu, one artifact of which is the steam shovel itself, as the former; and together, mixed and blended, so to speak, they create a mentality in which unrestrained environmental exploitation and degradation could almost be predicted in advance.

It seems obvious (especially to philosophers and historians of ideas) that attitudes and values *do* directly "determine" behavior by setting goals (e.g., to subdue the Earth, to have dominion) and, through a conceptual representation of the world, providing means (e.g., mechanics and other applied sciences). Skepticism regarding this assumption, however, has been forthcoming. Yi-Fu Tuan says in "Discrepancies Between Environmental Attitude and Behavior: Examples from Europe and China": "We may *believe* that a world-view which puts nature in subservience to man will lead to the exploitation of nature by man; and one that regards man as simply a component in nature will entail a modest view of his rights and capabilities, and so lead to the establishment of a harmonious relationship between man and his natural environment. But is this correct?"[29] Yi-Fu Tuan thinks not. The evidence from Chinese experience which he cites, however, is ambiguous. Concerning European experience, he marshals examples and cases in point of large scale transformations imposed, with serious ecological consequences, upon the Mediterranean environment by the Greeks and Romans. They were, of course, nominally pagans. He concludes this part of his discussion with the remark that "against this background of the vast transformations of nature in the pagan world, the inroads made in the early centuries of the Christian era were relatively modest."[30] I believe, nevertheless, that my discussion in part two of this paper has explained the environmental impact of Greek and Roman civilization consistently with the general thesis that world view substantially affects behavior! Among the Chinese before Westernization, the facts which Yi-Fu Tuan presents indicate as many congruencies as discrepancies between the traditional Taoist and Buddhist attitude toward nature and Chinese environmental behavior.

A simple deterministic model will not suffice with respect to the question, do cultural attitudes and values really affect the collective behavior of a culture? On the one hand, it seems incredible to think that *all* our conceptualizations, our representations of the nature of nature, are, as it were, mere entertainment, sort of epiphenomena of the mind, while our actions proceed in some blind way from instinctive or genetically programmed sources. After all, our picture of nature defines our theater of action. It defines both the possibilities and limitations which circumscribe human endeavor. On the other hand, the facts of history and everyday experience do not support any simple cause and effect relationship between a given conceptual and valuational set and what people do. My own view is that it is basic to human nature to both consume and modify the natural environment. Representations of the order of nature and the proper relationship of people to that order may have either a tempering, restraining effect on manipulative and exploitative tendencies or they may have an accelerating, exacerbating effect. They also give form and direction to these inherently human drives and thus provide different cultures with their distinctive styles of doing things. It appears to me, further, that in the case of the predominant European mentality, shaped both by the Judeo-Christian and Greco-Roman images of nature and man, the effect was to accelerate the inherent human disposition to consume and modify surroundings. A kind of "take-off" or (to mix metaphors) "quantum leap" occurred, and Western European civilization was propelled for better or worse into its industrial, technological stage with a proportional increase in ecological and environmental distress. The decisive ingredient, the *sine qua non,* may have been the particulars of the European world view.

If the predominant traditional Chinese view of nature and man is, as it has been characterized by Yi-Fu Tuan, "quiescent" and "adaptive," the American Indian view of the world has been characterized as in essence "ecological," for example, by Steward Udall, in the *Quiet Crisis.* In "First Americans, First Ecologists" Udall nostalgically invokes the memory of Thoreau and attributes to his ghost the opinion that "the Indians were, in truth, the pioneer ecologists of this country."[31] To assert without qualification that the American Indians were ecologists is, to say the least, overly bold. Ecology is a part of biology, just as organic chemistry is a part of chemistry. It is a methodic and *quantitative* study of organisms in a contextual, functional relationship to conditions of their several ranges and habitats. Udall, of course, disclaims that he means to suggest that Indians were scientists. One might prefer to say that American Indians intuitively acquired an essentially ecological "outlook," "perspective," or "habit of mind." That would be roughly to say that Indians viewed nature as a matrix of mutually dependent functional components integrated systemically into an organic whole. It would suggest a kind of global or holistic viewpoint; it would also imply an acute sensitivity to the complex factors influencing the life cycles of living things.

To attribute to American Indians, on the one hand, a highly abstract conceptual schematism and, on the other, disinterested, systematic, disciplined, and meticulous observation of minutiae is to press the romantic interpretation of American Indian thought much too far. Much of the material which I have already cited *does* indicate that both woodland and plains Indians were careful students of their natural surroundings. Knowledge of animals and their ways, particularly those of utilitarian value, and knowledge of plants, especially edible and medicinal ones, is a well-known and much respected dimension of traditional Indian cultures. The American Indian pharmacopoeia alone certainly testifies to Indian botanical acumen. My impression, nonetheless, is that the typically Indian representation of nature is more animistic and symbolic than mechanical and functional. The "rules" governing hunting and fishing seem more cast in the direction of achieving the correct etiquette toward game species than *consciously* achieving maximum sustained yield of protein "resources." Medicinal plants were sought as much for their magical, symbolic, and representational virtues as for their chemical effects. Of course, in the case of hunting and fishing, proper manners *are* behavioral restraints and, more often than not, the outcome of their being followed—of correct social forms in respect to bear, beaver, and so on, being observed—was to limit exploitation and, therefore, incidentally, to achieve sustained yield.

To suggest that the Indians were (intuitive or natural or pioneer or even primitive) ecologists, in other words, strikes me as being very much like saying that Indian healers, like Black Elk, were intuitive (etc.) physicians. Indian medicine was not at an earlier stage of development than European medicine, as if moving along the same path some distance behind. It followed a different path altogether. As Black Elk explains, "It is from understanding that power comes; and the power in the [curing] ceremony was in understanding what it meant; for nothing can live well except in a manner that is suited to the way the sacred Power of the World lives and moves."[32] The power that Black Elk employed was, in *his view,* ceremonial and symbolic—what it *meant* not what it *did* to the patient. The cure, thus, was effected through symbolism, not biological mechanism.

The general American Indian world view (at least the one central part of it to which I have called attention) deflected the inertia of day-to-day, year-to-year, subsistence in a way that resulted, on the average, in conservation. Conservation of resources may have been, but probably was not, a *consciously* posited goal, neither a personal ideal nor a tribal policy. *Deliberate* conservation would indeed, ironically, appear to be inconsistent with the spiritual and personal attributes which the Indians regarded as belonging to nature and natural things, since these are represented by most conservationists in the predominant Pinchot tradition as only commodities, subject to scarcity, and therefore in need of prudent "development" and "management." The American Indian posture toward nature was, I suggest, neither ecological nor conservative in the modern scientific sense so much as it was moral or ethical. Animals, plants, and minerals were treated as persons, and conceived to be coequal members of a natural social order.

My cautious claim that American Indians were neither deliberate conservationists nor ecologists in the conventional sense of these terms, but manifested rather a distinctly ethical attitude toward nature and the myriad variety of natural entities, is based upon the following basic points. The American Indians, on the whole, viewed the natural world as enspirited. Natural beings therefore felt, perceived, deliberated, and responded voluntarily as persons. Persons are members of a social order (i.e., part of the operational concept of a person is the capacity for social interaction). Social interaction is limited by (culturally variable) behavioral restraints, rules of conduct, which we call, in sum, good manners, morals, and ethics. The American Indians, therefore, in Aldo Leopold's turn of phrase lived in accordance with a "land ethic." This view is also maintained by Scott Momaday: "Very old in the Native American world view is the conviction that the earth is vital, that there is a spiritual dimension to it, a dimension in which man rightly exists. It follows logically that there are ethical imperatives in this matter."[33]

To point to examples of wastage—buffaloes rotting on the plains under high cliffs or beaver all but trapped-out during the fur trade—which are supposed to deliver the *coup de grace* to all romantic illusions of the American Indian's reverence for nature[34] is very much like pointing to examples of murder and war in European history and concluding therefrom that Europeans were altogether without a humanistic ethic of any sort. What is lacking is a useful understanding of the function of ethics in human affairs. Ethics bear, as philosophers point out, a normative relation to behavior; they do not describe how people actually behave, but rather set out how people ought to behave. Therefore, people are free either to act in accordance with a given ethic or not. The fact that on some occasions some do not scarcely proves that ethics are not on the whole influential and effective behavioral restraints. The familiar Christian ethic has exerted a decisive influence within European civilization; it has inspired noble and even heroic deeds both of individuals and whole societies. The documented influence of the Christian ethic is not in the least diminished by monstrous crimes on the part of individuals. Nor do shameful episodes of national depravity, like the Spanish Inquisition, and genocide, as in Nazi Germany, refute the assertion that a humanistic ethic has palpably affected behavior among members of the European civilization and substantially shaped the character of that civilization itself. By parity of reasoning, examples of occasional destruction of nature on the pre-Columbian American continent and even the extirpation of species, especially during periods of enormous cultural stress, as in the fur trade era, do not, by themselves, refute the assertion that the American Indian lived not only by a tribal ethic but by a land ethic as well, the *overall* and *usual* effect of which was to establish a greater harmony between Indians and their environment than enjoyed by their European successors.

V

This conclusion would not, perhaps, require further elaboration or defense had it not recently been specifically denied by two authors, Calvin Martin and Tom Regan. In this brief polemical epilogue, I therefore undertake to defend it against their criticisms. Martin writes:

> Land-use was therefore *not* so much *a moral issue* for the Indian as technique animated *by spiritual-social obligations* and understandings. . . . There is *nothing here to suggest morality;* certainly there is nothing to suggest the presumptuous, condescending extension of ethics from man-to-man to man-to-land, as the Leopoldian land ethic implies. When

Indians referred to other animal species as "people"—just a different sort of person from man—they were not being quaint. *Nature was a community of such "people"*—"people" for whom man had a great deal of *genuine* regard and with whom he had a contractual relationship to protect one another's interests and fulfill mutual needs. Man and Nature, in short, were joined by compact—*not by ethical ties*—a compact predicated on *mutual esteem.* This was the essence of the traditional Indian-land relationship.[35]

As we see, Martin denies point-blank the major conclusion reached in the previous discussion: that the American Indian world view in its general and common characteristics incorporated an environmental ethos or fostered an ethical attitude toward land and the plants and animals belonging to the land community. But his statement is very puzzling when we analyze it closely and compare it further with some of the things he says immediately before it, for example, that one shared aspect of traditional American Indian world views was "*a genuine respect* for the welfare of other life forms . . . ; [that] aboriginal man felt a *genuine kinship* and often *affection* for wildlife and plant-life . . . ; [and that] wildlife were revered and propitiated not only out of fear that their favors might be withheld, although there was some sense of that, but also because they were felt to be *inherently deserving of such regard.*"[36]

What more do we mean by *morality* or *ethics,* one wonders, than a sense of respect, kinship, affection, regard, and esteem? At the risk of sounding trite, I suggest that it may be merely a "semantical difference" that is involved here. I have called these American Indian attitudes toward wildlife and plant life, mountains and rivers, sky and earth, "moral" or "ethical" attitudes, while Martin apparently wishes to hold the terms *moral* and *ethical* in reserve (though for what he does not say). He does say, "Ethics were involved only when either party broke regulations, if even then"; but he does not explain this cryptic remark or what precisely he means here by *ethics.*[37] My view of what counts as an ethical attitude is more Humean, I suppose, while Martin's is, perhaps, more Kantian. Following Hume, I am willing to label behavior toward nature "ethical" or "moral" which is motivated by esteem, respect, regard, kinship, affection, and sympathy; Kant, on the other hand, regarded all behavior motivated by "mere inclination" (i.e., sentiment or feeling), however unselfish, as lacking genuine moral worth. For Kant, to be counted as ethical an action must be inspired solely by unsentimental duty toward some abstract precept, some categorical imperative, issued by pure reason unsullied by any empirical content. Perhaps this exalted Kantian standard for ethical behavior lies behind Martin's disclaimer. But only by some special and highly technical definition of *ethics,* such as Kant's, can Martin's discussion be rescued from the allegation that it is plainly incoherent, indeed, that it is blatantly self-contradictory.

That issue having been, if not settled, at least clarified, let us consider another of Martin's disavowals, viz., that, more specifically, the overall traditional American Indian attitude toward nature was not akin to Aldo Leopold's land ethic. In this case, the evidence which Martin himself has so masterfully assembled and presented earlier in his book plainly contradicts this negative claim and I can see no way to rescue his discussion from self-contradiction by semantical distinctions or by any other interpretive concessions.

For purposes of illustrating the similarity of his impression of Indian attitudes toward nature and the attitudes toward nature recommended by Leopold's land ethic, consider the following sample from Martin's very full account:

> Nature, as conceived by the traditional Ojibwa, was a *congeries of societies:* every animal, fish and plant species functioned in a *society* that was parallel in all respects to mankinds'. . . .[38]

> As we extend these ideas further, we come to realize that the key to understanding the Indian's role within Nature lies within the notion of *mutual obligation:* man and nature both had to adhere to a prescribed behavior toward one another. . . .[39]

> "According to Cree ideology . . . hunting rests on a kind of *social relationship* between men and animals. Throughout the cycle of hunting rites men emphasize their *respect* by means of symbolic expressions of their subordination to animals. . . ."[40]

To see just how similar the precepts of Leopold's land ethic are to American Indian attitudes, we need only take a closer look at the foundations of the Leopoldian land ethic. First, the primary feature of the land ethic is the representation of nature as a congeries of societies and human/nonhuman relationships as essentially social: "The land ethic simply enlarges the boundary of the *community* to include soils, waters, plants, and animals, or collectively: the land."[41] Second, it is social membership to which ethics and ethical attitudes are correlative: "All ethics so far evolved rest upon a single premise: that the individual is a member of a community of interdependent parts."[42] Third, Leopold takes a more Humean than Kantian approach to the concept of ethics and morality: "It is inconceivable to me," he writes, "that an ethical relation to land can exist without *love, respect,* and *admiration* for land and a high *regard* for its value."[43] As we see, according to the reconstruction that Martin himself so ably and persuasively presents (though he later unaccountably denies it), the traditional American Indian attitude toward nature was in its shared and general assumptions so similar to the essential notions of Leopold's land ethic as to be basically identical with it.

Martin does not explain why he finds Leopold's land ethic "presumptuous" and "condescending," nor shall I speculate on his reason for these epithets. I find Leopold's land ethic to be, if anything, the opposite of presumptuous and condescending. For the sake of comparison, there is a very different sort of "environmental ethic," the so-called animal liberation or animal rights ethic, that is based upon an arbitrary condition, "sentience," for moral considerability which all human beings paradigmatically exhibit, with moral standing then extended to higher "lower animals" on the grounds that they too manifest the same quality.[44] This humane ethic does seem to me to be condescending and presumptuous. In Leopold's land ethic, the *summum bonum* resides in the "biotic community" and moral value or moral standing devolves upon plants, animals, people, and even soils and waters by virtue of their membership in this (vastly) larger-than-human society.[45] As Leopold rather bluntly puts it, "A land ethic changes the role of *Homo sapiens* from conqueror of the land-community to plain member and citizen of it."[46] The privileged position of human beings in the natural order is, thus, in the Leopoldian land ethic, done away with in a single bold stroke. How can this be either presumptuous or condescending?

There is another unjustifiably skeptical remark which Calvin Martin makes as his parting shot at the neoromantic environmentalist view of Indians. He says that

> even if we absolve him of his ambiguous culpability in certain episodes of despoliation, invoking instead *his pristine sentiments toward Nature* [once more, are these not the very soul of an ethical attitude?], the Indian still remains a misfit guru. . . . The Indian's was a profoundly different cosmic vision when it came to interpreting Nature—a vision Western man would never adjust to. There can therefore be no salvation in the Indian's traditional conception of Nature for the troubled environmentalist.[47]

This statement, though brief and scarcely defended, has had wide influence. For example, one reviewer for a distinguished journal devoted to scholarship on American Indians, though thoroughly critical of Martin's ethno-historical methods and his controversial hypothesis of an Indian-animal war, assumes without question or criticism that "his epilogue disparages effectively contemporary views about the ecological Indian."[48]

After having so sharply contrasted the traditional Western European attitude toward nature with the traditional American Indian, perhaps I should wholeheartedly agree with Martin on this particular, especially as the basis of his claim goes back to cultural roots or fundamentals. Indeed, it is precisely because Western culture is grounded, according to Martin, in the Judeo-Christian tradition that "even if he [the Indian] were capable of leading us we could not follow."[49]

A full discussion of this issue goes far beyond the scope of this section. However, in view of Martin's pessimistic conclusion I will hazard a more optimistic suggestion. It may prove to be true that in its own fashion Western science, particularly ecology and the life sciences, but also physics and cosmology, is contributing to the development of a *new* Western world view remarkably similar in *some* ways (but only in some) to that more or less common to American Indian cultures. Science in the twentieth century has retreated from its traditional mechanistic and materialistic biases; indeed, twentieth-century science has been, in just this respect, "revolutionary." Popular Western culture still lags behind. Europeans and Euro-Americans remain, for the most part, nominally Christian and unregenerately materialistic and mechanistic, but the new biocentric and organic world view (embedded in a holistic cosmology and coupled with a field-theory ontology) has already begun to emerge. And there is, further, every reason to expect that eventually it will fully flower in the form of a wholly new popular culture. Present interest in environmental pollution, endangered species, popularized ecology, *and* American Indian environmental attitudes and values are all harbingers of this emerging consciousness.

By the foregoing criticisms I certainly do not intend to belittle Calvin Martin's major achievement in the main body of *Keepers of the Game,* which is a monumental contribution to the recent effort to reconstruct the outlines of the traditional American Indian outlook upon the world. Tom Regan, in a discussion which is very dependent upon Martin's, takes a step toward articulating the very real philosophical problem which Martin may have felt, but was able neither coherently to state nor effectively to resolve. According to Regan, "There is always . . . the possibility that it was fear of the keepers [spiritual warden's of game animals in woodland Indian metaphysics], not appreciation of nature's inherent values, that directed these people's behavior."[50] Regan, therefore, believes that this consideration contributes "an ineradicable layer of ambiguity to the respectful behavior of Native Peoples [toward nature]."[51]

With Regan's observations before us we can now formulate what may have been the actual basis of Martin's reluctance to call American Indian attitudes toward nature "ethical" or "moral." Indian self-interest alone may have dictated deference toward nature, since if such restraint were not forthcoming, nature, everywhere spiritually enlivened, as they believed, would withhold its sustenance or, worse, actively retaliate and the Indians would woefully suffer. Now, any pattern of behavior motivated by mere selfishness on all accounts (including Hume's, to say nothing of Kant's) is certainly not properly described as moral or ethical. Hence, for all their touted spiritualizing of nature and reverence and restraint in taking game and gathering plants, perhaps "there is nothing here to suggest morality," to quote Martin again.

Regan quite fairly points out that "the ambiguity of Amerind behavior is the ambiguity of human behavior, the ancient puzzle over whether, as humans, we are capable of acting out of disinterested respect for what we believe has value in its own right or whether, beneath all manner of ceremony, ritual and verbal glorification of the objects of our attention, there resides, in Kant's memorable words, 'the dear self', the true, the universal sovereign of our wills."[52] As this observation clearly suggests, to describe *any* human behavior whatsoever as "ethical" or "moral" may be naive and incautious. Personally, I think Regan and perhaps Martin (if this is in fact the basis of his reservations) are being overly cynical about human nature. I am more inclined to agree with Hume when he says, respecting human motives of behavior, that while

we may justly esteem our *selfishness* the most considerable, I am sensible, that, generally speaking, the representations of this quality have been carried much too far; and that the descriptions, which certain philosophers delight so much to form of mankind in this particular, are as wide of nature as any accounts of monsters, which we meet with in fables and romances. So far from thinking that men have no affection for anything beyond themselves, I am of opinion, that tho' it be rare to meet with one, who loves any single person better than himself; yet tis rare to meet with one, in whom all the kind affections taken together, do not over-balance all the selfish.[53]

Human beings are not, I think, incapable of acting from motives of affection, sympathy, regard, respect, fellow feeling, reverence, and so on, as well as from purely selfish motives; thus, I think human beings *per se* are not incapable of ethical or moral behavior.

Most folk ethics (as distinct from formal, philosophical theories) take account of and play upon both our moral and selfish sentiments. Take the familiar Christian ethic as an example. We are urged to love God and to love our neighbor as ourselves. Those whose moral sentiments "over-balance" the selfish probably do genuinely behave respectfully, for the most part, toward other persons because they love God and at least sympathize with (if not love) one another. On the other hand, there is an appeal to the dear self. If you do not obey God's commandments and at least act *as if you* respected other persons, God will punish you.

In this respect it seems to me that Indian land ethics are precisely analogous to Western humanitarian ethics. Nowhere in this discussion have I claimed that traditional American Indians were morally better than Westerners in the sense that they were more altruistic and Europeans and Euro-Americans more selfish. Rather, I have claimed that these two broad *cultural traditions* provide very different views of nature and thus very differently excite or stimulate the moral sentiments of their members. In persons belonging to both cultures there is, we may be sure, a mixture of selfishness and altruism. The ratio does not vary so much from culture to culture as from individual to individual. Some individuals in any culture may be very nearly devoid of benevolent feelings, while others are so filled with them that they willingly sacrifice themselves for the sake of their fellows. Hence, Indian land ethics, like the humanitarian religious folk ethic of Western culture, is in this respect bilateral.

In traditional American Indian cultures the animals and plants were commonly portrayed as fellow members of a Great Family or Great Society. They were "persons" worthy of respect, even affection. But if there were individuals (and in every human group there always are) incapable of other-oriented feelings, people who were narrowly selfish, then an appeal to fear of punishment was included, as it were, as a backup motivation to the same forms of action that others were motivated to do because of *moral* sentiments. Noble and generous American Indians would have been mortified to slaughter game animals wantonly and needlessly for sport alone, since the animals were fellow members of an extended family or extended society and had themselves been so generous and cooperative. On the other hand, less noble Indians might have been induced to submit to similar restraints because of fear of retribution. This retributive factor does not suggest, to me at any rate, that American Indian *world views* did not, therefore, include a land ethic (Martin's claim), or even that there is, therefore, an "ineradicable layer of ambiguity" in the average, manifestly restrained, behavior of traditional Indians toward nature (Regan's claim), an ambiguity which makes it impossible for us to decide if their restrained relations with nature were genuinely moral or merely selfish. Such restraints were doubtlessly of both the moral and selfish sorts and the balance between these two behavioral poles varied from person to person and, with respect to a given person, probably from time to time. The point is, American Indian *cultures* provided their members with an environmental ethical *ideal,* however much it may have been from time to time or from person to person avoided, ignored, violated, or for that matter, grudgingly honored because of fear of punishment.

Notes

Callicott teaches in the Philosophy Department of the University of Wisconsin, Stevens Point. Callicott's major professional interests are ancient Greek philosophy and environmental philosophy. He has written extensively on philosophical issues associated with Aldo Leopold and the land ethic. He is coauthor with Thomas Overholt of *Clothed-in-Fur and Other Tales: An Introduction to an Ojibwa World View* (Washington, D.C.: University Press of America, 1982).

First published in *Environmental Ethics* 4, no. 4. Permission to reprint courtesy of *Environmental Ethics* and the author.

1. Joseph E. Brown, "Modes of Contemplation Through Action: North American Indians," *Main Currents in Modern Thought* 30 (1973–74): 60.

2. Calvin Martin, *Keepers of the Game: Indian Animal Relationship and the Fur Trade* (Berkeley: University of California Press, 1978), p. 186.

3. W. Vernon Kinietz, *Indians of the Western Great Lakes, 1615–1760* (Ann Arbor: University of Michigan Press, 1965), p. 115.

4. Thomas S. Kuhn, *The Copernican Revolution: Planetary Astronomy and the Development of Western Thought* (Cambridge, Mass.: Harvard University Press, 1957), p. 237.

5. H. Paul Santmire, "Historical Dimensions of the American Crisis," reprinted from *Dialog* (Summer 1970) in *Western Man and Environmental Ethics,* ed. Ian G. Barbour (Menlo Park, Calif.: Addison-Wesley Publishing Co. 1973), pp. 70–71.

6. Empedocles, *Purifications,* DK 31 B 121, in *An Introduction to Early Greek Philosophy,* trans. John Mansley Robinson (New York: Houghton Mifflin, 1968), p. 152.

7. Aldo Leopold, *A Sand County Almanac and Sketches Here and There* (Oxford: Oxford University Press, 1949), p. 215.

8. Richard Erodes, *Lame Deer: Seeker of Visions* (New York: Simon and Schuster, 1976), pp. 108–09.

9. Ibid., p. 101.

10. Ibid., p. 124.

11. Ibid., pp. 102–03.

12. John G. Neihardt, *Black Elk Speaks* (Lincoln: University of Nebraska Press, p. 3.

13. Ibid., p. 6.

14. Ibid., p. 7.

15. N. Scott Momaday, "A First American Views His Land," *National Geographic* 149 (1976): 14.

16. Ruth M. Underhill, *Red Man's Religion: Beliefs and Practices of the Indians North of Mexico* (Chicago: University of Chicago Press, 1965). p. 40.

17. Diamond Jenness, *The Ojibwa Indians of Parry Island, Their Social and Religious Life,* Canadian Department of Mines Bulletin no. 78, Museum of Canada Anthropological Series, no. 17 (Ottawa, 1935), pp. 20–21. The (Parry Island) Ojibwa, Jenness earlier details, divided spirit into two parts—soul and shadow—though, as Jenness admits, the distinction between the soul and shadow was far from clear and frequently confused by the people themselves.

18. A. Irving Hallowell, "Ojibwa Ontology, Behavior, and World View," *Culture in History: Essays In Honor of Paul Radin,* ed. S. Diamond (New York: Columbia University Press, 1960), p. 26.

19. Kinietz, *Indians of the Western Great Lakes,* p. 126.

20. Hallowell, "Ojibwa Ontology," p. 19.

21. Ibid., p. 41.

22. Ibid., p. 32.

23. Ibid., p. 35.

24. Ibid., p. 47 (emphasis added).

25. Brown, "Modes of Contemplation," p. 64.

26. Ian McHarg, "Values, Process, Form," from *The Fitness of Man's Environment* (Washington, D.C.: Smithsonian Institution Press, 1968), reprinted in Robert Disch, ed., *The Ecological Conscience* (Englewood Cliffs, N.J.: Prentice-Hall, 1970), p. 25.

27. Ibid., p. 98.

28. Leopold, *Sand County Almanac,* pp. 225–26.

29. Yi-Fu Tuan, "Discrepancies Between Environmental Attitude and Behavior," in *Ecology and Religion in History,* eds. David Spring and Eileen Spring (New York: Harper and Row, 1974), p. 92.

30. Ibid., p. 98.

31. Steward Udall, "First Americans, First Ecologists," *Look to the Mountain Top* (San Jose, Calif.: Gousha Publications, 1972), p. 2.

32. Neihardt, *Black Elk Speaks,* p. 212.

33. Momaday, "First American Views," p. 18.

34. The most scurrilous example of this sort of argument with which I am acquainted is Daniel A. Guthre's "Primitive Man's Relationship to Nature," *BioScience* 21 (July 1971): 721–23. In addition to rotting buffalo, Guthrie cites alleged extirpation of pleistocene megafauna by Paleo-Indians, c. 10,000 b.p. (as if that were relevant), and his cheapest shot of all, "the litter of bottles and junked cars to be found on Indian reservations today."

35. Martin, *Keepers,* p. 187 (emphasis added).

36. Ibid., p. 186 (emphasis added).

37. Ibid., p. 187.

38. Ibid., p. 71 (emphasis added).

39. Ibid., p. 77 (emphasis added).

40. Ibid., p. 116 (emphasis added). Martin is here quoting Adrian Tanner with approval.

41. Leopold, *Sand County Almanac,* p. 204 (emphasis added).

42. Ibid., p. 203.

43. Ibid., p. 227 (emphasis added).

44. Cf. J. Baird Callicott, "Animal Liberation: A Triangular Affair," *Environmental Ethics* 2 (1980): 311–38.

45. Cf. ibid., p. 324.

46. Leopold, *Sand County Almanac,* p. 204.

47. Martin, *Keepers,* p. 188 (emphasis added).

48. Kenneth M. Morrison, *American Indian Culture and Research Journal* 3 (1979): 78.

49. Martin, *Keepers,* p. 188.

50. Tom Regan, "Environmental Ethics and the Ambiguity of the Native American Relationship with Nature," in Tom Regan, *All That Dwell Therein: Animal Rights and Environmental Ethics* (Berkeley: University of California Press, 1982), p. 234. Martin does, of course, mention such fears (see n. 38), but does not pursue the line of thought this psychological element suggests to Regan.

51. Ibid.

52. Ibid, p. 235.

53. David Hume, *A Treatise of Human Nature* (Oxford: Clarendon Press, 1960), pp. 486–87.

Part III

*Systematic Environmental Ethics
Reconsidered*

11

Before Environmental Ethics

Anthony Weston

I. Introduction

To think "ecologically," in a broad sense, is to think in terms of the evolution of an interlinked system over time rather than in terms of separate and one-way causal interactions. It is a general habit of mind. Ideas, for example, not just ecosystems, can be viewed in this way. Ethical ideas, in particular, are deeply interwoven with and dependent upon multiple contexts: other prevailing ideas and values, cultural institutions and practices, a vast range of experiences, and natural settings as well. An enormous body of work, stretching from history through the "sociology of knowledge" and back into philosophy, now supports this point.[1]

It is curious that environmental ethics has not yet viewed itself in this way. Or perhaps not so curious, for the results are unsettling. Some theories, in particular, claim to have transcended anthropocentrism in thought. Yet these theories arise within a world that is profoundly and beguilingly anthropocentrized.[2] From an "ecological" point of view, transcending this context so easily seems improbable. In part two this paper, I argue that even the best nonanthropocentric theories in contemporary environmental ethics are still profoundly shaped by and indebted to the anthropocentrism that they officially oppose.

I do not mean that anthropocentrism is inevitable, or even that nonanthropocentric speculation has no place in current thinking. Rather, as I argue in part three, the aim of my critique is to bring into focus the slow process of culturally constituting and consolidating values that underlies philosophical ethics as we know it. My purpose is to broaden our conception of the nature and tasks of ethics, so that we can begin to recognize the "ecology," so to speak, of environmental ethics itself, and thus begin to recognize the true conditions under which anthropocentrism might be overcome.

One implication is that we must rethink the practice of environmental ethics. In part four, I ask how ethics should comport itself at early stages of the process of constituting and consolidating new values. I then apply the conclusions directly to environmental ethics. In particular, the co-evolution of values with cultural institutions, practices, and experience emerges as an appropriately "ecological" alternative to the project of somehow trying to leapfrog the entire culture in thought. In part five, finally, I offer one model of a co-evolutionary approach to environmental philosophy: what I call "enabling environmental practice."

II. Contemporary Nonanthropocentrism

I begin by arguing that contemporary nonanthropocentric environmental ethics remains deeply dependent upon the thoroughly anthropocentrized setting in which it arises. Elsewhere I develop this argument in detail.[3] Here there is only room to sketch some highlights.

For a first example, consider the very phrasing of the question that most contemporary environmental philosophers take as basic: whether "we" should open the gates of moral considerability to "other" animals (sometimes just: "animals"), and/or to such things as rivers and mountains. The opening line of Paul Taylor's *Respect for Nature,* for example, invokes such a model. Environmental ethics, Taylor writes, "is concerned with the moral relations that hold between humans and the natural world."[4]

Taylor's phrasing of "the" question may seem neutral and unexceptionable. Actually, however, it is not neutral at all. The called-for arguments address humans universally and exclusively on behalf of "the natural world." Environmental ethics, therefore, is invited to begin by positing, not by questioning, a sharp divide that "we" must somehow cross, taking that "we" unproblematically to denote all humans. To invoke such a divide, however, is already to take one ethical position among others. For one thing, it is largely peculiar to modern Western cultures. Historically, when humans said "we," they hardly ever meant to include all other humans. Moreover, they often meant to include some individuals of other species. Mary Midgley emphasizes that almost all of the ancient life patterns were "mixed communities," involving humans and an enormous variety of other creatures, from dogs (with whom, she says, we have a "symbiotic" relationship) to reindeer, weasels, elephants, horses, and pigs.[5] One's identifications and loyalties lay not with the extended human species, but with a local and concretely realized network of relationships involving many different species.

Taylor might respond that his question is at least *our* question: the urbanized, modern, Westerner's question. So it is. But it is precisely this recognition of cultural relativity that is crucial. "The" very question that frames contemporary environmental ethics appears to presuppose a particular cultural and historical situation—which is not the only human possibility, and which may itself be the problem. Cross-species identifications, or a more variegated sense of "the natural world," fit in awkwardly, or not at all.

Consider a second example. A defining feature of almost all recent nonanthropocentrism is some appeal to "intrinsic values" in nature. Once again, however, this kind of appeal is actually no more neutral or timelessly relevant than an appeal to all, and only to, humans on behalf of the rest of the world. Intrinsic values in nature are so urgently sought at precisely the moment that the instrumentalization of the world—at least according to a certain sociological tradition[6]—has reached a fever pitch. It is because we now perceive nature as thoroughly reduced to a set of "means" to human ends that an insistence on nature as an "end in itself" seems the only possible response. We may even be right. Still, under other cultural conditions, unthreatened by such a relentless reduction of everything to "mere means," it at least might not seem so *obvious* that we must aspire to a kind of healing that salvages a few non-traditional sorts of ends while consigning everything else to mere resourcehood. Instead, we might challenge the underlying means-ends divide itself, turning toward a more pragmatic sense of the interconnectedness of all of our values.[7]

Also, unthreatened in this way, we might not be tempted to metaphysical turns in defense of the values we cherish. Jim Cheney has suggested that the turn to metaphysics in some varieties of contemporary environmental ethics represents, like the ancient Stoics turn to metaphysics, a desperate self-defense rather than a revelation of a genuine nonanthropocentrism. Cheney charges in particular that a certain kind of radical environmentalism, which he dubs "Ecosophy S," has been tempted into a "neo-Stoic" philosophy—an identification with nature on the level of the universe as a whole—because neo-Stoicism offers a way to identify with nature without actually giving up control. In this way, abstract arguments become a kind of philosophical substitute for "real encounter" with nature.[8]

Cheney argues that Ecosophy S reflects a profoundly contemporary psychological dynamic. I want to suggest that it also reflects the diminished character of the world in which we live. The experiences for which Ecosophy S is trying to speak are inevitably marginalized in a thoroughly anthropocentrized culture. They are simply not accessible to most people or even understandable to many. Although wild experience *may* actually *be* the starting point for Ecosophy S, there are only a few, ritualized, and hackneyed ways to actually speak for it in a culture that does not share it. Thus—again, under present circumstances—environmental ethics may be literally driven to abstraction.

Once again it may even be true that abstraction is *our* only option. Nonetheless, in a different world, truly beyond anthropocentrism, we might hope for a much less abstract way of speaking of and for wild experience—for enough sharing of at least the glimmers of wild experience that we can speak of it directly, even perhaps invoking a kind of love. But such a change, once again, would leave contemporary nonanthropocentric environmental ethics—whether neo-Stoic or just theoretical—far behind.

As a third and final example, consider the apparently simple matter of what sorts of criticism are generally regarded as "responsible" and what sorts of alternatives are generally regarded as "realistic." The contemporary anthropocentrized world, which is, in fact, the product of an immense project of world reconstruction that has reached a frenzy in the modern age, has become simply the taken-for-granted reference point for what is "real," for what must be accepted by any responsible criticism. The absolute pervasiveness of internal combustion engines, for example, is utterly new, confined to the last century and mostly to the last generation. By now very few Westerners ever get out of earshot of internal combustion engines for more than a few hours at a time. The environmental consequences are staggering, the long-term effects of constant noise on "mental health" are clearly worrisome, and so on. Yet, this technology has so thoroughly embedded itself in our lives that even mild proposals to restrict internal combustion engines seem impossibly radical. This suddenly transmuted world, the stuff of science fiction only fifty years ago, now just as suddenly defines the very limits of imagination. When we think of "alternatives," all we can imagine are car pools and buses.

Something similar occurs in philosophical contexts. Many of our philosophical colleagues have developed a careful, neutral, critical style as a point of pride. But in actual practice this style is only careful, neutral, critical in certain directions. It is not possible to suggest anything *different,* for the project of going beyond anthropocentrism still looks wild, incautious, intellectually overexcited. Anthropocentrism itself, however, is almost never scrutinized in the same way. Apparently, it just forms part of the "neutral" background: it seems to be no more than what the careful, critical thinker can *presuppose.* Thus, it is the slow excavation and the logical "refutation" of anthropocentrism that, perforce, occupy our time—rather than, for one example, a much less encumbered, more imaginative exploration of other possibilities, less fearful of the disapproval of the guardians of Reason, or, for another example, a psychological exploration of anthropocentrism itself, taking it to be more like a kind of lovelessness or blindness than a serious philosophical position. Anthropocentrism still fills the screen, still dominates our energies. It delimits what is "realistic" because in many ways it determines what "reality" itself is.

III. Ethics in Social Context

The conclusion of the argument so far might only seem to be that we need better nonanthropocentrisms: theories that rethink Taylor's basic question, theories that are not so easily seduced by intrinsic values, and so on. Although such theories would be useful changes, the argument just offered also points toward a much more fundamental conclusion, one upon which very large questions of method depend. If the most rigorous and sustained attempts to transcend anthropocentrism still end up in its orbit, profoundly shaped by the thought and practices of the anthropocentrized culture within which they arise, then we may begin to wonder whether the project of transcending culture in ethical thought is, in fact, workable *at all*. Perhaps ethics requires a very different self-conception.

Here, moreover, is a surprising fact: ethics generally *has* a very different self-conception. Most "mainstream" ethical philosophers now readily acknowledge that the values they attempt to systematize are indeed deeply embedded in and co-evolved with social institutions and practices. John Rawls, for example, who at earlier moments appeared to be the very incarnation of the philosophical drive toward what he himself called an "Archimedean point" beyond culture, now explicitly justifies his theory only by reference to its "congruence with our deeper understanding of ourselves and our aspirations, and our realization that, given our history and the traditions embedded in our public life, it is the most reasonable doctrine for us." For *us,* culture answers "our" questions. "We are not," he says, "trying to find a conception of justice suitable for all societies regardless of their social or historical circumstances." Instead, the theory "is intended simply as a useful basis of agreement in our society."[9] The same conclusion is also the burden, of course, of an enormous body of criticism supposing Rawls to be making a less culturally dependent claim. Rawls, thus, does not transcend his social context at all. His theory is, rather, in a Nietzschean phrase, a particularly scholarly way of *expressing* an already established set of values. That contemporary nonanthropocentric environmental ethics does not transcend *its* social context, therefore, becomes much less surprising. At least it is in good company.

Similarly, John Arras, in an article surveying Jonsen and Toulmin's revival of casuistry, as well as the Rawls-Walzer debate, remarks almost in passing that all of these philosophers agree that "there is no escape from the task of interpreting the meanings embedded in our social practices, institutions, and history."[10] Michael Walzer argues for a plurality of justice values rooted in the varied "cultural meanings" of different goods.[11] Alasdair MacIntyre makes the rootedness of values in "traditions" and "practice" central to his reconception of ethics.[12] Charles Taylor localizes the appeal to rights within philosophical, theological, and even aesthetic movements in the modern West.[13] Sabina Lovibond updates Wittgensteinian "form of life" ethics along sociologically informed "expressivist" lines.[14]

It may seem shocking that the "Archimedean" aspirations for ethics have been abandoned with so little fanfare. From the point of view of what we might call the "theology of ethics," it probably is. Day to day, however, and within the familiar ethics of persons, justice, and rights practiced by most of the philosophers just cited, it is less surprising. Operating within a culture in which certain basic values are acknowledged, at least verbally, by nearly everyone, there is little practical need to raise the question of the ultimate origins or warrants of values. Because the issue remains metaphilosophical and marginal to what are supposed to be the more systematic tasks of ethics, we can acquiesce in a convenient division of labor with the social sciences, ceding to them most of the historical and cultural questions about the evolution of values, while keeping the project of systematizing and applying values for our own. "Scholarly forms of expression" of those values—or at least systematic forms of expression, "rules to live by"—are then precisely what we want.

It now seems entirely natural, for example, to view persons as "centers of autonomous choice and valuation," in Taylor's words, "giving direction to their lives on the basis of their own values," having a sense of identity over time, and so on. It also seems natural to point to this "belief system" to ground respect for persons, as Taylor also points out. He does *not* ask how such a belief system came into being and managed to rearrange human lives around itself. He does *not* need to ask. But we need at least to remember that these are real and complex questions. It is only such processes, finally running their courses, that make possible the consensus behind the contemporary values in the first place. Weber traces our belief system about persons, in part, to Calvinist notions about the inscrutability of fate, paradoxically leading to an outwardly calculating possessiveness coupled with rigid "inner asceticism," both self-preoccupied in a fundamentally new way. In addition, he traces it to the development of a system of increasingly impersonal commercial transactions that disabled and disconnected older, more communal ties between people.[15] The cultural relativity of the notion of persons is highlighted, meanwhile, by its derivation from the Greek dramatic "personae," perhaps the first emergence of the idea of a unique and irreplaceable individual. A tribal African or Native American would never think of him or herself in this way.[16]

It may be objected that to stress the interdependence of ethical ideas with cultural institutions, practices, and experience simply reduces ethical ideas to epiphenomena of such factors. However, the actual result is quite different. The flaw lies with the objection's crude (indeed, truly "vulgar," as in "vulgar Marxist") model of causation. Simple, mechanical, one-way link-ages between clearly demarcated "causes" and "effects" do not characterize cultural phenomena (or, for that matter, *any* phenomena). Thus, the question is emphatically *not* whether ethical ideas are "cause" or "effect" in cultural systems, as if the only alternative to being purely a cause is to be purely an effect. Causation in complex, interdependent, and evolving systems with multiple feedback loops—that is, an "ecological" conception of causation—is a far better model.[17]

One implication of such a model, moreover, is that fundamental change (at least constructive, non-catastrophic change) is likely to be slow. Practices, habits, institutions, arts, and ideas all must evolve in some coordinated way. Even the physical structure of the world changes. Individualism and its asso-ciated idea of privacy, for example, developed alongside a revolution in home and furniture design.[18] Thus, it may not even be that visionary ethical ideas (or anything else visionary, e.g., revolutionary architecture) are impos-sible at any given cultural stage, but rather that such ideas simply cannot be recognized or understood, given all of the practices, experiences, etc. along-side of which they have to be placed, and given the fact that they cannot be immediately applied in ways that will contribute to their development and improvement.[19] To use Darwinian metaphor, all manner of "mutations" may be produced at any evolutionary stage, but conditions will be favorable for only a few of them to be "selected" and passed on.[20]

It may also be objected that any such view is hopelessly "relativistic." Although the term *relativism* now seems to be confused and ambiguous, there is at least one genuine concern here: if values are thoroughly relativized to culture, rational criticism of values may become impossible. In fact, how-ever, rational criticism remains entirely possible—only its "standpoint" is in-ternal to the culture it challenges, rather than (as in the Archimedean image) external to it. Much of what we tend to regard as radical social criticism rein-vokes old, even central, values of a culture rather than requiring us to somehow transcend the culture in thought. Weber, for example, reread Luther's conception of the individual's relation to God as an extension of the already old and even revered monastic ideal to society at large. Likewise, the challenges of the 1960s in the U.S. arguably appealed not to new values but to some of the oldest and most deeply embedded values of our culture. The Students for Democratic Society's "Port Huron Statement" persistently speaks in biblical language; the Black Panthers invoked the Declaration of Independence; the Civil Rights Movement was firmly grounded in Christianity. In his 1981 encyclical "Laborem Exercens," Pope John Paul II appealed to Genesis to ground a stunning critique of work in industrial soci-eties reminiscent of the early Marx.[21]

In general, those who worry about the implications of social-scientific "relativism" for the rationality of ethics should be reassured by Richard Bernstein's delineation of a kind of rationality "beyond objectivism and relativism," a much more pragmatic and processual model of reason built upon the historical and social embeddedness and evolution of ideas.[22] Those who worry that "relative" values will be less serious than values that can claim absolute allegiance might be reassured by the argument that it is precisely the profound embeddedness of our ethical ideas within their cultural contexts that marks their seriousness. For *us,* of course. Nevertheless, that is whom we speak of and to.

Although these last remarks are very sketchy, they at least serve to suggest that a sociological or "evolutionary" view of values is not somehow the death knell of ethics. Instead, such a view seems to be almost an enabling condition of modern philosophical ethics. At the same time, however, "mainstream" ethics does not need to be, and certainly *has* not been, explicit on this point. The actual origins of values are seldom mentioned at all, and the usual labels—for example, Lovibond's "expressivism" and even MacIntyre's "traditions"—only indirectly suggest any social-scientific provenance. But it is time to be more explicit. As I argue below, large issues outside the "mainstream" may depend upon it.

IV. The Practice of Ethics at Originary Stages

In order to begin to draw some of the necessary conclusions from this "evolutionary" view of values, let us turn our attention to the appropriate comportment for ethics at what we might call the "originary stages" of the development of values: stages at which new values are only beginning to be constituted and consolidated. In the case of the ethics of persons, for example, we must try to place ourselves back in the time when respect for persons, and persons themselves, were far less secure—not fixed, secure, or "natural" as they now seem, but rather strange, forced, truncated, the way they must have seemed to, say, Calvin's contemporaries. How then should—how *could*—a proto-ethics of persons proceed in such a situation?

First, such early stages in the development of a new set of values require a great deal of exploration and metaphor. Only later do the new ethical notions harden into analytic categories. For example, although the concept of the "rights" of persons now may be invoked with a fair degree of rigor, throughout most of its history it played a much more open-ended role, encouraging the treatment of whole new classes of people as rights holders—slaves, foreigners, propertyless persons, women—in ways previously unheard of, and in ways that, literally speaking, were misuses of the concept. (Consider "barbarian rights." The very concept of *barbarian* seems to preclude one of them being one of "us," i.e., Greeks, i.e., rights holders.) This malleable rhetoric of rights also in part *created* "rights holders." Persuading someone that he or she has a right to something, for example, or persuading a whole class or group that their rights have been violated, dramatically changes his, her, or their behavior, and ultimately reconstructs his, her, or their belief systems and experiences. Even now the creative and rhetorical possibilities of the concept of rights have not been exhausted. It is possible to read the sweeping and inclusive notion of rights in the United Nations Declaration of Human Rights in this light, for instance, rather than dismissing it as conceptually confused, as do legalistic thinkers.[23]

Moreover, the process of co-evolving values and practices at originary stages is seldom a smooth process of progressively filling in and instantiating earlier outlines. Instead, we see a variety of fairly incompatible outlines coupled with a wide range of proto-practices, even social experiments of various sorts, all contributing to a kind of cultural working through of a new set of possibilities. The process *seems* smooth in retrospect only because the values and practices that ultimately win out rewrite the history of the others so that the less successful practices and experiments are obscured—much as successful scientific paradigms, according to Kuhn, rewrite their own pasts so that in retrospect their evolution seems much smoother, more necessary, and more univocal than they actually were. Great moments in the canonical history of rights, for example, include the Declaration of Independence and the Declaration of the Rights of Man, capitalism's institutionalization of rights to property and wealth, and now the persistent defense of a non-positivistic notion of rights for international export. *Not* included are the utopian socialists many experimental communities, which often explicitly embraced (what *became*) non-standard, even anti-capitalistic notions of rights, such sustained and massive struggles as the labor movement's organization around working persons rights, and the various modern attempts by most social democracies to institutionalize rights to health care.

A long period of experimentation and uncertainty, thus, ought to be expected and even welcomed in the originary stages of any new ethics. Again, as I suggested above, even the most familiar aspects of personhood co-evolved with a particular, complex, and even wildly improbable set of ideas and practices. Protestantism contributed not just a theology, and not just Calvin's peculiar and (if Weber is right) peculiarly world-historical "inner-world asceticism," but also such seemingly simple projects as an accessible Bible in the vernacular. Imagine the extraordinary impact of being able to read the holy text oneself after centuries of only the most mediated access. Imagine the extraordinary self-preoccupation created by having to choose for the first time between rival versions of the same revelation, with not only one's eternal soul in the balance, but often one's earthly life as well. Only against such a background of practice did it become possible to begin to experience oneself as an individual, separate from others, beholden to inner voices and "one's own values," "giving direction to one's life" oneself, as Taylor puts it, and bearing the responsibility for one's choices.

Since we now look at the evolution of the values of persons mostly from the far side, it is easy to miss the fundamental contingency of those values and their dependence upon practices, institutions, and experiences that were for their time genuinely uncertain and exploratory. Today we are too used to that easy division of labor that leaves ethics only the systematic tasks of "expressing" a set of values that is already established, and abandons the originary questions to the social sciences. As a result, ethics is incapacitated when it comes to dealing with values that are *now* entering the originary stage. Even when it is out of its depth, we continue to imagine that systematic ethics, such as the ethics of the person, is the only kind of ethics there is. We continue to regard the contingency, open-endedness, and uncertainty of "new" values as an objection to them, ruling them out of ethical court entirely, or else as a kind of embarrassment to be quickly papered over with an ethical theory.

This discussion has direct application to environmental ethics. First and fundamentally, if environmental ethics is indeed at an originary stage, we can have only the barest sense of what ethics for a culture truly beyond anthropocentrism would actually look like. The Renaissance and the Reformation did not simply actualize some preexisting or easily anticipated notion of persons, but rather played a part in the larger *co-evolution* of respect for persons. What would emerge could only be imagined in advance in the dimmest of ways, or not imagined at all. Similarly, we are only now embarking on an attempt to move beyond anthropocentrism, and we simply cannot predict in advance where even another century of moral change will take us.

Indeed, when anthropocentrism is finally cut down to size, there is no reason to think that what we will have or need in its place will be something called *non*anthropocentrism at all—as if that characterization would even begin to be useful in a culture in which anthropocentrism had actually been transcended. Indeed, it may not even be any kind of "centrism" whatsoever, i.e., some form of hierarchically structured ethics. It is already clear that hierarchy is by no means the only option.[24]

Second and correlatively, at this stage, exploration and metaphor are crucial to environmental ethics. Only later can we harden originary notions into precise analytic categories. Any attempt to appropriate the moral force of rights language for (much of) the trans-human world, for example, ought to be expected from the start to be *im*precise, literally confused. (Consider "animal rights." The very concept of *animal* seems to preclude one of them being one of "us," i.e., persons, i.e., rights holders.) It need not be meant as a description of prevailing practice; rather, it should be read as an attempt to *change* the prevailing practice. Christopher Stone's book *Should Trees Have Standing? Toward Legal Rights for Natural Objects,* for example, makes a revisionist proposal about legal arrangements; it does not offer an analysis of the existing concept of rights.[25]

Something similar should be understood when we are invited to conceive not only animals or trees as rights holders, but also the land as a community and the planet as a person. All such arguments should be understood to be rhetorical, in a non-pejorative, pragmatic sense: they are suggestive and open-ended sorts of challenges, even proposals for Deweyan kinds of social reconstruction, rather than attempts to demonstrate particular conclusions on the basis of premises that are supposed to already be accepted.[26] The force of these arguments lies in the way they open up the possibility of new connections, not in the way they settle or "close" any questions. Their work is more creative than summative, more prospective than retrospective. Their chief function is to provoke, to loosen up the language, and correspondingly our thinking, to fire the imagination: to *open* questions, not to settle them.

The founders of environmental ethics were explorers along these lines. Here I want, in particular, to reclaim Aldo Leopold from the theorists. Bryan Norton reminds us, for example, that Leopold's widely cited appeal to the "integrity, stability, and beauty of the biotic community" occurs in the midst of a discussion of purely economic constructions of the land. It is best read, Norton says, as a kind of counterbalance and challenge to the excesses of pure commercialism, rather than as a criterion for moral action all by itself. Similarly, John Rodman has argued that Leopold's work should be read as an environmental ethic *in process,* complicating the anthropocentric picture more or less from within, rather than as a kind of proto-system, simplifying and unifying an entirely new picture, that can be progressively refined in the way that utilitarian and deontological theories have been refined over the last century.[27] Leopold insists, after all, that "the land ethic [is] *a product of social evolution. . . .* Only the most superficial student of history supposes that Moses 'wrote' the Decalogue; it evolved in the mind [and surely also in the practices!] of the thinking community, and Moses wrote a tentative summary of it. . . . I say 'tentative' because evolution never stops."[28] It might be better to regard Leopold not as purveying a general ethical theory at all, but rather as simply *opening* some questions, unsettling some assumptions, and prying the window open just far enough to lead, in time, to much wilder and certainly more diverse suggestions or "criteria."

Third and more generally, as I put it above, the process of evolving values and practices at originary stages is seldom a smooth process of progressively filling in and instantiating earlier outlines. At the originary stage we should instead expect a variety of fairly incompatible outlines coupled with a wide range of proto-practices, even social experiments of various sorts, all contributing to a kind of cultural working-through of a new set of possibilities. In environmental ethics, we arrive at exactly the opposite view from that of J. Baird Callicott, for example, who insists that we attempt to formulate, right now, a complete, unified, even "closed" (his term) theory of environmental ethics. Callicott even argues that contemporary environmental ethics should not tolerate more than one basic type of value, insisting on a "univocal" environmental ethic.[29] In fact, however, as I argued above, originary stages are the worst possible times at which to demand that we all speak with one voice. Once a set of values is culturally consolidated, it may well be possible, perhaps even necessary, to reduce them to some kind of consistency. But environmental values are unlikely to be in such a position for a very long time. The necessary period of ferment, cultural experimentation, and thus *multi*-vocality is only *beginning*. Although Callicott is right, we might say, about the demands of systematic ethical theory at later cultural stages, he is wrong—indeed, wildly wrong—about what stage environmental values have actually reached.

V. Enabling Environmental Practice

Space for some analogues to the familiar theories does remain in the alternative environmental ethics envisioned here. I have argued that although they are unreliable guides to the ethical future, they might well be viewed as another kind of ethical experiment or proposal rather like, for example, the work of the utopian socialists. However unrealistic, they may, nonetheless, play a historical and transitional role, highlighting new possibilities, inspiring reconstructive experiments, even perhaps eventually provoking environmental ethics equivalent of a Marx.

It should be clear, though, that the kind of constructive activity suggested by the argument offered here goes far beyond the familiar theories as well. Rather than systematizing environmental values, the overall project at this stage should be to begin *co-evolving* those values with practices and institutions that make them even *un*systematically possible. It is this point that I now want to develop by offering one specific example of such a co-evolutionary practice. It is by no means the only example. Indeed, the best thing that could be hoped, in my view, is the emergence of many others. But it is *one* example, and it may be a good example to help clarify how such approaches might look, and thus to clear the way for more.

A central part of the challenge is to create the social, psychological, and phenomenological preconditions—the conceptual, experiential, or even quite literal "space"—for new or stronger environmental values to evolve. Because such creation will "enable" these values, I call such a practical project *enabling environmental practice*.

Consider the attempt to create actual, physical spaces for the emergence of trans-human experience, *places* within which some return to the experience of and immersion in natural settings is possible. Suppose that certain places are set aside as quiet zones, places where automobile engines, lawnmowers, and low-flying airplanes are not allowed, and yet places where people will live. On one level, the aim is modest: simply to make it possible to hear the birds, the winds, and the silence once again. If bright outside lights were also banned, one could see the stars at night and feel the slow pulsations of the light over the seasons. A little creative zoning, in short, could make space for increasingly divergent styles of living on the land—for example, experiments in recycling and energy self-sufficiency, Midgleyan mixed communities of humans and other species, serious "re-inhabitation" (though perhaps with more emphasis on place and community than upon the individual re-inhabiters), the "ecosteries" that have been proposed on the model of monasteries, and other possibilities not yet even imagined.[30]

Such a project is not utopian. If we unplugged a few outdoor lights and rerouted some roads, we could easily have a first approximation in some parts of the country right now. In gardening, for example, we already experience some semblance of mixed communities. Such practices as beekeeping, moreover, already provide a model for a symbiotic relation with the "biotic community." It is not hard to work out policies to protect and extend such practices.

Enabling environmental practice is, of course, a *practice*. Being a practice, however, does not mean that it is not also philosophical. Theory and practice interpenetrate here. In the abstract, for example, the concept of "natural settings," just invoked, has been acrimoniously debated, and the best-known positions are unfortunately more or less the extremes. Social ecologists insist that no environment is ever purely natural, that human beings have already remade the entire world, and that the challenge is really to get the process under socially progressive and politically inclusive control. Some deep ecologists, by contrast, argue that only wilderness is the "real world."[31] Both views have something to offer. Nevertheless, it may be that only from within the context of a new practice, even so simple a practice as the attempt to create "quiet places," will we finally achieve the necessary distance to take what we can from the purely philosophical debate, and also to go beyond it toward a better set of questions and answers.

Both views, for example, unjustly discount "encounter." On the one hand, nonanthropocentrism should not become anti-anthropocentrism: the aim should not be to push humans out of the picture entirely, but rather to open up the possibility of reciprocity *between* humans and the rest of nature. Nevertheless, reciprocity does require a space that is not wholly permeated by humans either. What we need to explore are possible realms of *interaction*.

Neither the wilderness nor the city (as we know it) is "the real world," if we must talk in such terms. We might take as the most "real" places the places where humans and other creatures, honored in their wildness and potential reciprocity, can come together, perhaps warily, but at least openly. The work of Wendell Berry is paradigmatic of this kind of philosophical engagement. Berry writes, for example, of "the phenomenon of edge or margin, that we know to be one of the powerful attractions of a diversified landscape, both to wildlife and to humans." These margins are places where domesticity and wildness meet. Mowing his small hayfield with a team of horses, Berry encounters a hawk who lands close to him, watching carefully but without fear. The hawk comes, he writes, "because of the conjunction of the small pasture and its wooded borders, of open hunting ground and the security of trees. . . . The human eye itself seems drawn to such margins, hungering for the difference made in the countryside by a hedgy fencerow, a stream, or a grove of trees. These margins are biologically rich, the meeting of two kinds of habitat. . . ."[32] The hawk would not have come, he says, if the field had been larger, or if there had been no trees, or if he had been plowing with a tractor. Interaction is a fragile thing, and we need to pay careful attention to its preconditions. As Berry shows, attending to interaction is a deeply philosophical and phenomenological project as well as a practical one—but, nonetheless, it always revolves around and refers back to practice. Without actually maintaining a farm, he would know very little of what he knows, and the hawk would not—*could* not—have come to him.

Margins are, of course, only one example. They can't be the whole story. Many creatures avoid them. It is for this reason that the spotted owl's survival depends on large tracts of old-growth forest. Nonetheless, they are still *part* of the story—a part given particularly short shrift, it seems, by all sides in the current debate.

It is not possible in a short article to develop the kind of philosophy of "practice" that would be necessary to work out these points fully. However, I can at least note two opposite pitfalls in speaking of practice. First, it is not as if we come to this practice already knowing what values we will find or exemplify there. Too often the notion of practice in contemporary philosophy has degenerated into "application," i.e., of prior principles or theories. At best, it might provide an opportunity for feedback from practice to principle or theory. I mean something more radical here. Practice is the opening of the "space" for interaction, for the reemergence of a larger world. It is a kind of exploration. We do not know in advance what we will find. Berry had to *learn,* for example, about margins. Gary Snyder and others propose Buddhist terms to describe the necessary attitude, a kind of mindfulness, attentiveness. Tom Birch calls it the "primary sense" of the notion of "consideration."[33]

On the other hand, this sort of open-ended practice does not mean reducing our own activity to zero, as in some form of quietism. I do not mean that we simply "open, and it will come." There is not likely to be any single and simple set of values that somehow emerges once we merely get out of the way. Berry's view is that a more open-ended and respectful relation to nature requires constant and creative *activity*—in his case, constant presence in nature, constant interaction with his own animals, maintenance of a place that maximizes margins. Others will, of course, choose other ways. The crucial thing is that humans must neither monopolize the picture entirely nor absent ourselves from it completely, but rather try to live in interaction, to create a space for genuine encounter as part of our ongoing reconstruction of our own lives and practices. What will come of such encounters, what will emerge from such sustained interactions, we cannot yet say.

No doubt it will be argued that Berry is necessarily an exception, that small unmechanized farms are utterly anachronistic, and that any real maintenance of margins or space for encounter is unrealistic in mass society. Perhaps. But these automatically accepted commonplaces are also open to argumentation and experiment. Christopher Alexander and his colleagues, in *A Pattern Language* and elsewhere, for example, make clear how profoundly even the simplest architectural features of houses, streets, and cities structure our experience of nature—and that they can be consciously redesigned to change those experiences. Windows on two sides of a room make it possible for natural light to suffice for daytime illumination. If buildings are built on those parts of the land that are in the worst condition, not the best, we thereby leave the most healthy and beautiful parts alone, while improving the worst parts. On a variety of grounds, Alexander and his colleagues argue for the presence of both still and moving water throughout the city, for extensive common land—"accessible green," sacred sites, and burial grounds within the city—and so on. If we build mindfully, they argue, maintaining and even expanding margins is not only possible, but easy, even with high human population densities.[34]

VI. Conclusion

In the last section, I offered only the barest sketch of enabling environmental practice: a few examples, not even a general typology. To attempt a more systematic typology of its possible forms at this point seems to me premature, partly because ethics has hitherto paid so little attention to the cultural constitution of values that we have no such typology, and partly because the originary stage of environmental values is barely underway.

Moreover, enabling environmental practice is itself only one example of the broader range of philosophical activities invited by what I call the co-evolutionary view of values. I have not denied that even theories of rights, for instance, have a place in environmental ethics. However, it is not the only "place" there is, and rights themselves, at least when invoked beyond the sphere of persons, must be understood (so I argue) in a much more metaphorical and exploratory sense than usual. This point has also been made by many others, of course, but usually with the intention of ruling rights talk out of environmental ethics altogether. A pluralistic project is far more tolerant and inclusive. Indeed, it is surely an advantage of the sort of umbrella conception of environmental ethics I am suggesting here that nearly all of the current approaches may find a place in it.

Because enabling environmental practice is closest to my own heart, I have to struggle with my own temptation to make it the whole story. It is not. Given the prevailing attitudes, however, we need to continue to insist that it is *part* of the story. Of course, we might still have to argue at length about whether and to what degree enabling environmental practice is "philosophical" or "ethical." My own view, along pragmatic lines, is that it is both, deeply and essentially. Indeed, for Dewey the sustained practice of social reconstruction—experimental, improvisatory, and pluralistic—is the most central ethical practice of all. But that is an argument for another time. It is, nevertheless, one of the most central tasks that now calls to us.

Notes

Weston, who teaches in the Department of Philosophy at the State University of New York, Stony Brook, is the author of *Toward Better Problems: New Perspectives on Abortion, Animal Rights, the Environment, and Justice* (Philadelphia: Temple University Press, 1992) and *A Rulebook for Arguments,* 2d ed. (Indianapolis: Hackett Publishing Company, 1992). The author wishes to thank Holmes Rolston, III, Jennifer Church, Jim Cheney, Tom Regan, Tom Birch, and two anonymous referees for many helpful comments on an earlier version of this paper.

First published in *Environmental Ethics* 14, no. 4. Permission to reprint courtesy of *Environmental Ethics* and the author.

1. Some landmarks of this body of work come into view in the later discussion. For a general overview of work on ethical ideas in particular from this perspective, see Maria Ossowska, *Social Determinants of Moral Ideas* (Philadelphia: University of Pennsylvania Press, 1970).

2. I distinguish *anthropocentrism* as a philosophical position, issuing in an ethic, from the practices and institutions in which that ethic is embodied, which I call "anthropocen*trized.*"

3. See Anthony Weston, "Non-Anthropocentrism in a Thoroughly Anthropocentrized World," *The Trumpeter* 8, no. 3 (1991): 108–12.

4. Paul Taylor, *Respect for Nature* (Princeton, N.J.: Princeton University Press, 1986), p. 3.

5. Mary Midgley, *Animals and Why They Matter* (Athens: University of Georgia Press, 1983), p. 118. See also Arne Naess, "Self-Realization in Mixed Communities of Humans, Bears, Sheep, and Wolves," *Inquiry* 22 (1979): 231–41.

6. A tradition beginning with Max Weber, *The Protestant Ethic and the Spirit of Capitalism,* trans. Talcott Parsons (New York: Scribner's, 1958) and *Economy and Society: An Outline of Interpretive Sociology,* ed. G. Roth and C. Wittich (Berkeley: University of California Press, 1978), and carried into the present in different ways by, e.g., Morris Berman, *The Reenchantment of the World* (Ithaca, N.Y.: Cornell University Press, 1981) and Albert Borgmann, *Technology and the Character of Contemporary Life* (Chicago: University of Chicago Press, 1984).

7. For an argument in defense of this point, see Anthony Weston, "Beyond Intrinsic Value: Pragmatism in Environmental Ethics," *Environmental Ethics* 7 (1985): 321–39.

8. Jim Cheney, "The Neo-Stoicism of Radical Environmentalism," *Environmental Ethics* 11 (1989): 293–325.

9. John Rawls, "Kantian Constructivism in Moral Theory," *Journal of Philosophy* 77 (1980): 318; and "Justice as Fairness: Political, not Metaphysical," *Philosophy and Public Affairs* 14 (1985): 228.

10. John Arras, "The Revival of Casuistry in Bioethics," *Journal of Medicine and Philosophy* 16 (1991): 44.

11. Michael Walzer, *Spheres of Justice* (New York: Basic Books, 1983).

12. Alasdair MacIntyre, *After Virtue* (Notre Dame, Ind.: University of Notre Dame Press, 1981).

13. Charles Taylor, *Sources of the Self* (Cambridge, Mass.: Harvard University Press, 1989).

14. Sabina Lovibond, *Realism and Imagination in Ethics* (Minnesota: University of Minnesota Press, 1983).

15. Weber, *The Protestant Ethic and the Spirit of Capitalism* and *Economy and Society.*

16. For classic examples of selves in other keys, see Louis Dumont, *Homo Hierarchichus* (Chicago: University of Chicago Press, 1980) and Colin Turnbull, *The Forest People* (New York: Simon and Schuster, 1961).

17. Unavoidable here is the Kantian objection that ethical values actually offer "reasons" rather than anything in the merely "causal" universe. My dogmatic response is that, despite its patina of logical necessity, this insistence on seceding from

the phenomenal world actually derives from the same misconception of "causal" stories criticized in the text. Let me add, however, that, in my view, the idea that one can somehow understand and systematize ethical values in ignorance of their origins and social dynamics also partakes of the spectacular overconfidence in philosophical reason implicitly criticized in this paper as a whole. For some support on this point, see Kai Nielsen, "On Transforming the Teaching of Moral Philosophy," *APA Newsletter on Teaching Philosophy* (November 1987), pp. 3–7.

18. Witold Rybczynski, *Home: A Short History of an Idea* (New York: Viking Books, 1986).

19. I don't mean to deny that rapid change (both cultural and biological) occasionally does occur, perhaps precipitated by unpredictable but radical events. Drastic global warming or a Chernoble-type accident outside of Washington, D.C. might well precipitate a drastic change in our environmental practices. Still, even in moments of crisis we can only respond using the tools that we then have. From deep within our anthropocentrized world it remains hard to see how we can respond without resorting either to some kind of "enlightened" anthropocentrism or to a reflex rejection of it, still on anthropocentrism's own terms. Thus, when I speak of "fundamental" change, I mean change in the entire system of values, beliefs, practices, and social institutions—not just in immediate practices forced upon us by various emergencies.

20. For this way of putting the matter, I am indebted to Rom Harre.

21. In general, the possibility of invoking dissonant strands in a complex culture is part of the reason that radical social criticism is possible in the first place. Cf. Lovibond, *Realism and Imagination in Ethics;* Walzer, *Interpretation and Social Criticism* (Cambridge, Mass.: Harvard University Press, 1987); and Anthony Weston, *Toward Better Problems: New Perspectives on Abortion, Animal Rights, the Environment, and Justice* (Philadelphia: Temple University Press, 1992), pp. 167–74.

22. Richard Bernstein, *Beyond Objectivism and Relativism* (Philadelphia: University of Pennsylvania Press, 1983).

23. While Hugo Bedau (in "International Human Rights," in Tom Regan and Donald VanDeveer, eds., *And Justice Toward All: New Essays in Philosophy and Public Policy* [Totowa, N.J.: Rowman and Littlefield, 1982]) calls the declaration "the triumphant product of several centuries of political, legal, and moral inquiry into . . . 'the dignity and worth of the human person'" (p. 298), he goes on to assert that "It is . . . doubtful whether the General Assembly that proclaimed the UN Declaration understood what a human right is," since in the document rights are often stated loosely and in many different modalities. Ideals, purposes, and aspirations are run together with rights. At the same time, moreover, the declaration allows considerations of general welfare to limit rights, which seems to undercut their function as protectors of individuals against such rationales (p. 302n). In opposition to Bedau's position, however, I am suggesting that the General Assembly understood what rights are very well. Rights language is a broad-based moral language with multiple purposes and constituencies: in some contexts a counterweight to the typically self-serving utilitarian

rhetoric of the powers that be; in others, a provocation to think seriously about even such often-mocked ideas as a right to a paid vacation, etc.

24. See, for example, Bernard Williams, *Ethics and the Limits of Philosophy* (Cambridge, Mass.: Harvard University Press, 1985); Walzer, *Spheres of Justice;* and Karen Warren, "The Power and Promise of Ecofeminism," *Environmental Ethics* 12 (1990): 125–46.

25. Christopher Stone, *Should Trees Have Standing? Toward Legal Rights for Natural Objects* (Los Altos, Calif.: William Kaufmann, 1974). G. E. Varner, in "Do Species Have Standing?" *Environmental Ethics* 9 (1987): 57–72, points out that the creation of new legal rights—as, for example, in the Endangered Species Act—helps expand what W. D. Lamont calls our "stock of ethical ideas—the mental capital, so to speak, with which [one] begins the business of living." There is no reason that the law must merely reflect "growth" that has already occurred, as opposed to motivating some growth itself.

26. See Chaim Perelman, *The Realm of Rhetoric* (Notre Dame, Ind.: University of Notre Dame Press, 1982) and C. Perelman and L. Olbrechts-Tyteca, *The New Rhetoric* (Notre Dame, Ind.: University of Notre Dame Press, 1969) for an account of rhetoric that resists the usual Platonic disparagement.

27. Bryan G. Norton, "Conservation and Preservation: A Conceptual Rehabilitation," *Environmental Ethics* 8 (1986): 195–220; John Rodman "Four Forms of Ecological Consciousness Reconsidered," in Donald Scherer and Thomas Attig, eds., *Ethics and the Environment* (Englewood Cliffs, N.J.: Prentice-Hall, 1983), pp. 89–92. Remember also that Leopold insists that ethics are "products of social evolution" and that "nothing so important as an ethic is ever 'written'"—which again suggests that we ought to rethink the usual reading of Leopold as an environmental-ethical theorist with a grand criterion for ethical action.

28. Aldo Leopold, *A Sand County Almanac* (New York: Oxford University Press, 1949), p. 225.

29. J. Baird Callicott, "The Case Against Moral Pluralism," *Environmental Ethics* 12 (1990): 99–124.

30. On "ecosteries," see Alan Drengson, "The Ecostery Foundation of North America: Statement of Philosophy," *The Trumpeter* 7, no. 1 (1990): 12–16. On "re-inhabitation," a good starting point is Peter Berg, "What Is Bioregionalism?" *The Trumpeter* 8, no. 1 (1991): 6–12.

31. See, for instance, Dave Foreman, "Reinhabitation, Biocentrism, and Self-Defense," *Earth First!* (August 1, 1987); Murray Bookchin,"Which Way for the US Greens?" *New Politics* 2 (Winter 1989): 71–83; and Bill Devall, "Deep Ecology and Its Critics," *Earth First!* (December 22, 1987).

32. Wendell Berry, "Getting Along with Nature," in *Home Economics* (San Francisco: North Point Press, 1987), p. 13.

33. Gary Snyder, "Good, Wild, Sacred," in *The Practice of the Wild* (San Francisco: North Point Press, 1990); Tom Birch, "Universal Consideration," paper presented at the International Society for Environmental Ethics, American Philosophical Association, December 27, 1990; Jim Cheney, "Eco-Feminism and Deep Ecology," *Environmental Ethics* 9 (1987): 115–45. Snyder also speaks of "grace" as the primary "practice of the wild"; Doug Peacock, *The Grizzly Years* (New York: Holt, Henry, and Co., 1990), insists upon "interspecific tact"; Berry writes of an "etiquette" of nature; and Birch of "generosity of spirit" and "considerateness." All of these terms have their home in a discourse of manners and personal bearing, rather than moral discourse as usually conceived by ethical philosophers. We are not speaking of some universal categorical obligation, but rather of something much closer to us, bound up with who we are and how we immediately bear ourselves in the world—though not necessarily any more "optional" for all that.

34. Christopher Alexander et al., *A Pattern Language* (New York: Oxford University Press, 1977). On windows, see secs. 239, 159, and 107; on "site repair," sec. 104; on water in the city, secs. 25, 64, and 71; on "accessible green," secs. 51 and 60; and on "holy ground," secs. 24, 66, and 70.

12

Moral Pluralism and the Course of Environmental Ethics

Christopher D. Stone

I. Introduction

With this volume, *Environmental Ethics* concludes its first decade. It may be a good time to ask what the environmental ethics movement has to show for itself. Where is it, and where should it be heading? Without doubt, and particularly in view of the short time span, the contributions assembled are impressive. Many (some might surmise all) of the basic issues have been clarified. Perhaps most valuable is the body of literature focusing attention on what I will call "the obstacles" (below).

Good work continues, to be sure, but I fear we have reached a plateau. The signs include a tendency to reiterate the well-worn "need" for an environmental ethic "whose time has come," and then to work over the increasingly familiar themes about the restricted reach of mainstream theories, et cetera. Part of the problem is that we have yet to establish a clearly defined sense of mission. Where does environmental ethics situate itself within the larger world of moral philosophy?

As an applied ethics is one response. But, if so, we still need to ask what such a status entails.[1] Does it mean we are to regard environmental ethics as applying certain invariant moral principles—"core principles," let us say—to deal with the peculiar properties of nature, the way mathematic's core principles (of algebra and topology) are said to be extended and refined by statistics and probability theory to suit them for application to their special "materials"?[2] If that is the commitment, then certain other questions follow. What are the invariant moral principles that environmental ethics, as an applied field, is applying? (In whose service do we place ourselves?) What leeway do the appliers have to supplement and deform the "purest" and most abstract propositions in the core when they bruise against the concrete riddles of the world?

An alternate, considerably larger ambition is to assemble forces under the banner of a new, independent ethic and proceed to mount an assault on the core itself with an aim either to overthrow and replace the reigning premises or to establish some sort of co-regency.

A third alternative is the most far-reaching. It would use the environmental ethics movement as the occasion to reexamine the metaethical assumptions that underlie all of moral philosophy.

It is my position that each of these missions has some validity, but the third must dominate attention now, for we have not yet made clear, neither to ourselves nor to others, what exactly are the aims and ground rules that govern the composition of an ethical viewpoint.

II. The Obstacles

Certainly I am not going to presume to summarize the body of literature that has appeared to date. The writers of the past ten years have identified a cluster of obstacles that environmental ethicists face. Most of these are familiar to readers of *Environmental Ethics* and require, therefore, only a brief recapitulation here.

First is the question of putting the *objective* into coherent form. On this score the proponent of an environmental ethic is tempted to fall back upon negatives, to speak of what such an ethics is *not:* the aim is to inject into moral reasoning considerations that are not sheerly homocentric, that do not appeal solely or decisively to human preferences or utility. Here the first difficulty appears. Even if the environmentalist can persuade others that trees and trout *have value* (in some sense), only humans *do the valuing;* it is, after all, humankind, not trees or trout, that the environmentalist is seeking to persuade. Does this requirement to appeal to human consciousness and preferences land us in a contradiction, a sort of homocentrism after all?

Second is the related question of *foundation.* Even if we can intelligibly express an environmental ethic's objective, on what rational basis can it possibly rest? We could conceive ourselves to be working within an applied field, and then figure out which dominant ethic to apply. Subordination to utilitarianism is unappealing because it is an alliance that values nature only so far as it is instrumental to human welfare. Union with the neo-Kantians is rebuffed, for while we are glad that they do not kick their dogs, the justification—duties to their own selves, not the dog's—is unacceptable. The prevailing mood is to uncover some "good" that is not wholly instrumental either to human welfare or to human virtue, one that is somehow situated outside ourselves in nature. The challenges of identifying and legitimating such an intrinsic or inherent good are substantial, however, and increase the further we wander beyond intelligence or life as its foundation. The animal rights advocate has, at least, some of the goods of familiar moral theory to work with: a life that can be snuffed out, a plan that can be frustrated, a nerve that can transmit pain. The person who supports the moral considerateness of an inanimate object confronts the task of identifying some comparable basis, some "intrinsic worth" of something that cannot be killed, frustrated, or pained.

Third, what is being sought is not just a moral viewpoint that accounts for nature in principle. We need a moral viewpoint detailed and ingenious enough to maneuver us through the *ontological conundrums*. By reference to what principles is the moral and legal world to be carved up into those "things" that count and those that do not? This is a problem that can be approached as one of ethic's *boundaries:* that is, if self-consciousness is not the key to moral considerateness, nor sentience, nor life, . . . how does one draw the line, so that an argument favoring a lake does not apply with equal force to a lamp? The same sort of dilemma crops up in other forms: is the unit of our concern the individual ant, the anthill, the family, the species, or the ant's habitat?

Fourth, suppose that we can do the carving up correctly, that is, identify those objects towards which some prima facie moral regard is justified, e.g., perhaps a certain mountain. There will remain the question, even if moral obligations to a mountain are conceded to exist in principle, how they can be *discharged?* In familiar, interpersonal moralities, the discharge of duties toward another is connected with respect for other's wants and welfare. But how does one "do right by" a mountain?

Fifth, there are the *distributional dilemmas*. It is not enough to carve up the world, establishing what is to be morally considerate. Nor is it enough to agree how that regard translates into prima facie good and bad acts. What are we to do in the case of conflicting indications? For example, one can imagine a life-respecting moral framework whose basic principle is "more life is better than less." One can imagine, too, support for the preservation of a singular, pristine desert. But then, how do we judge an irrigation project that offers to transform the desert into a habitat teeming with vegetation? In general terms, the problem is the familiar one of weighing: even if the continued existence of a species or the state of a river is demonstrated to be a (noninstrumental) good, how strongly does that good withstand the moral force of other, competing goods?

While each of these questions is hard—the fact we are in the tenth volume of this journal says as much—we can take some heart from the fact they are, in kind, no more formidable than those with which the proponents of every moral theory have been vexed: how to establish the meaning and legitimacy of moral reasoning in general, to demonstrate that it is cogent and defensible to sacrifice evident ego-pleasures to further something else. Those who appreciate the difficulties of substantiating the human community as that "something else" cannot sniff at those who find some plausible candidacy in the biotic. That granted, the development of an ethic that gives good moral guidance for our conduct respecting nature is not a quantum leap more perplexing than the task of putting together (or discovering) an ethics for our conduct respecting persons.

III. The Metaethical Assumptions

The larger—in all events, prior—questions require further consideration of the implicit metaethical assumptions. What are environmental ethicists trying to achieve, and what are the standards for success? In other words, what, more exactly, is an ethics supposed to look like and do? To illustrate, for years environmental ethicists have been stimulated by Aldo Leopold's conviction that we should develop a "land ethic." But how much thought has been given to what such a project implies? Are the proponents of a land ethic committed to coming up with a capacious replacement for all existing ethics, one capable of mediating all moral questions touching man, beast and mountain, but by reference to a grander, more all-encompassing set of principles? Or can the land ethic be an ethic that governs man's relations with land alone, leaving intact other principles to govern actions touching humankind (and yet others for actions touching, say, lower animals, and so on)?

If we are implying that there are different ethics, then there are a host of questions to face. What is an ethical system, and what are its minimum requirements? Need its "proofs" be as irresistible as a geometry's? Is it required to provide for each moral dilemma that it recognizes as a dilemma, one right, tightly-defined answer? Or is it enough to identify several courses of action equally acceptable, perhaps identifying for elimination those that are wrong or unwelcome? How—by reference to what elements—can one ethic differ from another? What possibilities of conflicting judgments are introduced by multiple frameworks, and how are they to be resolved?

These are among the questions that, sooner or later, environmental ethicists will have to confront. Upon their answer hinges nothing less than the legitimacy of environmental ethics as a distinct enterprise.

IV. Moral Monism

The environmental ethics movement has always known that if it were to succeed it has to challenge the prevailing orthodoxy. But the orthodoxy it has targeted is only the more obvious one, the orthodoxy of morals: that man is the measure (and not merely the measurer) of all value. Certainly calling that gross presumption to question is a valid part of the program. But the orthodoxy we have to question first is that of metaethics—of how moral philosophy ought to be conducted, of the ground rules.

Note that I am not claiming that we lack controversy at the level of morals. There is no shortage of lively contention in the philosophy literature. But underneath it all there is a striking, if ordinarily only implicit agreement on the metaethical sense of mission. It is widely presumed, by implication when it is not made explicit, that the ethicist's task is to put forward and defend a single overarching principle (or coherent body of principles), such as utilitarianism's "greatest good of the greatest number" or Kant's categorical imperative, and to demonstrate how it—the one correct viewpoint—guides us through all moral dilemmas to the one right solution.

This attitude, which I call moral monism, implies that in defending, say, the preservation of a forest or the protection of a laboratory animal, we are expected to bring our argument under the same principles that dictate our obligations to kin or the just deserts of terrorists. It suggests that moral considerateness is a matter of either-or; that is, the single viewpoint is presumably built upon a single salient moral property, such as, typically, sentience, intelligence, being the subject of a conscious life, etc. Various entities (depending on whether they are blessed with the one salient property) are *either* morally relevant (each in the same way, according to the same rules) *or* utterly inconsiderate, out in the moral cold.[3]

Environmentalists, more than most philosophers, have an at least intuitive reason for supposing that this attitude is mistaken, for it is they whom the attitude is first to bridle. Environmentalists wonder about the possible value in a river (or in preserving a river), but cannot rationalize those feelings in the familiar anthropocentric terms of pains and life-projects that they would apply to their own situations. By contrast, mainstream ethicists, concentrating on interpersonal relations, constrict their attention to a relatively narrow and uncontroversial band of morally salient qualities. Persons can speak for themselves, exercise moral choice, and—because they share a community—assert and waive many sorts of claims that are useful in governing their reciprocal relationships. Orthodox ethics has understandably tended to identify all ethics with this one set of morally salient properties: the paradigmatic moral problems historically have been interpersonal problems; the paradigmatic rules, person-regarding.

Thus, while vying camps have arisen within the orthodox tradition, none is ordinarily forced to account for the significance of properties that lie outside the common pool of human attributes. It is only when one starts to wonder about exotic clients, such as future generations, the dead, embryos, animals, the spatially remote, tribes, trees, robots, mountains, and art works, that the assumptions which unify ordinary morals are called into question. Need the rules that apply be in some sense, and at some level of generality, "the same" in all cases? The term *environmental ethics* suggests the possibility of a distinct moral regime for managing our way through environment-affecting conduct. But in what respects that regime is distinct from other regimes and how conflicts among the regimes are to be mediated are crucial matters that have not been generally and directly addressed.

In default of well-worked out answers, the prevailing strategy of those who represent nonhumans is one of extension: to force one of the familiar person-oriented frameworks outward and apply one of the familiar arguments to some nonhuman entity. But such arguments too often appear just that— forced. Utilitarianism's efforts to draw future generations under its mantle (a relatively easy extension, one would suppose) ties it in some awkward, if not paradoxical knots: Do we include, for example, those who might be born— obliging us to bring as many as possible of them into existence in order to aggregate more pleasures? Nor is it clear that utilitarianism, unqualified by a complex and ill-fitting rights appendage, can satisfy the concerns that drive the animal liberation movement.

The shortcomings of (let us call it) moral extensionism[4] are not peculiar to utilitarianism. Extensions of utilitarianism's principal contenders all require, in various ways and with various justifications, putting oneself in the place of another to test whether we can really wish the conduct under evaluation if we assumed the other's position, role, and/or natural endowment. While such hypothetical trading of places and comparable techniques of thought experiment are always problematical, they are most satisfactory when we are trading places with (or universalizing about) persons who share our culture, whose interests, values, and tastes we can therefore presume with some confidence. But even that slender assurance is destined to erode the further we venture beyond the domain of the most familiar natural persons. With what conviction can we trade places with members of spatially and temporally remote cultures, or with our own descendants in some future century? And, of course, if we wish to explore our obligations in regard to the dead, trees, rocks, fetuses, artificial intelligence, species, or corporate bodies, trading places is essentially a blind alley. It is one thing to put oneself in the shoes of a stranger, perhaps even in the hooves of a horse—but quite another to put oneself in the banks of a river.

Certainly, the fact that orthodox moral philosophies, each with its own ordinary-person orientation, have difficulty accommodating various nonhumans is not, in itself, proof that the conventional moral schools are wrong, or have to be amended beyond recognition. One alternative, the position of an ardent adherent to one of the predominant schools, is that any unconventional moral client that it cannot account for, except perhaps in a certain limited way, cannot (save in that limited way) have any independent moral significance or standing.

But there is another response to the dilemma, one that is more challenging to the assumptions that dominate conventional moral thought. In accordance with this approach we need to ask several new questions. How imperialistic need a moral framework be? Need we accept as inevitable that there be one set of axioms or principles or paradigm cases for all morals—operable across all moral activities and all diverse entities? Are we constrained to come forward with a single coherent set of principles that will govern throughout, so that any ethic we champion has to absorb its contenders with a more general, abstract and plenary intellectual framework? My own view is that monism's ambitions, to unify all ethics within a single framework capable of yielding the one right answer to all our quandaries, are simply quixotic.

First, the monists's mission sits uneasily with the fact that morality involves not one, but several distinguishable *activities*—choosing among courses of conduct, praising and blaming actors, evaluating institutions, and so on. Is it self-evident that someone who is, say, utilitarian in his or her act evaluation is committed to utilitarianism in the grading of character?

Second, we have to account for *the variety of things* whose considerateness commands some intuitive appeal: normal persons in a common moral community, persons remote in time and space, embryos and fetuses, nations and nightingales, beautiful things and sacred things. Some of these things we wish to account for because of their high degree of intelligence (higher animals); with others, sentience seems the key (lower life); the moral standing of membership groups, such as nation-states, cultures, and species has to stand on some additional footing, since the group itself (the species, as distinct from the individual whale) manifests no intelligence and experiences no pain. Other entities are genetically human, either capable of experiencing pain (advanced fetuses) or nonsentient (early embryos), but lack, at the time of our dealings with them, full human capacities. Trying to force all these diverse entities into a single mold—the one big, sparsely principled comprehensive theory—forces us to disregard some of our moral intuitions, and to dilate our overworked person-wrought precepts into unhelpfully bland generalities. The commitment is not only chimerical; it imposes strictures on thought that stifle the emergence of more valid approaches to moral reasoning.

V. Moral Pluralism

The alternative conception toward which I have been inviting discussion, what I call moral pluralism,[5] takes exception to monism point by point. It refuses to presume that all ethical activities (evaluating acts, actors, social institutions, rules, states of affairs, etc.) are in all contexts (in normal interpersonal relations, across large spaces and many generations, between species) determined by the same features (intelligence, sentience, capacity for emotions, life) or even that they are subject, in each case, to the same overarching principles (utilitarianism, Kantianism, nonmaleficence, etc.). Pluralism invites us to conceive the intellectual activities of which morals consist as being partitioned into several distinct frameworks, each governed by its own appropriate principles.

Certainly, one would expect pain-regarding principles to emerge as pivotal in establishing obligations toward all those things that experience pain. Not pain alone, but preferences of some sort, e.g., the projection of a life plan, have to be accounted for in our relations with a second level of creature. Still richer threads (such as a sense of justice, and rights of a sort that can be consensually created, extinguished, traded, and waived) form the fabric of the moral tapestry that connects humans who share a common moral community. Other principles, perhaps invoking respect for life, for a natural unfolding, seem fit as a basis for forming our relations with plants.[6] Indeed, should we pursue this path, we would multiply subdivisions even within the interpersonal realm. The Kantians, emphasizing the place of nonwelfarist duties, make rightful ado about our not saving our child from drowning because it is "best on the whole." But this does not mean that classic utilitarianism is wrong. Maybe it is of only limited force in parsing out obligations among associates and kin. Utilitarianism strikes me as having considerable validity for legislation (an activity) affecting large numbers of largely unrelated persons (an entity set) who are therefore relatively unacquainted with each other's cardinal preferences.

That monism should have become so firmly established in morals is understandable (it echoes one God, one grand unified theory) but is hardly inevitable. Geometers have long relinquished the belief that Euclid's is the only geometry. "This discovery led to the pluralization of mathematics (itself already a strangely plural noun); where we once had geometry, we how have geometries and, ultimately, algebras rather than algebra, and number systems rather than a number system."[7]

A comparable partitioning has taken place in the empirical and social sciences. The body politic is commonly viewed as being comprised of groups: groups of humans, each of which is made up of more groups, groups of cells, molecules, atoms, and subatomic particles, and/or waves. What happens at one level of description is undoubtedly a product, in some complex way, of what is occurring at another. Many, perhaps most scientists feel that "in principle" there is a single unifying body of law—the laws of nature— that at some level of simple generality holds throughout. If so, one may harbor the hope not only of abolishing all lingering pockets of ignorance and chaos, but of connecting phenomena on every plane with phenomena on another, of someday unifying, say, the laws that govern the movement of subatomic particles with those that govern social conduct. But we are far from it. What we actually work with, for all intents and purposes, and to almost everyone's satisfaction, are separate bodies of law and knowledge.

The issue I am raising is this. If, as I maintain, ethics comprises several activities and if it has to deal with subject matters as diverse as persons, dolphins, cultural groups, and trees, why has ethics not pursued the same path as the sciences—or, rather, paths? That is, why not explore the possibility that ethics can also be partitioned?

Perhaps the analogy is simply too weak. However free science may be to partition, one might argue, ethics is under peculiarly strong constraints to remain monistic. The argument might go like this. Alternative descriptions of how the world is (or might be) can peacefully coexist over a broad latitude without logical conflict—e.g., in most contexts, one can indulge either in a particle or a wave version of light without chafing. And even where apparently irreconcilable conflict does erupt at one level (say, at the subatomic) the participants at other levels (those doing cellular biology) can ordinarily remain agnostic. By contrast, ethics (one is tempted to say) is not merely descriptive. It has as its ultimate aim choosing the right *action.* Unlike describing, in which subtly overlapping nuances of adjective and predicate are tolerable, acting seems to lend itself to, if not to demand, binary yes/no, right/wrong alternatives.

If this is the argument why morals require monism, it appears to me unpersuasive. There is, to begin with, the question of agenda: one wants from moral reasoning not merely the verdict, whether or not to do act *a,* but also what the choice set is: *a, b, c, . . .* ? Moral thought is a service when it is populating and clarifying the range of morally creditable alternatives. Hence, attention to plural approaches would find justification if, by stimulating us to define and come at problems from different angles, it were to advance our grasp of alternatives.[8]

Perhaps most importantly, let us remind ourselves that actions are in the physical world; the evaluation of them is intellectual. Many persons (are these the "moralists"?) would probably be pleased if our moral reasoning had the power to map a unique, precise moral evaluation for each alternative action. It would give us much the same pleasure (tinged with a not entirely ingenuous surprise) that mathematicians derive from confirmation that the world "out there," while theoretically at liberty to go its own haphazard way, is conforming in general to the elegant inventions of our intellects.[9] Why, when we set out to apply our best moral theories to the unruly world of human conduct should we confidently expect more—a more meticulous isomorphism, more freedom from inconsistency, more power of resolution?

Specifically, it may be a (not terribly interesting) truth that an act can be defined in such a way that we are left with no alternative but to do it or not—a feature of the world that makes monism superficially attractive. But even if so, it is a fact about the world that our best moral reasoning may just not be able to rise to or to map. The rightness and wrongness of some acts may lie beyond our power to deduce or otherwise discover. Key moral properties may not lend themselves to produce a transitive ordering across the choice set.

VI. The Variables

If we are to explore bringing our relations with different sorts of things under different moral governances, then we face the question: by reference to what intellectual elements might governances vary domain to domain?

(a) Grain of Description

Morals are concerned with comparing actions, characters, and states of affairs. To compare alternatives, as a logical first step, we have to settle upon the appropriate vocabulary of description. For example, in evaluating our impact on humans, we consistently adopt a grain of description that individuates organisms: each person counts equally. In evaluating other actions, there is often intuitive support for some other unit, e.g. the hive or the herd or the habitat. I am not claiming that these intuitions are self-validating, only that they, and their implications, merit sustained and systematic attention. Each vying grain of description is integral to a separate editorial viewpoint. Suppose that a bison naturally (of its own action) faces drowning in a river in a national park. Should we rescue it, or let "nature take its course"? One viewpoint emphasizes the individual animal; another (favored, apparently, by the Park Service)[10] consigns the individual animal to the background and emphasizes the larger unit, the park ecosystem. Another viewpoint emphasizes species. Each focus brings along its allied constellation of concepts. In invoking the finer grain, focusing upon the individual animal, we scan for such properties as the animal's capacity to feel pain, its intelligence, its understanding of the situation, and its suffering. None of these terms apply to the park. Instead, the ecosystem version brings out stability, resilience, uniqueness, and energy flow.

(b) Mood

What I mean by mood may best be illustrated by a contrast between morals and law. Law, like morals, often speaks in negative injunctions, i.e., "Thou shalt not kill . . ." and "Thou shalt not park in the red zone. . . ." But the law always proceeds to specify, in each case, a sanction which expresses the relative severity of the offense, viz., ". . . or face the death penalty," ". . . or face a $12 fine." The result is a legal discussion endowed with fine-tuned nuances. By contrast, much of moral philosophy, inspirited with monism, is conducted at a level of abstraction at which every act is assumed to be either-or, either good or bad; there is either a duty to do *x* or a duty not to do *x;* a right to *y* or no right to *y*. Monist moral discourse, then, lacks the refinements of expression that enrich legal discourse. As long as monism reigns, significant distinctions between cases, distinctions marked by nuances of feeling and belief that moral reflection might investigate and amplify, lack a semantic foothold.

By contrast, pluralism welcomes diversified material out of which moral judgments can be fashioned, particularly as we cross from one domain to another. Moral regard for lakes may seem silly—or even unintelligible—if we are required to flesh it out by reference to the same rules, and express our judgments in the same mood, as those that apply to a person. But there are prospective middle grounds. Our lake-affecting actions might have to be judged in terms of distinct deontic operators understood to convey a relatively lenient mood, perhaps something like "that which is morally welcome" or that which will bring credit or discredit to our character.

(c) Logical (Formal) Texture

Every system of intellectual rules is girded on a number of properties that endow it with a distinct logical texture. These range from whether it is subject to closure (whether it is capable of yielding one unique solution for each question that can be opened within it) to its attitude on contradictions and inconsistencies. As to closure, the monist implicitly assumes that morals must be modelled on ordinary arithmetic. There is one and only one solution to 4 + 7; so too there should be, for each dilemma of morals, one right answer. And monism rejects, too, any system of ethical postulates from which we could derive conflicting and contradictory prescriptions. After all, what would we think of a system of geometry from whose postulate we could derive both that two triangles were, and that they were not, congruent?

Pluralism is not so dogmatic—or perhaps one should just say not so "optimistic"—about the prospects of assimilating morals to (slightly idealized conceptions of) arithmetic or geometry. We simply may not be able to devise a single system of morals, operative throughout, that is subject to closure, and in which the laws of noncontradiction[11] and excluded middle[12] are in vigilant command.[13]

VII. Reconciling the Differences

There are many problems with this pluralistic approach. Many of the stumbling blocks—those that I could identify myself, or with a little help from my friends—are dealt with in *Earth and Other Ethics*.[14] It can be defended from the obvious charge that it must stumble into moral relativism of the rankest sort.[15] But it faces comparable problems that are not so easy to dismiss. It would appear that a pluralist, analyzing some choice situation in one framework (say, one that accounts for species in an appropriate way) may conclude that act *a* is right. The same person, analyzing the situation in another framework (one built, say, from a person-regarding viewpoint) concludes *b*. Are not such conflicts paralyzing? And do they not therefore render pluralism methodologically unacceptable?

To begin with, the fact that morals might admit of several allowable viewpoints does not mean that each and every dilemma will require several competing analyses. Assuming that remotely probable and minimal consequences can be ignored, some choices may be carried through solely within one framework. For example, whatever morality has to say about whether to uproot an individual plant could be provided, presumably, by the appropriate one-plant framework. No excursion into the agent's obligations to the plant's species, or to mankind, or to kin or whatever would be called for.

We can anticipate myriad other circumstances in which thorough analysis requires defining and processing the situation in each of several frameworks. But in some of those situations each of the various analyses will endorse the same action. We all know that vegetarianism, for example, can be supported both within a framework that posits the moral considerateness of animals and one that values humans alone, viz., that by eating animals the planet uses protein inefficiently, therefore reducing aggregate human welfare, even robbing badly undernourished persons of a minimally human existence. (What we do not know—and ought to examine—is why approaching such a question from several angles, a technique well-accepted in other areas,[16] should be indicted as an ignoble and impure way to go about doing philosophy.)

There is a third set of cases in which more than one framework will appear appropriate, and the different frameworks, rather than mutually endorsing the same result, reinforce different, even inconsistent actions. The potential for conflicts is there—but no more so than in any moral system that deems the proper choice to be a function of several independent criteria: welfare maximization, duties to kin, respect for life, the values of community, and friendship. How do we "combine," where rights analysis says one thing, utility analysis another?

One possibility is to formulate a lexical ordering rule. For example, our obligations to neighbor-persons, as determined on a framework built on neo-Kantian principles, might claim priority up to the point where our neighbor-persons had reached a certain level of comfort and protection. But when that level has been reached, considerations of, say, species preservation as determined per another framework, or of future generations per another, would be brought into play.

One might claim, with partial justification, that in those circumstances in which we accepted mediation by reference to a master rule, we are reintroducing a sort of monism "after all." But even in these cases, it is an "after all" significant enough to keep pluralism from collapsing into monism. Under monism, a problem is defined appropriately for evaluation by the relevant standard, in such a way that all the "irrelevant" descriptions are left behind from the outset. The problem, so defined, is worked through to solution without further distraction. Under pluralism, a single situation, variously described, may produce several analyses and various conclusions. If a master rule is to be introduced, it is to be introduced only after the separate reasoning processes have gone their separate ways to yield a conflicting set of conclusions, *a, b, c, d*. The master rule is brought to bear on that set, none of whose members would necessarily have been constructed had the procedure been subjected to the monist stricture that a single standard, such as utilitarianism, had to be applied consistently and exclusively from the start.

Finally, and most troublesomely, there are quandaries for which each of our multiple analyses not only endorse inconsistent actions, but for which no lexical rule is available, and for which further intuitive reflection[17] reveals no further, best-of-all, alternative. We can imagine as a "worst case scenario," an outcome not merely of the form *a* is mandatory per one framework and b is mandatory per the other (and we cannot do both), but rather of the form that *a* is mandatory and *-a* is mandatory (*a* is impermissible). One must, and must not, pull the trigger. What then?

This much is clear: those two edicts, taken together, tell us (logically) nothing. We would say of the total system of beliefs that it had *disappointed us in the particular case.* We would have to agree, too, that if such out-and-out conflicts were in each and every case endemic to pluralist methodology, the whole system we constructed would have to be abandoned. But suppose that such outcomes, while possible, should prove exceptional. Then we could regard their occasional occurrences as a particularly poignant indication of the total system's indeterminacy.

This prospect illustrates one of the principal monist-pluralist dividing lines referred to earlier: How fatal is it to a system of moral rules if it fails to furnish a single unambiguous answer to each choice we recognize as morally significant? If we cannot devise a whale-regarding moral framework that gives us one confident right answer to every action affecting whales, do we have to withdraw whales from consideration (except as resources in a human-oriented-framework) entirely? If our whale-regarding and our person-regarding edicts conflict, does one or the other or both of the systems responsible have to be dismantled?

As I have already indicated, such a standard, if to be applied with an even hand (and fin) throughout, would cramp the range of morals significantly.

Better to come right out and consider the alternative: that we may have to abandon the ambition to find perfect consistency and the "one right answer" to every moral quandary, either because a single answer does not exist, or because our best analytical methods are not up to finding it.[18]

In some circumstances, if we can identify and eliminate the options that are morally unacceptable, we may have gone as far as moral thought can take us. It may be that the choices that remain are equally good or equally evil or equally perplexing.[19]

This does not mean that as a moral community we are relieved from striving for a higher, if ultimately imperfect consensus on progressively better answers.[20] Nor does it mean that, as regards the indeterminate set, one can be arbitrary—as though, from that point on, flipping a coin is as good as we can do. It is by the choices we affirm in this zone of ultimate uncertainty that we have our highest opportunity to exercise our freedoms and define our characters. Particularly as the range of moral considerateness is extended outward from those who are (in various ways) "near" us, people who take morals seriously, who are committed to giving good reasons, will come to irreconcilably conflicting judgments on many issues. But the main question now is this: what model of decision process provides the best prospect for constructing the best answers we can furnish?

Notes

Stone teaches in the School of Law at the University of Southern California, Los Angeles. He is the author of *Should Trees Have Standing?* and *Earth and Other Ethics: The Case for Moral Pluralism* (New York: Harper and Row, 1987). His current research interest is in the development of institutional responses to global pollution. He serves on USC's Institutional Animal Care and Use Committee and is a Member of the Editorial Advisory Board of Environmental Ethics. The author would like to thank Homes Rolston, III and Martin Krieger for criticisms of particular aspects of the manuscript.

First published in *Environmental Ethics* 10, no. 2. Permission to reprint courtesy of *Environmental Ethics* and the author.

1. See J. Baird Callicott, "Non-Anthropocentric Value Theory and Environmental Ethics," *American Philosophical Quarterly* 21 (1984): 299–300.

2. See Lynn Arthur Steen, "Mathematics Today," in *Mathematics Today,* ed. L. A. Steen (New York: Springer-Verlag, 1970), pp. 7–8. Note that in the model of mathematics Steen presents, the flow of ideas and valuable information runs in two directions: the inventory of the most highly abstract ideas in the core area available for equipping application in the outer regions; in turn, the core is fueled with the new ideas that concrete application sends back from the field.

3. Consider the argument that a proponent of using animals in medical research throws up to the animal rights advocate: "If all forms of animal life . . . must be treated equally, and if therefore . . . the pains of a rodent count equally with the pains of a human, we are forced to conclude (1) that neither humans nor rodents possess rights, or (2) that rodents possess all the rights that humans possess." Carl Cohen, "The Case for the Use of Animals in Biomedical Research," *New England Journal of Medicine*, 315 (1986): 865, 867. An alternative "pluralist" position would examine the possibility that a laboratory bred animal has "rights," but not the same as humans. This distinction could be operationalized by saying that the proponent of an experiment that took a laboratory animal's life painlessly would only have to show a clear likelihood of an advance of human welfare; animal suffering, however, would (alternatively) never be allowed, or allowed only when it could be shown that there was a very high probability that the experiment would result in the saving of human lives or the reduction of human suffering—never because it would alleviate mere inconveniences in human life, such as baggy eyelids.

4. The term was suggested to me by Holmes Rolston.

5. Moral pluralism ought not to be confused with moral relativism, the view, roughly, that all morals are context-dependent. A pluralist can be agnostic with respect to the moral realist position that there are absolutely true answers to moral quandaries, as invariable across time, space, and communities as the value of pi. There may be "really right" and not just relatively right answers, but the way to find them is by reference not to one single principle, constellation of concepts, etc., but by reference to several distinct frameworks, each appropriate to its own domain of entities and/or moral activities (evaluating character, ranking options for conduct, etc.).

6. See Paul Taylor, *Respect for Nature* (Princeton, N.J.: Princeton University Press, 1986); J. L. Arbor presents a coherent and persuasive plea for plants—coldly logical, however heartfelt—in "Animal Chauvinism, Plant-Regarding Ethics, and the Torture of Trees," *Australasian Journal of Philosophy* 64 (1986): 335.

7. Steen, "Mathematics Today," pp. 4–5. To pursue the mathematical model for a further moment, Gödel and others have laid to rest the hope of ever producing a complete and consistent formal system powerful enough to prove or to refute every statement it can formulate. Although what happens in math is hardly a conclusive model of what should go on in morals, it does make one wonder how much of moral philosophy implicitly proceeds on the assumption that a morality not only has axioms (or even solider starting points), but that they are axioms more powerful than math's! And if that is not the assumption, what takes its place?

8. Note that this rationale for pluralism could be endorsed on heuristic grounds by a monist, even by a moral realist who presumed (as I do not) that all the candidates for truth *disclosed* by this many-angled attack on the problem will in the end be submitted to a single adjudicatory principle to decide which of them is *uniquely and truly right*. Compare the position Paul Feyerabend adopts with respect to the natural sciences, viz., that the history of sciences reveals an incompleteness and even inconsistency of each framework which should be regarded as routine and inevitable, and that

a pluralism of theories and metaphysical viewpoints should be nourished as a means of advancing on the truth. Feyerabend, *Against Method* (London: Verso, 1978), pp. 35–53.

9. See E. P. Wigner, "The Unreasonable Effectiveness of Mathematics in the Natural Sciences," in Wigner, *Symmetries and Reflections* (Cambridge, Mass.: M.I.T. Press, 1970).

10. See Jim Robbins, "Do Not Feed the Bears?" *Natural History* (January 1984): 12.

11. The law of contradiction holds that it cannot be the case that both a proposition *p* and its negation, *-p,* hold.

12. The law of excluded middle maintains that either a proposition *p* or its negation, *-p* must be true; there is no middle possibility.

13. See Freidrich Waismann, "Language Strata," in *Logic and Language,* ed. Anthony Flew (New York: Anchor Books, 1965), p. 237. The notion I present of multiple conceptual planes with systematically varying formal requirements owes much to Waismann's musings about "language strata."

14. Christopher D. Stone, *Earth and Other Ethics* (New York: Harper and Row, 1987).

15. See note 5 above.

16. I do not mean only lawyers, who do this sort of thing unabashedly all of the time. As for the natural sciences, see Feyerabend, *Against Method.* In mathematics, Gorg Polya, *How to Solve It* (Princeton, N.J.: Princeton University Press, 1957) is a classic exposition of how mathematicians may stalk a single problem with widely assorted techniques (indirect proofs, reductio ad absurdums, analogy), ultimately to be convinced of the truth of a solution by the dual standards of formal proof and intuition.

17. I mean by intuitive reflection a process of analysis that leads to a right-feeling judgment, but one for which, even after the conclusion, we cannot offer any proof, perhaps not even specify the premises.

18. As Hilary Putnam puts it, "The question whether there is one objectively best morality or a number of objectively best moralities which, hopefully, agree on a good many principles or in a good many cases, is simply the question whether, given the desiderata . . . [of] the enterprise . . . will it turn out that these desiderata select a best morality or a group of moralities which have a significant measure of agreement on a number of significant questions." Hilary Putnam, *Meaning and the Moral Sciences* (Boston: Routledge and Kegan Paul, 1978), p. 84.

19. See Leibniz's stumper: "It is certain that God sets greater store by a man than a lion; nevertheless it can hardly be said with certainty that God prefers a single man in all respects to the whole of lion-kind." *Theodicy,* trans E. M. Hoggard (New Haven, Conn.: Yale University Press, 1952), sec. 118.

20. One might even expect this endeavor to take the form of integrating, or at least striving to integrate, originally independent "plural" frameworks into something grander and more unified—much as the theoretical physicist will continue to scout about for a grand unified field theory. But in the meantime, the practical and even playful work of significance will take place on humbler levels.

13

Cheney and the Myth of Postmodernism

Mick Smith

I. Preliminaries

The entrance of postmodernism into the world of environmental ethics is both inevitable and auspicious. Jim Cheney's intricate, and sometimes obscure paper, "Postmodern Environmental Ethics: Ethics as Bioregional Narrative," raises important considerations, including, among other things, its emphasis on context, or *place,* in determining ethical values.[1] Unfortunately, however, as I argue, Cheney's paper is marred in certain respects which hamper his avowed aim of *recontextualizing* ethical discourse.

His paper centers on an explicit thesis which divides human history into three epochs: primitive, modern, and postmodern. According to Cheney, although the change from the "primitive" to the "modern" period began "some nine or so millennia" ago with the appearance of agriculture, the change from the "modern" to "postmodern" has occurred only very recently. The dominant world view of the whole of Western society, and consequently all Western philosophy until now, has been modern.[2] These historical epochs are associated with radical changes in social ethos. Postmodernism represents a long awaited return to a primitive understanding of our place in the world. Although historically and sociologically disparate, being separated by an age of modernist domination, these world views are linked by a number of supposedly "shared affinities": "With the advent of postmodernism, contextualized discourse seems to emerge as our mother tongue; totalizing, essentializing language emerges as the voice of the constructed subjective self, the voice of disassociated gnostic alienation."[3] If such a structural axis is represented as primitive and postmodern versus modern, then the homologous associations implicit in the above passage can be represented as follows: *contextual discourse* versus *totalizing discourse, female* versus *male, nature* versus *culture,* and *at home* versus *the alienated.* In all cases, Cheney wishes to re-privilege the left hand side of the dichotomies. These qualitative divisions remain constant throughout

Cheney's paper, and reinforce one another. Thus, the boundary between primitive and modern corresponds to a change from contextual discourse to a totalizing discourse and from female influence in society to male control. In addition, it marks the point at which the individual subject appeared as a fundamental *given* (i.e., the "intuitive obviousness of the Cartesian privitized self"[4]) as well as the point at which language lost its rootedness in natural place.[5] Conversely, postmodernism supposedly heralds a return to primitive homologies, especially contextual discourse.

According to Cheney, the primitive paradigms of contextual discourse are tribal mythologies. For this reason, a mythological approach can "significantly inform postmodern thought on discourse."[6] Myths are both fabulous stories with moral connotations and forms of "knowledge shaped by transformative intent."[7] They are "historically sociologically and geographically shaped system[s] of reference that allow . . . us to order and thus comprehend perception and knowledge."[8] Mythic narratives are the "primitive" alternative to theory; they reflect upon, and are tied to, specific contexts. By contrast, totalizing discourses are forms of theory abstracted from place and context. Once divorced from the specific settings and practices that originally gave them meaning, "language closes in on itself, becoming inbred."[9] Totalizing discourses tend to be universalizing and acontextual and possess an internal autonomous logic or grammar that often claims to *represent* the world's underlying structure. As far as Cheney is concerned, the blame for environmental destruction lies firmly on the shoulders of totalizing discourses and the societies that have developed them.

Cheney's paper is, at heart, a defence of mythical narrative and its concomitant associations against totalizing discourse. He presents a myth of a past Golden Age and in terms of it describes a prehistorical tribal humanity at one with itself and nature, a modern alienated society uprooted from the natural world, and a future postmodern millennium.[10] Each stage is epitomized by the form of language it uses. In an attempt to bolster this position Cheney cites Heidegger's parallel distinction between *primordial* and *fallen* languages. *Fallen* obviously carries with it all the moral overtones he requires to disparage the discourse of modernism.

II. The World and Language

Cheney deconstructs subjectivity and replaces it with a concept akin to Heidegger's "being-in-the-world." This deconstruction takes the form of rejecting the traditionally accepted division between the world and language. A frequently cited aspect of postmodernism is its refusal to accept any taxonomic divisions as absolute givens—i.e., there are no *facts of the matter* upon which we can safely ground argument. Cheney takes this line in his discussion of the relationship between ontology and language.[11] He accurately portrays the general postmodern consensus that it is best to "practice ontological abstinence," to treat language without epistemological presuppositions about just how it relates to the world. The usually cited postmodern alternatives are to treat language as "either a set of tools" or the "free creation of conscious persons and communities."[12] Cheney is dissatisfied with these options and favors instead a "more useful . . . feminist standpoint epistemology" as an alternative in which "objectivity is defined negatively in relation to those views which oppositional consciousness deconstructs. A voice is privileged to the extent that it is constructed from a position that enables it to spot distortions, mystifications, and colonizing and totalizing tendencies within other discourses."[13] This conception of objectivity, or rather *privilege,* is not a "claim to having access to the way things are," but a positional concept describing the world as it seems from a particular *place.* Cheney's form of standpoint epistemology recognizes that there is no wholly objective position from which we can determine how the world really is. At the same time, it alters the role of the human subject. The voice we hear is not that of an atomistic individual separated from the surrounding environment. Rather, the particular contexts within which persons have developed are supposed to speak through them.[14] At least, Cheney argues, this development occurs in primitive conditions where the surrounding environment is natural. Primordial language represents the original contextualizing language with which the "world speaks through us." It results from a "meditative openness to the world." In primordial language we are not trapped but "free." Primitive societies residence in natural contexts ensures the contextuality of their discourse: "the world discloses itself by our being *rooted* in the world."[15]

By contrast, fallen (modernist) language as the opposite structural pole "uproots itself." Because it is abstract, it becomes a vehicle for repressive power that can be exported from one context to another. Modern societies utilize their discourses in the colonization of other areas and cultures. This activity causes environmental problems because the colonizing language almost certainly has developed in surroundings very different from its new circumstances. The practices it enjoins, therefore, disrupt the delicate balance which, Cheney thinks, was reached between primitive humanity and its natural environment.

The unhealthy tendency for discourses to become bases for oppressive power needs to be overcome. However, Cheney believes that simply deconstructing the current dominant paradigm is not enough, for as soon as one totalizing discourse is overthrown, another takes on its oppressive role. How then can we avoid this need for constant recontextualization? "Is there any setting, any landscape, in which contextualizing discourse is not constantly in danger of falling prey to the distortions of essentializing, totalizing discourse?

Perhaps not. A partial way out might be envisioned, however, if we expand the notion of a contextualizing narrative of place so as to include nature—nature as one more player in the construction of community."[16] In other words, Cheney tries to ground the notion of *place* in particular natural regions: "Our position, our *location,* is understood in the elaboration of relations in a non-essentializing narrative achieved through a grounding in the geography of our lives."[17] Also, "Bioregions provide a way of grounding narrative. . . ."[18]

In the foregoing outline of Cheney's "myth" of the postmodern and the primitive, there are a number of problems associated with the dissolution of the world/language barrier and its replacement by Cheney's dichotomy between narrative and totalizing theory. Perhaps the most obvious problem is the status of Cheney's own proposals. How do they fit within his own taxonomy of discourses, which seems itself to conflate a number of concepts with very different meanings: *totalizing* versus *contextual, essentialist* versus *non-essentialist, colonizing* versus *in place,* and *foundational* versus *non-foundational?* The first terms in each pair are used almost synonymously for any form of modernist discourse and the second terms for what is postmodern and primitive. It is possible to argue, nevertheless, that the dichotomies as they are used in Cheney's own discourse are not mythological, but rather are themselves part of a modern abstract theory. First of all, the theory is foundationalist insofar as it makes bioregions the necessary grounds for all properly contextual discourse. Second, it is colonizing to the extent that it appears in an international journal written in English, the most widespread colonial language. Finally, it is essentializing in its conception of all modernism as *inherently* divorced from place.[19] Viewed in this way, it is easy to begin wondering how Cheney can possibly defend his monolithic treatment of modernism and his view of primitive peoples as uniformly environmentally friendly.

It is difficult to enter a debate upon the nature of discourse in prehistoric societies. Evidence of whether such societies were contextual, as Cheney claims, or totalizing is simply unavailable, for by definition prehistoric societies leave no discourse for posterity. Cheney, nevertheless, does hold that there is some evidence for his claims, namely, that the discourse of contemporary "primitive," i.e., tribal peoples, is contextual. I would argue, however, that such a claim involves a parochialism reminiscent of Victorian anthropology. Other cultures are taken as anachronisms, survivals from the evolutionary past of our own society, rather than as separate peoples with their own cultural development. In effect, by privileging tribal world views, the Victorian assumption of modern superiority over the primitive is simply reversed. More importantly, by generalizing about primitive peoples and their language, Cheney is in danger of engaging in a kind of essentialist discourse himself. Instead of noting the vast cultural differences between tribal peoples, he simply buries these under the weight of a supposed *essential* similarity, namely, their possession of contextual discourse!

What is the nature of contextual discourse? Cheney'seems to confuse the context that produces a particular statement, its epistemological standpoint, with the content of that statement (in particular, whether or not it makes universal claims). He certainly cannot hold that primitive peoples do not make universal generalizations. Indeed, consider the example Cheney offers of a contextual discourse, that of the Ainu, an indigenous people of Japan, who, according to Cheney, claim that "everything is a Kamui [spirit] for the Ainu." This claim is an abstract statement that is just as universal as any claim a contemporary scientist might make. The Ainu may be contextual in the sense that they come from a particular locale and have a language specific to that context, but they are certainly not contextual in the sense that they do not use totalizing generalizations.

For Cheney, the totalizing discourse of modernism is indelibly associated with the artificial, the unnatural, and the colonizing, that which is abstracted and applied outside its own remit—a remit that in natural circumstances is bounded within a biogeographical region. He states that "[t]he possibility of totalizing, colonizing discourse arises from the fact that concepts and theories can be abstracted from their paradigm settings and applied elsewhere."[20] By contrast, it is simply not possible for contextual discourses to be applied out of *place*. "[T]hey are not thought of as exportable."[21] In one way this claim makes perfect sense. The carrying of a language from that part of the world in which it developed to another might well cause serious problems. Just as a tropical plant *may* not be *at home* in a temperate climate—either languishing near death, at one extreme, or destroying indigenous flora, at the other—taxonomies designed for one place *may* be disruptive in other places.

But there is no reason to suppose, in general, that a language of *place* (biogeographically) need be environmentally friendly. Places are not static; environments change: the development of language and place hand-in-hand *may* have produced the destruction of many features of the original prehuman landscape. It *may* be that stable ecological relationships tend to evolve only when language, people, and place have been associated for long periods. In any event, to hold *a priori* that this relationship is universally the case for all tribal cultures is surely unwarranted.

For Cheney, totalization is a consequence of language closing in on itself as it gets farther from the natural world.[22] Nevertheless, to operate at all, language to some degree has to be closed in on itself. Because language is a means of communication between different *places* (people, social groups, etc.) in the world, it has to be abstracted as a condition of its existence. It has to be a *relatively autonomous* aspect of the world. Cheney provides no anthropological evidence to show that tribal languages are less abstract than other languages. Rather, his argument merely shows that mythic narrative frequently incorporates metaphors of natural place. *All* languages are abstracted from place insofar as they *can* be carried by human vectors. Thus, any kind of distinction that can be made between mythic narrative and modern theory on the grounds of abstraction seems likely to be one of degree rather than of kind. Cheney needs to recognize that any language is potentially exportable and *could* become colonizing.

Primitive taxonomies are not necessarily less rigid than modernist ones. Further, not all primitive peoples live statically in one geographical locale. Most have moved at some period, and when they moved they took their language with them. In such circumstances, a language that is less general and more tied to bioregional place seems to have just as much potential to be disruptive as a more generalized language. One reason why it might have this potential is that general languages might of necessity tend to be more flexible in constructing boundaries than those that are specifically tied to locale. The best sort of language to export, if any, is one that is not essentialist, that reflexively recognizes the need to be flexible and to fit language into place wherever it might end up. This anti-essentialist form of contextuality is not inevitably tied to residence in particular bioregional locales. In short, it is not totalizing discourses *per se* that are at fault, but their acontextual application.

Next, consider whether, as Cheney suggests, close contact with specific natural environments leads, via a meditative openness, to a mythical account of the relations between people and the world. It is at the level of this mythical narrative that moral norms are supposedly expressed and justified. This suspicion, that abstract theory somehow creates a barrier between the world and our speaking of it, is not only characteristic of some postmodernists, but was common to many romantics. In general, the romantic answer was to re-privilege the feeling side of a perceived dichotomy between reason and feeling. Attentiveness to primitive feelings was seen as an antidote to rationally imposed structures. For example: "[L]ike the other Romantics, Herder idolised early language and literature, from a time when these had still been direct expressions of inner feeling, not yet spoiled by the sophistication of reason and reflection."[23] Others saw the answer not in terms of inner feelings, but in a meditative openness to nature, which seems very close indeed to Cheney's and Heidegger's prescription. There can be few better examples to show the complexity of the modern traditions lumped together by Cheney than the writings of Jean-Jacques Rousseau, a figure central to Enlightenment thought who was also a profound romantic. His philosophy, like Cheney's, is inspired by an Arcadian myth of a prehistoric society rooted in nature. In addition, meditative openness to nature also plays an important role. In *Reveries of a Solitary Walker,* for example, Rousseau provides a paradigm for letting the world speak through him:

The more sensitive the soul of the observer, the greater the ecstasy aroused in him by this [natural] harmony. At such times his senses are possessed by a deep and delightful reverie, and in a state of blissful self-abandonment he loses himself in the immensity of this beautiful order, with which he feels himself at one. All individual objects escape him; he sees and feels nothing but the unity of all things. His ideas have to be restricted and his imagination limited by some particular circumstances for him to observe the separate parts of this universe which he was striving to embrace in its entirety.[24]

This passage is particularly striking with its talk of self-abandonment, sensitivity, and reverie. It could be read as a romantic version of the deconstruction of the self, the rejection of taxonomic boundaries, and an openness to the world that allows it to speak through us.[25]

The links between Cheney and Rousseau go still deeper. Both have very partial views on the advantages of primitive societies. Both overestimate the quality of life and the degree of freedom obtainable in such societies. The well-known depiction of the "noble savage" was itself influenced by the findings of contemporary explorers. For example, when Bougainville brought reports back to France of Tahiti and its populace, it seemed as if a primitive Arcadia had been found. Nevertheless, Bougainville himself only had the most superficial acquaintance with the customs of the islanders. That Tahitian society had strong class and gender divisions and was adept at human sacrifice only emerged as contacts with the culture became more prolonged. Nor were Tahitians relations with the natural world all that the romantics at first envisaged. At the time of Tahiti's "discovery" by Europeans it had a massive population of approximately 200,000: "A single bread-fruit tree was often owned by two or more families, who disputed each others rights of property over the branches. Infanticide was habitual."[26] Closeness to nature and the absence of theoretical orthodoxy is no guarantee of human freedom. Indeed, the absence of theory may actually exclude the possibility of voicing heterodoxy, of questioning the ideological assumptions incorporated in that society's world views, ethical values, etc.[27]

If there is anything to the analogy just drawn, it might suggest that Cheney's distinction between postmodernism and modernism is certainly one that is difficult to justify on grounds of philosophical concerns.[28] Although modern traditions influence him more deeply than Cheney admits, my point is not to claim that Cheney is a modernist. Rather, I am suggesting that the dichotomy between modernism and postmodernism is itself unconvincing.

III. Modernism and Its Context

Modernism itself needs to be seen in the context of its specific histor-ical and cultural origination. Modernism has its own myths, no doubt in part influenced by particular biogeographies. There is no *a priori* reason why modernism does not deserve attention as an example of the world *speaking through* people, a world of artifice, no doubt, but, nonetheless, a part of na-ture in the wider sense in which humanity is natural too. Cheney is willing to extend this contextual privilege in some instances of modernist discourse, when the predominant influence is supposedly natural. One example is "The Land Ethic," where Leopold states, "A thing is right when it tends to preserve the integrity, stability, and beauty of the biotic community. It is wrong when it tends otherwise."[29] Even though Cheney sees this ethic as formed, in part, by a *rootedness* in the sand counties of Wisconsin, at the same time he un-doubtedly also believes that it is meant to apply beyond Wisconsin's bound-aries. Thus, it is a "colonizing discourse" in the sense that Cheney gives to this phrase—and, moreover, as a principle abstracted from the practice in which it originated that theoretically is supposed to prescribe our relations to the world, it is also a "totalizing discourse."

Can other modernist claims be seen as analogously *rooted?* Why can modernism's totalizing discourses not be regarded as instances of particular places operating, in Cheney's words, "all the way up"? The answers to such questions lie in Cheney's acceptance of the particular set of hard and fast ho-mologies outlined above. He has not yet begun the work of social negotiation for his own culture because his overt acceptance of the nature/culture and modern/postmodern dichotomies does not permit it.[30] To escape the necessity for a constant recontextualizing of social discourse, he depends upon an ide-alized picture of a timeless natural environment as opposed to the historicized artificial environment of our cities. This division, however, is merely a con-tinuation of a myth that is undoubtedly modernist in origin, even in his own terms: if it was modernism that broke the connections between the human, qua abstract subject, and the world, then the nature/culture division upon which Cheney relies is very much a modernist creation.[31]

Cheney's Arcadian myth of a primitive people rooted in nature is asso-ciated with a utopian vision of a return to contextuality that is supposed to take place with the advent of postmodernism. What, however, can such a re-turn mean for the majority of people who live in urban and agricultural envi-ronments? Is it impossible for *place* to speak through mediating subjects in modern cultures? To be sure, the city environment is not one populated with salmon, unless they lie cold on the supermarket slab; rather, it is populated with its own ecology of cars preying upon pedestrians, the rich upon the poor. In Britain, we live in an environment with no wilderness left. *All* the geography and landscapes are human influenced; yet, the land, its history, and its occupants—human and otherwise—can still speak through us. Like Cheney, I can speak out against the horrors of the city and against much of the history that made me. We are free to produce our own myths, or, alternatively, we are all tied to producing the myths of our personal *place*. Each of us is a product of our particular place in the world. The place can be described in terms of geography, history, family, biology, and so forth. Yet, the product is also *to a degree* self-constructed, internally motivated, etc. The world does not *just* speak through us; we also form an active part of it.[32]

To the extent that we are a product of a particular society at a certain historical period (a *social formation*), both the theoretical/mythic pictures we draw and our everyday actions are ideologically infused. There is no reason why theories, like myths, cannot be seen as an *expression* (rather than a *representation*) of a particular modern place. Correspondingly, theory also forms an important part of the modern environment that can be ideologically incorporated at the very heart of the individual. Although our dispositions and ethical values are constructed in and influenced by place, they, in turn, influence place, including our theoretical place. Insofar as such values and perspectives are theoretically articulated, they attain a relative paradigmatic autonomy while remaining open to transformative criticism inspired by alternative theoretical expressions and by practical experiences of the nonhuman and the non-theorized.

The importance of place is not an invention of postmodernism. Rather, to the contrary, "place" in this sense has to be something much wider than bioregionalism. Cheney excludes important aspects of Martin and Mohanty's multifaceted conception of the contextual background of discourse, which they call *home*. Their original concept includes "geography, demography and architecture, as well as the configuration of . . . relationships to particular people," that is, elements of both "nature" and "culture."[33] In contrast, Cheney's conception of bioregionality places exclusive emphasis on the importance of "natural" contexts. Thus, it might be appropriate to question his bioregional foundationalism by re-privileging one of Martin and Mohanty's "cultural" elements, namely, architecture. Consider the following remarks of Le Corbusier, who is unquestionably a doyen of modernism:

> Every modern man has the mechanical sense. The feeling for mechanics exists and is justified by our daily activities. This feeling in regard to machinery is one of respect, gratitude and esteem. . . .

> Machinery includes economy as an essential factor leading to minute selection. There is a moral sentiment in the feeling for mechanics. . . .

> The man who is intelligent, cold and calm has grown wings to himself.[34]

Here are all the hallmarks of modern (humanist) discourse, the emphasis upon the abstract human subject and "his" calculating rationality, the reference to *essential* factors inherent within machinery, etc. However, from another perspective, it can be read as a piece of contextual writing about the condition of a group of people *placed* within a modern environment. According to Corbusier, the world "speaking through" these particularly placed people has come to regard some of the mechanical constituents of that world in a moral light, has come to entertain a certain epistemology, has engaged in particular practices, and so on. In this world, even machinery *can* be spoken of in ethical terms. Our ethical values have come to incorporate our practical relations to the modern world. Viewing his writings in this way, Corbusier can be seen as a mythographer of modernity.

Cheney's problem is that if *all* geographical (or wider) environments are admitted to be influential, to speak through people, then how can he privilege the natural and its concomitant contextual (geographically speaking) discourse above artificial (and sometimes totalizing) discourse? His only recourse is to view any discourse espousing opposition to "modernism" as being privileged just because it is oppositional. Although doing so allows almost any position whatsoever to be positionally privileged, given a certain characterization of modernism, it provides no grounds at all for accepting these views as being objectively right. It merely permits us to claim that all discourse comes from place, which is precisely what he seems to deny in the case of modernism.

Cheney is caught in a bind, despite his standpoint epistemology, because he is loath to admit that there is no way of being objectively right. To make such an admission in no way lessens the importance that nature might have for us. Nor does it entail that we should worship machines. Nor need it weaken criticism of those forms of foundationalism according to which nature is not morally considerable. The paradox in Cheney's position lies in his attempt to privilege an oppositional mythical narrative—i.e., his own theory. This attempt opposes the general tendency of his thought toward a much more radical *positionality,* a relational view of taxonomy and discourse in which "nature" is "one more player [among many] in the construction of community." The reason for this problem is Cheney's desire to present an environmentally friendly stance, one that maintains close connections with nature, that is objectively correct. The "correct" stance toward the environment, in this case, is supposed to be a myth that is able to transcend boundaries and cultures. Insofar as his position depends crucially upon the opposition of contextual myth to totalizing and foundational discourse, Cheney has to be judged inconsistent.

By contrast, a broader and less constrained positionality than Cheney's has great potential. Such an account would not be identical to a cultural relativism in which one ethic cannot be judged better than another. Such anthropological relativism takes cultures as isolated and essentially incommensurable. In an account with a modest positionality, however, there could be similarities and differences at all levels. Moral values in different communities might converge because of similarities in geography, biology, cultural practices, problematics, histories, or any combination of these or other aspects of place.

In terms of this modest account, it is possible to develop a conception of place with similarities to Wittgenstein's idea of "forms of life." In such an account, *form of life* would not be a narrowly defined concept grounded in either human culture or the natural world, but rather would include a wider conception of community, including all relevant aspects of past and present environment. Humans tend to have similarities with each other on many levels in their practical as well as discursive encounters with the world. These similarities make communication possible. Without such similarities at some level, discourse becomes impossible. In addition, communication entails a meeting of places, an expression of different perspectives.

Human social practices, including discursive practices, do not just exist in place, but themselves form a part of place. As Hans Peter Duerr puts it, "The questions that have meaning within a particular form of life are not *determined* by that way of life, but constitute themselves *elements of life* of that world view."[35] We can expand Wittgenstein's concept to provide a vague perspectival standpoint in which forms of life are the background in which and against which humans function as nodes of positionality.[36] A broadly similar interpretation has already been offered by Lynne Rudder Baker, who writes: "The idea of a form of life emerges as the result of a kind of transcendental argument: We have language that we use to communicate; . . . meaning requires a community. 'Form of life' is Wittgenstein's way of designating what it is about a community that makes possible meaning. Given this role of the idea of a form of life, it is hardly surprising that little meaningfully can be said about it."[37] In this sense, we can treat Wittgenstein's statement, "What has to be accepted, the given, is—so one could say—*Forms of life*," in a much less anthropocentric and sociological way than is usual.[38] Such an admittedly vague form of totalizing, but, nevertheless, anti-essentialist and anti-foundationalist myth seems a more promising ground for understanding the complexities of morality than any such narrow concept as bioregionalism. We can see that bioregionalism is only one among many aspects of community that can be used to recontextualize social discourse. Finally, this *positional holism* does not reduce the human subject to a completely functional role as the voice of nature. To quote Duerr once more: "It seems a mistake on which extreme relativists and dogmatists of the 'transcendental' bent agree . . . to be convinced that the form of life is the framework in the strict sense of the word *within* which all questions have to find their meaning. . . . Dogmatists tend to hold . . . that we do not think the myths but the myths think themselves in us."[39]

IV. Afterword

It is ironic, important, and probably not accidental that there is a current reemphasis on context in philosophy. This development has occurred at a moment in history when global uniformity is proclaimed from the offices of governments and powerful multinationals. If and when *place* comes to mean nothing more than how close one is to the nearest McDonald's, the totalizing discourse of mass communication, of television and radio, will have triumphed. In such a world, we will not even be free to create our own modernist myths. They will be created for us by the commercial exploiters of our planet as they encourage us to join them in the death of the "natural" world.

The most devastating myth we are fed is that of economic humanism, the reduction of all value to economic value, determined by a "free" market of isolated selfish individuals. Although this myth has already become a part of the ideological place of many people, we may be able to resist it if we are able to see the oversimplified essentialist nature of the discourse. To this extent, I agree with Cheney, not with the privilege accorded to this opposition, but with its necessity for those who have and wish to promulgate different world views. In this sense, those of us who value nature for itself cannot but oppose this particular modernist myth. However, while insisting upon the value of nature, we must forgo any claim to step outside of ideology, to obtain a transcendental perspective via privileged access to nature and the natural. The strength of the environmentalists' argument is that similar conclusions come from many different places, providing an overdetermination of natural value and environmental policies and decisions.

Notes

Smith is an ecologist, in the Philosophy Department of the University of Stirling, Scotland, who is currently completing a doctoral dissertation on humanism and anti-humanism in accounts of environmental values. His philosophical perspective is particularly influenced by Louis Althusser's conception of ideology and the later philosophy of Wittgenstein. The author thanks Andrew Brennan and the anonymous referees for their encouragement and their valuable criticisms.

First published in *Environmental Ethics* 15, no. 1. Permission to reprint courtesy of *Environmental Ethics* and the author.

1. Jim Cheney, "Postmodern Environmental Ethics: Ethics as Bioregional Narrative," *Environmental Ethics* 11 (1989): 117–34 [Chapter 1 in this book]. I con-

centrate almost entirely on this paper as an expression of Cheney's philosophy rather than on his later paper, "The Neo-Stoicism of Radical Environmentalism," *Environmental Ethics* 11 (1989): 293–325, which is a more specific critique of certain deep ecological approaches.

2. Cheney, "Postmodern Environmental Ethics," p. 122. Although Cheney names 7000 B.C. as the starting point of modernism, his evidence is hardly supportive of this claim. For example, one author cited declares that a unified concept of the *self* developed between the composition of the *Iliad* and the *Odyssey,* i.e., some 6000 years later!

3. Ibid.

4. Ibid, p. 120.

5. Ibid., p. 122. Barbara Bender, in T. Douglas Price and James A. Brown, eds., *Prehistoric Hunter-Gatherers: The Emergence of Cultural Complexity* (Orlando, Fla.: Academic Press, 1985), challenges the anthropological evidence for such a division into so-called "hot" and "cold" societies, those with history and those without, those that change and those that supposedly do not.

6. Cheney, "Postmodern Environmental Ethics," p. 122.

7. Ibid, p. 121. Throughout I use Cheney's conception of myth rather than introduce any of the many technical meanings that the term has in anthropological literature or structuralist writings. See, for example, Roland Barthes, *Mythologies* (London: Paladin, 1990).

8. Paula Gunn Allen, *The Sacred Hoop: Recovering the Feminine in American Indian Traditions* (Boston: Beacon Press, 1986), pp. 103–05; Cheney, "Postmodern Environmental Ethics," p. 121.

9. Cheney, "Postmodern Environmental Ethics," p. 126.

10. Cheney's reference to male domination and intratribal violence in contemporary tribal societies as a "deterioration" exemplifies this Arcadian myth. In calling it deterioration, he implies that these tribes enjoyed a past in which these vices were absent.

11. Cheney, "Postmodern Environmental Ethics," pp. 118–20.

12. Ibid, p. 118. These are not the only "postmodern" options, but it should be recognized that to treat language in these ways hardly eschews ontology or makes a radical break with modernism. Instead, these options resurrect elements of modern philosophical traditions. The former alternative is an example of pragmatism; the latter is a type of anthropocentric idealism.

13. Ibid, p. 118.

14. Ibid, p. 119.

15. Ibid, p. 119 (emphasis added).

16. Ibid, p. 128.

17. Ibid, p. 126 (emphasis in original).

18. Ibid, p. 128. The concept of bioregional foundationalism has a distinctly modernist ancestry. According to Malcolm Nicholson, "The earth was one whole. But geographers also recognized the existence of regionality. Phenomena peculiar to a particular region were the causes of other equally regional phenomena—for example, climatic and environmental conditions influenced human society so that, as Kant wrote, 'in the mountains, men are actively and continuously bold lovers of freedom and their homeland.'" Malcolm Nicholson, "Alexander von Humboldt and the Geography of Vegetation," in Andrew Cunningham and Nicholas Jardine, eds., *Romanticism and the Sciences* (Cambridge: Cambridge University Press, 1990), p. 170. Cheney would probably abjure Kant's simplistic causality of place determining personality, but replace it with place "speaking through" people. But is this change really any less naive? Both see *place* primarily as a bioregional concept. (I do not mean to disparage bioregionality per se, merely certain formulations of it.)

19. It is also inconsistent, for how can Cheney repudiate totalizing attempts to give one true picture of the world while endorsing Ridington's remark that "the *true* history of these people [the Beaver Indians] will have to be written in mythic language"? Cheney, "Postmodern Environmental Ethics," p. 123; Robin Ridington, "Fox and Chickadee," in Calvin Martin, ed., *The American Indian and the Problem of History* (Oxford: Oxford University Press, 1987), pp. 134–35.

20. Cheney, "Postmodern Environmental Ethics," p. 126.

21. Ibid, p. 120.

22. Ibid.

23. Nicholas A. Rupke, "Caves, Fossils and the History of the Earth," in Cunningham and Jardine, eds., *Romanticism and the Sciences,* p. 253.

24. Jean-Jacques Rousseau, *Reveries of a Solitary Walker* (Harmondsworth: Penguin Books, 1979), p. 108.

25. Ibid, pp. 110–11. It is a great shame that this work, which was Rousseau's last, seems to have been overlooked in the literature on environmental ethics. Among other things, it contains beautifully expressed and witty passages on the distinction between the instrumental and intrinsic valuation of nature. "There is one further thing that helps to deter people of taste from taking an interest in the vegetable kingdom. This is the habit of considering plants only as a source of drugs and medicines. . . . No one imagines that the structure of plants could deserve any attention in its own right. . . . Linger in some meadow studying one by one all the flowers that adorn it, and people will take you for a herbalist and ask you for something to cure the itch in children, scab in men, or glanders in horses. . . . These medicinal associations . . . tarnish the colour of the meadows and the brilliance of the flowers, they drain the woods of all freshness and make the green leaves and shade seem dull and disagreeable. . . . It is

no use seeking garlands for shepherdesses among the ingredients of an enema."
Rousseau was also aware of the dangers of such instrumental evaluation. "This attitude which always brings everything back to our material interest, causing us to seek
in all things either profits or remedies, and which if we were always in good health
would leave us indifferent to all the works of nature. . . ." Ibid, pp. 109–10.

26. Henry Adam, *Tahiti* (New York: Scholars' Facsimiles and Reprints, 1976),
p. 6. Bougainville touched only the Eastern side of Tahiti at Hitiau in April 1768.
Douglas C. Oliver, *Ancient Tahitian Society* (Honolulu: University of Hawaii Press,
1974), reports that violence was endemic and mass rape of those females on the losing
side in battle a common occurrence. "Sometimes when a warrior felled his opponent
he would beat the body to a flat pulp, cut a slit through it large enough for his own
head to pass through, and then wear it, poncho fashion as a triumphant taunt."

27. For a detailed anthropological discussion of this question, see Pierre
Bourdieu, *Outline of a Theory of Practice* (Cambridge: Cambridge University Press,
1991), pp. 159–71.

28. Cheney also characterizes all modernist philosophy as accepting a subject/ob-
ject divide. He endorses Paula Gunn Allen's description of the modernist position, in
which "there is such a thing as determinable fact, natural—that is right explanations—
and reality that can be determined outside the human agency of discovery and fact
finding." Cheney, "Postmodern Environmental Ethics," p. 121. See also Cheney's own
remarks on p. 120. Cheney's paper drastically underrates the complexity of modern
Western world views. He rightly notes the connections frequently found between *representational* epistemology—according to which theory is a wholly autonomous realm
mirroring the world—and conceptions of a rational autonomous human subject.
However, in equating this "humanism" with modernity, he overlooks the many alternative problematics. There are many philosophies that deny these humanist presuppositions, but cannot, by any stretch of the imagination, be termed postmodern. For example, Althusser's anti-humanism specifically denies the autonomy of the subject and
develops an epistemology based on social practice. See *For Marx* (London: New Left
Books, 1979) and *Essays on Ideology* (London: Verso, 1984), esp. ch. 1.

29. Aldo Leopold, *A Sand County Almanac* (New York: Oxford University
Press, 1949), pp. 224–25.

30. In a different context, Cheney has asked a similar question: "*Might* we listen
with the same ear to the residents of Harlem (or to the corporate executives engaged
in the destruction of the old-growth forests) with which we listen to the voices of a
tall-grass prairie in southern Wisconsin? What would such a listening be like?" He
seems to think that we might and must achieve this listening. "Even the strategies of
the colonizers must be understood ecologically. They are not to be understood or condemned using timeless and ahistorically 'true' criteria." Unfortunately, he does not
seem to have realized the implications of this answer for his own methodology. He
criticizes deep ecology for "its [modernist] dualistic opposition of anthropocentric and
ecological consciousness" and its acontextuality while working with just such rigid
dualisms himself. Cheney, "Neo-Stoicism," pp. 317–18.

31. The intuitive obviousness of this culture/nature dichotomy is being broken down in many respects. Bill McKibben suggests that with the advent of the greenhouse effect and ozone depletion, we see *The End of Nature* (London: Penguin Books, 1990). Human influence is now so widespread as to preclude the existence of untouched wilderness.

32. Cheney's reduction of individuals to vectors of a mythological language originating in natural structures can be seen as a naturally grounded version of the social anti-humanism promoted by structural Marxists such as Althusser. It similarly underestimates the degree of individual human autonomy.

33. Cheney, "Postmodern Environmental Ethics," p. 126.

34. Le Corbusier, *Towards a New Architecture* (London: The Architectural Press, 1974), pp. 115–19.

35. Hans Peter Duerr, *Dreamtime: Concerning the Boundary Between Wilderness and Civilisation,* trans. Felicitas Goodman (Oxford: Basil Blackwell, 1985), p. 96.

36. Cheney alludes to this view of the positional subject in the work of Linda Alcoft. Cheney, "Neo-Stoicism," p. 318.

37. Lynne Rudder Baker, "On the Very Idea of a Form of Life," *Inquiry* 27 (1984): 277–89.

38. Ludwig Wittgenstein, *Philosophical Investigations* (Oxford: Basil Blackwell, 1958), p. 226e.

39. Duerr, *Dreamtime,* p. 97.

14

Quantum Theory, Intrinsic Value, and Panentheism

Michael E. Zimmerman

I. Introduction

J. Baird Callicott has recently examined attempts to resolve what he considers to be "the most critical and recalcitrant theoretical problem of environmental ethics, the problem of intrinsic value in nature."[1] He points out that these attempts commit the "naturalistic fallacy" of identifying moral value with this or that natural property. As a plausible alternative to the theory of intrinsic values, i.e., values that inhere in entities independently of any evaluator, Callicott offers Hume's theory of moral sentiments. Hume maintains that good and evil are evaluations grounded in the feelings that someone or something evokes in the subject. While Hume often speaks as if utility evokes the feeling that a person or thing is "good," he makes clear that people also regard other persons and things as good *for their own sakes.* Callicott argues that just as parents value their child for its own sake, and not merely for its utility, so too other people might value a forest, river, or bioregion for its own sake, and not merely for its utility. Callicott uses the term *inherent value* to describe the value that accrues to people and things that are appreciated *for themselves.* This term *intrinsic value* continues to refer to the value that things are alleged to have independently of any evaluator. Making use of the notion of inherent value, Callicott argues, we can develop an environmental ethics that does not fall prey to the naturalistic fallacy, and that is not based merely on prudential, anthropocentric concerns. Such an environmental ethics can be discovered in the work of Aldo Leopold, who owes much to Darwin, who, in turn, was himself considerably influenced by Hume.

Yet, having defended this Humean-based theory of environmental ethics, Callicott then shows that it has shortcomings because "the Humean fact-value dichotomy is logically and historically ancillary" to "the Cartesian subject-object dichotomy."[2] Callicott argues that while classical physics adopted this subject-object dichotomy, quantum physics does not. Quantum physics provides the framework necessary for "a wholly new axiology which does not rest, either explicitly or implicitly, upon Descartes' obsolete bifurcation."³ There are two parts to Callicott's argument from quantum physics: a conservative and a radical part. According to the conservative part, quantum physics by overcoming the subject-object dualism also overcomes the value-fact dualism. Just as the "objective" properties of atomic particles are in fact the result of interactions between the knower and the thing known, so too we can understand the "valuational" properties of things in terms of the interaction between thing and evaluator. Values then are neither subjective nor objective, but are "the progeny of two complementary potentialities: receptive but active consciousness and an exciting but excitable physical plenum."

In the second, more radical part of his argument, Callicott claims that quantum physics views the universe as an internally related cosmic "web." The dualistic view of the "I" as residing inside of a skin bag and thus separate from everything else has been undermined by the insight of contemporary physics (and ecology) that in some sense the world is my body: I and world interpenetrate. Since we have traditionally assumed that the "I" is intrinsically valuable (not merely "inherently" valuable), and since the "I" is internally related to all of nature, then we can arguably regard nature, too, as intrinsically valuable. The findings of quantum physics, thus, appear to provide a startling new basis for environmental ethics.

In the present essay, I examine critically both Callicott's conservative and radical use of quantum physics for environmental ethics. I argue that Western humanity will develop an attitude of respect toward nonhuman reality only as we move from atomistic, dualistic ego consciousness toward relational, nondualistic consciousness. Although new scientific theories compatible with a metaphysics of interrelatedness may help prepare the ground for such a move, and in addition may give humanity prudential reasons for treating the biosphere with more care, a change in scientific understanding alone cannot produce the needed change of consciousness. I believe that Callicott is right, nevertheless, in suggesting that trends in science—and in other fields as well—may be a harbinger of humanity's continuing evolution toward a more inclusive, less dualistic mode of consciousness.

At the outset, let me acknowledge how much I have learned from Callicott's excellent work. I regard the present essay as part of a continuing conversation with him.

II. Callicott's Conservative Approach

It is often said that subject-object, mind-body dualism went hand-in-glove with the development of the scientific view of the universe as a collection of atoms that are externally related according to invariant causal laws. Yet such dualism is not at all required by modern science, for a thorough-going materialism obviates the need for mind-body dualism.[4] Nevertheless, for a variety of reasons (including those associated with the rise of *Homo oeconomicus*), Descartes' dualistic interpretation of classical physics had an enormous influence on metaphysical and ethical theory. According to Galileo, Descartes, Locke, and many others, the "primary" qualities of natural objects are those (such as position, momentum, extension, and mass) that belong to the objects intrinsically, i.e., independently of being observed. These primary qualities are the "facts" of physical reality. "Secondary" qualities are those (such as color, smell, taste, sound) that at first *seem* to be ingredients of the objects themselves, but turn out to be experiences (or representations or ideas) that result when the sense organs of a perceiving subject are stimulated by some object (as when sound waves stimulate the eardrum). Without a perceiver, the physical universe would be noiseless, soundless, tasteless, and colorless. In addition, some philosophers eventually began using the term *tertiary qualities* to describe values that subjects attribute to natural objects. Insofar as these qualities are wholly the product of the evaluating subject, the realm of facts (nature) is without value of its own. This view of nature can help to justify what many people regard as the "exploitation" of nonhuman beings.

Callicott observes that Hume accepted both subject-object dualism and the value-fact distinction and therefore concluded that moral evaluations do not concern the primary or intrinsic properties of objects. Instead, those evaluations are extrinsic to the object and subjective in origin. Callicott argues, however, that for Hume these evaluations are not merely arbitrary, but are rooted in the human heart, and that this view influenced Darwin, who was familiar with Hume's moral philosophy and maintained that human sentiments help to promote the formation of society. Similarly, contemporary sociobiologists argue that altruism is a function of kin selection: animals and humans tend to behave not only in self-interested ways, but also in ways that protect their offspring and other relatives in order to enhance the reproduction of the family DNA.[5]

According to Callicott, altruistic behavior—the original importance of which lay in promoting reproduction of one's own kin—forms the basis for valuing something "for itself." Valuing something "for itself" amounts to ascribing *inherent worth* to something, i.e., valuing it not instrumentally but "for its own sake." In accordance with sociobiology, altruism itself was originally "instrumental" in character, since it served the purpose of insuring the propagation of the parents' own genes. Nevertheless, even though altruism might have been instrumental in propagating one's own genes, the people behaving in altruistic ways were not necessarily *conscious* of the underlying adaptive-biological motives. The *experience* of such people would have been that they loved their offspring "for themselves," not merely as carriers of familial DNA. Once altruism had emerged as a constituent feature of humankind, the scope and nature of altruism could be transformed by *cultural* developments.

Leopold seized on the notion of expanded altruism as the basis for an environmental ethics, i.e., an ethic that values nature not only instrumentally, but also as having inherent value. Callicott writes that "Leopold masterfully played upon our open social and moral sentiments by representing plants and animals, soils, and water as "fellow members" of our maximally expanded "biotic community." Hence, to those who are ecologically well-informed, nonhuman natural entities are inherently valuable—as putative members of one extended family or society. And nature as a whole is inherently valuable—as the one great family or society to which we belong as members or citizens."[6] It would appear that in addition to valuing nonhuman natural entities as inherently valuable, Leopold also believed that prudence requires that we transform our treatment of those entities. Nature is not only valuable "for itself," but also as an instrument necessary for sustaining the human species. Hence, it would be adaptive behavior for humanity to begin treating nature with respect—and what better way to achieve this than to speak of nonhuman entities as having "inherent value"? To conclude that valuing nonhuman human entities "for themselves" is *really* to value them instrumentally, however, is a reductionistic move that Hume himself rejected. He concluded that it is misguided to interpret all human behavior solely in self-interested, instrumental terms; much human behavior can be best explained by saying that human beings naturally care about others for their own sake.

We cannot pursue any further the twists and turns of this old dispute about egoism vs. altruism. Suffice it to say that Callicott is satisfied that the views of Hume-Darwin-Leopold can provide a genuine environmental ethics, one concerned with nature "for itself." Nevertheless, Callicott concludes that this trio of thinkers was deeply affected by the fact-value and the subject-object dichotomies associated (rightly or wrongly) with modern science. As a scientist influenced by the dualistic interpretation of science, Leopold took it for granted that nature is "in itself" value-neutral. According to Callicott, however, there have been significant changes in twentieth-century physics which undercut the dualistic metaphysics and science that were the basis for the work of Hume, Darwin, and Leopold:

> Hence, although Hume's classical subjectivist axiology, evolutionarily explained by Darwin, and ecologically informed by Leopold, provides for inherent value in nature and thus a serviceable axiology for a properly *environmental* ethic, it is not consistent with a *contemporary* or

post-*revolutionary* scientific world view. Moreover, as Warwick Fox has recently argued, ecology and certain interpretations of quantum theory provide "structurally similar" or analogous representations of terrestrial organic nature and cosmic micro-physical nature, respectively. The essentially Humean *axiological* foundation of Leopold's land ethic is actually, therefore, an insidious theoretical legacy of classical mechanics in a larger fabric of ideas which has succeeded and indeed transcended mechanism.[7]

Callicott notes that Descartes' dualistic interpretation of classical physics provided a metaphysical paradigm or model which deeply influenced modern moral theory. For example, Hume took it for granted that the fact-value, object-subject dichotomies were descriptive of reality. To remain plausible during the Enlightenment, moral theory had to take account of what science was allegedly saying about reality. While Aldo Leopold developed environmental ethics to the utmost within the constraints imposed by metaphysical dualism, Callicott suggests that we must now take seriously the fact that such dualism has been undermined by the appearance of quantum theory. Quantum theory allegedly overcomes the subject-object dualism responsible both for humanity's exploitation of nature and for Leopold's attempt to curb that exploitation. Just as a certain interpretation of classical mechanics provided a paradigm for the development of moral theory in the previous era, so too Callicott proposes to interpret quantum theory in a way that makes it available as a new paradigm for developing a new moral theory to guide contemporary humanity's relation with the rest of reality. This new moral theory, based upon a nondualistic metaphysical view, would go well beyond the limits of Leopold's "land ethic" which is still rooted in dualistic metaphysics.

Callicott maintains that quantum theory, including its so-called "Copenhagen interpretation," no longer speaks of "intrinsic" or "objective" qualities of atomic structures as if those qualities existed independently of the interaction between atomic structures and the measuring apparatus of the scientist. Prior to making a measurement, a physicist cannot say that an atomic "particle" (a term that must be used with care when speaking about subatomic reality) has a definite location or momentum; instead, it only has "tendencies" (measured in terms of probability functions) to have a particular location or momentum. The very act of measuring is responsible for "collapsing" the probability function in such a way as to give the "particle" in question a specific location. Yet the nature of these so-called particles is such that when they take on a relatively precise location, their momentum becomes relatively more indeterminate. The "objectivity" of atomic phenomena, the qualities that Newton (and Einstein, too) regarded as "primary" and "independent of the observer," is constituted by the very act of measuring. Since the Humean

distinction between fact and value was based, at least in part, on the notion
that science discloses objective facts about physical reality, and since
quantum physics has undermined the doctrine of such objective facts, we can
conclude that quantum physics undermines the radical fact-value distinction,
too. In light of quantum physics,

> *All* properties, in short, could be conceived as the classical secondary
> qualities were supposed to be, not dichotomous, existing actually either
> on the side of the object or on the side of the subject, but potential and
> dipolar requiring for their realization the interaction between erstwhile
> subjects and erstwhile objects. To borrow a metaphor from Plato, ac-
> tual reality in its quantitative, qualitative, and valuational manifesta-
> tions is the issue, the progeny of a marriage . . . of two complementary
> potentialities: receptive and active consciousness and an exciting but
> excitable physical plenum. Mass and motion, color and flavor, good
> and evil, beauty and ugliness, all alike, are equally potentialities which
> are actualized in relationship to us or to other similarly constituted or-
> ganisms. . . .
>   . . . Borrowing . . . from the vocabulary of quantum theory, we
> may assert . . . that values are virtual. Virtual value is an ontological
> category . . . encompassing the entire spectrum of instrumental and in-
> herent values . . . In other words, nature affords a range of potential
> value, i.e., some things are potentially instrumentally valuable . . . and
> some things are *inherently* valuable, i.e., are in themselves potentially
> valuable for their own sakes.
>   . . . The advantage of the quantum theoretical axiology lies in the
> fact that it renders an account of value which puts value on an ontolog-
> ical par with other properties, including culturally revered quantitative
> properties. . . . Physics and ethics are, in other words, equally descrip-
> tive of nature.[8]

In this ingenious interpretation, Callicott "solves" the problem of the
intrinsic value of nonhuman beings by showing that there are no intrinsic
properties of any sort, whether they be physical or axiological. *All* properties
are interactive in origin; *nothing* is "intrinsic" in the sense of being independent of such interaction. With the notion that axiological and even physical
properties are products of *relationships,* Callicott undermines traditional substance metaphysics and its subject-predicate scheme. Substance metaphysics
was the mainstay both of the doctrine of intrinsic value and of the doctrine of
primary qualities. Even if a backer of the doctrine of intrinsic value admits
that it has been sunk along with substance metaphysics, however, he or she
might remain uncomfortable with Callicott's "solution" to the value question.

While neither radically relative nor merely subjectivistic, Callicott holds that the value of nonhuman beings is only "actualized" through interaction with human (or other) evaluators. Critics might object that the real force of the doctrine of intrinsic values was that it made the worth of things *independent* of human evaluators. Callicott addresses such critics in his more radical interpretation of quantum theory.

Before we examine that interpretation, however, we must pause to examine Callicott's contention that quantum theory overcomes subject-object dualism. This examination is important not only for introducing Callicott's second, more radical interpretation of quantum theory, but also for our paving the way for my own contention, viz., that quantum theory does not involve the nondualistic *experience* necessary for overcoming the subject-object dualism. In other words, quantum theory (and its practical utilization) does not in and of itself bring about a new attitude toward nature on the part of quantum theorists. A quantum theorist can remain committed to an anthropocentric, dualistic attitude in his or her everyday life. Yet it is precisely this anthropocentric, dualistic attitude, apparently responsible for humanity's destructive treatment of nature, that Callicott hopes will be changed by quantum theory. Let us now turn to the question of whether quantum theory overturns subject-object dualism.

III. Quantum Physics and Subject-Object Dualism

While physicists agree on the mathematical formalism of quantum theory, they are in disagreement about how to interpret the metaphysical implications of that formalism. There are at least eight interpretations of quantum physics, all of which are absurd by common-sense standards.[9] According to the interpretation that Callicott favors, what we call "objects" are constituted as the result of the activity of measurement. Niels Bohr, one of the founders of quantum physics, agreed with this interpretation of quantum theory. Bohr, nevertheless, would not be so quick to say that quantum theory overcomes subject-object dualism, although certain other physicists would say that it does. Bohr held that quantum physics *does* overcome the dualism of classical physics, according to which there is a precisely knowable reality existing independently of the subject. Bohr stated that what is *observed* results from the interaction between atomic structure and measuring apparatus. Yet, as Henry Folse maintains, despite this interactionist view, Bohr remained a *realist,* although not a classical realist, since he did not hold that "the ontological status of independently real objects is the same as that of 'objects' represented by the classical concept of the state of the isolated system . . . defined as possessing the classical mechanical properties."[10] Bohr contended that we cannot make unambiguous use of the vocabulary of classical physics to describe subatomic reality. What we describe as the "position" and "momentum" of a particle do not correspond to subatomic reality, but are ways of representing in terms of classical physics the results of the interaction between subatomic reality and measuring apparatus. Classical physics sought to describe atoms as tiny substances with properties in three-dimensional space. In contrast, Bohr held that while we must represent reality that way, we are wrong to think that subatomic reality is in fact like that. Folse concludes:

> Freeing the concept of a reality behind the phenomena from the presupposition that such a reality must be described as a substance possessing properties removes the temptation to concede that a realistic defense of quantum theory is impossible. But our language is so influenced by the character of the descriptions of phenomenal objects that a verbal communication referring to the reality symbolized in the formal mathematical structures of the theory is quite difficult. Nevertheless, whatever else the nature of an independent reality might entail, the assumption that such a reality is endowed with the power to interact with other physical systems to produce the phenomena we observe is directly required by [Bohr's framework of] complementarity. The formal theoretical structures from which we can predict descriptions of observed phenomena provide a symbolic expression for the characteristics of such an activity.[11]

Hence, despite the fact that subatomic reality can only show up for us in the laboratory as a result of interactions between reality and measuring apparatus, this does not mean that the reality itself is *constituted* by that interaction. What we call "objective" features of that reality are those properties that are constituted by the measuring activity. For Bohr, there was still a "reality" independent of us, but it could only manifest itself objectively, i.e., as an object within the space-time parameters of classical physics, in terms consistent with the entire experimental situation established by the investigator.

Trouble arises if we speak as if the *consciousness* of the human subject is what interacts with atomic reality, because in fact the interacting "agent" is a complex and often enormous *machine*. The human subject notices and interprets the findings of such interactions; those findings remain an "object" for the knowing "subject." We can say, of course, that the human subject chooses what, when, and where to measure so that consciousness has a role in directing the measuring apparatus; and such apparatus can even be conceived as an extension of human sense organs. Some interpretations of quantum physics go so far as to say that reality only becomes objectified and realized insofar as it is measured, known, and studied by the human subject; hence, the history of the universe becomes finalized only when human subjects interpret and "objectify" the still indeterminate processes of that history.[12] Such interpretations, however, are highly controversial. Even the relatively conservative approach adopted by Callicott can be construed as going too far, for the experience of mind-body, subject-object dualism is *not* overcome simply because atomic structures are "objectified" in the process of measuring them. Here we are not talking about the interaction between atomic structure and consciousness, but about the interaction between atomic structure and measuring apparatus: two physical structures. The majority of physicists continue to speak in dualistic terms; their work in quantum physics does not necessarily lead to any shift in their relationship with or their appraisal of nonhuman reality.

It is possible that the continuing dualistic thinking of quantum physicists is merely an uncritical residue of habitual practices, much like what happens when astronomers who are theoretically aligned with Copernicus still use Ptolemaic categories in everyday language ("the sun rises earlier in the summer"). I would maintain, however, that quantum physicists continue to speak in everyday situations in ways that are inconsistent with their own theoretical findings precisely because their everyday experience has not been affected by those insights. Despite the nondualistic implications of quantum theory, its practitioners continue to experience themselves and the world dualistically, as ego-subject standing over against the object-world. To move beyond this dualistic mode, an experiential insight is required that is not available from quantum theory. Nevertheless, quantum theory, especially now that it is being made more accessible to non-experts, may well help to demonstrate the limits of certain aspects of dualistic and rationalistic thought and encourage increasing numbers of people to begin exploring nondualistic alternatives to dualistic rationality, even though in and of itself quantum theory does not produce the experience of nondualism. In the next section, I discuss some of these issues in more detail.

IV. Mysticism, Quantum Theory, and Nondualism

Although quantum theory does not overcome dualism in the way Callicott seems to suggest, many leading twentieth-century physicists appear to have been drawn to mysticism, which is a mode of experience that always includes the transcendence of subject-object dualism. Is this tendency an indication that quantum physics does in fact go beyond such dualism? Fritjof Capra offers a qualified "yes" to this question in his popular work, *The Tao of Physics,* to which Callicott makes reference.[13] Other authors, however, are more cautious in attempting to draw parallels between mystical experience and quantum physics. Ken Wilber, for example, argues that physicists such as Jeans, Shroedinger, Einstein, Pauli, Eddington, Heisenberg, and Planck were drawn to mysticism precisely because physics *failed* to lead them beyond subject-object dualism and toward a direct experience of reality.[14] Wilber uses Plato's metaphor of the cave to explain the limitations of quantum physics. Despite the fact that quantum physics has discovered many extraordinary things about matter-energy, and despite the fact that matter-energy only becomes "objectified" as a result of interaction with apparati of our own devising, all of these findings have to do with the realm of matter-energy, which is represented by the shadows on the walls of Plato's cave. Plato insisted that gaining wisdom involved more than understanding the play of shadows, i.e., the activity of material reality, however interesting it might be. The seeker of wisdom had to make his (or her) way outside of the cave in a journey up through higher levels of reality toward an experience that transcended rational categories that are inherently dualistic. These "higher" levels are higher because they are nondualistic, i.e., they include domains of reality that are excluded from lower levels of consciousness.

Ego consciousness, which is necessarily dualistic, is a major achievement in human evolution. Characteristic of ego consciousness is the ego's tendency not merely to *differentiate* itself from the body, from nature, and from woman (all of which are associated by the ego with death and limitation), but to *dissociate* itself from them.[15] Dissociated from nature, body, and woman, the ego regards them both as threats to its survival and as intrinsically inferior to the ego, whose major feature is rational consciousness. The ego, having emerged from an earlier collective consciousness, experiences death anxiety as a result of its apparent isolation. To protect itself against death, the ego engages in what Ken Wilber has called the "God project," i.e., the attempt to turn the intrinsically mortal ego into an eternal substance.[16] The God project is linked to culture, science, technology, and money. While quantum theory provides aspects of the theoretical basis for a relational metaphysics that is inconsistent with dualistic thinking, quantum theory, nevertheless, has arisen within the stage of history characterized by such dualistic thinking and cannot move us beyond that stage.

Some have argued that the proximity of quantum theory and nondualistic experience (experience that occurs outside Plato's cave) is evidenced by the fact that both quantum theory and nondualistic experience are characterized by puzzles and paradoxes. But the paradoxes of quantum physics are not the paradoxes involved in nondualistic experience. As perplexing as the quantum paradoxes might be, Wilber has argued that they concern the interactions of fields of matter-energy, interactions which require mathematical intelligence—but not personal transformation—to be understood. By way of contrast, the paradoxes encountered outside the cave disclose levels of reality that are far more inclusive than matter-energy, and that can only be understood through experience that surpasses dualistic rationality.

In his initial, relatively conservative use of quantum theory for environmental ethics, Callicott does not emphasize that nondualistic understanding requires a radical shift of experience, a shift that is not required for doing quantum physics. Instead, he is concerned to argue that just as all "properties" of objects are determined as the result of interaction between knower and known, so too the value of objects can be said to arise from that interaction. Values then are neither merely subjective nor purely objective; indeed, the distinction between subjectivity and objectivity is blurred by the interactional model of properties. Hence, even if quantum theory does not require a radical shift in consciousness, and even if it does not go beyond subject-object dualism in the way some have suggested that it does, nevertheless, it can serve as a model or paradigm for understanding value as an interactional product. The major drawback is that this model remains operative only at the *cognitive* or *rational* level; the model does not transform dualistic rationality. Still, the emergence in our century of scientific theories that emphasize internal relatedness may well be a sign that a gradual evolution is occurring toward a more inclusive, less dualistic mode of consciousness.

Earlier, I said that rationality is inherently dualistic. It would take a separate essay to defend this claim; in support of it, I will mention only the following points. By rationality I do not mean "wisdom," which arrives when one moves beyond the limits of dualistic thinking, but the calculating, discriminating activity of the self-conscious ego subject. Rationality and ego consciousness developed together in human history. Descartes provided the paradigmatic interpretation of rationality and its relation to dualism. While Cartesian dualism owes much to Plato's metaphysics, Plato himself seems to have retained the idea that rationality (discursive, calculating, categorizing consciousness) is not the highest form of thought, but only a stage along the way. He held that the higher stages could not be understood in terms of the categories operative at the lower stages. This is why it is impossible for the rational man (or woman) to imagine a higher mode of consciousness than that of ego consciousness. The failure of modern philosophy to find its way out of dualism does not arise out of a lack of rational genius, but from the fact that modern philosophers have operated primarily from within the domain of rational ego consciousness. Modern philosophers dismiss as "irrational" and "mystical" and "regressive" those states of consciousness that both include and go beyond the rational. Such a dismissive attitude is understandable because of the tenacity with which the ego seeks to maintain its identity. Indeed, greater rationality can prove an impediment to moving beyond the confinement of rational consciousness, unless the rational ego can be convinced to assist in the process of its own displacement.

Though dualistic, rationality is a powerful and important stage in the development of humanity. Moving to a level beyond such rationality does *not* mean becoming irrational. Like earlier elements retained in our own development, inclusive levels of awareness will also include ego consciousness. Dualistic rationality is a stage that must be attained before higher stages are possible. Since many human beings are still struggling to attain the stage of dualistic rationality or ego consciousness, such rationality must not be disparaged but encouraged. On the other hand, we must be cautious about any claims to finality or ultimacy that we make with respect to that level of consciousness. Human evolution is still taking place. Keeping all of this in mind, we are prepared to consider Callicott's second, more radical interpretation of quantum theory.

V. Callicott's More Radical Interpretation

In his first interpretation of quantum theory, Callicott maintains that quantum theory overcomes fact-value dualism by providing an interactionist paradigm for the emergence of properties, including "intrinsic value." In his second, more radical interpretation, he argues that quantum theory offers a cosmological-metaphysical paradigm of the total interrelationships of all things. This new paradigm undermines the notion of the separate "I" that opposes itself to nature. Hence, the new paradigm undermines subject-object dualism and calls for a new sense of "self" that goes beyond the separate "I." As we shall see, the emergence of this new sense of self cannot occur solely on the basis of cognitive insight into the "interrelatedness" of all things. Instead, the new self sense requires transformational insight that goes beyond the limits of cognitive rationality, which is inherently dualistic. In my view, it is only through such transformation—which may nevertheless be anticipated and in some measure encouraged by changes in scientific understanding—that a new humanity-nature relationship can be established.

Consistent with this viewpoint, Callicott suggests that quantum theory contributes to environmental ethics not simply by providing a new approach to physical reality, but also by offering a new paradigm for understanding experience. This new paradigm emphasizes the importance of moving beyond dualistic thinking. Hence, even if practitioners of quantum physics continue to think dualistically in everyday life (even in their interpretations of results obtained in experiments based on quantum theory), nonscientists might nevertheless be *inspired* by quantum theory to think in less dualistic, more inclusive terms.

An important instance of such inclusive thinking is the doctrine of internal relationships developed more than sixty years ago by Alfred North Whitehead.[17] Whitehead maintained that only a metaphysical doctrine of internal relationships could be made consistent with the findings of quantum theory. He accused classical physics of committing the fallacies of "simple location" and "misplaced concreteness." Whitehead's writings did not have the influence they deserved, not only because of their intrinsic difficulty, but also because many philosophers were still wedded to the paradigms of classical physics and positivism. Today, however, there is a renewal of cosmological and metaphysical speculation, fueled at least in part by the increasing accessibility and influence of quantum theory, and because of discoveries in many other scientific fields that seem to parallel the doctrine of internal relations belonging to quantum theory.[18]

As Callicott points out, reality at the atomic level is interrelated in ways that cannot be pictured in terms of the common-sense paradigms that have been influenced by classical physics. We cannot properly even speak of atomic "particles" as if they are separate entities. It is more appropriate to describe such "particles" as concentrated moments of energy within the internally related field from which all atomic structures emerge in a constant cosmic "dance." Further, just as we cannot speak of particles as separate from the field from which they arise, so too we cannot speak of terrestrial organisms as separate from the niche from which they emerge and on which they depend for life. The science of ecology, then, provides a model of internal relationships at the level of terrestrial life that is analogous to the model of internal relationships that quantum theory offers for the atomic level of reality. Lovelock and Margulis, moreover, argue that life on Earth regulates its own environment.[19] The temperature of the atmosphere, its gaseous contents, the mineral contents of the oceans—all are kept at equilibrium by homeostatic processes taking place in the plant and animal realms.

The paradigm of internal relations lets us view ourselves as manifestations of a complex universe; we are not apart, but are moments in the open-ended, novelty-producing process of cosmic evolution. As the universe evolves, there arise ever more complex domains of reality with "emergent" qualities. Emergent qualities are characteristics of entities at a new level of reality that are not found in, and cannot be predicted on the basis of, the entities at the level of reality from which the new level emerges. For example, molecular properties are not deducible from atomic properties; cultural properties are not deducible from the properties of organisms; and so on. Nobel Prize winning physical chemist Ilya Prigogine argues that order arises out of chaos: complex, apparently random situations are capable of spontaneously producing new levels of organization that exhibit properties not found in the earlier level.[20]

The paradigms of internal relationships, evolution, emergent qualities, and spontaneous generation of order stand in striking contrast to the nineteenth-century view of the universe as a gigantic clockwork whose character and destiny are prefigured according to strict, unchanging causal laws. Contemporary physics also acknowledges, of course, that there are law-like patterns at work in the universe, but these patterns do not appear to be eternal. Instead, they seem to have been precipitated out as the universe cooled during the first few thousand years after the "Big Bang." The entire universe then appears to be evolving. In light of modern scientific paradigms, contemporary cosmologists are asking: if everything is interrelated, and if the universe is evolving into ever more complex forms, can it be considered merely an *accident* that intelligent life forms have evolved that are capable of bearing witness to and understanding the universe? Is the emergence of self-conscious forms of life an inevitable result of the self-organizing activity of the universe? Does the existence of human life *mean something?*

From the viewpoint of a number of nineteenth-century scientists, such questions are teleological and thus have no place in scientific thinking. For mechanistic science, the human species is simply a cosmic "accident" that doesn't mean anything. According to this "naturalistic" view, human beings are simply clever animals competing for survival on the planet. Humans are not worth more than anything else, since the universe has no value or purpose. Many nineteenth-century naturalists distinguished themselves from their scientific predecessors by abandoning reference to the Divine Creator's plan for creation. By way of contrast, many earlier scientists, including such luminaries as Newton, regarded themselves as doing "natural theology." By understanding creation, they sought to gain insight into the divine. For such scientists, the Great Chain of Being remained an important paradigm. More than one author has pointed out, moreover, that Western science is grounded in the concept of a transcendent God whose creation works according to rational laws discoverable by human beings. Many nineteenth-century scientists, despite disclaimers about teleology and the divine, continued to make use of the Great Chain of Being in their thinking. For example, while many scientists may have concluded that the universe did not "mean" anything, they continued to speak of the human being as the "highest" animal because of its "complexity." A number of other scientists continued to be guided by the sense that they were uncovering the secrets of divine creation. As recent scholarship has made clear, the so-called "war" between science and religion has been much overstated.[21]

There is no denying, however, that modern science has had a profound impact on Western humanity's religions in particular and on humanity's self-understanding in general. Science explains reality by observation and reasoning, without appeal to revelation. The extraordinary success of scientific explanation, and the impact of applied science on technology, has led many people to discard traditional belief systems, or else to separate the world of science from the world of faith. Those who have abandoned traditional religion have often replaced it with a new one: anthropocentric humanism, which holds that humans are the origin of all value, purpose, and meaning.[22]

When such anthropocentric humanism is combined with naturalism, the following world view results: the human animal is the source of all meaning, value and purpose and, as a result, the human animal has the "right" to do whatever it chooses to other entities in order to insure its own survival and security. On the one hand, humans are merely a part of nature: on the other hand, they are radically distinct from nature and are justified in using it in any way they please. This humanity-nature dualism has played an important role in transforming natural science, which was originally motivated at least in part by the desire to understand and to appreciate the structure of creation, into a tool for exploiting nature for cultural, economic, and military purposes.

Historically, anthropocentric-naturalistic humanism has helped to heighten modern humanity's new sense of self. This new self, already defined in important respects by Descartes, is the autonomous, intrinsically valuable, self-made "I," which is essentially different from merely "natural" entities. The new self is defined as wholly separate, distinct, independent; in this manner, it mirrors the view that reality is composed of atoms that move according to mechanical principles. This privileged, intrinsically valuable, security-seeking "I" has gradually arrogated to itself the characteristics formerly belonging to the divine by engaging in the God project mentioned earlier. Modern Western humanity, as a result, is essentially schizophrenic.[23] On the one hand, we speak of ourselves as natural things in a meaningless universe; on the other hand, we speak of ourselves as intrinsically valuable persons in a universe that is ours for the taking. By regarding nature merely as raw materials for enhancing human power and security, and by regarding humans (in part) as merely natural things, humanity ends up regarding people as the most important "raw material" for the achievement of the highest human "goals."

As I pointed out earlier, however, new paradigms may be replacing both the old atomistic-mechanistic ones and the anthropocentric ones. According to these new paradigms, everything is an aspect of the same cosmic web or fabric. Hence, it is an illusion to think of the "I" as radically separate from everything else. Einstein had this in mind when he said that "A human being is a part of the whole, called by us 'Universe'; a part limited in time and space. He experiences himself, his thoughts and feelings as something separated from the rest—a kind of optical delusion of consciousness. This delusion is a kind of prison for us, restricting us to our personal desires and to affection for a few persons nearest us. Our task must be to free ourselves from this prison."[24]

Extending beyond my "skin bag," I am constituted by a matrix of internal relations. So long as I think I am encapsulated in my own body, I will care for it, but often at the expense of other bodies: mineral, plant, animal, and human. But if I see that I am in fact internally related with everything else, then everything is my body. Even my "I" is constituted by these internal relationships. Hence, there is no radical divide between self and nature. Callicott explains:

> Now if we assume, (a) with [Paul] Shepard and [Fritjof] Capra that nature is one and continuous with the self, and (b) with the bulk of modern moral theory that egoism is axiologically given and that self-interested behavior has a *prima facie* claim to be at the same time rational behavior, then the central axiological problem of environmental ethics, the problem of intrinsic value in nature, may be directly and simply solved. If quantum theory and ecology both imply in structurally similar ways in both the physical and organic domains of nature the continuity of self and nature, and if the self is intrinsically valuable, then nature is intrinsically valuable. If it is rational for me to act in my own best interest, and I and nature are one, then it is rational for me to act in the best interests of nature. . . . Since nature is the self fully extended and diffused, and the self, complementarily, is nature concentrated and focused in one of the intersections, the "knots," of the web of life or in the trajectory of one of the world lines in the four dimensional space-time continuum, nature is intrinsically valuable, *to the extent that the self is intrinsically valuable.*[25]

Note that Callicott is not saying that the "I" as traditionally understood *is* intrinsically valuable; instead, he is speaking conditionally. If we assume, as do most modern moral theorists, that the "I" is intrinsically valuable, then in light of the paradigm of internal relations we can conclude that *everything* is intrinsically valuable. Hence, the "I" ought to treat all things with respect, just as the "I" treats itself and other "I's" with the respect deserving of entities with intrinsic value. Callicott, then, uses the notion of the intrinsic value of the "I" to beat anthropocentric humanists at their own game.[26] Even if Callicott does not necessarily agree with the notion of the intrinsic value of the "I," it is clear that he regards the paradigm of internal relations as crucial for overcoming the subject-object, value-fact dualisms responsible for the human domination of nature. Henceforth, in light of the internal relatedness of all things, *whatever* ethical theory humans develop will have to take into account nonhuman beings as well.

VI. The Contribution of Nondualism to Environmental Ethics

The deep ecologists Arne Naess and Warwick Fox have argued that only a process of wider identification with all beings can provide the basis for a satisfactory environmental ethics. In a commentary on Callicott's quantum theory essay, Fox says that the problem of justifying intrinsic value could be said to shift from the environmental axiological question "What is it about the nature or being of x that makes it intrinsically valuable?" to the normative "auto-logical" question "Why ought one relate to x as to one's self (or in an 'I-Thou' rather than an 'I-It' manner)?" . . . Thus the term "intrinsic value" can still do useful philosophical work in deep ecological theo-rizing if it is understood as making a claim about the nature of the rela-tionship that one has or ought to have with x (and, hence, about the *state of being to which one ought to aspire*), rather than as making a claim about the nature of being or x.[27]

The paradigm of internal relationships is, in Fox's point of view, important in overcoming previous delusions about the separateness of the self from na-ture. Yet Fox acknowledges that cognitive insight into internal relatedness is not in itself sufficient to bring about a new relationship between oneself and the rest of the world. This new relationship requires a new "state of being," one that is nondualistic. But how to bring about this new state of being?

Callicott argues that knowledge about the interrelatedness of all life may lead a rational humanity to a deeper appreciation of the need to live on Earth appropriately. Knowledge about the paradoxes of quantum theory, moreover, may have the effect of showing the limits to dualistic thinking and of promoting cosmological speculation that is consistent with a metaphysics of internal relations. As I've already mentioned, these trends in the sciences may be helping to prepare the way for the emergence of a more inclusive, nondualistic level of awareness.

Nondualistic awareness involves direct apprehension of the fact that there are no boundaries, that all dualisms are artificial (though often helpful). Even the division between ego states (thoughts, memories, fantasies, etc.) and so-called external objects is revealed as artificial. All things, including ego states and external objects, are seen as manifestations emerging from what is apprehended as a fertile "no-thing-ness." The "I" itself appears as a temporary phenomenon, an energy pattern maintaining itself according to certain intentions and habits. The true "self" is not the ego, but instead the "no-thing-ness" from which all things emerge.

Within Eastern and Western nondualistic traditions there is disagree-ment about the meaning of the "non-thing-like" source for all beings, a source that is itself not "located" anywhere, but provides the context for space, time, matter, energy, perception, and ego consciousness. Some non-dualistic Eastern traditions, such as Buddhism, refer to this nothingness (*sun-yata*) in metaphysical terms as the nonpersonal awareness that perceives/en-genders all things. In some nondualistic Western traditions, including Western mysticism, the primordial "no-thing-like" source is conceived in more personalized terms, as the Godhead beyond God. Mystical Christianity claims that the ordinary concept of God (a divine entity in heaven) is a misleading product of dualistic consciousness. The God beyond God cannot be said to "be" at all, but instead must be conceived as "no-thing-ness," as beyond but somehow inclusive of all creatures. The apparent proximity of the Buddhist and mystical Christian view has not gone unnoticed. Recent decades have witnessed an extraordinary dialogue between Buddhists and Christians, who have discovered such a remarkable convergence of themes from their nondualistic traditions.[28]

Nondualistic experience leads to compassion and love for all beings. Nondualistic awareness no longer identifies itself with a particular entity (the rational ego) and so no longer is forced to adopt a defensive posture toward entities that are other than ego. Freed from false identification with a dualistic state (ego consciousness), awareness can now discern and have compassion for the suffering undergone by people who remain at dualistic levels of awareness. Nondualistic awareness does not cling or hinder, but instead lets all things come forth as they are. The Christian mystical tradition maintains that such awareness is divine, and to the extent that humans share such awareness, they participate in the divine. This is the esoteric meaning of Jesus' claim that "I and the Father are One."[29] Nondualistic awareness would not only lead humanity to treat all beings, human and nonhuman, with a profound respect, but would also free humanity from many of the cravings, aversions, and delusions that are responsible for wars and for production methods that threaten to destroy the biosphere.

As I mentioned earlier, while the experiential dimension of nondualism is reported to be the same by various traditions, those traditions have different interpretations of the "meaning" of such nondualistic experience. Certain versions of mystical Christianity, for example, hold that nondualistic experience reveals the truth of the doctrine of *panentheism*. Panentheism, seeking to reconcile divine transcendence with divine immanence, maintains that God is present in but not identical with creation. Divine awareness gives rise to creatures and in some measure participates in the life of those creatures, but is not wholly identical with them. Evolutionary panentheists, whose doctrines resemble those of Hegel, claim that God is present in and continues to develop through the evolving existence of creatures, thereby overcoming the otherworldliness of traditional Christianity.

In one essay, Callicott maintains that traditional Christianity has promoted the human exploitation of nature, but nevertheless recognizes that

> Historically the first and theoretically the most obvious possibility [for a nonanthropocentric axiology] is theistic axiology. If God is posited as the arbiter of value, anthropocentrism is immediately and directly over-

come. If God, moreover, is conceived as in the Judeo-Christian tradition to be the creator of the natural world, and to have declared his creation to be *good,* then the creation as a whole, including, as its centerpiece, the biosphere, and the components of the creation, species prominently among them, have, by immediate inference, intrinsic value. . . .

This theistic axiology has one main drawback as a nonanthropocentric value theory for environmental ethics. It is primitive, essentially mythic, ambiguous, and inconsistent with modern science, and more especially with modern ecological, evolutionary biology. It is therefore metaphysically discordant with the world view in which environmental problems are perceived as fundamentally important and morally charged in the first place.[30]

Callicott is right in suggesting that theocentrism provides the basis for a nonanthropocentric axiology: everything is good if it is a manifestation of and in relationship with the divine. Callicott agrees with theocentrism that modern humanity is arrogant, but—at least in the essay from which the quotation is taken—he does not accept the theocentric diagnosis of or solution to such arrogance. He identifies theocentrism as such with a particular interpretation of Judeo-Christian theocentrism. He then dismisses that tradition as "primitive, essentially mythic, ambiguous, and inconsistent with modern science. . . ."

It is important to note that nondualistic panentheists would agree with much of Callicott's assessment of traditional Christianity. The Christian panentheist would say that Christ was indeed the Son of God, the first human being to make his way back to the highest level of consciousness. Yet Christ's nondualistic awareness could not be shared by later "Christians," who were still struggling to move beyond the stage of collective consciousness to dualistic ego consciousness and were deeply influenced theologically by neo-Platonic disdain for matter and preference for soul. Because of their soul-matter dualism, early Christians tended to dissociate themselves from creation and to seek an otherworldly home. This dissociation, when combined with the doctrine that humanity had been given "dominion" over creation, helped to justify modern exploitation of the natural world.[31] Such exploitation was spurred on by Reformation doctrines regarding the necessity of "developing" one's talents and the Earth through industry. Indeed, the quest to create a technological-industrial "paradise" on Earth can be regarded as a secular version of the Judeo-Christian promise of a New Jerusalem.[32]

Fortunately, the Judeo-Christian tradition can be interpreted panentheistically, in such a way that the tradition calls for humans to do God's will "on Earth as it is in Heaven." For panentheism, obeying the "will of God" on Earth means accepting and respecting all beings as the fruit of God's creative activity. Such obedience stems automatically from nondualistic awareness, which discerns that divine awareness is not radically separate, but merely concealed from dualistic human awareness.

As a theory, panentheism cannot in and of itself bring about nondualistic experience any more than quantum theory can. Nevertheless, the growing interest on the part of Christian theologians in panentheistic doctrines may be yet another sign of the emergence of nondualistic awareness. Some panentheists describe the evolution of creation in the following way.[33] For "reasons" beyond rational comprehension, the timeless presence of the divine is disturbed by a "disturbance" or "ripple" in which a separate level comes forth from the divine. This separate level falls into still lower levels until it manifests itself as the level of matter-energy. This manifestation may correspond with what Genesis calls creation, and with what nondualistic thinkers call "involution." In creation, as Arthur Peacocke has argued, God surrenders or empties Himself/Herself to the lowest level of reality, that of matter-energy.[34] Then, over billions of years of cosmic evolution, matter-energy moves toward ever greater complexity; later stages of development include the earlier stages. Life emerges, and then self-conscious life. The emergence of self-conscious life is a crucial stage in the divine process of reconstituting the levels of reality that were temporarily forgotten when God emptied Himself/Herself into the level of matter-energy and "forgot" Himself/Herself.

Ego consciousness is a constricted form of the self-awareness that is emerging through the history of creation. Even at the level of ego consciousness, humanity has some sense of the divine presence. But ego conscious humanity is stricken with the death anxiety that comes with sensing itself to be separate from and threatened by everything else. Inflated by self-importance and driven by anxiety, the ego engages in the God project: the attempt to turn the finite, mortal ego into the infinite, eternal Divine. Denying its own mortality, the ego projects mortality onto nature: by controlling and even by destroying nature, the ego thinks that it will somehow conquer its own mortality. In addition, the ego projects its mortality and evil onto enemies: by destroying the enemy, the ego believes it destroys its own mortality and evil. This is an important key for understanding the nuclear arms race.[35]

To avoid self-destruction, it would appear that humanity must evolve into a more inclusive, nondualistic level of awareness which dissolves the dualisms of ego vs. nature, and of ego vs. ego. Nondual awareness includes, but transcends the level of ego consciousness. Just as someone existing at a collective level of consciousness cannot conceive of what it means to be an autonomous individual, a self-directed ego consciousness, so too someone existing at the stage of ego consciousness cannot appreciate what the next level of consciousness might be. According to panentheists, nondualistic experience discloses that the ego's isolation is illusory and that the ego is not a substantial entity at all, but instead merely a temporary, constricted mode of divine experience.

An important question for panentheists is the degree of independent "reality" that creatures have with respect to their divine source.[36] Many Christian panentheists maintain that although creatures are manifestations of the divine, they also make their own contribution to the creative unfolding of God through creation. Other types of panentheists emphasize that even the relative independence of creatures is an illusion; all creation is a phenomenal form through which the will of God is at work. This view is more typical of certain Vedantic versions of panentheisms.

Such considerations are not a problem for those nondualists who are not panentheists, for example, the Buddhists. Buddhism does not ascribe divinity to the openness/emptiness (*sunyata*) in which all things emerge and dwell. Callicott seems to be more comfortable with Eastern forms of nondualism, as can be seen in his recently published essay on Asian religions and environmental ethics.[37] In this essay, Callicott seems to agree with the view for which I have been arguing: namely, that a transformation of rational awareness is necessary to achieve the nondualism consistent with a doctrine of internal relations.

Warning against a naive conflation of the multifarious Asian traditions into a lump called "Eastern thought," Callicott makes important distinctions among Vedanta, Confucianism, Taoism, Buddhism, and Zen Buddhism. While he regards Vedanta as too given to monism, and Buddhism as too life denying, Callicott suggests that Confucianism, Taoism, and Zen Buddhism are capable of providing the foundation for a profound environmental ethics. Zen Buddhism, for example, which was influenced by Taoism, offers a nondualistic, aesthetic appreciation of all phenomena, an appreciation that promotes right treatment of all beings. Callicott notes that "The inherent aesthetic quality of the momentary/eternal state of *satori* in Zen distinguishes it from the apparent negativity of *nirvana* in traditional Indian Buddhism."[38] *Satori* is not achieved by cognitive insight into "internal relations," but involves direct, noncognitive, nondualistic experience. There is no longer a cognitive subject contemplating the "fact" of internal relations; instead, there is the *direct manifestation* of this internal relatedness.

Similarly, we can conceive of the relationship between Creator and creation nondualistically. Traditionally, God has been conceived as an entity "out there," while creation is another entity "over here." This dualistic conception was motivated by the proper insight that God cannot be identified with any creature, not even with creation. Pantheism makes such an identification. Panentheism, however, claims that the Creator is both transcendent of and immanent in creation. This state of affairs is paradoxical for cognitive rationality, but not for nondualistic awareness. Panentheistic seers proclaim that while the "Godhead" transcends all creation, creation, nevertheless, is a completely sufficient manifestation of God within the limitations of matter and energy. An "enlightened" human being, then, experiences the divine in the here and now. No longer identifying with the separate "I," and hence no longer driven to protect the "I" from its inevitable death, the enlightened person becomes, in effect, the divine openness in which all creatures can manifest themselves and "be" what they are. Such a person is godlike insofar as he or she bears witness to, marvels at, and participates in the ongoing event of creation. Here we may think of St. Francis of Assisi.

Callicott seems to be moving toward a nondualistic position, one that is consistent with many of the principles of panentheism. His preference for religious traditions—such as Taoism and Zen Buddhism—which both appreciate nature and do not appeal to a transcendent creator, and his antipathy toward the transcendent deity of traditional theocentrism, can be reconciled in a properly constituted panentheistic view. Western people, however, are unlikely to be converted to Zen or Taoism. If an evolution of Western awareness is to occur, it may well need to take place in terms of the Judeo-Christian tradition. A Christian panentheism offers a different interpretation of the meaning of Jesus Christ than do more traditional anthropocentric views. For example, the doctrine of Christ's Incarnation can be interpreted as meaning that the divine is present in creation, not removed from it, and that God is present in *all* creation, not just in human beings. Christ was resurrected only after he had surrendered to his incarnate, mortal status. Hence, redemption does not mean that the eternal soul flies off to an otherworldly heaven; instead, redemption means experiencing eternity here and now in incarnate form.

For the panentheist, the history of the universe is purposive, but its details are not planned in advance. Hence, panentheists are comfortable with recent cosmological speculation which holds that the universe is open-ended, creative, and characterized by novelty. Evidently, God trusts that the interaction of matter-energy will eventually give rise to self-conscious forms of life that will evolve toward divine awareness. Although it was not necessary that *human* life emerge, an increasing number of scientists as well as theologians are saying that it appears to have been inevitable that in a universe like our own *some* form of self-consciousness would emerge.[39]

Recently, cosmologists have been discussing the "anthropic principle," the "strong" version of which maintains that our universe inevitably produces beings capable of observing and in some sense capable of helping to complete that universe.[40] Human interaction with the rest of creation/nature would then not only give rise to new forms of value, but would also *recognize* the value of creation/nature as it was before human life emerged.

Panentheism affirms that creation/nature has intrinsic value, although as noted above panentheists differ with respect to the degree of relative independence to assign to creatures.

While I have not provided an exhaustive account of nondualism, I have shown that a certain kind of nondualistic panentheism is consistent with the wider sense of identification that Callicott holds as the necessary basis for environmental ethics. The search for a solution to the problem of the intrinsic value of nonhuman beings leads to a nondualistic solution. One interpretation of nondualism is panentheism, one form of which holds that all creatures are valuable both in and of themselves *and* insofar as they are manifestations of the divine, and another form of which holds that all creatures are intrinsically valuable only because they are manifestations of the divine. Panentheists tend to agree that humankind has evolved as a result of self-organizing processes of the physical universe, the history of which is the history of God remembering Himself or Herself. Our present, dualistic-anthropocentric level of awareness is an inevitable stage of the evolution toward a more inclusive level of awareness.

Quantum theory and ecology are in many respects consistent at the rational-dualistic level with the experiential insight into internal relationships at the level attained by the awakened person. That increasing numbers of people, even in our anthropocentric age, are recognizing the intrinsic value of nature, suggests that humanity is continuing to evolve toward a more inclusive level of awareness.

VII. Concluding Remarks

In closing, I want to entertain two objections to what I have been saying: first, that my talk of nondualism, panentheism, and human transformation is utopian and provides no guidance for life in the present; second, that talk of a new, nondomineering humanity-nature relationship is usually accompanied by talk about the need for humanity to become passive with regard to nature.

The first objection correctly perceives the need for moral guidance in the here and now for the great number of people who still operate primarily at the level of ego awareness. At this level of awareness, prudential appeals are most effective for protecting the biosphere from human abuse. Reform environmentalism, which seeks to preserve the environment for human use, will be with us for a long time. There is no contradiction in seeking to reform current ways of using nature while simultaneously seeking a shift toward a more inclusive level of awareness, in light of which nature would manifest itself as something other than an object for domination. Moreover, there is no contradiction between promoting human "rights" while at the same time preparing the way for a new level of awareness in which *all* beings are accorded more respect; indeed, winning universal human rights is a necessary step in consolidating ego awareness. Before such consolidation has taken place, humanity will not be capable of moving to a more inclusive stage of awareness, one that will engender respect for nonhuman reality.

The level of attainment of those who promote a shift to higher consciousness can be discerned, in part, by their attitude toward the ego, dualism, and rationality. If the promoters condemn and call for the destruction of ego consciousness, if they dissociate themselves from rationality, then they themselves remain caught in dualistic thinking. A higher consciousness does not dissociate itself from prior stages, but instead *includes* those stages within itself.

According to the second objection, talk of enlightenment is tied to human passivity and such passivity is incompatible with the obvious need for the human organism to be active in using nature. Moreover, a passive person cannot fulfill or realize him/herself. Hence, so the argument goes, the search for nondualistic awareness and for a more profound humanity-nature relationship ends up stifling human existence.[41]

I reply to this objection by arguing that nondualistic awareness neither leads to passivity nor stifles human existence. Indeed, a level of awareness that is more inclusive than ego consciousness promotes a more profound activity and makes possible a more fulfilled human existence than is possible at the level of ego consciousness. Arne Naess, a deep ecologist and student of nondualistic pathways, maintains that a way of life rooted in domination corrupts the master as well as the slave.[42] An awakened humanity would presumably seek to develop the technical means necessary to provide for human welfare and self-development in ways that would not treat the rest of nature/creation merely as raw material. Learning to "let beings be" is not at all incompatible with an active human life that utilizes trees, animals, water, and minerals for life-sustaining, creative, and self-fulfilling purposes.[43] As contrasted with ego consciousness which has no sense of limits, however, enlightened awareness respects the limits proper to him/herself as well as those proper to the rest of creation. Existing fully within one's limits is the sign of wisdom.

In essence, religion promotes more inclusive levels of awareness which overcome the separateness, isolation, and fragmentation caused by dualisms. All too often historical forms of theocentrism have been governed by dualistic thinking (heaven vs. Earth, man vs. nature, man vs. woman, God vs. creation, etc.). In contrast, nondualistic traditions (including panentheism) point beyond the limits of such dualism. Essentially, religion is a linking up (*religio*), a "re-membering" of what has been disassociated. A glance at any newspaper will reveal the consequences of such disassociation. Whether or not the "re-membering" necessary for a sense of limits will occur in time to avert ecological disaster remains to be seen. If the theocentric traditions are right, however, a disaster that would be catastrophic for our civilization would not be a permanent obstacle to the process whereby the divine "re-members" itself through world history. It may well be that what we have been taught to regard as the pinnacle of the history of consciousness—rational, scientific, technological civilization—is in fact a temporary stage that will be *aufgehoben* as a more inclusive stage comes on the scene. Yet it is also possible that a less painful process is already underway, one that will help to move us away from the paradigm of power to the paradigm of mutuality, from the drive toward an always receding goal of total control to the appreciation of loving creativity present in the here and now. It is this process that Callicott seeks to further in his admirable quest for a nondualistic basis for humanity's relation with nature.

Notes

Zimmerman, author of *Eclipse of the Self: The Development of Heidegger's Concept of Authenticity,* teaches in the Department of Philosophy, Newcomb College, Tulane University. He thanks J. Baird Callicott for his encouragement, for his generous assistance in criticizing earlier versions of this essay, and for the use of unpublished work that helped more fully indicate the direction of his thinking. He also thanks John D. Glenn, Henry J. Folse, Teresa A. Toulouse, Warwick Fox, and an anonymous reviewer for *Environmental Ethics* for their critical reading of this essay.

First published in *Environmental Ethics* 10, no. 1. Permission to reprint courtesy of *Environmental Ethics* and the author.

1. J. Baird Callicott, "Intrinsic Value, Quantum Theory, and Environmental Ethics," *Environmental Ethics* 7 (1985): 271. See also "Elements of an Environmental Ethic," *Environmental Ethics 1* (1979): 71–81 and "Hume's Is/Ought Dichotomy and the Relation of Ecology to Leopold's Land Ethic," *Environmental Ethics* 5 (1982): 163–74.

2. Callicott, "Intrinsic Value," p. 272.

3. Ibid., p. 267.

4. I would like to thank Henry Folse for having pointed out that modern science is not necessarily committed to mind-body dualism.

5. The ground-breaking work in sociobiology is Edward O. Wilson's *Sociobiology: The New Synthesis* (Cambridge, Mass.: Harvard University Press, 1975). See also Wilson, *On Human Nature* (Cambridge, Mass.: Harvard University Press, 1978); Charles Lumsden and Edward O. Wilson, *Promethean Fire: Reflections on the Origins of Mind* (Cambridge, Mass.: Harvard University Press, 1983); John D.

Baldwin, *Beyond Sociobiology* (New York: Elsevier, 1981); David Barash, *Sociology and Behavior* (New York: Elsevier, 1977) and *The Whisperings Within* (New York: Harper and Row, 1979); Richard Dawkins, *The Selfish Gene* (New York: Oxford University Press, 1976); Richard Morris, *Evolution and Human Nature* (New York: Seaview/Putnam, 1983).

6. Callicott, "Intrinsic Value," p. 264. For an interesting critique of Callicott's essay, see Warwick Fox, "Deep Ecology and Intrinsic Value: A Postscript to the Overview of My Response to Sylvan," unpublished manuscript. Fox, an Australian philosopher, has made important contributions to environmental ethics. Correspondence between the two of us concerning Callicott's article helped give rise to the present essay.

7. Callicott, "Intrinsic Value," p. 267. While Callicott finds considerable merit in the sociobiological approach to ethics, others find that it lacks such merit. The critical literature on sociobiology is enormous in scope. A sampling includes: Martin Barker, *The New Racism: Conservatism and the Ideology of the Tribe* (London: Junction Books, 1981); Kenneth E. Bock, *Human Nature and History: A Response to Sociobiology* (New York: Columbia University Press, 1980); Arthur L. Caplan, *The Sociobiology Debate: Readings on Ethical and Scientific Issues* (New York: Harper and Row, 1978); Michael S. Gregory, Anita Silvers, and Diane Sutch, eds., *Sociobiology and Human Nature* (San Francisco: Jossey Bass Publishers, 1978); Jeffrie G. Murphy, *Evolution, Morality, and the Meaning of Life* (Totowa, N.J.: Rowman and Littlefield, 1982); Evelyn Reed, *Sexism and Science* (New York: Pathfinder Press, 1978); Michael Ruse, *Sociobiology: Sense or Nonsense?* (Dordrecht: D. Reidel, 1979) and *Is Science Sexist?* (Dordrecht: D. Reidel, 1981); Peter Singer, *The Expanding Circle: Ethics and Sociobiology* (New York: Farrar, Straus, and Giroux, 1981); Gunther Stent, ed., *Morality as a Biological Phenomenon* (Berkeley: University of California Press, 1980); Robert J. McShea, "Biology and Ethics," *Ethics* 88 (1977–78): 139–49; "The Is/Ought Question," *Zygon* 15, no. 2 (1980): 99–234; "The Challenge of Sociobiology to Ethics and Theology," *Zygon* 19, no. 2 (1984): 115–232.

8. Callicott, "Intrinsic Value," p. 271.

9. Nick Herbert discusses these eight interpretations in *Quantum Reality: Beyond the New Physics* (Garden City, N.Y.: Anchor/Doubleday Books, 1985). For further literature on the new physics, see Heinz Pagel, *The Cosmic Code: Quantum Physics as the Language of Reality* (New York: Bantam Books, 1983) and *Perfect Symmetry: The Search for the Beginning of Time* (New York: Simon and Schuster, 1985); Paul Davies, *God and the New Physics* (New York: Simon and Schuster, 1983), *Superforce: The Search for the Grand Unified Theory of Nature* (New York: Simon and Schuster, 1985), and *Other Worlds* (New York: Simon and Schuster, 1982); John Gribben, *In Search of Schroedinger's Cat: Quantum Physics and Reality* (New York: Bantam Books, 1984); Fritjof Capra, *The Tao of Physics* (New York: Bantam Books, 1982); John P. Briggs and F. David Peat, *The Looking Glass Universe: The Emerging Science of Wholeness* (New York: Simon and Schuster,

1984); Roger S. Jones, *Physics as Metaphor* (New York: New American Library, 1982); David Bohm, *Wholeness and the Implicate Order* (London: Routledge Kegan and Paul, 1983).

10. Henry J. Folse, *The Philosophy of Niels Bohr: The Framework of Complimentarity* (Amsterdam: North-Holland, 1985), p. 255. Folse provides an excellent interpretation of the philosophical importance of Bohr's work.

11. Ibid., pp. 256–57.

12. Eugene Wigner and John Wheeler have made this kind of claim. For a brief discussion of this point of view, see Gribbin, *In Search of Schroedinger's Cat,* pp. 208–13. Also see Frank Tipler and John Barrow, *The Anthropic Cosmological Principle* (New York: Oxford University Press, 1986), for a very important, if controversial, treatment of the idea that the presence of humankind in the universe is directly related to the character and even the origin of that universe. I am not claiming that these more radical and controversial interpretations of quantum theory and the cosmological theories based upon them are wrong. My point is that since the *meaning* of quantum theory remains very much in dispute, philosophers ought to be very careful in appropriating this or that interpretation of quantum theory for ethical theory. It might, in fact, turn out that the Wigner-Wheeler interpretations of quantum theory will become increasingly accepted by the community of physicists, in which case the implications for cosmology would be profound. More and more physicists are concluding that the findings of contemporary physics and astronomy have enormous implications for humanity's understanding of itself and the universe. Callicott makes a speculative contribution to the widespread discussion of the cosmological and ethical implications of modern science.

13. Fritjof Capra, *The Tao of Physics,* 2d ed. (New York: Bantam Books, 1984).

14. Ken Wilber, "Introduction: Of Shadows and Symbols," *Quantum Questions: Mystical Writings of the World's Great Physicists* (Boulder, Colo.: Shambhala, 1984) and "Physics, Mysticism and the New Holographic Paradigm: A Critical Appraisal," in *The Holographic Paradigm,* ed. Ken Wilber (Boulder, Colo.: Shambhala, 1982). In *The Holographic Paradigm* Wilber includes interviews with physicists such as David Bohm and Fritjof Capra, who discuss the relevance of quantum physics for new modes of thought. Capra in particular disagrees with Wilber's rejection of the notion that quantum theory can be shown to be parallel with the great wisdom-mystical traditions.

15. Ken Wilber analyzes the negative consequences of the phenomenon of dissociation in *Up from Eden: A Transpersonal View of Human Evolution* (Boulder, Colo.: Shambhala, 1981).

16. Ken Wilber, *The Atman Project* (Wheaton, Ill.: Quest Books, 1980).

17. Alfred North Whitehead, *Science and the Modern World* (New York: Macmillan Company, 1927) and *Process and Reality* (New York: Macmillan Company, 1929). See Susan Armstrong-Buck, "Whitehead's Metaphysical System as a Foundation for Environmental Ethics," *Environmental Ethics* 7 (1986): 241–59.

18. Callicott pursues many of these themes in a very interesting essay, "The Metaphysical Implications of Ecology," *Environmental Ethics* 8 (1986): 301–16. See also Briggs and Peat, *The Looking Glass Universe,* Stephen Toulmin, *The Return to Cosmology: Postmodern Science and the Theology of Nature* (Berkeley: University of California Press, 1982); and the references in note 9.

19. J. E. Lovelock, *Gaia: A New Look at Life on Earth* (New York: Oxford University Press, 1979); Dorion Sagan and Lynn Margulis, "Gaia and Philosophy," in *On Nature,* ed. Leroy S. Rouner (Notre Dame, Ind.: University of Notre Dame Press, 1984); "The Gaian Perspective of Ecology," *The Ecologist* 13 (1983): 160–67, and *Microcosmos* (New York: Summit Books, 1986); David Abram, "The Perceptual Implications of Gaia," *The Ecologist* 15 (1985): 96–103; and John Gibbin, ed., *The Breathing Planet* (London: Basil Blackwell and New Scientist, 1986).

20. Ilya Prigogine and Isabelle Stengers, *Order out of Chaos: Man's New Dialogue with Nature* (New York: Bantam Books, 1984). See also the remarkable book by Erich Jantsch, *The Self-Organizing Universe: Scientific and Human Implications of the Emerging Paradigm of Evolution* (New York: Pergamon Press, 1980).

21. See, for example, the excellent collection of essays edited by David C. Lindberg and Ronald L. Numbers, *God and Nature: Historical Essays on the Encounter Between Christianity and Science* (Berkeley: University of California Press, 1986). Contemporary discussions of the importance of the hierarchical ordering of reality can be found in Huston Smith, *Beyond the Post-Modern Mind* (New York: Continuum, 1982); Jacob Needleman, *A Sense of the Cosmos: The Encounter of Modern Science and Ancient Truth* (New York: E. P. Dutton and Co., 1975); Arthur M. Young, *The Reflexive Universe: Evolution of Consciousness* (New York: Delacorte Press, 1976).

22. For a critique of anthropocentric humanism and of its destructive effects on the biosphere, see David Ehrenfeld, *The Arrogance of Humanism* (New York: Oxford University Press, 1981).

23. On this schizophrenia, see Needleman, *A Sense of the Cosmos.*

24. Albert Einstein, cited by Wilber, *Up from Eden,* p. 6.

25. Callicott, "Intrinsic Value," pp. 274–75. Emphasis added.

26. On the egocentrism of modern moral philosophy, see Kenneth E. Goodpaster, "From Egoism to Environmentalism," in K. M. Goodpaster and K. M. Sayre, eds. *Ethics and Problems of the Twenty-first Century* (Notre Dame, Ind.: University of Notre Dame Press, 1979). For an overview of the problems encountered by modern moral philosophy in relation to environmental ethics, see Michael E. Zimmerman, "The Critique of Natural Rights and the Search for a Non-Anthropocentric Basis for Moral Behavior," *Journal of Value Inquiry* 19 (1985): 43–53. See also John Rodman "The Liberation of Nature?" *Inquiry* 20 (1977): 83–131, and "The Counter-Revolution in Natural Right and Law," *Inquiry* 22 (1979): 3–22.

27. Fox, "Deep Ecology and Intrinsic Value." Emphasis added. By *autological* Fox means "having to do with self."

28. See, for example, Hans Waldenfels, *Absolute Nothingness: Foundations for Buddhist-Christian Dialogue,* trans. J. W. Heisig (New York: Paulist Press, 1980); J. K. Kadowaki, S.J., *Zen and the Bible: A Priest's Experience,* trans. Joan Rieck (London: Routledge and Kegan Paul, 1980); Dom Aelred Graham, *Zen Catholicism* (New York: Harcourt Brace and World, 1963); Thomas Merton, *Mystics and Zen Masters* (New York: Dell Publishing Co., 1967).

29. On this topic, see Wilber, *Up from Eden;* Fritjof Schuon, *The Transcendent Unity of Religions* (Wheaton, Ill.: Quest Books, 1984); Alan Watts, *The Supreme Identity* (New York: Vintage Books, 1972).

30. J. Baird Callicott, "Non-Anthropocentric Value Theory and Environmental Ethics," *American Philosophical Quarterly* 21 (1984): 302.

31. It is important to note that feminist authors interpret this soul-body dualism, along with other features of ego consciousness, as symptoms of the primary dichotomy in Western civilization: male vs. female. Patriarchalism is allegedly responsible for the domination of nature. To a large extent, the nondualistic mode of awareness described in the present essay is consistent with the nonsexist mode of awareness called for by eco-feminists. On this topic, see my essay "Feminism, Environmental Ethics, and Deep Ecology," *Environmental Ethics* 9 (1987): 21–44. See also Marti Kheel, "The Liberation of Nature: A Circular Affair," *Environmental Ethics* 7 (1985): 135–49; Rosemary Radford Ruether, *New Woman New Earth* (New York: Seabury Press, 1975); Ynestra King, "Toward an Ecological Feminism and a Feminist Ecology," in *Machina Ex Dea: Feminist Perspectives on Technology,* ed. Joan Rothschild (New York: Pergamon Press, 1983); Ariel Kay Salleh, "Deeper than Deep Ecology: The Eco-Feminist Connection," *Environmental Ethics* 6 (1984): 339–45; Naomi Flax, "Political Philosophy and the Patriarchal Unconscious," *Discovering Reality: Feminist Perspectives on Epistemology, Metaphysics, Methodology, and Philosophy of Science,* ed. Sandra Harding and Merrill Hintikka (Boston: D. Reidel Publishing Company, 1983); Marilyn French, *Beyond Power: On Women, Men, and Morals* (New York: Summit Books, 1985); Carol Gilligan, *In a Different Voice* (Cambridge, Mass.: Harvard University Press, 1982).

32. The pioneering essay criticizing the Judeo-Christian tradition is Lynn White, Jr.'s "The Historical Roots of Our Ecologic Crisis," *Science* 155 (1967): 1203–07. See also David Crownfield, "The Curse of Abel," *North American Review* 258 (1973): 58–63; and John Passmore, *Man's Responsibility for Nature* (New York: Charles Scribner's Sons, 1974). Passmore argues that the Jewish tradition was more respectful of creation, while the Christian tendency to dominate nature can be traced back to the influence of Greek stoicism on Christian theology. For the most famous feminist critique of patriarchal Christianity, see Mary Daly, *Beyond God the Father* (Boston: Beacon Press, 1973). Since the appearance of White's article in 1967, an enormous literature has arisen to defend the Judeo-Christian tradition against the charge that it justifies the domination of nature. See, for example, Thomas S. Derr,

"Religious Responsibility for Ecological Crisis: An Argument Run Amok," *Worldview* 18 (1975): 39–45; Gordon Kaufman, "A Problem for Theology: The Concept of Nature," *Harvard Theological Review* 65 (1972): 337–66; Daniel O'Connor and Francis Oakley, eds., *Creation: The Impact of an Idea* (New York: Scribner, 1969); Alfred Stefferud, ed., *Christians and the Good Earth* (New York: Friendship Press, 1972); Zachary Hayes, *What Are They Saying About Creation?* (Ramsey, N.J.: Paulist Press, 1980); Loren Wilkinson, *Earthkeeping: Christian Stewardship of Natural Resources* (Grand Rapids, Mich.: Eerdman, 1980); Wesley Granberg-Michaelson, *A Worldly Spirituality: The Call to Redeem the Earth* (New York: Harper and Row, 1985); and David Spring and Eileen Spring, eds., *Ecology and Religion in History* (New York: Harper and Row, 1974).

33. See Wilber, *Up from Eden;* and Watts, *The Supreme Identity.* Other panentheists, such as Charles Hartshorne, offer a rather different account of creation and evolution. See also the important book by Charles Birch and John Cobb, Jr., *The Liberation of Life* (Cambridge: Cambridge University Press, 1981).

34. A. R. Peacocke, *Creation and the World of Science* (New York: Oxford University Press, 1979).

35. See Michael E. Zimmerman, "Humanism, Ontology, and the Nuclear Arms Race," *Research in Philosophy and Technology* 6 (1983): 157–72; Zimmerman, "Anthropocentric Humanism and the Arms Race," *Nuclear War: Philosophical Perspectives,* ed. Michael Fox and Leo Groarke (New York: Peter Lang Publishers, 1985).

36. For this point, and for others as well, I am indebted to an anonymous reviewer of this essay. It would take another essay to develop sufficiently the many important suggestions by the reviewer.

37. J. Baird Callicott, "Conceptual Resources for Environmental Ethics in Asian Traditions of Thought: A Propaedeutic," *Philosophy East and West* 37 (1987): 115–30. See also Callicott, "The Metaphysical Implications of Ecology," *Environmental Ethics* 8 (1986): 301–16. Because of constraints of time and space, I have not been able to fully to incorporate into the present essay the important ideas found in these recent works by Callicott.

38. Callicott, "Conceptual Resources."

39. See Peacocke, *Creation and the World of Science.*

40. Barrow and Tipler, *The Cosomological Anthropic Principle.*

41. See Richard Watson, "A Critique of Anti-Anthropocentric Biocentrism," *Environmental Ethics* 5 (1983): 245–56, and "Eco-Ethics: Challenging the Underlying Dogmas of Environmentalism," *Whole Earth Review,* no. 45 (March 1985): 5–13.

42. Arne Naess, "A Defence of the Deep Ecology Movement," *Environmental Ethics* 6 (1984): 265–70.

43. The philosopher Martin Heidegger made a significant contribution to the humanity-nature relation with his notion of "letting beings be." On this topic, see Michael E. Zimmerman, "Towards a Heideggerean *Ethos* for Radical Environmentalism," *Environmental Ethics* 5 (1983): 99–131, and "Ontology, Science, and the Humanity-Nature Relationship," *The Modern Schoolman* 64 (1986): 19–43. See also Neil Evernden, *The Natural Alien* (Toronto: University of Toronto Press, 1985).

15

Christian Existence in a World of Limits

John Cobb, Jr.

I. Introduction

A world which once seemed open to almost infinite expansion of human population and economic activity now appears as a world of limits. Christians are hardly more prepared for life and thought in this world than are any other group despite the fact that Christian understanding and ethics were shaped in a world of limits. Those of us who are Christian need to recover aspects of our heritage that are relevant to our current situation and to offer them for consideration in the wider domain as well. Accordingly, this paper first describes the recognition of limits as these now appear to many sensitive people and then reviews features of the Christian tradition that may today inform appropriate responses.

The finitude of our planet requires us to work toward a human society that accepts limits and seeks a decent life for all within them. Such a society should live in balance with other species and primarily on the renewable resources of the planet. It should use nonrenewable resources only at a rate that is agreed upon in light of technological progress in safe substitution of more plentiful resources. The emission of waste into the environment should be within the capacity of that environment to purify itself. By shifting primarily to solar energy, thermal pollution would be kept to a minimum.

Whereas the goal of universal affluence has led to increasing economic interdependence of larger and larger regions, until we have become a global economic unity, the goal of living within renewable resources points in the opposite direction. Relative economic independence of smaller regions is preferable. Whereas the goal of universal affluence has directed industry and agriculture to substitute energy and materials for human labor, the new goal will severely qualify this. Labor-saving devices are certainly not to be despised, but much production will need to be more labor-intensive than is that of the overdeveloped world today. Whereas the goal of universal affluence has led us to encourage the application of scientific knowledge about chemistry and physics to technology and production, restricting this only when the dangers could be demonstrated beyond reasonable doubt, the goal of living within renewable resources will put the burden of proof on the other side. A new product will be allowed only when it is shown beyond reasonable doubt not to damage the long-term capacity of the planet to support life. Whereas we have pursued universal affluence chiefly by increasing the total quantity of goods and services available, and we have concerned ourselves only secondarily about their distribution, the goal of living within renewable resources forces a reversal. Since global growth will be limited, and since in many areas there must be substantial reduction of production, appropriate distribution of goods to all becomes the primary concern.

Clearly these shifts are drastic. Our present economic system is geared to the goal of affluence and is quite inappropriate to the new goal. Our political system is intimately bound up with our economic system. Our agriculture has now been largely absorbed by our industrial capitalism. Our cities are designed so as to require maximum amounts of consumption and hence of production. Our international policies are geared to support this way of life.

Merely to sketch some ingredients of the order which is needed is to become aware of limits at another point. We have limited ability even to conceive a way of moving to the kind of society we need or to enter seriously into willing the steps that would be required. We are like passengers on a train whose brakes have failed and which is rushing down a slope toward a broken bridge. We point to a spot above us on the mountainside, reached by no tracks, and say that should be our destination.

Further, even these changes would not work without stability of global population, and the limits beyond which a decent life for all is impossible will almost certainly have been reached in some parts of the globe before voluntary control will effect such stability. In addition, even if adverse effects on planetary climate by human activity are greatly curtailed, the favorable weather of these past decades is not likely to last, and we must reckon with the probability that it will be difficult to continue to increase food production. Hence, implementation of the policies indicated, while curtailing catastrophe, would not prevent large-scale suffering. The recognition of limits must include the recognition that we cannot prevent the occurrence of manifold types of evil.

The notion of the limits of human capacity to overcome poverty or even to prevent starvation comes to us as a shock. This shock shows how deeply we have been shaped by our recent history. It presupposes that we view ourselves as the creators of history, able to fashion it according to our rational purposes. Such an idea was unknown prior to the late-eighteenth century. Already in the mid-nineteenth century it was subject to ridicule by leading humanists and philosophers who saw in supposed human progress the death of Western civilization. Nevertheless, the continuing increase in human capacity to exploit and alter the environment, the advance of science, the extension of creature comforts, and the "conquest" of space have reinforced the sense of human omnipotence that came to expression in the idea of progress. We Americans, especially, feel that we *should* be able to prevent the deterioration of the world.

The assumption of responsibility for the world, even in its nineteenth-century expressions, was bound up with a sense that there is a force for progress that is deeper than our individual choices. Marx found a dialectical process at work in the economic order. Comte envisaged an evolution from the theological to the metaphysical stages of history, which is now realizing the positive stage. People are called to join in a struggle where the winning cards are already on their side. In this view, history is now triumphing over its age-old limits.

If instead we see that the dominant forces of history are rushing toward catastrophe, we confront the question of limits in a new way. Even if there are conceivable forms of society that would make possible a just and attractive life in a physically limited world, are we human beings capable of personal changes of the magnitude required for the constitution of such societies? The old debate about human nature takes on new importance. Are we naturally good, so that when distorting social pressures are removed we will enter into humane and appropriate patterns of life? Are we naturally competitive and acquisitive, so that only imposed social controls can maintain a measure of order? Are we naturally capable of either good or evil, so that everything depends on our individual acts of will?

Only the first of these three theories offers hope for a successful adaptation to physical limits, and unfortunately the evidence does not support it. Our genetic endowment is shaped by earlier epochs in which those communities survived that nurtured affection and cooperation within, but enmity toward competing groups. Those communities whose males were adverse to violence did not survive in the more desirable regions of the globe. Genetic tendencies have been accentuated in those cultures which have been most successful in history, so that deeply entrenched cultural conditioning reenforces personal attitudes and habits that resist needed changes. Viewed naturalistically and historically there is reason to doubt that the human species has the requisite capacity to change.

There is danger today that those who understand our situation most profoundly will despair. Despair leads to inaction. Unless hope can live in the midst of openness to truth, our situation is indeed desperate. The Christian faith has been one important way in which people have lived with hope in the midst of conditions that appeared, objectively, hopeless. It is the way which I know as a participant, and it is to the exposition of this way that the remainder of this paper is devoted.

Christianity does not underestimate the strength of tendencies which in the course of history have become anti-human and now threaten our survival. Viewing our ordinary ways of feeling, thinking, and acting in the light of Jesus, Christians have used language such as "natural depravity." But we also recognize in ourselves a transcendence over genetic endowment and cultural conditioning that makes us both responsible and, in principle, free to change. We recognize in ourselves also a profound resistance to change, such that our freedom is not a matter of simple choice between good and evil. Our self-centeredness distorts our use of our freedom. But we discover that there is a power at work in us that can transform even our distorted wills. This transformation is not subject to our control but comes as a gift. We call it grace, and we can place no limits on the extent to which grace can make us into new men and new women.

Apart from the transformative power of grace, there would be no grounds of hope. We would have to resign ourselves to the inevitable or seek release from an unendurable world in mystical transcendence. Because of grace, resignation and release are not acceptable choices for Christians. We know that we are not masters of history, but we are not mere victims either. We need to identify appropriate options recognizing (1) the physical limits of our context and (2) the limits of our own capacities to envision needed change or to adopt even those changes we can envision, but also (3) the openness of the future and the unlimited power of transformation that is the grace of God. In this paper, I propose five images of appropriate Christian response. There is some tension among them, and none of us is called to enter equally into all of them. It is my hope that we can support one another in our varied Christian decisions.

II. Christian Realism

By Christian realism I mean to point to that style of action described so brilliantly by Reinhold Niebuhr.[1] Niebuhr knew that the quest for justice in human affairs would not be consummated by the achievement of a just society. Every attainment of relative justice produces a situation in which new forms of injustice arise. There is no assurance that any amount of effort will lead to a society that is better than our own, and, even if it does, there is no assurance that the improvement will last. But this is no reason to relax our efforts. The maintenance of relative justice requires constant struggle.

In this struggle moral exhortation is of only limited use. People in large numbers are motivated by self or group interest. Relative justice is obtained only as the competing groups within society arrive at relatively equal strength. Thus organized labor now receives relative justice in this society because labor unions have power comparable to that of capital.

Christian realists do not appeal to the United States on idealistic grounds alone to supply food to a world food bank. They form alliances with those groups that stand to gain financially by such an arrangement or see political advantages to be won. Furthermore, they realize how fragile will be any agreement on the part of this country that is not clearly in its self-interest, and they work accordingly to strengthen the political power of those countries most in need of American largesse. Perhaps other suppliers of raw materials can follow the model of the OPEC countries in banding together, so as to be able to bargain better for what they need.

Christian realists know that influencing government policy requires hard work and shrewdness. They employ the best lobbyists they can find and bring as much sophisticated understanding as possible to bear on issues while exerting pressure through influencing public opinion. They know that the problems we are dealing with will be with us for the foreseeable future, and hence they settle in for the long haul rather than rely on a quadrennial emphasis on hunger or a special plea for compassionate action.

Christian realists see that the church itself has its own independent capacity to deal with global issues and that there are other nongovernmental organizations with which it needs to work closely. Rightly directing the energies of these private institutions may be as important as directly influencing government policy. Often government policy will follow directions pioneered by other institutions.

III. The Eschatological Attitude

Although Christian realism is a more appropriate response for American Christians than either moral exhortation or revolution, it has limitations. Its maximum achievement will be ameliorative. Since it accepts the existing structures of power, and since these structures are part of the total world-system that moves toward catastrophe, Christian realism alone is not an adequate Christian response. Although any direct attempt to overthrow the existing system would be counterproductive, that system may well collapse of its own weight. It would be unfortunate if Christians became so immersed in a "realistic" involvement in existing institutions that they could not respond creatively to the opportunity that may be offered to build different ones.

Some Christians may elect to live now in terms of what they envision as quite new possibilities for human society even when they do not know how to get from here to there. We may not know how to bring about a society that uses only renewable resources, but we can experiment with life styles that foreshadow that kind of society. We may not know how to provide the Third World with space and freedom to work out its own destiny, but in the name of a new kind of world we can withdraw our support from the more obvious structures of oppression. We may not know how to shift from a growth-oriented economy to a stationary-state economy, but we can work out the principles involved in such an economy.

To exert energies in these ways is not to live in an irrelevant world of make-believe. It is to live from a hopeful future. It may not affect the course of immediate events as directly as will the policy of Christian realism, but it may provide the stance that will make it possible, in a time of crisis, to make constructive rather than destructive changes. Even if the hoped-for future never comes, the choice of living from it may not be wrong. The Kingdom expected by Jesus' disciples did not arrive, but the energies released by that expectation and the quality of lives of those who lived from that future deeply affected the course of events in unforeseen and unintended ways. To live without illusion in the spirit of Christian realism may turn out in the long run to be less "realistic" than to shape our lives from visions of a hopeful future.

To live eschatologically in this sense is not simply to enjoy hopeful images from time to time. The hope for the Kingdom freed early Christians from concern for success or security in the present order. Similarly for us today to live from the future will mean quite concretely that we cease to try to succeed and to establish our security in the present socioeconomic order. For most of us that would be a radical change, and many would say it is "unrealistic." But, unless there are those Christians who have inwardly disengaged themselves from our present structures, we will not be able to offer leadership at a time when there might be readiness for such leadership.

IV. The Discernment of Christ

Most dedication to social change has involved the belief that history is on the side of the change. Christians have made the stronger claim that they were working to implement God's will. When God is understood as omnipotent, Christians have an assurance of ultimate success for their causes regardless of the more immediate outcome of the efforts. But today we do not perceive God as forcing his will upon the world. Every indication is that the human species is free to plunge into catastrophes of unprecedented magnitude if it chooses to do so.

If we no longer think of God as on our side insuring the success of our undertakings, we can and should seek all the more to discern where Christ as the incarnate Logos is at work in our world. When we look for Christ we do not seek displays of supernormal force but quiet works of creative love, or the still small voice. Bonhoeffer did well when he pointed away from a controlling deity, and spoke of the divine suffering. But he was dangerously misleading when he spoke of the divine as powerless. The still small voice and the man on the cross have their power, too, only a different sort of power from that of the thunderbolt and the insurance company's "acts of God."

If our eyes are opened by faith, we see Christ wherever we look. We see him in the aspirations for justice and freedom on the part of the oppressed and in the glimmering desire of the oppressor to grant justice and freedom. He appears most strikingly in the miracle of conversion when something radically new enters a person's life and all that was there before takes on changed meaning. But we see him less fully formed in a child struggling to understand, or in a gesture of sympathy to an injured dog. Wherever a human being is reaching out from herself or himself, wherever there is growth toward spirit, wherever there is hunger for God, wherever through the interaction of people a new intimacy comes into being, we discern the work and presence of Christ. Equally, we experience Christ in challenges that threaten us and in opportunities we have refused. Christ appears also in the emergence of new ideas and insights, in the creativity of the artist, and in the life of the imagination. For Christ is that which makes all things new, and without newness there can be no thought, art, or imagination.

In a situation where habits, established institutions, social and economic structures are leading us to destruction, Christ is our one hope. In quietness and in unexpected places Christ is bringing something new to birth, something we cannot foresee and build our plans upon. As Christians we need to maintain an attitude of expectancy, open to accepting and following the new work of Christ. It may even be that Christ wants to effect some part of that important work in us, and we must be open to being transformed by it. We cannot produce that work, but we can attune ourselves and practice responsiveness to the new openings that come moment by moment.

The attitude I am now describing is different from Christian realism and Christian eschatology, but it is contradictory to neither. Ultimately, we should adopt the realist or eschatological stance only as we are led to do so by Christ, and we should remain in those postures only as we find Christ holding us there. That is to say, to live by faith is to live in readiness to subordinate our past plans and projects, even those undertaken in obedience to Christ, to the new word that is Christ today.

In the discernment of that word we need one another. It is easy to confuse Christ with our own desires or impulses or even our fears. Our ability to discriminate Christ is heightened by participation in a community which intends to serve him and which remembers the failures as well as the achievements of the past. But finally Christians know that they stand alone with Christ responding or failing to respond to the offer of new life through which they may also mediate Christ to others.

V. The Way of the Cross

Moltmann followed up his great book on *The Theology of Hope* with another on *The Crucified God*.[2] He rightly recognized that, for the Christian, hope stands in closest proximity to sacrifice. Whereas in the sixties it was possible for some oppressed groups to believe that the forces of history were on their side and that they had suffered enough, the course of events has reminded us all that hope is not Christian if it is tied too closely to particular events and outcomes. We cannot circumvent the cross. Now as we face more clearly the limits of the human situation and the fact that poverty and suffering cannot be avoided even by the finest programs we could devise, we are forced to look again at the meaning of the cross for us. Have we affluent middle-class American Christians been avoiding the cross too long?

I am not suggesting that we should court persecution or that we adopt ascetic practices in order to suffer as others do. There is enough suffering in the world without our intentionally inflicting it upon ourselves. Whatever the future, we are called to celebrate all life, including our own, not to repress it. But the celebration of life does not involve participation in the luxury and waste of a throwaway society that exists in the midst of world poverty. More important, it does not mean that we float on down the stream because the current carries us effortlessly along. We are called to swim against the stream, at personal cost, and without expectation of understanding and appreciation. That is a serious and authentic way of bearing a cross.

Furthermore, in a world in which, globally, poverty is here to stay, we are called as Christians to identify with the poor. That has always been Christian teaching, but when we thought that our own affluence contributed to the spread of affluence around the world, we could evade that teaching. Now we know that riches can exist in one quarter only at the expense of the poverty of others. In a world divided between oppressor and oppressed, rich and poor, the Christian cannot remain identified with the oppressor and the rich.

The rhetoric of identification with the poor and the oppressed has been around for some time. We have to ask what it means, and here diversity is legitimate. For some it means functioning as advocates for the cause of the poor; for a few, joining revolutionary movements; for others, embracing poverty as a way of life. I believe this third meaning needs to be taken by Christians with increasing seriousness. I also believe in the Protestant decision. The one who actually becomes poor will be a better advocate for the cause of the poor and freer to respond to other opportunities for identification.

I do not have in mind that we should dress in rags, go around with a begging bowl, or eat inferior food. That, too, may have its place, but I mean by poverty two things: first, and chiefly, disengagement from the system of acquiring and maintaining property and from all the values and involvements associated with it, and, secondly, frugality. The Catholic church has long institutionalized poverty of this sort. Protestants tried to inculcate frugality and generosity as a form of poverty to be lived in the world, but that experiment failed. Today we need to reconsider our earlier rejection of special orders so as to develop new institutions appropriate for our time. We can learn much from the Ecumenical Institute as well as from Taize.

I believe that the actual adoption of poverty as a way of life, supported by the churches, would strengthen the capacity of Christians to respond in all the ways noted above. The Christian realist is limited not only by the political powers with which he or she must deal but also by his or her own involvement in a way of life that the needed changes threaten. The Christian voice will speak with greater clarity and authenticity when it speaks from a life situation that is already adapted to the new condition that is needed. Although a life of poverty is not by itself a sufficient definition of living from the hoped-for future, it is an almost essential element in such a life. Our capacity to be sensitive to the call of Christ can be enhanced when we do not nurse a secret fear that he will speak to us as he did to the rich young ruler. Of course, there will be danger of self-righteousness and otherworldliness, but we have not escaped these dangers by abandoning special orders.

VI. Prophetic Vision

"Where there is no vision, the people perish" (Proverbs 29:18). That proverb has a frighteningly literal application to our time. We simply will not move forward to the vast changes that are required without an attracting vision. But such vision is in short supply. There are still proposed visions of a future of increasing global affluence, but they are irrelevant to our present situation and encourage the wrong attitudes and expectations. There are images aplenty of catastrophe, but they breed a despair that is worse than useless. We need a prophetic vision of a world into which God might transform ours through transforming us.

This means that one particularly important response to our situation is openness to the transformation of our imagination. We live largely in and through our images. Where no adequate images exist, we cannot lead full and appropriate lives. In recent centuries church people have not been in the forefront of image making. We have increasingly lived in and from images fashioned by others. Our traditional Christian images have been crowded into special corners of our lives. Recognizing our poverty we need to find Christ at work in other communities in the new creation of images by which we can be enlivened. We can hope also that as we confess our nakedness and gain a fresh appreciation for the creative imagination, the sickness of the church in this respect may be healed and our Christian faith can be released to share in the fashioning of the images so urgently needed.

Concretely we in this country need a prophetic vision of an economic order that is viable and humane with respect to our own people without continuing economic imperialism and environmental degradation. We need a vision of a global agriculture that can sustain the health of an increased population in the short run without worsening the opportunities of future generations or decimating other species of plants and animals. We need a vision of urban life that maximizes the social and cultural opportunities of cities while minimizing the destructive impact of our present cities both upon their inhabitants and upon the environment. We need a vision of personal existence in community that brings personal freedom into positive relation with mutual intimacy and individual difference into positive relation with mutual support. We need a vision of how the finest commitments of one generation can be transmitted to the next without oppression and so as to encourage free responsiveness to new situations.

We have bits and pieces of the needed vision. In my personal search I have found the most impressive breakthrough in the work of Paolo Soleri. But in all areas most of the work remains to be done. Vision in no sense replaces the need for rigorous reflection on details of both theory and practice. Instead, it gives a context in which hard work of mind and body takes on appropriate meaning.

Without vision the other types of reason I have mentioned degenerate into legalism and self-righteousness. As the bearer of prophetic vision, the church could again become a center of vitality in a decaying world. But to bear prophetic vision is costly. It is not possible apart from some of the other responses noted above.

VI. Conclusion

Perhaps the deepest level of our response to the awareness of limits is the recognition that we cannot free ourselves from guilt. We are caught in a destructive system, and we find that even our will to disidentify with that system is mixed with the desire to enjoy its fruits. None of us is innocent either in intention or behavior. At most we ask that we may be helped to open ourselves to re-creation by God, but we also depend on grace in another sense. It is only because we know ourselves accepted in our sinfulness that we can laugh at our own pretenses, live with a measure of joy in the midst of our halfheartedness, and risk transformation into a new creation.

Notes

Cobb is a noted American theologian and process philosopher who teaches at the School of Theology and Claremont Graduate School. He has served as coeditor and publisher of *Process Studies* and is now director of the Center for Process Studies. He is the author of *Is It Too Late? A Theology of Ecology* (Beverly Hills, Calif.: Bruce, 1972).

First published in *Environmental Ethics* 1, no. 2. Permission to reprint courtesy of *Environmental Ethics* and the author.

1. Reinhold Niebuhr, *The Nature and Destiny of Man: A Christian Interpretation* (New York: Charles Scribner's Sons, 1941).

2. Jürgen Moltmann, *Theology of Hope: On the Ground and the Implication of a Christian Eschatology* (New York: Harper and Row, 1967); *The Crucified God* (New York: Harper and Row, 1974).

Index

shaped by production, 80; and communication, 110, 113; as sociohistori-
cally conditioned, 174; and
Democritus, 196; and Amerinds, 202;
and nondualism, 293
person, and language, 23; and the group,
33; in Third World, 86; mentioned,
169; and the meaning of texts, 191; as
the essential self, 198; in relation to
nature, 198, 205; and social relations,
203, 209; and dreaming, 204; as animal others, 211; mentioned,
215–216; as agent of choice, 228;
planet as, 233; and moral considerateness, 245; in moral philosophy, 248,
252; person-regarding edicts, 255;
Hume's view of, 277; as enlightened,
298
phenomenology, of perceptual experience, 12; of nature, 45; and the primacy of perception, 57–59, 61, 64,
66, 69, 72–73; human, 85
philosophy of ecology, 73, 158
philosophy of nature, 57, 197
philosophy of science, 125, 134, 305
picture of nature, the, 193, 197, 207
Pietila, Hilkka, 90, 99n39
place, and language, 9, 262; importance
of living in, 10–11, 176; and communicative reason, 13; metaphysics of,
16; and Amerinds, 26, 52; land ethic
tied to, 29; contextualized narrative
of, 31–33, 37, 261, 263–266, 274n18;
and the Desert Fathers, 34; humankind's, 47, 51, 104, 200, 261; and
perception, 72, 75, 80; mentioned,
111, 186n7, 191n71; specificity of,
123–124, 263; as prison or asylum,
142, 145, 147–148; as outside the imperium, 153–155; and dreams, 203;
and natural setting, 235–237; and
modernism, 268–272
Plato, 55, 69, 122, 174, 197–200, 282,
286–287
Platonism, 83; neo-Platonism, 295
political philosophy, 124, 134, 305

politics, postmodern, 13; of wilderness
preservation, 14; gender, 87, 89,
95–96; monkey-wrench, 92; and communicative rationality, 101, 105, 110,
114; of radical environmentalism,
121, 178; mentioned, 125; of difference, 130, 134–135
population, overgrowth of, 9, 91,
129–130, 309–310, 318; Third World,
80; control issues, 85–86, 103; prison,
159n20; on Fire Island, 163–164; optimum, 168–169; and environmental
practice, 237; of Tahiti, 267
positivism, 49, 83, 117, 289
post-Enlightenment, 9, 49, 103
postmodern environmental ethics, definition of, 1–2; and the linguistic turn, 6;
as reconstructive, 7; as effective discourse, 8; situated in language, 9; as
bioregional narrative, 11; criticism of,
13, 17, 181; as ignoring poststructural
theory, 15, 274n19, 275n28; as practice, 16; and the politics of difference,
134; and place, 261. See also ethics as
bioregional narrative; language
"Postmodern Environmental Ethics:
Ethics as Bioregional Narrative," 10,
17, 23–42, 134n22, 26, 189nn48, 54,
261, 272n1
postmodern philosophy, 4, 19, 49
postmodernism, definition of, 1–2, 122;
and the linguistic turn, 2–5; deconstructive and reconstructive, 6–8; political roots of, 13; myth of, 17,
261–262, 267–269; and standpoint
epistemology, 24; and language, 25,
28–29; as transformed, 30; and bioregional contextualization, 38; and radical environmentalism, 122–123, 125,
131, 133n2; and relation of knowledge and power, 126–128; and community, 130–131; and hypervisibility,
188n30
poststructural theory, 15, 173, 188–189
poststructuralism, 175, 181–182,
184–187, 190

and story, 14, 137; locked up, 141–142, 169–170; as speaking, 153

Wilson, Edward O., 2, 20, 301n5

witches, 87. *See also* shamanism.

Wittgenstein, Ludwig, 4–5, 20, 271, 272, 276n38

woman (women), and nature, 12, 82, 84, 92, 96; as silenced, 44; mentioned, 70, 95; and oppression, 79, 89; labor of, 80–81, 86–88; and spirituality, 83; and rights, 85, 93, 230; as a class, 90–91; hating, 94; as modelled, 102; preferential hiring of, 127; in literature, 148; attributions of beauty, 179; and ego consciousness, 286–287; vs. man, 300; and grace, 312

world, the, knowledge of, 2, 35, 82; in process, 3; scientific account of, 4, 285; and language, 5, 11, 24–27, 37, 51, 124, 263–265; recovery of, 12; human place in, 12, 123, 261, 269–270, 293; embracing rationally, 13; as threatened, 15, 311; and Heidegger, 25; and myth, 28, 266; and monotheism, 34; perception of, 36, 59, 69–70; descriptions of, 37, 47, 207; and Amerinds, 37, 43, 202, 205, 208–209, 214; mentioned, 45, 63, 137, 148, 225, 245, 290; speaking of, 46; and "Man," 48–49; as surrounding, 58; metaphysical detachment from, 60; and truth, 61, 71; as carnal, 65, 278; participation in, 70, 114; and women, 80–81, 90–91; "scapegoats" for problems with, 89; disenchantment of, 102; living with, 112, 157; as property, 129–130; iden-

tification with, 132; alienation from, 144; and "others," 164; as artifactual, 167; as nonartifactual, 169; Hemingway's characterization of, 174; and poststructuralism, 175, 178, 181–183, 185n3, 267; picture of, 199, 274n19; as hierarchy, 200; diminished character of, 225; structure of, 229; bearing ourselves in, 242n33; riddles of, 243; alternative descriptions of, 251; and monism, 252; and modernism, 268, 274n28; and forms of life, 271; its intrinsic value, 292; and God's will, 314. *See also* chiasm, the; flesh of the world

world view, premodern, 2; storied residence as, 11; modern Western, 2–3, 13, 15, 196–198, 208, 261, 275n28, 291, 295; postmodern, 5, 261; as language games, 15; animistic, 53n15; anthropocentric, 101, 166; Amerind, 193, 202–203, 207, 209, 211; as affecting behavior, 207; new Western, 214, 281; dominant, 261; tribal, 264, 267; and Duerr, 271; promulgating different, 272

Worster, Donald, 139, 158n7

Zen, 297–298, 305n28

Zimmerman, Michael E., commentary on, 17–18; mentioned, 39, 97nn7, 9, 18, 98n20, 99nn38, 40, 43, 46, 51, 100nn58–60, 301, 306n35; his oversights, 81, 84–85, 88, 90–94; on moral philosophy, 304n26; on Heidegger, 307n43